# H.D.'s Freudian Poetics

# Reading
## WOMEN
# Writing

a series edited by Shari Benstock and Celeste Schenck

*H.D.'s Freudian Poetics: Psychoanalysis in Translation*
by Dianne Chisholm

*Reading Women Writing* is dedicated to furthering international feminist debate. The series publishes books on all aspects of feminist theory and textual practice. *Reading Women Writing* especially welcomes books that address cultures, histories, and experiences beyond first-world academic boundaries. A full list of titles in the series appears at the end of this book.

# H.D.'s Freudian Poetics

*Psychoanalysis in Translation*

**Dianne Chisholm**

*Cornell University Press*

ITHACA AND LONDON

First published 1992 by Cornell University Press.

International Standard Book Number 0-8014-2474-7 (cloth)
International Standard Book Number 0-8014-8009-4 (paper)
Library of Congress Catalog Card Number 91-55558
Printed in the United States of America
*Librarians: Library of Congress cataloging information appears on the last page of the book.*

∞ The paper in this book meets the minimum requirements
of the American National Standard for Information Sciences—
Permanence of Paper for Printed Library Materials, ANSI Z39.48-1984.

*For my mother and father,*
Helen and Earl Chisholm

*and in memory of my uncle,*
Bruce Steele

# Contents

# Acknowledgments

My deepest gratitude to Elizabeth Wright and to Toril Moi for their assistance during the first stages of this work; to Rosalind Ballaster and to Karen Van Dyck for their stimulating conversation and resourceful collegiality; to the diversely committed participants of the Oxford Feminist Theory Reading Group (1985–1988), without whose lively forum this book would have been composed in dull, monological silence. I owe thanks to Gillian Beer and to Terry Eagleton for their encouraging critical evaluations. Forbes Morlock, Athena Economides, Marni Stanley, and especially Deborah Wills have won my eternal thanks for their painstaking proofreading, as have Anne Richardson and Astrid Blodgett for their computer wizardry and Tim Heath for his steady research assistance. I also thank the editors of this series, Celeste Schenck and Shari Benstock, for their enthusiastic reception and supportive correspondence. Finally, special acknowledgment must go to Susan Stanford Friedman for her thorough and instructive reading of the manuscript.

D.C.

*Edmonton, Alberta*

*H.D.'s Freudian Poetics*

# Introduction

This is not the first book to address the relationship between H.D. (Hilda Doolittle) and Sigmund Freud, but to my knowledge, it is the first full-length reading of the intertext "H.D.-Freud," or what I call H.D.'s translation of Freud.[1] From one signifying practice (in)to another, there being no universal language that encompasses both and each being irreducible to the other, "Freud" exchanges with "H.D." Since this exchange takes place primarily when Freud is no longer alive, he can say little about her style of appropriation. His writing lives on, occupying the shelves of H.D.'s library, but it has none of the textual authority that characterizes her transcriptions of their sessions together. The "Freud" who authorizes a major transition in H.D.'s writing life is the deferred and revisionary subject of her departure from the original scene of analysis.

Since the publication of *Literature and Psychoanalysis: The Question of Reading: Otherwise* edited by Shoshana Felman, it has become fashionable among psychoanalytic literary critics to consider the literariness of psychoanalysis while psychoanalyzing literature. Reading for the poetics of Freud implicates the psychoanalytic reading of literature, deauthorizing any methodological or theoretical priority while disclosing the precise rhetorical and structural features that constitute the specifically psychoanalytic discourse(s). Felman explains:

> In view of this shift of emphasis, the traditional method of *application* of psychoanalysis to literature would here be in principle ruled out. The notion of *application* would be replaced by the radically different notion of *implication*: bringing analytical questions to bear upon literary questions, *involving* psychoanalysis in the scene of literary analysis, the

interpreter's role would here be, not to *apply* to the text an acquired science, a preconceived knowledge, but to act as a go-between, to *generate implications* between literature and psychoanalysis—to explore, bring to light and articulate the various (indirect) ways in which the two domains do indeed *implicate each other*, each one finding itself enlightened, informed, but also affected, displaced by the other.[2]

I do not, then, take my cue from Marie Bonaparte's classic application of psychoanalysis to the works of Edgar Allan Poe (*Edgar Poe: Étude psychanalytique*, 1933), as did Edmund Wilson in his reading of Henry James's *Turn of the Screw* ("The Ambiguity of Henry James," 1962), the reading that Shoshana Felman so rigorously undoes in her exemplary illustration of the new approach ("Turning the Screw of Interpretation"). I follow Felman, herself, reading H.D. and Freud side by side in search of interimplications. My purpose, broadly speaking, is to examine works by H.D. in light of Freud's psychoanalytic writings, and vice versa: to reread Freud in light of H.D.'s revisionary psychoanalysis.[3] My procedure involves tracing Freudian figures, concepts, techniques, narratives, and theories in H.D.'s writing, marking the similarities between her "poetic" and his "psychoanalytic" texts, revealing and interpreting differences.

H.D. addresses and emphasizes a wholly different Freud from that of orthodox Freudianism, calling for a critical rereading of the *Standard Edition* and any standard understanding of the historical reception of psychoanalysis; Freud's entry into H.D.'s writing effectively displaces her imagism and informs her autobiography: after *Tribute to Freud* (1944), there is no H.D. without Freud, and for the psychoanalytic critic who reads this tribute and the later verse whose poetics it outlines, there is no Freud without H.D.

Neither the particulars of this intertext nor the fact that H.D. was actually in analysis with Freud implies, however, a unique conjunction in the history of literature and psychoanalysis. While I was preparing this book for publication, Elizabeth Abel's *Virginia Woolf and the Fictions of Psychoanalysis* (1989) appeared, featuring different characters (Woolf and Melanie Klein as well as Freud) but arguing for a similar "intertextual" reading of the same historical period.[4]

What, then, are the particulars of this intertext? I should like to say at the outset that *H.D.'s Freudian Poetics* is not a study in structuralism. With Felman, I look for the uncanny in H.D.-Freud but I do not follow Lacan's tracing of the displacement and repositioning of the phallus. A telltale sign of intertextuality, H.D.'s "uncanny" involves much more than the subject's horrifying discovery of the lack of something she always assumed to be there, standing in its proper place as a signpost of self-originality. One of the most subversive aspects of her translation is its recovery and privileging of those works of Freud which undermine the metapsychology of presence as conditioned by rhetorical dependence on or idealization of the terms of a binary opposition (masculine/feminine; having/not having the phallus); these are works that address the riddling language of the dream, the archaic, antithetical content of maternal fantasy, the perverse eroticism of Count von Zinzendorf's Moravians, breaking through the familiar repressions of a phallic desire for self-identity and enlightenment.

She foregrounds neither a confirmed theoretician nor even an established clinician but a "blameless physician," whose healing practice bears redeeming traces of a heterogeneous genealogy, of roots in hermeticism, Moravianism, romanticism, kabbalism, Egyptology, and even witchcraft. By analogy, I recall Lisa Ruddick's observation of Gertrude Stein's relationship to William James as "more complex than that of a disciple": "His theories helped her to develop as a 'modern' novelist, but she used him in ways he would not have anticipated. Her very modernism is finally what distances her from him. . . . Her rebellion may be summarized as a form of antipragmatism. Yet . . . James himself was capable of exhibiting an antipragmatist streak. . . . It is to be found not in his *Psychology* but in his religious writings. In his quasi-mystical vein."[5]

H.D.'s Freud is not the (post) structuralist hero who claims today's legacy of psychoanalysis; he is a "psychic" or "feminine" medium of individual and racial self-expression, more like Nietzsche's artist than like the founding father of an institute. This is the Freud who calls on the poets, especially Goethe, to back up his speculations, who illustrates and formulates his theories with modern or romantic "psychological" literature, who relies on his schooling in classical philology, folklore, and mythology to interpret the symptomatic dreams of his patients, who employs figurative language no less than the technical discourse of conventional medicine and traditional philosophy to conceptualize operations of the psyche.

Instead of cross-referencing a consistent use of structure, I present a radical comparison of the use of concept metaphors. Freud's figurative language borrows from multiple sign systems, some scientific and technological (such as optics, thermodynamics, neurophysiology, zoology, pharmacology, anthropology, archaeology), some textual and bibliographical (oneirocriticism, biblical and classical literary criticism), some occult (telepathy, totemism, animism, magic). H.D. develops these figures with her own heuristic application of the vocabularies of the avant-garde (imagism, vorticism, cinematography) as well as the sign languages of mysticism and astrology. The play of figures affects the structural framework in both texts, be they case study (Freud's "Dora"; H.D.'s *Her*), narrative history (*Moses and Monotheism; Helen in Egypt*), speculative autobiography (*The Interpretation of Dreams* or *Beyond the Pleasure Principle; The Gift*), subverting and surpassing the fixtures of method and theory and opening doors to further exploration. Where this subverting and surpassing takes H.D. is what this book intends to disclose.

Indebted as I am to Susan Stanford Friedman's pioneering work *Psyche Reborn: The Emergence of H.D.* (1981), half of which is concerned with "H.D. and the Psychoanalytic Tradition," I differ in my understanding of the dialectics of engagement between H.D. and Freud. Friedman's position may be summarized in the following passage: "To reiterate the pattern of influence, H.D. took Freud's theories, dismissed their evaluative framework, and developed his ideas in a direction ultimately antithetical to his own perspective."[6] My own position is less oppositional. As I see it, in turning to Freud for the words to shape her writing, H.D. implicates herself in his ideas and evaluations. In reconstructing childhood memories, maternal fantasies, narrative histories, she takes on the same subjects that perplexed Freud, resolving to extend his more occult or archaic or feminine speculations while developing the same figures of speech. In some dramatic way, H.D. *becomes* Freud, curing herself of the blocks and gaps that infect the telling of her life story and, at the same time, healing Freud of discursive foreclosures in scientific skepticism, Schopenhauerian pessimism, and metapsychological misogyny.

Although demonstrating that H.D.'s engagement with Freud's text (the text of her analysis as well as the *Standard Edition*) is primarily an engagement with Freudian figures, I do not confine this book to an exercise in formalism. Rhetorical analysis alone will not disclose what is at stake for the woman in this act of translation. Feminist criticism looks for signs of ideological and historical suppression in the canny belief that it is suppression that commits women to writing in the first place, either as a substitute for participation in public and cultural life still denied them (or from which they are discouraged) or as a medium for healing an internalized oppression.

H.D., I contend, applies certain analytic skills that she acquires *through writing* in order to expand her autobiography and to displace the dissatisfying and disabling normative life story by which she had come to know and judge herself. Deeply unhappy with the role of muse or objet d'art assigned her by male modernists bent on materializing their amorous and artistic fantasies, she adapts the techniques of dream interpretation and symptom analysis to help articulate desires and aspirations of her own.[7] With "Freud," she reconstitutes the suppressed and repressed subject of a woman's history. Beginning with what she calls her "personal heritage," I trace this other autobiography onto the stage of world history as represented by the (dis)contented civilization of her war trilogy and by the prehistoric projections of *Helen in Egypt*.

My critical attention falls on those works H.D. composed after her analysis with Freud in 1933–1934. Since the account her life among analysts has been documented, I do not venture over old biographical ground but refer almost exclusively to her transcription of analysis in verse narrative, prose fiction, dramatic reminiscence, and speculative commentary.[8] Though Freud may be traced in all of her writing from the mid-1930s on, I select for close reading those texts whose Freudian poetics I find fundamental to the figures and structures of her writing, including *Her* (1926–1927), *Kora and Ka* (1930), *Nights* (1931, 1934), *The Gift* (1941–1943), *The Walls Do Not Fall* (1942), *Tribute to the Angels* (1944), *Tribute to Freud* (1944), *Flowering of the Rod* (1944), and *Helen in Egypt* (1952–1956).

Each chapter of this book is organized around key structuring figures, explored in one or more of H.D.'s texts. Chapter 1 considers the primary figure and function of translation. *Translation* is the term Freud uses to refer to his concept and technique of dream and symptom interpretation; H.D. adapts the semiotics and hermeneutics of Freudian translation to her poetic practice. It is the interweaving of analytical and hermetic components of this practice which interests me, especially its transformation of the dream work's secondary revision into a re-visionary dream-poem. Since "Freud" was already at play in her writing before 1933–1934, I do not regard H.D.'s analysis as a turning point in her production, although I do consider the "delayed analysis" of *Tribute to Freud* a turning point in her formulation of a Freudian poetics. The chapter begins by tracing the entry of "Freud" (as text) into H.D.'s early prose, particularly *Notes on Thought and Vision* and *Kora and Ka*. It then examines how "Freud" is translated into the figure of hermetic talisman and how this figure charms her exploratory autobiography as occult muse and analytic interlocutor before proceeding to investigate another key sign of intertextuality, H.D.'s hieroglyph, drawn from a double source in American transcendentalism and Freudian oneirocriticism. The chapter ends with a discussion of H.D.'s changing representation of writing (her "grammatology") and the particular psychoanalytic techniques of sign analysis and text production (free association, wordplay, transference) she uses in her poetic semiology.

Chapter 2 focuses on the figure of fantasy as a medium of intertextual exchange. In her projected autobiography, H.D. fantasizes a chiasmus of psychic genealogies, creating the illusion of a genetic interlocking between herself and Freud, relocating the origins of psychoanalysis in mystic Moravia. In this chapter I show how H.D. "occults" Freud not only by claiming the same motherland but also by elaborating his conceptualization of fantasy with that of "projection," as derived from cinematography and telepathy. Moreover, I show how H.D. adapts psychoanalytic narrative, including that of Freud's *Autobiographical Study*, to her own life-writing, tracing the "hysterical" delusions of *Her* to the "mysteria" of *Nights* and the "necromancy" of *The Gift*, which anticipate the maternal imaginary of Western prehistory in *Trilogy* and *Helen in Egypt*.

Chapter 3 turns to the figures of mourning and melancholia, particularly as they appear in *The Gift*, showing how H.D. transcribes her Freudian autobiography with therapeutic efficacy. Like Julia Kristeva's study of mournful or melancholic writers (Gérard de Nerval, Fyodor Dostoevsky, Marguerite Duras) in *Black Sun: Depression and Melancholia* (1987), I explore the cathartic and curative facility of H.D.'s writing.[9] But unlike Kristeva, who extends her clinical practice to literary criticism without problematizing the morbid character of the Freudian view of civilization and especially of women, I examine the figure of *double* treatment in H.D.'s writing cure. *The Gift*, and the autobio-/historiography it subsequently inspires, administers its medicine of translation to the repressed melancholic text of a girlhood fantasy-reminiscence of female sexuality *and* to the misogynous, metaphysical subtext of Freud's solemn discourses on femininity. In rehabilitating her maternal memory, H.D. challenges Freud's diagnosis of woman's symptomatic inferiority, disputes his prognosis of her inevitable (f)rigidity as the natural effect of her oppression by manmade, man-centered civilization. In place of this untreatably depressive femininity, she offers a wholly affirmative vision of woman's libidinal resources and her capacity for creative sublimation.

Chapter 4 traces the figures and structures of treatment, specifically as they arise in *Helen in Egypt*, H.D.'s most ambitious translation. Here she administers the terms of her analysis to the Western literary tradition of representing women as the specular objects of male fantasy. Tracing her "hieroglyph of the unconscious" back to its roots in an age that predates both Oedipus and Moses, I uncover a plot to subvert the classical foundations of the Western imagination. Like Deborah Kelly Kloepfer, I examine the revolutionary semiotics of a maternal prehistory, the "unspeakable language" of maternal desire and its radical undermining of patriarchal discourses of so-called enlightenment.[10] Unlike Kloepfer, however, I consider H.D.'s reverse treatment of psychoanalysis, how she critiques Freud's superstitious antifeminism in ironic figures of the *pharmakeus*, the sorceress, the prophetess, and the witch. The "H.D." who emerges could, I conclude, be listed among the revisionists who identify and expand the radical implications of Freud's writing on eros and dreams as (poetic) antidote to civilization and its discontents, namely, Otto Rank, Wilhelm Reich, Herbert Marcuse, Norman O. Brown, and Leo Bersani.[11] Moreover, she could also be listed among feminist revisionists such as Melanie Klein and contemporary French psychoanalysts Julia Kristeva, Hélène Cixous, Catherine Clément, and Luce Irigaray.

Having outlined the purpose and procedure of *H.D.'s Freudian Poetics*, I should like to draw attention to the occasionally understated feminism that mobilizes this critical interweaving and unraveling of texts. As I mentioned in the beginning, my criticism entertains a poststructuralist reading of Freud which draws less from Lacan than from Derrida. But is it not a contradiction to present deconstruction and feminism as critical companions? Whereas deconstruction hurls a radical critique at the residual metaphysics or phallogocentrism of Lacan's neo-Freudianism, it is not sympathetic to feminism's rehabilitation of a "woman's imaginary," to its strategies of reverse mystification. As a way of clarifying my position, I offer a brief evaluation of Joseph Riddel's Derridean reading of H.D.

In his essay "H.D.'s Scene of Writing—Poetry as (and) Analysis" (1979), Riddel argues, much as I do, that *Tribute to Freud* "translates" the first scene of analysis, restoring, reworking, and thus replacing the "original" text of memory: there is no original memory, and *Tribute* has no author, save the operations of a deferred analysis. Taking his cue from two works by Derrida, "Freud and the Scene of Writing" (1968) and *Spurs: Nietzsche's Styles* (1978), Riddel proceeds to identify H.D.'s metaphors of writing as the true subject of her memoir. As he reads her, H.D. presents herself less as a patient come for treatment than as a Freudian writing style, emblematizing the role of woman in the dissemination and dissimulation of his word in theory and in practice. There is no woman outside the text, Riddel decrees, going so far as to say that

> all the women in Freud's life—Anna, Marie Bonapart [sic], H.D. herself—become for H.D. the fecund multiplicity of his utterance, the virulence and the cure of writing. The woman, then, is the doubled center of the Freudian scene, the sign of the always displaced center of the Freudian scene of analysis. She is not an alternative to the father, but uncanny, the sign of a translation that does not reproduce presence or meaning but disperses meanings, like a text. She is the sign, as Derrida says of Nietzsche's woman, of a castration that does not take place.[12]

In speaking for H.D., outlining what "woman," including herself, means to herself as well as to Freud, Riddel oversteps his bounds as textual critic. Without questioning the authority, however imaginary, with which he endows the mythic father, he authorizes her "castration" from the specific history and genealogy that prompts this particular negotiation in writing. He repeats Freud's dismissive gesture to the women attending his lecture "Femininity" (1932), telling them they might as well leave since they have nothing either to gain from or to contribute to this riddling subject that they themselves constitute.[13] But in dismissing the woman's perspective, and the story of how it came to be formulated, Riddel also dismisses her potential intervention in and transformation of psychoanalysis. "The tainted (and for some chauvinist) vocabulary, which we have borrowed directly from H.D. and from Freud, can never itself have any direct reference to sexual politics," he taunts "for H.D.'s poetics, like her dream, appropriates Freud's 'family romance.'"[14] Searching only for the signs of her parasitic emendations of Freud's text, Riddel neglects to see how H.D. resets the stage of analysis for the uncanny return of the mother of prehistory, the mother from whom Freud withdrew in horror and despair, the mother who brings with her a song even more "originary" than that of the prehistoric father. In his overzealous denial/deconstruction of the fantasy of presence, he censors the work of mystification in H.D.'s writing, overlooking her articulation of a primary female imaginary and its psychic genealogy in the mother-daughter romance. His erasure of the testament of her will to recover the gifts of her maternal inheritance, of her promise to restore the *Spiritus Sancti* to psychical reality, reflects his desire to preserve the anti-feminist bias that informs the "double displacement of woman" in Derrida.[15]

One of my strongest motives for undertaking the study of H.D.'s Freudian poetics is to disclose the politics as well as the aesthetics and the therapeutics of translation, examining the effects of that other imaginary and showing how Derrida might, after all, be fruitfully applied to a feminist reading of a historically conditioned intertextuality.

# 1

# Telltale Signs of
# Intertextuality

H.D. makes a deceptive proposition in *Tribute to Freud*: "We can read my writing, the fact that there was writing, in two ways or in more than two ways. We can read or translate it as a suppressed desire for forbidden 'signs and wonders.' . . . Or . . . merely [as] an extension of the artist's mind, a *picture* or illustrated poem, taken out of the actual dream or daydream content and projected from within . . . really a high-powered *idea* . . . over-stressed . . . a 'dangerous symptom'" (51). The choice she presents to "we"—that is, to her and Freud, the collaborative readers of her traumatic memory of a visionary or hallucinatory "writing on the wall"—the choice between two ways of reading her writing, is not really a choice at all. Posed as a question of reading either this way or that, H.D.'s proposition actually points to a conjunction and proliferation of readings (two ways and more than two ways) at once symptomatic and poetic. In taking up her proposition, "we" disclose, instead of a demon or a diagnosis, a signifying practice that weaves together the productive and interpretative activities of reading and writing in a process of re-vision.

This process of writing, reading, translating is emphatically collective: the "we" who engage in the process are H.D. *and* Freud. Neither functions without the other: it is H.D.'s dream text that is read in the light of Freud's dream interpretation. Without Freud's theory and technique of reproducing the dream work, there would be no dream memory, no "writing," and without H.D.'s dream text, there would be no reading, no material for translation.

Freud, moreover, participates in the writing: it is his scene of transference which enables the recall of the "writing on the wall" memory in the first place. H.D.'s recollection of the writing is inscribed on the palimpsest of preconscious and unconscious memory whose cryptic visibility/readability the transference facilitates. Moreover, his theory or method of dream and symptom analysis has already entered into the re-production of the manifest text, so that in being re-presented, the recovered writing undergoes secondary revision, a screening onto *The Interpretation of Dreams* and other texts of Freud's collected works. Theory, here, is constitutive, shaping the trace of memory, conducting the retrieval of hieroglyphic sources from semiotic roots in linguistic material accessible not only to the symbolist poet but also to the practiced oneirocritic.

Finally, "we"—including the collective reader of *Tribute to Freud*—can translate this writing as a sign of subversion as well as a sign of suppression. H.D.'s *suppressed* (in place of the more properly psychoanalytic term *repressed*) emphasizes the sense of political repression and the subversiveness of the semiotic practice that signifies forbidden desire. Freud is a collaborator in more than one or two ways. He helps facilitate transference and the re-presentation of the manifest text of dream memory; he helps interpret this text; he also helps affirm, perhaps in spite of himself, the poet's wishful image of herself as a prophetess: "We can read or translate [my writing] as a suppressed desire for forbidden 'signs and wonders,' breaking bounds, a suppressed desire to be a Prophetess, to be important anyway, megalomania they call it" (*TF* 51). Freud collaborates in authorizing her dream of writing visionary poetry, a kind of "projective verse" that has the capacity to signify more than merely the neurosis or nostalgia of a modern, discontented ego.[1] Freud is implicated in the collective translation of her writing, a "high-powered" projection and extension of psychic and artistic potential, "dangerous" for the suppressive culture to which her prophecies may be addressed, as for the individual who may suffer from "megalomania."

In another passage H.D. recalls a different dream of writing.[2] "I had a dream about my little bottle of smelling-salts, the tell-tale transference symbol. In my dream, I am *salting* my typewriter. So I presume I would salt my savorless writing with the salt of the earth, Sigmund Freud's least utterance" (*TF* 148). This time writing figures more precisely as a writing machine, a typewriter, or as writing production, the fruits of which are "salted" with Freudian significance. The "tell-tale transference symbol" signals the intertextuality of H.D.'s dream-work revision. What she confesses about her relation to Freud is as overtly textual as it is covertly sexual. The seeds of the saltcellar may, to the crude psychoanalytic interpreter, symbolize woman's hopeless and inevitable envy for the pen(is), but to a more poetic reader, they signify not semen but semiosis. In this dream rebus, H.D.'s poetic generativity is salted, or supplemented, by Freudian utterances: her type (of) writing is a dissemination of Freudian discourse. We might translate this figure not simply as a sign of H.D.'s repressed desire for Freud the man or the father but also as a sign that she has determined how to conceive of their relationship as a desirable intertextuality. Freud's salting of H.D.'s type (of) writing reads allegorically as a combination of semiotic practices, an intertextuality in Julia Kristeva's sense of the term, "a permutation of texts," in which "in the space of a given text, several utterances, taken from other texts, intersect and neutralize one another."[3]

We might proceed to read H.D.'s dream as a pronouncement that from now on her text will inscribe Freud's text, his "least utterance," that her text should be read as a typology of texts, of utterances taken from Freud's text as well as from the text of her own dream-vision. This dissemination, salting the text with Freud's utterances, is not a figure of mimetic transcription, of recording Freud's authoritative word, his logos, the discursive or diagnostic language of psychoanalysis. Instead, scattered utterances are sprinkled into the writing machine, where they will be processed and transformed through an intertextual semiosis or poiesis: the significance of Freud's utterances will be translated as they translate.[4] Dreaming of salting her text with his, H.D. wishes to add to the significance of her own "savorless" text: it is added taste, significance, that she desires, not a clinical tongue, a clarifying *langue*. She envisions a writing that is, to borrow a Kristevan distinction, translinguistic rather than discursive, a tasteful play of semiotic practices that "operate through and across language, while remaining irreducible to its categories as they are presently assigned" (*Desire* 36).

In place of critical theory, poetic manifesto, doctrinal methodology, H.D. presents translation as the basic formulation of her writing practice. It appears throughout *Tribute to Freud* in demonstrations of her work with Freud and in commentary that explains her Freudian poetics. Translation is hardly a new activity for H.D.; her earliest training as an imagist involved extensive translation of ancient Greek texts. But in the course of her career, her art of translation changes from being something like interpretation, involving the transfer of significance between historical or national languages, to a heuristic device of self-discovery, involving the decoding of the "hieroglyph of the unconscious" (*TF* 93).[5]

The first passage quoted at the beginning of this chapter appears midway in the simultaneous tracing and deciphering of the cryptic writing on the wall for which this section of *Tribute* is named. It is one of several passages that comment on the translation in process, partly to explain Freud's conception and procedure of translation in dream and symptom analyses and partly to ensure that "we," the readers of *Tribute*, understand the intertextuality at work. What is performed in *Tribute* is not simply the translation from one language into another, H.D.'s discourse into Freud's or vice versa. In a parenthetical aside, H.D. affirms the acuteness of Freud's decoding acuteness with this significant qualification: "The Professor was right (actually he was always right, though we sometimes translated our thoughts into different languages or mediums)" (47). There is no universal language, no standard grammar or critical discourse for interpreting her dream-text. Together, she and Freud produce a reading that derives from the semiotics of the writing, the telltale "hieroglyphics" of the manifest text, through a collaborative evocation and employment of sign systems—hers hermetic and heretical, his classical and canonical; hers Moravian, his Judaic; hers American transcendentalist, his German romantic; and both autobiographical.[6]

Near the end of "Writing on the Wall," following a series of translations of troubling dream-texts, H.D. presents a model translation:

> She asks the question. Each verse of the lyric is a question or a series of questions. Do you know the Land? Do you know the House? Do you know the Mountain?
>
> *Kennst du den Berg und seinen Wolkensteg*
>
> 'Do you know the mountain and its cloud-bridge?' is an awkward enough translation but the idea of the mountain and bridge is so very suitable to this whole *translation* of the Professor and our work together. (*TF* 108)

There are several translations at work here. First, H.D. translates the question-and-answer format of analysis into verse from Goethe's *Wilhelm Meister*, which, in turn, begs translation from the German back into English, as well as an interpretation of the symbols. The translation proceeds: " '*Steg*' really means a 'plank'; *foot-bridge* is the most accurate rendering. It is not a bridge for a great crowd of people" (108). The common language, however, is neither German nor English, not even the language of psychoanalysis: it is Goethe's poetry and a certain dialogism that transfers a play of sound and sense across his lyrics. This bridge of translatable meaning is not for everyone: the intertextual reading is not generic. Moreover, it is "not built and hammered and constructed," not a methodological framework or a theoretical structure but a semiotic network "flung" across a gap opened by personal and cultural difference and the inaccessible unconscious. "We are dealing here with the realm of fantasy and imagination, flung across the abyss, and these are the poet's lines" (108).

But why does H.D. feature Goethe in this allegory of translation? Perhaps because Freud frequently quotes from Goethe's lyrics to support his speculations about human nature: H.D. stresses Freud's poetic sources as something they have in common, a bridge over an otherwise untranslatable abyss of cultural and personal difference. Perhaps also because this particular lyric features a question-and-answer dialogue that illustrates the style of interrogation in analysis.[7] Just as Goethe assigns priority to the questioner (Mignon) and her question, Freud leaves it to the analysand to intiate analysis. That "the question must be propounded by the protagonist himself," that "he must dig it out from its buried hiding-place . . . before it could be answered," is what H.D. observes to be the distinguishing feature of transference dialogue, as distinct from the mentor-centered Socratic dialogue (TF 84). The student, not the master, initiates the process of self-discovery; the poet, not the philosopher, mediates the dialogue of transference and translation.

H.D. suggests that we regard *Tribute* itself as an attempt to translate her appreciation of Freud, as she was unable to do in his lifetime for lack of a poetic intertext. She had not only to acquire an analytical appreciation of the transference but also to reformulate this appreciation in the poet's own words, "to express [an appreciation of Freud's enduring significance] adequately would be to delve too deep, to become involved in technicalities, and at the same time would be translating my admiration for what he stood for . . . into terms too formal . . . conventional . . . banal . . . *polite*" (63). To adequately translate her admiration of what Freud stood for, H.D. had to translate psychoanalysis. This translation, she knew, would please the Professor, judging by his enthusiasm for Marie Bonaparte, "the Professor's French translator" (39), whose translations extended his work not only to another European language but also to another discipline, literary criticism (with her *Edgar Poe: Étude psychanalytique* [1933], which Freud prefaced). But H.D.'s translation presents no orthodox representation. She has none of the fidelity of the guardians and canonizers of his discourse, those idolaters whom she caricatures in "The Master":

they will discuss all his written words,
his pen will be sacred
they will build a temple
and keep all his sacred writings safe.
                                    (CP 457)

In her translation, Freud's written word is not locked in a safe, but it is encrypted in the hieroglyphic intertext of her hermeticism. While subjecting Freud to a certain heterodoxy, endangering the "truth"— the fixed code—his disciples would like to administer, H.D.'s translation also transforms and enlivens. No dogmatic ideologue, H.D. adapts Freud's language and (psycho)logic for heuristic purposes. She knows what any lexicographer of Freud's work has shown, that his terms are less definitive than tentative and evolving.[8] Underlining his poetic use of language, his inventive play with words to open realms of the unknown, H.D., like Freud, supplements what she borrows from the crucible of existing sign systems, "so the impact of a language, as well as the impact of an impression may [not] become 'correct,' become 'stylized,' lose its living quality" (15).

Elsewhere, in *Bid Me to Live*, the autobiographical novel she wrote in response to Freud's prescription of a "writing cure," she testifies to her unorthodox sense of translation:

> Anyone can translate the meaning of the word. She wanted the shape, the feel of it, the character of it, as if it had been freshly minted. She felt that the old manner of approach was as toward hoarded treasure, but treasure that had passed through too many hands, had been too carefully assessed by the grammarians. She wanted to coin new words.
> She pushed aside her typewriter and let her pencil and her notebook take her elsewhere. (163)

Here, the typewriter symbolizes the mechanical reproduction of grammarians, whereas in the passage from "Advent" quoted earlier, it signified the incorporative machinery of intertextual production. In both cases, however, writing appears to operate "through and across language"; it does not appear to be put in the service of discourse or restricted to recording a transcendental signified. Moreover, in both cases, intertextual production is presented as appropriation. The profound humility that H.D.'s dream of salting her typewriter with "Sigmund Freud's least utterance" seems to express merely cloaks the profound arrogance of the dreamer's wish to incorporate selected utterances into her transformative typology of texts. A writing machine and a mint, the typewriter or pen and notebook are set to coin new words, to translate Freud's written word into heuristic neologism. The passage from *Bid Me to Live* makes it explicit that in performing her translation the poet is at once "arrogant and . . . humble" (163), "self-effacing" and "ambitious" (162).

In *Tribute to Freud*, H.D. attests to appropriating or adapting Freud's signifying practice: "I must find new words as the Professor found or coined words to explain certain as yet unrecorded states of mind or being" (145). She neologizes Freud's neologisms in an effort not merely to disguise an anxiety of influence or to satisfy a megalomania but to maximize her "self" as exploratory medium, just as Freud explored his "self," his unconscious self, with the heuristic device of concept metaphors. No one accuses Freud of being megalomaniacal; yet his method of dream interpretation is self-extending. H.D. emphasizes the "I, Maximus" character of Freud's oneiric research:

> With precise Jewish instinct for the particular in the general, for the personal in the . . . universal, for the *material* in the abstract, he had dared to plunge into the unexplored depth, first of his own unconscious. . . . From it, he dredged, as samples of his own theories, his own dreams, exposing them as serious discoveries, facts, with cause and effect, beginning and end, often showing from even the most trivial dream sequence the powerful dramatic impact that projected it. (71–72)

It is delusory to think of oneself as a prophetess if there is nothing upon which to base this assumption but one's own "signs." In Freud's semiotic theory of dreams, however, H.D. found an oracular source for her own unconscious and preconscious memory. The collaborative translation of her dream writing simultaneously enacted the translation of a haunted soul into *spiritus mundi*, a treasure-source of transpersonal signification. The poet humbly worships "the Professor" who showed her the way to her self-maximizing dreams:

> He had said, he had dared to say that the dream had its worth and value in translatable terms, not the dream of a Pharaoh . . . , not merely Joseph's dream or Jacob's dream of a symbolic ladder, not the dream only of the Cumaean Sibyl of Italy or the Delphic Priestess of ancient Greece, but the dream of everyone, everywhere. He had dared to say that the dream came from an unexplored depth in man's consciousness and that this unexplored depth ran like a great stream or ocean underground, and the vast depth . . . produced inspiration, madness, creative idea, or the dregs of the dreariest symptoms. . . . *even if not stated in so many words*, he had dared to imply that the dream-symbol could be

interpreted; its language, its imagery were common to the whole race, not only of the living but of those ten thousand years dead. (70–71, my emphasis)

What Freud gave H.D., what she especially attributes to his genius and daring, is access to the universal myths of (pre)history through her own symptomatic dream symbols. In transference with Freud, she learns the technique of invoking and translating the hieroglyphs of fantasy-vision, observing that her own personal dream could come up with the universal "Goods" or "Gods" (12, 63) to heal disillusion-ment, the disease to which her age was particularly susceptible. Freud taught her that "the dream of everyone, everywhere" had universal value (71). He helped her realize that her dream could, and even should, be regarded with as much prognostic weight as the Sibyl's, the oracle's, and Freud's own dream.

He helped affirm her own sense of *spiritus mundi*, which modernist male poets plundered as an exclusively male domain. Their access to this treasure-source of symbols, primarily through recovery and translation of a masculinist mythos/logos, was not her access, not her way of reading the palimpsest of the Western mind. *Tribute to Freud* is a woman poet's late defense of her Freudian translation of the mod-ernist tradition that Eliot traced from Magdalenian rock drawings through Homer onward. *Tribute* defends H.D. from charges of mega-lomania,[9] and more important, it defends her heterodox sense of descent from prehistoric sources in the "Magdala" of matriarchal mystery cults, whose mythos/logos and signs she would endeavor to recover through the (mother) transference. "In any case," she pro-tests,

> he had opened up . . . that particular field of the unconscious mind that went to prove that the traits and tendencies of obscure aboriginal tribes, as well as the shape and substance of the rituals of vanished civiliza-tions, were still inherent in the human mind—the human psyche, if you will. But according to his theories the soul existed explicitly, or showed its form and shape in and through the medium of the mind, and the body, as affected by the mind's ecstasies or disorders. (12–13)

Freud uncovers another palimpsest with which to retrace and re-cover the signifying practices of the past. Instead of having to turn exclusively to the "tradition" of male-dominated literary history to compose her modernist text, H.D. discovers, through Freud and the medium of her own symptomatic mind/body processes, an other realm for semiotic excavation and translation.

H.D. defends Freud[10] against the growing institutionalization of psychoanalysis, which threatens, paradoxically, to stifle the growth of his creative word. "In our talks together," she testifies, "he rarely used any of the now rather overworked technical terms, invented by himself and elaborated on by the growing body of doctors, psychologists, and nerve specialists who form the somewhat formidable body of the International Psycho-Analytical Association" (87). She also defends him against the self-elected high priests of literary modernism, in particular D. H. Lawrence and Ezra Pound.[11] It is a careful defense that does not seek to oppose or polarize differences, since Lawrence and Pound also find their way into H.D.'s intertext. Her tactic is to revise the character of Freud which Lawrence so viciously inscribes in *Psychoanalysis and the Unconscious* (1921), and to translate the image of Freudian thought, which Pound dismisses as so much vile bunk. In her text Freud is an alchemist of the word, a charismatic healer, and above all a poet-seer—figures that ironically contest the modernist masters' self-images.

Finally, another important feature of H.D.'s Freudian translation merits introductory attention. *Tribute to Freud* also asks that we read the collaborative efforts of analyst and analysand, professor and poet, as therapeutic. Readings and revisions of dream symptoms are presented in these pages as cathartic and enabling translations of an inexpressible and irrepressible traumatizing memory. Early in the text, H.D. discloses why she sought out Freud. During the war years, 1914–1919, she suffered several disturbing events from which she had not yet recovered in the thirties: "I had had a number of severe shocks; the news of the death of my father, following the death in action of my brother in France, came to me while I was alone outside London in the early spring of that bad influenza winter of 1919. I myself was waiting for my second child—I had lost the first in 1915, from shock and repercussions of war news broken to me in a rather brutal fashion" (40). In the same period, she also suffered the dissolution of her marriage and the breakup of her literary circle in London (v). Failure to assign these events sufficiently satisfying meaning resulted in the recurrence of "borderline" perceptual experiences. To master these experiences, and to claim them as creative activity, she put them into writing, but, for want of a technique, in vain:

I have tried to write of these experiences. . . . The fear of losing them, forgetting them, or just giving them up as neurotic fantasies, residue of the war, confinement and the epidemic . . . drives me on to begin again and again. . . .

I can decide that my experiences were the logical outcome of illness, separation from my husband, and loss of the friendship of Lawrence; but even so I have no technique with which to deal with the vision. (153)

In her 1933–1934 sessions with Freud, however, H.D. found no antidote for these phantasmal experiences.[12] By her account, the onset of World War II prevented her analysis from ever really getting under way. Moreover, she noted, Freud "saw 'from signs' that [she] did not want to be analyzed" (139). This reluctance, together with her dread of shocking or worrying him to death with her premonition of a Jewish holocaust (134, 139), put severe constraints on the transference: "My sessions with the Professor were barely under way, before there were preliminary signs and symbols of the approaching ordeal. And the thing I wanted to fight in the open . . . was driven deeper. With the death-head swastika chalked on the pavement, leading to the Professor's very door, I must, in all decency, calm as best I could my own personal Phobia . . . of war-terror" (93–94). In the end, she decided to settle for a " 'delayed' analysis" (139), whose enactment we are invited to read in *Tribute to Freud*, and in subsequent writing whose poetics elaborate the techniques of translation presented there.

## "Freud" Enters H.D.'s Writing

"Freud" makes his explicit entry into H.D.'s text with the composition of *Her* (1926–1927), although, as the narrative informs us, the author had been reading his books long before. Susan Stanford Friedman explains that "H.D.'s earliest acquaintance with psychoanalysis probably began in the home of her friend Frances Josepha Gregg sometime before they left for Europe in 1911. In *Her*, the autobiographical novel dealing with the years 1909 and 1910, H.D. wrote that Gregg had given her some psychoanalytic books in German. Since she had difficulty with the language, Gregg's uncle translated sections for the two friends."[13] It seems that H.D. first engaged with psychoanalysis *in translation*. Not content, however, with someone else's translation and uninterested in the original German and the problems of standardized foreign-language editions,[14] H.D. started "translating" Freud and psychoanalysis for herself when she began to formulate a poetics at the end of World War I.

H.D. became familiar with Freud's library long before she arranged to meet the man in person, and even before "those astounding Freudian and post-Freudian volumes" were a familiar feature on the common bookshelf (*Her* 18). Friedman finds that "H.D.'s work with the Professor was the central point around which a forty-year involvement with psychoanalysis revolved," but she maintains that this work must be viewed in context of H.D.'s "previous and subsequent exposure to psychoanalysis" in order to illuminate "Freud's significance for the transformation of H.D.'s art" (*Psyche Reborn* 17). I would like to add that whereas *Tribute to Freud* may signify the formulation of a poetics and thus may occupy a certain theoretical locus in H.D.'s writing life, this achievement must be read in the context of a lengthy practice of translation before and after her sessions of apprenticeship/analysis with Freud, in order to disclose the changing textual strategies H.D. employs in her appropriation and transformation of Freud's text.

Friedman points to variable biographical sources of psychoanalytic influence, including H.D.'s "friendships with proponents of Freud's new science,[15] her extensive reading in the psychoanalytic literature, her experiences with other psychoanalysts, . . . her reflections on Freud in her memoirs and notebooks," as sources that "laid the foundation for his impact" (17). I would like to consider as well H.D.'s Freudian "pre-texts," the writing she did before and around the time of her analysis in 1933–1934, with the purpose of exploring the process of translation and its interimplications: how Freud's entry into her writing changes her writing, how her selection and revision of his texts changes our reading and reception of him.

H.D. first implies a knowledge of Freudian theory in *Notes on Thought and Vision* (1919). In this text she attempts, among other things, to formulate what she called her "'jelly-fish' experience" (116), one of those she feared "giving . . . up as neurotic fantasies, residue of the war, confinement and the epidemic" (153). *Notes* idealizes this experience as heightened aesthetic consciousness whose psychogenesis finds its source in the jellyfishlike "womb-brain or love-brain" of the body (*NTV* 22). Not entirely satisfied however, with a first, impressionistic description (which echoes Emerson, Nietzsche, de Gourmont, Lawrence and Pound), she tries again, this time outlining the topography of her jellyfish in endopsychic terms that vaguely allude to a Freudian topography: "I visualize my three states of consciousness in a row, 1. Over-conscious mind / 2. Conscious mind / 3. Sub-conscious mind" (*NTV* 46). Revision does not stop here but is repeated again and again until, in "Advent," it employs an explicitly psychoanalytic rhetoric. The following passages might loosely be read as references to such psychoanalytic concepts as the splitting of the ego in the process of defense, projection, transference, and preoedipal fantasy:

> I had what Bryher called the 'jelly-fish' experience of double ego; bell-jar or half-globe as of transparent glass spread over my head like a diving-bell and another manifested from my feet, so enclosed I was for a short space in St. Mary's, Scilly Isles, July 1918, immunized or insulated from the war disaster. (116)[16]

> I felt the double globe come and go and I could have dismissed it at once and probably would have if I had been alone. . . . It was being with Bryher that projected the fantasy. (130)

> When I told [Freud] of the Scilly Isles experience, the transcendental feeling of the two globes . . . enclosing me, I said I supposed it was some form of pre-natal fantasy. Freud said, 'Yes, obviously; you have found the answer, good—good.' (168)

Whether or not H.D.'s use of these concepts is technically correct, her writing shows a willingness to apply them to her own personal equation and a degree of satisfaction in learning to name her experience. She does not, however, give up the feeling that she had discovered the dream source or "womb-brain" or, to use Goethe's botanical metaphor, the *Urpflanze* of all creative production: "Are we psychic coral-polyps?" she muses. "Did I (sub-aqueous) in the Scilly Isles, put out a feeler? Did I die in my polyp manifestation?" (133).

It is important to note that this jellyfish experience, like all her visionary experiences, originates in the presence of an enabling companion. What might have been merely a disturbance of consciousness becomes with encouragement an experiment in autohypnosis, hallucination, and hypnoid states. Bryher, her ever-steady partner and the instigator of their explorations in psychoanalysis, saw her through at least two of these experiences (130, 48–49). But in the case of the jellyfish experience, she also had Havelock Ellis in mind (129). H.D. had been seeing Ellis for treatment and "all the time . . . was thinking that this would be an interesting bit of psychological data for [him]" (130). From this time on, she appears to write for an actual or imaginary audience of psychologists, as if posing her self and her work as specimen material for a new science. She did not, however, aspire to become a fascinating "case" like André Breton's Nadja or Josef Breuer's Anna O. "If I had been a little maladjusted or even mildly deranged, [the visionary experience] would have been no small wonder" (41), she reflects; not maladjusted but gifted, she would be mistress of these experiences, bringing them under her control as poetic technician.

Ellis declined to show any interest in her jellyfish experience.[17] Nevertheless, H.D. continued to transcribe her experiences and to seek further treatment (first, twenty-four sessions with Mary Chadwick in 1931 in London and later with Hanns Sachs in Berlin [vii]). Her writing displays ambivalence towards psychoanalysis. Much of the prose written over the years 1925–1935 assumes an exploratory and symptomatic form; these are the texts that, as she says, "ghosted" for the "story or the novel of [her] war experience, [the] first, still-born child and the second, born so fortunately" (148), pointing to *Palimpsest* (1926) and *Hedylus* (1928). During this period she also produced *Her* (1927), the story of her "slight breakdown" at the end of her second year at Bryn Mawr (x); *Kora and Ka* (1934), a narrative that interweaves ritual initiation into the Eleusinian Mysteries and the psychoanalytic process; and *Nights* (1935), a narrative study of borderlines between ecstasy and disorder. All these texts display a clinical interest in her own writing-subject, but none goes so far as to adopt a psychoanalytic orientation without equivocation. Still, each presents a serious commitment to an intertextual experimentation that in some way(s) incorporates Freud's text.

*Her* opens with a barrage of pseudoanalytic vocabulary, highlighted by quotation marks as if to indicate their foreignness as well as their failure to identify, explain, or even certify the protagonist's insufferable condition: " 'I am Her, Her, Her.' Her Gart had no word for her dementia. . . . 'failure complex,' 'compensation reflex,' and that conniving phrase 'arrested development' had opened no door to her" (*Her* 3). Appropriating and adapting "overworked technical terms," the narrator tests both the language and the theory of clinical psychology. In *Nights* the urge to name the other becomes even more compelling and the terminology more specifically psychoanalytic, if occasionally bracketed by quotation marks. *Nights* displays a sophisticated willingness to consider "the language of the unconscious" (*N* 15), "the fabulous hieroglyph of the Freudian technology" (18), and mechanisms of "repression" and "inhibition" (4), with the implied intention to extend "explorations into the new doctrines of the unconscious" (6) and to champion "the much misunderstood medium of psycho-analysis" (18). The most ambitious intertextual project of this period, however, is *Kora and Ka*.[18]

*Kora and Ka* works with at least five "texts": autobiography, psycho-analysis, modernist quest, Egyptian and Eleusinian mysteries. A telling rhetoric that includes such terms as "guilt-complex" (23), "mother complex" (24), "sadism" (26), "inhibited" (28), "analysis" (30, 31), and "dissociation" (35) and such phrases as "if I could encourage the subconscious to break into consciousness" (30) signal the inscription of psychoanalytic utterance. Intertextuality operates at the narrative and discursive levels but not at the level of lexemes and graphemes displayed in the more sophisticated semiotics of *Trilogy* and *Helen in Egypt*. Nonetheless the interweaving of multiple sign systems in the novel prefigures H.D.'s later, Freudian translations of dream symbols through a proliferation of linguistic and mythic sources.

The narrative consists of three parts, each narrated by a different psychic aspect of the narrating subject, John Helforth: dead soul, analysand, and Eleusinian initiate. Helforth is also the name of the narrator of the Prologue to *Nights*, though this Helforth plays the different role of psychoanalytic literary critic. In *Kora and Ka*, Helforth is a modernist quester who journeys neurotically through the London underworld as through an Egyptian/Eleusinian "hell" en route to catharsis and rebirth.

The initiation/analysis/underworld passage is methodically ritualistic. H.D.'s narrative follows the modernist "mythic method" of shaping its pastiche of quotations and collage of historical correspondences by mapping them onto an archetypal quest pattern. The three parts of her novel chart three parts of the quest: descent into hell, ritual initiation or rite of passage, revelation and resurrection with the final apotheosis attesting to the prominence of the Eleusinian text. That the narrative clearly charts a *progress* throws doubt on the significance of the reference to analysis whose movement is hardly so straightforward as Freud presents it, with its interminable blockages, displacements, regressions, fixations, and ambivalence. Though all the later major poetry, *Helen in Egypt*, *Trilogy*, and *Hermetic Definition*, adopts this tripartite mystery structure, the route of passage is not so mappable as it is in *Kora and Ka*. *Helen in Egypt*, in particular, embodies the interminable analysis, the three-phase highway toward revelation and transcendence fading among the details of surfacing palimpsests of memory.

Narrative navigation rather than translation might more precisely describe the intertextuality of this novel. The rite of passage takes place in a haunting landscape interwoven with features of Osiris' journey across water, Demeter-Persephone's harvested cornfields and burnt grasslands, London's labyrinthine back streets, as well as the maze of personal memory.[19] Scenes of passage are viewed through the narrator's changing state of mind. Part 1 navigates/narrates the descent into hell, whose stages include a drastic visit to the eye/I doctor, a diagnosis of failed "vision," and a blind taxi ride through smoky alleys to the entrance of a "neolithic" temple site. The point of view is that of Helforth's dissociating consciousness or disembodied soul, "that sort of shadow they used to call a Ka, in Egypt." As the shade itself explains: "A Ka lives after the body is dead. I shall live after Helforth is dead" (7).[20] Part 2 furthers the ritual initiation, which is also analytic, as experienced by Helforth's resisting ego: "I, John Helforth, go on existing. . . . Ka is far off now; Ka partook of symptom, was neurotic breakdown" (21) and "I insist on my masculinity and brutality. . . . I will burn away my soul with my mind, or should I say my body" (23) I have meant to be robust" (24). A drink from Mnemosyne's waters induces an onrush of memory, over whose painful narrative course Kora presides. She is Helforth's maternal confidante and engaging interlocutor with whom he enacts a mother transference; she is also an avatar of Koré-Persephone, priestess of the matriarchal mysteries of birth, death, and rebirth. To Kora, Helforth reveals his primal love for his mother (28) and attendant oedipal conflicts arising out of his family romance, complicated by the First World War (26–32). Kora serves at once as mythic inspiration ("Kora is everything. Without Kora, Ka would have got me. . . . I am on familiar terms with Kora, with Ka, likewise. . . . Some . . . primordial Three-in-One" [21]) and as analyst-prompter ("Kora says my attitude is fantastic and linked up with mother-complex" [28]). Part 3 charts the final stage of the mystery, ending with revelation and resurrection as perceived by the Eleusinian intitiate. Ka, Kora, and Helforth are reintegrated, as are mind and body, in a culminating moment of cathartic and ecstatic recognition which is chiefly Eleusinian in character: "We were Kora of the Underworld and Dionysos, not yet risen. . . . Now we are Kore and the slain God . . . risen" (43).[21]

Like *Hedylus* (1924), which H.D. mentions in *Tribute to Freud*, *Kora and Ka* attempts to retell and work through unassimilated material of her war experience in the figures of classical personae who "ghosted" for it (*TF* 148). Gary Burnett sees *Kora and Ka*, along with *Nights*, as a transitional work that brought H.D. "out" of a solitary, imaginary confinement, where she had been drawn by the spirit of the old Greek and Egyptian mysteries, into a public world where her spirit would have to be aired before demanding and discriminating audiences.[22] H.D., he confirms, "chooses the world. Such a return carries with it the responsibility of translating the terms of vision into the terms of the world, of testifying to the efficacy of revelation in a world which would otherwise deny it" (144). Burnett subtly argues that both author and narrator undergo a therapeutic process. In the case of Helforth, his "Ka returns, now transmuted from symptomatic sign of 'neurotic breakdown' to instrument of vision. The Ka's ability to see the deadened Helforth at the story's opening becomes a new power to 'see' Kora in mythological guise; . . . the entire situation changes from the world of breakdowns, husbands, and dead brothers to the eternal world of mysteries and rebirth" (152–53). As for H.D., her (w)rite of passage between "private vision and public constatation" has been intitiated and will continue with the writing of her "mysteries into speech" in the poems of the thirties (155). The finding of a public voice, however, is not the only therapeutic benefit of these transitional works. Interweaving these mysteries and the war experiences they "ghost" into the analytic process makes analysis "speak" to H.D., so that she can lend herself to analysis. *Kora and Ka* reflects H.D.'s serious commitment to finding a writing cure and sets the stage for the work of translation which she will perform with Freud in analysis.

It is significant that H.D.'s Eleusinian initiate is male,(her "only male pseudonym," as Burnett points out [144]), that it is a man who undergoes a transformative rite of passage, whose "mother complex" derives from a masculinity complex ("I insist on my masculinity and my brutality" [23]), with its death drive toward willful individuation and dis-integration ("I will burn away my soul with my mind" [23]; "I curse Ka. . . . I hate . . . Kora" [24]), a phallic thanatos opposed to a maternal eros, figured as bovine swamp ("I say, 'rushes and reeds and cows.' . . I go on, I say, 'cow,' I say, 'mother, mother, mother'" [24]). It is significant that it is the memory of a primal mother which re-members Helforth's body (Osiris) and soul (disembodied Ka, dissociated ego), that this primal mother is not a phallic mother, who threatens to devour the life potency of her sons but a preoedipal, pantheistic deity, whose power is chthonic, abundant, and regenerative. Helforth's initiation into the matriarchal mysteries is a subversion not only of the phallic mysteries propounded by the male modernists but also of the psychoanalytic cult of the father.

A similar subversion occurs in "The Master" (1934–1935), where Freud first enters H.D.'s poetry. Here, the poet testifies to her enthusiasm for the "master's" subtle powers of dream interpretation. She implies her willingness to be initiated into the higher mysteries of psychoanalysis, confident that he "will bring a new world to birth" (*CP* 457)—until she discovers and confronts his masculinist discourse:

> I was angry with the old man
> with his talk of the man-strength,
> I was angry with his mystery, his mysteries,
> I argued till day-break.
>
> (455)

The poem proceeds to perform not a dialogue or a debate but a radical translation of these male mysteries into female mysteries in which man is not represented:

> no man will be present in those mysteries,
> yet all men will kneel,
> no man will be potent,
> important,
> yet all men will feel
> what it is to be a woman.
>
> (460)

Most significantly, the master himself appears to go through some sea change, transformed from phallic priest to "Lord become woman" (461). Freud affirms the poet (455, 458) and also becomes the woman who translates his mysteries into her art.

## Thrice-Greatest: Hippocratic-Hermeneutic-Hermetic Freud

The "Freud" who emerges from *Tribute to Freud* is a figure of radical translation. In one suggestive passage "our Professor" reads as a symbolic equation between the seal of Hippocrates, the caduceus of Hermes, and the Tau cross of Thoth:

> I learned recently . . . that 'the seal of the Hippocratic University bears the Tau-cross, entwined with serpent—exactly the figure used by. . . .'

＃33333

. . . Asklepios of the Greeks who was called the *blameless physician*. He was the son of the sun, Phoebos Apollo, and music and medicine were alike sacred to this source of light. This half-man, half-god . . . went a little too far when he began actually to raise the dead. . . . Our Professor stood this side of the portal. He did not pretend to bring back the dead who had already crossed the threshold. But he raised from dead hearts and stricken minds and maladjusted bodies a host of living children. . . .

Leader of the Dead? That was Hermes of the Greeks who took the attribute from Thoth of the Egyptians. The *T* or Tau-cross became caduceus. (*TF* 100–101)

Before our very (reading) eyes, Freud undergoes a (w)rite of passage, from professor-physician to hermetic talisman. "Freud," whether the man or the text, is Hippocratic-hermeneutic-hermetic, a modern Hermes Trismegistos, H.D.'s "thrice-greatest" charismatic healer. In this section, I examine the therapeutics as well as the aesthetics (especially the stagecraft) of this translation/transfiguration of Freud into modern shaman and hermetic symbol.

In H.D.'s revisionary analysis, Freud uncannily assumes the role of the Old World pharmacist who induces waking dreams and who raises the dead and buried past from the crypts of memory. This is his guise as Hermes-Thoth, god of sleep and dreams and conductor of souls to the underworld.[23] "Perhaps I will be treated with a psychic drug, will take away a nameless precious phial from his cavern," H.D. muses. "Perhaps I will learn the secret, be priestess with power over life and death" (117). The "cavern" she refers to is the dark room off Freud's office which houses his amulets, charms, and idols from ancient Greece and Egypt: this is Freud's "pharmacy," the tomb to which he periodically withdraws to gather the precise treasure or combination of treasures to enchant deep memory. His charm, moreover, compares with that of the magic of word pharmacists Poe and Coleridge, two of H.D.'s favorite poets, "both alleged drug-addicts, Poe with his Lenores and haunted Ushers, and Coleridge with his Xanadu, his Khubla Khan" (132).

Freud enchants H.D. with his otherworldliness. In his presence, she feels the very essence of psyche applied to or extracted from her forehead: "Today, lying on the famous psychoanalytical couch, I have a feeling of evaporating cold menthol, some form of ether, laid on my 'morbid' brow," she writes (132), and later, "Again, I feel, lying on this couch that a sort of phosphorescence is evaporating from my forehead and I can almost breathe this anodyne, this ether. Am I reminded of happy release from pain and . . . fortunate auspices?"

(137). Freud's charm is embodied in his name. But the charm is not entirely Freud's. H.D.'s uncanny sensation of her physician's cold and ethereal psychic powers must derive, in part, from her poetic knowledge of etymology: she implicitly refers to the Greek *psuche*, meaning, in Gregory Ulmer's words, "cold breath, a gust of wind, which remains after life is gone, as its twin word *psuchos* [frost, chill] indicates," the ethereal subject of analytic treatment.[24]

Lined with etchings and paintings and with cabinets of ancient vases and signet rings, housing stacks full of leather-bound books, and featuring a desk top circled with bronze and stone idols, as well as a back room full of archaeological discoveries, Freud's office helps stage and shape H.D.'s most illuminating visions. It is not just he but also his "things" that conjure forth her Egyptian dreams, restore the dead to the living and the ancient past to present memory:

> The child in me has gone. The child has vanished and yet it is not dead. This contact with the Professor intensifies or projects this dream of a Princess, the river, the steps, the child. The river is an Egyptian river, the Nile; the Princess is an Egyptian lady. Egypt is present . . . actually or by inference or suggestion, in the old-fashioned print or engraving of the Temple at Karnak, hanging on the wall above me, as well as in the dimly outlined egg-shaped Ra or Nut or Ka figures on the Professor's desk in the other room. (38–39)

The personal dream is invoked and amplified by Freud's charms, is in part the *effect* of setting the scene with Egyptian props. When, on another occasion, H.D. identified the house or cathedral of a dream as himself, Freud answers "No . . . not me—but analysis" (147), prompting her further comment: "It is, as he had said of my grandfather, 'an atmosphere. . . .' The gnomes or gargoyles, the Gothic dragons, bird, beast, and fish of the inner and outer motives, the images of saints and heroes all find their replicas or their 'ghosts' in this room or in these two rooms" (147).

What her *Tribute* makes emphatically clear is that to remember herself and to (have) access (to) memories beyond her "self," to make the personal-transpersonal equation, she must remember "Freud," his words, his physical and psychical presence, and above all his things. To perform her delayed analysis, she must occupy her memory of him as though she were visiting the underworld home of Hermes Psychopompos. Norman Holmes Pearson, H.D.'s editor and correspondent in later years, observes in his Foreword to the 1974 edition of *Tribute*: "With him, the desk and walls of his consulting room filled with bibelots which were tokens of history, she had gone back to her childhood, back to the breakup of her marriage and the birth of her child, back to the death of her brother . . . of her father, and back to the breakup of her literary circle" (v).

Joseph Riddel reads H.D.'s "dream-house" as a product of reconstruction and translation, noting the play of distortion at work in the memory of analysis. Memory is not simply recalled: it is housed, framed, conditioned by the imaginary and symbolic exchange between H.D. and Freud (his space, his things):

> Freud's study, filled with Etruscan and Egyptian artifacts, is like a Cathedral reduplicating a mausoleum, a pyramid. . . . Freud's house/ Cathedral is the only space where reconstruction takes place. It begins with signs, memory objects but also artifacts antedating all personal memory. . . . The analysis has also been a kind of re-entombment . . . which reduplicates her childhood house . . . a scene of analysis, where the forces of reconstruction and distortion are simultaneously at play.[25]

The site of construction is also one of deconstruction. The cathedral of the dream is a sign that the scene of analysis is not just a reconstruction but also a *product* of imaginary distortion and translation in need of further analysis: "For reconstruction (whether it suggests recuperation of a forgotten or repressed memory or a mimetic repetition of some earlier state) is not separable from de-construction, since the process of re-working involves not only a distortion but a re-marking of the distortion. The Cathedral of 'analysis' marks itself as a 'dream,' and the 'dream is already an image-substitution and distortion in need of analysis" (45). But why should this house embodying H.D.'s memory of analysis take the specific form of a pyramid or a cathedral? Why should H.D. be so particularly charmed by them? Riddel apparently overlooks the "personal equation" of the universal formula of dream building. However cryptic and in need of further translation and analysis, these houses are precisely those images that signify to H.D. the personal and transpersonal dream content. They are the charismatic signs, the emblematic cryptograms that work specifically for her with the potency of a conjurer, opening the doors of memory's storehouse, setting the ball of analysis rolling.

Freud does not always facilitate conventionally Freudian memory and understanding. It is not necessarily the oedipal structure of the so-called typical dream of analysis on which H.D.'s memory is recast. In H.D.'s revised analysis, Freud's "sanctum" sets the stage for another scene in another house, perhaps the "House of Atreus" *before* the gods (Athene and Apollo) have decreed that patriarchal law shall overrule the maternal bonds of blood and love. (There are other, older gods besides the Olympian ones sitting atop his desk.) In one such recast scene, H.D. remembers her mother as "choragus" as well as Aphrodite or Clytemnestra (her mother's name was Helen, and the Helen of Greek legend was Clytemnestra's sister) and remembers her brother as the rebellious Orestes. She casts herself as a perplexed, potentially subversive Iphigenia:

> It seems odd that my mother should be laughing. My brother has defied her. He is seated firm on the curb-stone. He is not going home. As he repeats this solemnly, my mother laughs more. People stop and ask. . . . My mother tells them and they laugh too. . . . She obtains supporters; strangers and near-strangers repeat her words like a Greek chorus, following the promptings of their leader.
>
> There is a slight, whispered conspiracy. . . . My brother . . . has told her that he is going away to live by himself, and he has moreover told her that his sister is coming with him. . . . But though her brain is in a turmoil of anxiety and pride and terror, *it has not even occurred to [the sister] that she might throw her small weight into the balance of conventional behavior by following her mother and leaving her brother to his fate.* (28–29, my emphasis)

Freud's "Greek" artifacts may set the stage for childhood memory, but they do not always produce a classic psychoanalytic interpretation. "Oedipus" is not so spellbinding that he blocks the possibility of a radical revision. "In this scene," Deborah Kelly Kloepfer observes, H.D. "finds the seed of all her subsequent revisionism, a way of turning the tables on tragedies, myths, tales, and translations."[26] With this unconventional memory, H.D. prompts Freud to confirm that she "had not made the conventional transference from mother to father, as is usual with a girl at adolescence" (*TF* 136) and to remember the history of psychoanalysis, "how mistakes were made in the beginning, as it was not sufficiently understood that the girl did not invariably transfer her emotions to her father" (175).

Freud also helps her conjure forth a more charming father than the cool-tempered professor of mathematics and astronomy who lived in his study-observatory in intellectual abstraction, a remote soul among the heavenly stars (24–27). "Our Professor" translates this first professor into another order of memory, beyond the chilling personal recollection. "Freud" injects charisma into this ghost, by facilitating the play of transference between professor and father and by inducing archaic memory with provocative transference symbols. The magnifying glass on her father's desk becomes the "sacred *ankh*, the symbol of life in Egypt":

> He used this very sign, the circle with the supporting straight line, with an added little line, a cross, to indicate the planet Venus. I do not know if our father knows that the *ankh* is the symbol of life. . . . He writes columns and columns of numbers, yet at the top of one column he will sketch in a hieroglyph. . . . It is only now as I write this that I see how my father possessed sacred symbols, how he, like the Professor, had old, old sacred objects on his study table. (25)

H.D. equates the ankh with the astronomical sign for Venus, which is also the generic sign for female or woman. That she should "remember" her father signing his columns with the life/female/love symbol helps heal her sense of alienation in the paternal symbolic order of desire and difference. As she relates in *Her*, it was her brother, not she, who was enabled by the patriarchal structure of the Doolittle family romance to distinguish himself as heir to the father's profession.

In this recast scene of analysis, Freud's hermetic pharmacy, H.D. proceeds to stage the collaborative hermeneutical translations of her symptomatic dreams. The most "dangerous" of these dreams is the so-called writing-on-the-wall experience (42), which she had on holiday in Corfu with Bryher in 1920. Like the jellyfish experience, it cannot be written off as simply hallucinatory ("I could not get rid of the experience by writing about it. I had tried that" [40]). It occupies center stage of the tribute, signifying the *mise en abyme* structure of her "writing." *Tribute* re-presents a disturbing dream of writing through a vision/memory/distortion of analysis, which reveals a "suppressed desire for forbidden 'signs and wonders'" under the collaborative auspices of a (re)visionary Hermes-Freud: a complex translation designed (consciously? unconsciously?) to authorize a woman's transgressive wish to compare with her professional brother, to equal her modernist male colleagues, to be a poet-prophetess.[27]

From her description of the effort of concentration ("my own head is splitting with the ache of concentration. I know that if I let go, lessen the intensity of my stare . . . or even blink . . . the pictures will fade out" [49]), it is clear that H.D. is now, as then, in a hypnotic trance. The "shadow- or light-pictures" that are "projected" (41) before her in the form of lines, graphs, dots, circles, and symbolic figures are not unlike what one of Freud's hysterics sees under his "pressure-technique" of recall: symbols bathed in a "shimmer of light," "curious signs . . . like Sanskrit; figures like triangles," stars and crosses and snakes of "allegorical meaning."[28] But what H.D. projects are the graphic signs of poetic aspiration. Along with the lines and graphs and dots, there are figures of a hand that draws and of a head that hovers over the drawing like an emblematic muse (44–46). The head is "visored," suggesting an "airman" (Mercury? Hermes?), and he is accompanied by further projections of a lamp and a tripod (45).

A possible explanation of this hallucinated writing is the optical illusion of "eidetic vision," about which H.D. likely learned in her psychic research. What she describes as resembling the "colorless transfers or 'calcomanias' she played with as a child (45), as shadow-light reflections-of-reflections of ordinary objects in the room (an oillamp, a washstand) (45–46), suggests "the artistic products of a group of people whom the psychologists term eidetics." According to R. W. Hutchinson,

> This condition is very rare among European adults, and not very common among children, but is a well-attested phenomenon. Just as anybody who looks at the sun or a lighted lamp and then at a blank wall will see a little purple lamp or sun for a second or two, so an eidetic person will retain the vision of a whole picture or landscape if he transfers his gaze from it to a blank surface. This vision, which is not merely a mental picture, is termed an *eidos* and the people who are liable to such visions are termed "eidetics."[29]

This notion, says Hutchinson, was used to explain "the uncanny qualities of Minoan art" (129). The German scholar E. R. Jaensch was the first to study the condition; he published his findings in the first year of H.D.'s analysis, 1933. But although H.D. notes having discussed Minoan Crete with Freud (175), she mentions nothing about eidetics. Not content, perhaps, to be gifted merely as an eidetic (although *eidos* is a figure in her later poetry, "Eidolon" being the title of the third part of *Helen in Egypt*), she pursues the transcription of her wish to be the source of *oracular* vision. The Delphic tripod and the spirit lamp translate and make visible her forbidden desire "to be a Prophetess."

She beholds what she perceives to be a psychic projection instead of an optical illusion, and the "writing" continues; graphs, strokes, lines form a ladder that the dreamer's eye ascends before alighting on the winged Nike fluttering about the top rung (53–55). This is the climax of her experience, the completion of her vision, which she perceives with utter satisfaction. According to Freud's lexicon of dreams, ladders, staircases, symbols of ascent are frequently veiled images of sexual arousal and satisfaction (*SE* 5:364–66, 369–72). This meaning does not escape H.D.'s transcription and is one possible explanation of the "explosion" or near blackout that comes with the final revelation she shares with Bryher:

> So far—so good. But this is enough. I drop my head in my hands; it is aching with this effort of concentration, but I feel that I have seen the picture. I thought, "Niké, Victory." . . . And I shut off, "cut out" before the final picture, before (you might say) the explosion took place. . . . Bryher, who has been waiting by me, carries on the 'reading' where I left off. . . . as I relaxed, let go, from complete physical and mental exhaustion, she saw what I did not see. (55–56)

This mental and physical climax of vision carries over to Bryher, who, playing the part of Freud in the relay of transference, sees "telepathically" what H.D. wants him (now as then) to see: a figure of a man within a disk "reaching out to draw the image of a woman (my Niké) into the sun beside him" (56). This is her triumph: aided by Freud's implicit, retrospective mediation (in the figure of Bryher) she projects an image of self-enlightenment. "Niké, Victory," she reflects, "seemed to be the clue, seemed to be my own especial sign or part of my hieroglyph"; she cues the "last concluding symbol," the sun figure—perhaps that " 'determinative' that is used in the actual hieroglyph, the picture that contains the whole series of pictures in itself or helps clarify or explain them" (56).

Does this determinative hieroglyph signify H.D.'s initiation into the Freudian mysteries? Her victory sign is a hieroglyphic compound of Apollo's sun-son (Asklepios-Freud) *plus* the image of a woman (H.D. victrix) drawn (by her own projected writing hand) into Freud's inner circle. It is not quite the "Circle" whose members include analysts of established reputation such as Hanns Sachs (vii) or "the Princess," Marie Bonaparte (10), the institutional heirs of Freud's legacy, (in)to which she sees herself drawn. She would be his spiritual heir, reading the hieroglyph as a "clue" that she has been welcomed into the semi*circle* of Greek and Egyptian priestesses and prophets, gods and goods, idols and eidolons, which Freud had carefully arranged on his desk. She sees herself, as she sees Freud, to be an avatar of Thoth, bearing the stylus-caduceus of hermetic transcription. Moreover, her hieroglyph signifies a collaborative translation, "our hieroglyph, our writing" (88), our victory, with the hidden implication that the writing is on the wall: in the future, H.D. will translate-transcribe "Freud," his hieroglyphic method, into the poetry of prophecy and healing.

With the decipherment of "our hieroglyph," H.D. opens the way to the translation of another dream and another graphic symbol of her desire to be another, if not *the*, oracle of modernity. This is what she refers to as her "serpent and thistle" dream, not, she says, "a very sensational experience," though it qualifies as "visionary or supernormal" nonetheless:[30] "The vision or picture was simply this: before sleeping or just on wakening, there was a solid shape before my eyes, no luminous cloud-pictures or vague fantasy, but an altar-shaped block of stone. . . . In one half or section, there was a serpent, roughly carved . . . conventionally coiled with head erect; on the other side, there was a roughly incised, naturalistic . . . thistle" (64). This is an old recurrent dream whose hieroglyph she regards as a personal insignia, like "H.D.," and whose full meaning she pursues in cryptographic life-writing. At first she calls on Ezra Pound (then her mentor in literature, her tormentor in love) to help in the decoding, but after consulting references he can only determine half of the picture, confirming that the serpent, "the sign or totem, through the ages, of healing" was linked to Asklepios (65). On her own, she discovers in the Louvre a Greco-Roman signet ring bearing the same heraldic seal, confirming further that her personal vision had historical, material reality. But it was Freud who ultimately answers her hermeneutic quest to know the whole of the determinative hieroglyph.

To arrive at that answer, H.D. must recall and reconstruct another scene of analysis. This is the scene of one of those rare occasions when Freud beckons her into the other room, where he keeps his treasures. Presenting her with one of the statues, a small bronze of Athene, from his circle of idols, she reports, " 'This is my favorite. . . . She is perfect,' he said, 'only she has lost her spear' " (68–69). H.D. hesitates before responding; she rejects (or resists) reading the vulgar, conventional meaning of penis envy into this transference symbol, believing instead that Freud presents her with a gift in the spirit of affirmation and affection without any intent to clip her wings. She receives his symbol as a sign that he has read her hieroglyphic Nike with approval, has recognized her victory, and is welcoming her home to a healing self-knowledge: "He knew that I loved Greece. He knew that I loved Hellas. I stood looking at Pallas Athené, she whose winged attribute was Niké, Victory, or she stood wingless, Niké A-pteros. . . . Niké A-pteros, she was called, the Wingless Victory, for Victory could never, would never fly away from Athens" (69).[31] "He too had climbed those steps once," H.D. notes with empathy and self-justification (69).[32] He too had aspired to such heights, entertained remote fantasies of joining the gods and heroes; so why should he wish to constrain her in thinking so highly of her own? He was helping bring home to her the realization that she no longer had to take "flight" in neurotic fantasies. "Perhaps my trip to Greece," she at first skeptically suggests, "might have been interpreted as a flight from reality. Perhaps my experiences there might be translated as another flight—from a flight" (44). But retrospective to her re-transcription of analysis, she decides unequivocally that she has found the perfect medium, the visionary gift of writing. Her victory was her sign, her reading was her victory: in the *mise en abyme* of self-signification in the mise en scène of analysis, she recovers and affirms her sense of significance.

And once victory is brought home, the stage is finally set for deciphering the "thistle" of her vision. In the following passage, she gives an exemplary demonstration of the hieroglyphic method of translation which she attributes to Freud:

> There was Victory, our sign on the wall, our hieroglyph, our writing. There was the tiny bronze, his favorite among the semicircle of the Gods or '. . . Goods' on his table. There was Niké, Victory, and Niké A-pteros, the Wingless Victory. . . . There was Athens. . . . There were designs, weren't there, of acanthus leaves to crown upright Corinthian capitals? And the Latin *acanthus*, and the related Greek word *akantha*, is thorn or prickle. . . . as from *aké*, a point . . . a prickly plant, thistle; also a thorny tree. *A thorny tree.* . . . Perhaps even . . . that . . . Tree of the Knowledge of Good and Evil . . . with its attendant Serpent. . . . There was, among many others, that serpent of Wisdom that crouched at the feet of . . . Athené and was one of her attributes, like the spear (*aké*, a point) she held in her hand . . . that . . . might have been a rod or staff. (88–89)

This play of free association is also a display or replay of the metonymic displacement Freud observes in the primary symbolism of dream language. As Riddel pointed out, the translation is as hieroglyphic as the original dream symbol and stands in want of further interpretation ("H.D.'s Scene" 45). What, we are prompted to wonder, does her rewriting of analysis conceal that it should slip so elusively from sign to sign? Is it symbolic of her silent resistance to

Freud's all-too-Freudian presentation of the *spearless* Athene? But seeing that my own intention is not to analyze H.D., I would determine from this translation what it is that H.D. recovers for her poetic self-definition. With her equation spear = staff = rod = thistle and serpent = totem animal of healing, we are back to where we started: Hermes' caduceus, the Hippocratic symbol that has come down from Thoth to Freud and finally to H.D. herself. The only "thing" that has been missing, it seems, is a woman to bear the sign.

Her later "Hermetic Definition" once more reformulates this Hippocratic hieroglyph:

> Athené stands guardian,
> and there is ecstasy and healing
>
> in her acceptance of the ποιητής fantasy
> her serpent feeding
> from a cup.
>
> (33)

## Mixing Hieroglyphics: American Transcendentalism and Freudian Oneirocriticism

"Writing on the Wall" demonstrates H.D.'s familiarity with Freud's reading of dream symbols as hieroglyphics, but what Freud presents as an analogy H.D. re-presents as literal: for her, the "shapes, lines, graphs" (93), the luminous "glyphs" of the unconscious are actual characters of an archaic script, charmed into conscious memory by the techniques of transference and free association. From where, then, does this inspiration to literalize Freud derive? Does H.D. "see" through Freud's scientific façade to a hankering after the metaphysical? "He is Faust, surely," she muses. "We retreat from the so-called sciences and go backward or go forward into alchemy. . . . He was turning a heavy seal-ring on his finger" (145). Does she translate "Freud" into hermetic presence or do his duplicitous self-presentations, his slipping from science to poetry (to his favorite, Goethe), to natural philosophy, and even to occult speculation, belie another, transcendental "Freud" to whom H.D. was especially sensitive?[33]

In writing her tribute, H.D. approaches Freud's weltanschauung in good faith. "About the greater transcendental issues, we never argued," she notes reassuringly, after risking the claim that "the mind," "the psyche," and "the soul" are interchangeable terms in Freud's schema (*TF* 13). She relies on more than mere poetic license to make the equation between psychic and "spiritual realities" (*WDNF* 51). "According to his theories the soul existed explicitly" (*TF* 13), she insists. The unconventional syntax stresses her own metaphysical bias, the explicit existence of the soul implicitly overruling any scientific positivism his theories may signify. Moreover, such phenomenological phrasing as "the medium of the mind" emphasizes a double intention in Freud's world view, searching "Janus faced" (*TF* 100) in two directions: "forward," to the positive decipherment and treatment of the hieroglyph of the unconscious as a symptom of neurosis, and "backward," to the undecipherable mystery of the hermetic logos, the eternal, charismatic script of the pharaohs.

To appreciate the extent to which the "source and shape" of her poetic medium derives and differs from Freud's symbolic order, I trace her use of the "hieroglyph of the dream" (71) as well as her Professor's use of it, emphasizing the Faustian character of Freud who once declared his fascination with "the 'magical power of words.' "[34] What word magic, what medicine do H.D.'s hieroglyphics apply?

H.D.'s understanding of the "hieroglyph of the dream" substantially conforms to *The Interpretation of Dreams*, one of the heavily annotated texts in H.D.'s library.[35] When she attributes to Freud the opening up of a "vast, unexplored region" of "the unconscious mind" and the first attempts to "decipher and decode" it (93), she is not being merely rhetorical. She is echoing Freud himself in the *Traumdeutung* when he proposes an alternative to the symbolic method of dream interpretation, which "considers the content of the dream as a whole and seeks to replace it by another content which is intelligible and in certain respects analogous to the original one." Freud's alternative is "the '*decoding*' method, since it treats dreams as a kind of cryptography in which each sign can be translated into another sign having a known meaning, in accordance with a fixed key."[36] Freud proposes to read each pictorial sign of the dream as a letter in a hieroglyphic rebus and to decipher with a lexicon that he himself provides (through self-analysis, classical philology, and hermeneutical semiotics) in subsequent pages of his study,[37]—but not without underlining the difficulty of translation: ". . . the productions of the dream-work, which it must be remembered, *are not made with the intention of being understood*, present no greater difficulties to their translators than do the ancient hieroglyphic scripts to those who seek to read them" (SE 5:341).

Like Freud, H.D. employs Greek and Latin lexicons to decipher dream symbols without conforming to the positive science of lexicography. She avoids fixing meanings to symbols, so as to prohibit the variability of signfication following what she understands to be Freud's open method of decoding: "He himself—at least to me personally—deplored the tendency to *fix* ideas too firmly to set symbols, or to weld them inexorably" (93). Though she hints that this is a personal revelation, she is, here again, reciting Freud, who makes the following qualification:

> The question is bound to arise of whether many of these symbols do not occur with a permanently fixed meaning, like the "grammalogues" in shorthand; and we shall feel tempted to draw up a new "dream-book" on the decoding principle. On that point there is this to be said: . . . In a number of cases the element in common between a symbol and what it represents is obvious; in others it is concealed and the choice of the symbol seems puzzling. . . . the peculiar plasticity of the psychical material must never be forgotten. (*SE* 5:351–52)

H.D.'s conception of the dream work as transcription and translation vividly underlines Freud's own analogies. She describes her princess dream as a luminous "picture-writing" (51), as a "scene or picture [that] . . . 'wrote itself.'" "an exquisite, endless sequence from an *illuminated manuscript*" (92) whose pictoideographic script translates an otherwise indecipherable "suppressed desire." Understanding that the symbolic dream material is already a translation of the latent dream thought and that these symbols, cryptic glyphs or graphs, beg further translation into common language ("symptom or inspiration. . . . It is admittedly picture-writing, though its symbols can be translated into terms of today" [51]), clarifies Freud's explanatory metaphor:

> The dream-thoughts and the dream-content are presented to us *like* two versions of the same subject-matter in two different languages. Or, more properly, the dream-content seems *like* a transcript of the dream-thoughts into another mode of expression, whose characters and syntactic laws it is our business to discover by comparing the original and the translation. . . . The dream-content . . . is expressed *as it were* in a pictographic script, the characters of which have to be transposed individually into the language of the dream thoughts. (*SE* 4:277, my emphasis)

What is peculiar about H.D.'s illustration of the dream work is her literalization of Freud's figurative use of "transcript," "translation," dream "language," "pictographic script," erasing any clear distinction between dream thought (the desire for signs) and dream content (the signs of desire): the cryptic symbols of her dream are also the objects of her desire.

How much has H.D.'s reading of Freud, before and after analysis, influenced and informed the transcript of her dream? To what extent is her dream transcription a retranscription of Freud's writing on dreams, an application of his decoding method to her own personal equation? She repeatedly points to her princess dream as exemplary dream work, isolating each individual character as if tracing hieratic Egyptian:

> She is Egyptian. She appears at the top of a long staircase; marble steps lead down to a river. She wears no ornament, no circlet or scepter shows her rank, but . . . *this is a Princess.* . . . She has nothing in her arms, there is no one with her; there is no extraneous object with her or about her or about the carved steps to denote any symbolic detail or side issue involved. There is no detail. The steps are geometrical, symmetrical and she is as abstract as a lady could be. . . . There, in the water . . . is a shallow basket or ark or box or boat. There is . . . a baby. (36–37)

Her exemplary dream features nothing but "luminous" detail, unlike the muddle of ordinary dreams, whose clutter of merely ornamental detail must be searched through like false jewelry in order to find the gems. An illuminated manuscript, her princess is representatively Freudian, a brilliant transcription of his figure of the dream's hieroglyphic rebus:

> Suppose I have a picture-puzzle, a rebus, in front of me. It depicts a house with a boat on its roof, a single letter of the alphabet. . . . Now I might be mislead into . . . declaring that the picture as a whole and its component parts are nonsensical. . . . But obviously we can only form a proper judgement of the rebus if . . . we try to replace each separate element by a syllable or word that can be represented by that element in some way or other. The words which are put together in this way are no longer nonsensical but may form a poetical phrase of the greatest beauty and significance. (*SE* 4:277–78)

Did reading this passage prompt H.D. to dream such exemplary dream content? Or did it prompt an exemplary revision in writing her tribute to Freud? In the circularity of representation, the original transcript is lost, but a hieroglyphic method is recovered, one that literally recasts Freud in the tradition of Jean François Champollion.

H.D. invites the Freudian reader to consider each character of her princess dream—princess, staircase, river, boat, baby—as a letter in a picture puzzle inscribing a cartouche of hieroglyphs whose syllabic or phonetic values, if we knew them, would spell out the secret name or "signature" of the presence behind the cryptic veil.[38]

This is the method H.D. later uses to decode another princess, the Helen of her dream-poem *Helen in Egypt* whose written character, like the palimpsest or Rosetta stone, transcribes a double Greek-Egyptian text. H.D.'s revisionary writing, unlike Western literary history, is not dominated by the Greek text, by the legendary femme-fatale figure of Helen of Troy, who appears in classical epic and tragedy. Instead, H.D.'s personal dream retraces Helen's Egyptian character, decoding her name into hieroglyphic syllables, letters, and lyrical images. The result is a semioclastic translation and trans-figuration of the canonical character into a new iconography, "a poetical phrase of the greatest beauty and significance":

> the harp-strings will answer
> the chant, the rhythm, the metre,
> the syllables H-E-L-E-N-A;
> Helena reads the decree,
> shall be shrined forever.
>
> *(HE 95)*

According to Freud, the dream content cannot be deciphered di-rectly but must be arrived at through a series of intermediary steps. Since two primary processes, condensation and displacement, of which metaphor and metonymy are the poetic equivalents, operate the dream formulation, decoding must entail both free association and interpretation.[39] Likewise, H.D. supplements a free association of personal elements with interpretative knowledge, deriving from her study of languages and mythology. Freud suggests that it is the role of the analyst to facilitate interpretation by adding his or her (universal) knowledge of symbols to the analysand's limited (per-sonal) apprehension of the dream: "We are thus obliged, in dealing with those elements of the dream-content which must be recognized as symbolic, to adopt a combined technique, which on the one hand rests on the dreamer's associations and on the other hand fills the gaps from the interpreter's knowledge of symbols" (*SE* 5:353).

Perhaps her extensive knowledge of symbols contributes to H.D.'s sense of having collaborated with Freud in translating her signs and symptoms—"our hieroglyph." Her own knowledge of "*Astrologie,*

*Alchimie, Magie"* (*HD* 41) is as extensive as Freud's familiarity with classical sources, prompting her to note parenthetically that, "the Professor was . . . always right, though we sometimes translated our thoughts into different languages or mediums" (*TE* 47). Yet, the point she stresses about dream interpretation is the Freudian point that there is no limit to the horizon of translation; "The use of a common symbol extends further than the use of a common language" (*SE* 5:352). To interpret the symbols of her serpent and thistle dream precisely, she turns to her Greek and Latin grammalogues and dictionaries, but for her princess dream, she must rely on a wholly symbolic interpretation, pointing to what Freud calls the "genetic character" of dream language: "Things that are symbolically connected to-day were probably united in prehistoric times by conceptual and linguistic identity. The symbolic relation seems to be a relic and a mark of former identity. . . . A number of symbols are as old as language itself, while others . . . are being coined continuously down to the present time" (*SE* 5:352).

In analysis, her "imagination wandered at will," while her interpretative function drew primarily "on classical or biblical symbolism" (14); but the desire to trace back farther, to recover a more primal, more elemental, picto-ideo-phonographic language, the "Egyptian" hinted at in her princess dream, is elaborated more fully in the later *Helen in Egypt* (see Chapter 4). This desire is not unlike that of the philologist's dream that Freud himself entertained. According to John Forrester, once Freud discovered that "the exact relation of the symbol to its 'determining word' is not always the same," that, as Freud puts it, "it may appear in an older and now obsolete use of the same word, in the root from which the word was derived, or from other words cognate with it," that "even then we may not have found the association that brings the symbol into connection with language . . . thus fix[ing] its reference," and that "the sphere of linguistic usage in which one might have to cast one's net in search of the word grows wider and wider: jokes, folklore . . . foreign languages . . . a path mapped out . . . as far as ancient Egyptian," he arrives at "the strange spectre of a quasi-universal language (perhaps not even restricted to the Aryan tongues) in which . . . the dreamer 'knows' the linguistic connections that underlie these symbols, even though he may be uncultured and unilingual in everyday life. The unconscious seems to have become a receptacle for all the languages and usages of a historically determined group of tongues. The next step is to posit a primary or primal language that supports the polyglottism of the unconscious."[40] Neither uncultured nor unilingual (though more of a dabbler in foreign tongues than an actual polyglot), H.D. writes her tribute in support of this strange specter/speculation of Freud's, believing she "knows" the prehistoric language of her dreams and needs only to be reminded.

In dreaming of a primal language, Freud envisions a mental archaeology: he doubts "whether any psychical structure can be the victim of total destruction," believing that things of the mind have almost limitless power of preservation.[41] This is the "mind" to which H.D. alludes in *The Walls Do Not Fall*, part 1 of her war trilogy:

> still the Luxor bee, chick and hare
> pursue unalterable purpose
>
> in green, rose-red, lapis;
> they continue to prophesy
> from the stone papyrus:
>
> there, as here, ruin opens
> the tomb, the temple; enter,
> there as here, there are no doors:
>
> the shrine lies open to the sky,
> the rain falls, here, there
> sand drifts; eternity endures.
>
> (3)

Inspired by her day-to-day survival of the bombing of London in 1942 and less immediately by her visit to Karnak in 1923, her daydream attests to the power of primal symbols to endure ruin, today's as well as yesterday's. The walls that do not fall are the strata of the psyche, which Freud imagined to be as permanent as the walls of the ancient *Roma quadrata*, or so he speculates in the opening pages of *Civilization and Its Discontents*.[42] Her figure is more literal and more graphic: these are the walls of an even more ancient and more enduring Egypt, whose tombs are permanently inscribed in hieroglyphics. These are also the walls among which Helen of *Helen in Egypt* walks; with a foot in both past and present worlds, she transcribes hieroglyphs as she travels, hoping to revive modernity's disenchanted postwar psyche with their everlasting charm. Here are the opening lyrics:

Do not despair, the hosts
surging beneath the Walls
(no more than I) are ghosts;

.   .   .   .   .

yet in this Amen-temple,

.   .   .   .   .

. . . long corridors of lotus-bud
furled on the pillars,
and the lotus-flower unfurled,

with reed of the papyrus . . .
the old enchantment holds.

(HE 1–2)

H.D.'s tendency to literalize Freud's metaphors of writing, representing his "hieroglyph" as transpersonal, transhistorical symbol of the mind, betrays a transcendentalist emphasis that is not strictly Freudian. Though transcendentalist leanings can be found in Freud's work, they seldom and certainly never unequivocally dominate the progressive or scientific character of his theory. H.D. lends to Freud as much as she derives from him, reinforcing and adapting his metaphysics to fit her hermetic formula, which has poetic roots outside of Freudianism, in Neoplatonism, romanticism, French symbolism, Moravianism, and American transcendentalism.[43] It is to this transcendentalism, to Emerson, Thoreau, and Whitman, that I should now like to turn.

To my knowledge, H.D. does not refer to Emerson in any of her writing, though in *Tribute to Freud* she names Poe as her "favorite among American writers" (132) whose works she read during her school years.[44] If she read Poe, who was then considered uncanonical ("unwholesome, morbid" are her words [132]), she would also have read the leading poets of the American Renaissance. It was the Emerson-Whitman legacy from which she and Pound would struggle to disinherit themselves in their attempt to formulate an objectivist, post-transcendentalist, imagist poetics. Determined to place the accent on her other sources, she also names Baudelaire and his *Fleurs du mal* (132) as a poetic (Poe-tic) companion. She names these poets in context, or to put it another way, the context conditions her poetic memory; Poe and Baudelaire are conjured into thought by the "atmosphere" Freud's presence induces, his transference cues sounding "bell-notes" while "the fumes of the aromatic cigar waft above [her] . . . head" (132). Both Poe and Baudelaire were practitioners of a hieroglyphic method.[45] From *Fleurs du mal* H.D. would have known Baudelaire's celebrated "correspondences," his mystifying equation between natural symbols and symbols of the mind: "Nature is a temple where living columns / Sometimes murmur indistinct words [allow confused words to escape]; / There man passes through forests of symbols / That watch him with familiar glances."[46] It is Emerson, however, who speaks most directly about hieroglyphics; and who hails the poet descendants of Champollion.

Emerson's idea of the Poet as gifted diviner of the secrets of natural symbols contributes to H.D.'s idea of the apocalyptic scribe. In "Poetry and Imagination," Emerson pronounces that the poet "shall use Nature as his hieroglyphic," reiterating Shelley in "A Defence of Poetry," who sees poets as "those who have employed language as the hieroglyphic of their thoughts," and as "the hierophants of an unapprehended inspiration; the mirrors of the gigantic shadows which futurity casts upon the present."[47] Emerson observes in "The Poet" that "nature offers all her creatures to him as a picture-language" and that "things admit of being used as symbols because nature is a symbol, in the whole, and in every part. Every line we draw in the sand has expression; and there is no body without its spirit or genius."[48] This is the sort of transcendental wisdom that H.D. reads back into Freud in "The Master"; like the poet, he notes that every "thing" about his client has symbolic expression:

> whether I wore simple garments
> or intricate
> nothing was lost,
> each vestment had meaning,
> "every gesture is wisdom,"
> he taught;
>
> .  .  .  .  .
> how could he have known
> how each gesture of this dancer
> would be hieratic?
> words were scrawled on papyrus,
> words were written most carefully.
>
> (CP 451, 454)

"Freud" affirms that she herself has divined (danced) the hieratic: "It was he, himself, he who set me free / to prophesy, . . . (he said) / 'you are a poet'" (458). With that affirmation, she invokes the hieroglyphics of her transcendentalist predecessors "to discover . . . a new Master: / His, the track in the sand / from a plum-tree in flower" (*WDNF* 10). It is the Emersonian poet who divines the picture language of nature in the following lines from *Helen in Egypt*:

> when the bird swooped past,
> that first evening,
> I seemed to know the writing,
>
> as if God made the picture
> and matched it
> with a living hieroglyph.
>
> (23)

And Baudelaire echoes in this later passage:

> the mystery of a forest-tree,
> whispering its secrets upon Cithaeron,
>
> holds subtler meaning
> than this written stone
> or leaves of the papyrus
>
> (108)

The work of Emerson's upon which H.D. appears to draw most is *Nature*, where he meditates on the origins and ends of poetry:

> As we go back in history, language becomes more picturesque, until its infancy, when it is all poetry; or all spiritual facts are represented by natural symbols. The same symbols are found to make the original elements of all languages. . . . And as this is the first language, so it is the last. . . . The corruption of man is followed by the corruption of language. . . . When the sovereignty of ideas is broken up by the prevalence of secondary desires,—the desire of riches, of pleasure, of power, and of praise . . . new imagery ceases to be created, and old words are perverted to stand for things which are not. (33)[49]

Perhaps she detected a common idea of a primal language in Emerson and Freud, but it is an Emersonian prejudice toward a "perverted" modernity, and particularly its "corruption of language," which characterizes the aesthetic ideology of her war trilogy:

> Evil was active in the land,
> Good was impoverished and sad;
>
> Ill promised adventure,
> Good was smug and fat;
>
> Dev-ill was after us,
> .   .   .   .   .
>
> so let us search the old highways
>
> for the true-rune, the right-spell,
> recover old values.
>                                    (*WDNF* 5)

In the midst of war terror, when the corruption of language meant literally the burning of books, H.D. invokes the stylus-caduceus of the hermetic scribe. As poet, she would create new imagery, recover the full power of primal words and restore the source of all idea and invention, the transcendental content of the original "Dream, Vision":

> Thoth, Hermes, the stylus,
> the palette, the pen, the quill endure,
>
> though our books are a floor
> of smouldering ash under our feet;
>
> though the burning of books remains
> the most perverse gesture
>
> and the meanest
> of man's nature,
>
> .   .   .   .   .
> And Hatsheput's name is still circled
> with what they call the cartouche.
> .   .   .   .   .
>
> so what good are your scribblings?
> this we take them with us
>
> beyond death; . . .
> .   .   .   .   .

Without thought, invention,
you would not have been, O Sword,

without idea and the Word's mediation
you would have remained

unmanifest in the dim dimension
where thought dwells

and beyond thought and idea,
their begetter,

Dream,
Vision.

(*WDNF* 16–18)

The figure of the poets as "keepers of the secret, / the carriers, the spinners / of the rare intangible thread / that binds all humanity / to ancient wisdom" (*WDNF* 24), transfigures "Freud," who "took the events of the day preceding the night of the dream . . . unravelled from the mixed conditions and contacts of the ordinary affairs of life the particular thread that went on spinning its length through the substance of the . . . *buried* . . . unconscious or subconscious mind" (*TF* 72), who "dared to say that . . . this consciousness proclaimed all men one; all nations and races met in the universal world of the dream" (71). But the reverse is also true: H.D.'s transcendentalism is also affected by her Freudianism. The dream-vision of *The Walls Do Not Fall*, for instance, is re-presented in *Tribute to Freud* as the product of a psychological mechanism (projection) whose nature is undecidably psychopathological and spiritual.

Emerson's hieroglyphic pastoral can be seen everywhere in "The Walls do Not Fall." Harking back to the primal language-landscape of Egypt—"Take me home / where canals / flow / between iris-banks: / where the heron / has her nest: / where the mantis / prays on the river-reed: / where the grasshopper says / *Amen, Amen, Amen*" (32)— H.D. echoes *Nature*, where, Irwin says, "the air is full of sounds; the sky of tokens; the ground is all memoranda and signatures, and every object covered over with hints which speak to the intelligent" (*American Hieroglyphics*, 25). Clearly it is the transcendentalist who is moved to rapture by a "grass-blade," who finds paradise in the "valley of a leaf" (*WDNF* 11), who asks, "shall we lift rapt face and clasp hands / before laurel or oak-tree" (50) and who observes that "insignia / in the heron's crest, / the asp's back, / enigmas, rubrics promise as before, / protection for the scribe" (15).

H.D.'s "living hieroglyph" relives the world of *Walden*, where, according to Thoreau, "the earth is . . . living poetry like the leaves of a tree, which precede flowers and fruit—not a fossil earth, but a living earth."[50] It also recalls the cosmos of Walt Whitman, for whom the grass "is a uniform hieroglyphic" and "every object, mountain, tree and star—every / birth and life . . . / A mystic cipher."[51] In answer to Thoreau's rhetorical question, "What Champollion will decipher this hieroglyphic for us, that we may turn over a new leaf at last?" (308), H.D. points to herself as the poet of her age. But it is not from singing the "Song of Myself" with an all-American troupe of troubadours, the phallic poets ("spermatic" men) whom Emerson awaited,[52] but from analysis with Freud that she found her self-confidence. I repeat her lines: "it was he, himself, he who set me free / to prophesy, . . . (he said) / 'you are a poet.'" It is Freud she brings into her revision of transcendental nature, stressing individual psychogenesis over the universal prototype, or "uniform hieroglyphic":[53]

> but my mind (yours)
> has its peculiar ego-centric
>
> personal approach
> to the eternal realities,
>
> and differs from every other
> in minute particulars,
>
> as the vein-paths on any leaf
> differ from those of every other leaf
>
> in the forest, as every snow-flake
> has its particular star, coral or prism shape.
> (*WDNF* 51–52)

Freud sets her free to help "map out the field . . . of the hieroglyph of the unconscious," but Whitman leads the way as far afield as Egypt:

> I see Egypt and the Egyptians, I see the pyramids
>     and obelisks,
> I look on chisell'd histories, records of conquering kings,
>     dynasties, cut in slabs of sand-stone, or on
>     granite-blocks,

I see at Memphis mummy-pits containing mummies embalm'd,
  swathed in linen cloth, lying there many centuries,
I look on the fall'n Theban, the large-ball'd eyes.

                        (*Leaves of Grass*, 145)

"Freud" reinforces H.D.'s roots in American transcendentalism, which had been choked with disturbing visions following the events of World War I. At least some of her reasons for seeking Freud out had been "to dig down and dig out, root out my personal weeds, strengthen my purpose, reaffirm my beliefs, canalize my energies" (*TF* 91). In "Freud," H.D. finds the affirmation of both hermetist and scientist, as well as of a literary father who, in place of Whitman, recognized the arrival of the poet our age has been waiting for:

After the seas are all cross'd, (as they seem already cross'd,)
After the great captains and engineers have accomplish'd their work,
After the noble inventors, after the scientists, the chemist, the
      geologist, ethnologist,
Finally shall come the poet worthy that name
The true son of God shall come singing his songs.

Then not your deeds only O voyagers, O scientists
  and inventors, shall be justified.

                        (*Leaves of Grass*, 415)

But was H.D. compelled to make a god of Freud ("I had to recognise that he was beyond all-men, / nearer to God" [*CP* 452]), to see herself, the subject of his affirmation, as a viable link in a tradition from which, as a daughter, a woman, she felt excluded? For her to see herself as poet is not merely an issue of gender, not just a matter of feminizing "Song of Myself" into "Song of Herself," but a matter of recovering vital (re)sources. H.D.'s visionary Egypt is the product of one woman's psychic research into the deepest stratum of "soul" or "the mother-layer of fixation" (*TF* 175), using her mixed analytic-poetic hieroglyphic method to invoke prehistoric memory and revelation. With her we circumnavigate a field opened up but not yet charted by the new science of psychoanalysis; and having taken the plunge we are quite at sea:

        we are voyagers, discoverers
        of the not-known,

the unrecorded;
we have no map.
                    (*WDNF* 59)


## Semiology, Grammatology, Psychoanalysis

In *Tribute to Freud*, the poet begins to outline a semiology that is at once analytic and productive:

SIGNET—as from sign, a mark, token, proof; signet—the privy seal, a seal; signet-ring—a ring with a signet or private seal; sign-manual—the royal signature, usually only the initials of the sovereign's name. (I have used my initials H.D. consistently as my writing signet or sign-manual. . . .) Sign again—a word, gesture, symbol, or mark, intended to signify something else. Sign again—(medical) a symptom, (astronomical) one of the twelve parts of the Zodiac. Again sign—to attach a signature to, and sign-post—a direction post; all from the French, *signe*, and Latin, *signum*. And as I write that last word, there flashes into my mind the associated *in hoc signum* or rather, it must be *in hoc signo* and *vinces*. (66)

Starting with signet, signet ring, and sign manual, whose function she equates with her use of the initials H.D., she draws attention to her writing as a (self-)signifying practice—or practices—since she presents more than one: gestural, verbal, symbolic, medical, astrological, directional. H.D.'s semiology is intertextual, as the conjunctive "sign again" and "again sign" repeatedly indicate. Moreover, she points to the foreign-language roots of the word *sign*, implying that her semiology is polylingual. Finally, she offers the recognition that writing is metonymic or associative, that writing the word *signum* calls other words or phrases to mind: writing is not conscious, discursive, or thetic so much as associative, inscribing itself through the medium of the unconscious, the treasure-house of language and of pre- or nonverbal signs.

Later, she points to Freud as if he were the ultimate signpost of this complex signifying practice: "*S* for *s*eal, *s*ymbol, *s*erpent certainly, *s*ignet, *S*igmund" (88). *In hoc signo* ("in this word"), *in hoc vinces* ("in this we conquer"), in Sigmund, the sign reader, the oracle, "the *Siegmund*, the victorious voice or utterance" (105). This is testimony that in Sigmund Freud, H.D. finds direction, a method of (self-)signification, a way adequately to translate the sign manual and symptoms of her writing life. From the crypt of private symbols, she moves into an order of communication that does not limit (self-)definition: H.D. pays tribute in these passages to a liberating and satisfying collaboration between her writing and Freud's translation. One of the purposes of this final section is to consider how H.D.'s later poetry incorporates a psychoanalytic semiology.

The other purpose of this section is to inquire into the role psychoanalysis plays in mediating the history of change in the course of H.D.'s writing, in other words, to present a grammatology. The term *grammatology* was originally coined to refer to the history of writing, although it now has currency among literary critics as the theory of the history of writing and the application of that theory, Jacques Derrida being its most widely known exponent.[54] Theory considers the contributions philosophy has made to the history of writing in an attempt to resolve the confusion between the questions what is writing? and how did writing originate? It redresses the philosophical priority given the phonological over the grammatological and stresses, instead, the forgotten or suppressed pictoideographic (pictorial, tropical, metonymic) element that is (still) a constitutive component of languages that have "evolved" from the hieroglyphic. According to Gregory Ulmer, Derrida

> identifies two major breakthroughs leading to the current status of grammatology. The first occurred in the eighteenth century, [and] . . . had to do with a theological prejudice—the myth of an original, primitive language given to man by God. The other . . . concerned the period's "hallucinatory" misunderstanding of hieroglyphics. Far from being rejected owing to ethnocentric scorn of things non-Western, the hieroglyph was excessively admired as a form of sublime, mystical writing. Derrida credits the work of Freret and Warburton (one working with Chinese and the other with Egyptian writing) with creating an "epistemological break" that overcame these obstacles, thus "liberating a theoretical field in which the scientific techniques of deciphering were perfected by the Abbé Barthélemy and then by Champollion." (*Applied Grammatology*, 6)

From imagist ideogram to autobiographical complex and palimpsestic cryptogram, H.D.'s evolving hieroglyph provides the material for a grammatology, a microhistory of writing. H.D.'s emphasis on writing does not go so far as Derrida's in counter-privileging writing over discourse or logos, and therefore I would not describe her oeuvre as a grammatology in the theoretical sense. But her conception of writing changes over time in a way that is not merely a shift in genre: the change in her representation of writing constitutes a grammatology in the historical sense and is distinguished from her writing or semiotic practice. In retracing the evolution of her hieroglyphics, I make no attempt to deconstruct her semiology. Although heuristic, her transcription of hieroglyphs derives not from the demystifying works of Abbé Frerét and William Warburton but from both enlightened and mystical sources, from "objectivist" imagism and hermetic symbolism.

## Image and Ideogram

According to Ezra Pound, the movement's chief theoretician and first historian, the imagists developed a "science" of writing in opposition to the "mushy technique" of the symbolists. They aspired to present "the direct treatment of the 'thing.' "[55] Words were to be used as "primary pigment" (86, 88) that gave a thing, whether subjective or objective, its specific tone and form.[56] It was not mimesis or the representative function of imagining which they emphasized but its creative and constitutive function, the capacity to present things that would otherwise remain unperceived or inconceivable (86). Imagism also sought a reduction of "mystification" (92): the image was not to be a sign of a sign, or a symbol, or an icon; the image was to be iconoclastic, the most objective and most immediate verbal presentation of the thing perceived or of the perceiving subject.

Pound offers his hokkulike "In a Station at the Metro" as an example:

> The apparition of these faces in the crowd:
> Petals, on a wet, black bough.
>
> (89)

This " 'one image poem' " is a form of super-position," he explains; "that is to say, it is one idea set on top of another" (89). He adds that "in a poem of this sort one is trying to record the precise instant when a thing outward and objective transforms itself, or darts into a thing inward and subjective" (89). H.D.'s "Oread," Pound notes, is especially direct in its presentation of phenomenological immediacy and intensity (89). Here are the lines:

> Whirl up, sea—
> whirl your pointed pines,
> splash your great pines

on our rocks,
hurl your green over us,
cover us with your pools of fir.
                    (*CP* 55)

"Oread" casts the perfect illusion of presence; there seems to be no verbal mediation between the figurative vertigo of the dancing subject (Oread) and the literal action of the natural object (the sea and pines), no abstract border separating the things of the world from the things of poetry. Image displaces image without adding up to a subjective or artful gestalt of images, commanding the reader to follow the transitive flow of the "natural" (verbal) object in the spirit of the dancing nymph (O-read!).

H.D.'s exemplary lyric prompted Pound and others to formulate a dogmatic method—the famous dos and don'ts of imagism—to enable and ensure its reproduction.[57] While editing Ernest Fenollosa's *Chinese Written Character as a Medium For Poetry* (1918), Pound discovered a theory of the ideogram which he proceeded to elaborate into a poetics. His rendition of Fenollosa may in turn have reinformed H.D.'s conceptualization of the image, though I would not go so far as to argue the case for primary influence.

"Chinese notation," Fenollosa observes, "is something much more than arbitrary symbols. It is based upon a vivid shorthand picture of the operations of nature. In the algebraic figure and in the spoken word there is no natural connection between thing and sign; all depends upon sheer convention. But the Chinese method follows natural suggestion."[58] In *The ABC of Reading* (1934), Pound underlines Fenollosa's emphasis on the pictorial in Chinese writing, explaining that this is what makes the ideogram the most concrete script:

The Egyptians finally used abbreviated pictures to represent sounds, but the Chinese still use abbreviated pictures AS pictures . . . of a thing in a given position or relation, or of a combination of things. . . . Thus

人    man

木    tree

日    sun

東    sun tangled in the tree's branches, as at sunrise, meaning now the East. (21)

For Fenollosa, the most striking character of Chinese writing is its "concrete *verb* quality" (10). "The eye sees noun and verb as one:

things in motion, motion in things, and so the Chinese conception tends to represent them" he writes, pointing to the ideogram for east which Pound illustrated.[59]

It is Fenollosa's emphasis on the concrete verb quality of Chinese writing which Derrida sees as a breakthrough in modern grammatology. Fenollosa, Derrida writes, shows how the Chinese written language is essentially a pictoideographic script, whose continued existence and evolution calls into question the dominance of logical-grammatical structures assumed in the West, and he quotes Fenollosa: "Should we pass formally into the study of Chinese poetry, . . . we should beware of English [occidental] grammar, its hard parts of speech, and its lazy satisfaction with nouns and adjectives. We should seek and at least bear in mind the verbal undertone of each noun. We should avoid the 'is' and bring in a wealth of neglected English verbs" (*Of Grammatology*, 334 n. 44). Fenollosa adds that "the moment we use the copula, the moment we express subjective inclusions, poetry evaporates" (28).[60]

Pound shares, or rather informs, Derrida's reading of Fenollosa,[61] placing further emphasis on the capacity of Chinese writing which Fenollosa identifies as its "use of material images to suggest immaterial relations" (22), the function of catachresis. Pound asks:

> When the Chinaman wanted to make a picture of something more complicated, or of a general idea, how did he go about it? He is to define red. How can he do it in a picture that isn't painted in red paint?
> He puts (or his ancestor put) together the abbreviated pictures of
>
> ROSE                                        CHERRY
> IRON RUST                                   FLAMINGO
> . . . The Chinese "word" or "ideogram" for red is based on something everyone KNOWS. (*ABC of Reading*, 21–22)

Thus, taking their cue from Fenollosa, Pound and Derrida reverse the Western emphasis on an abstract, idealizing logos in favor of the ideogram's concrete powers of signification. Taking the Chinese written character as the medium for poetry, Fenollosa argues that poetry must necessarily differ from discourse: "Poetry differs from prose in the concrete colors of its diction. It is not enough for it to furnish a meaning to philosophers. It must appeal to emotions with the charm of direct impression, flashing though regions where the intellect can only grope" (21).[62]

Theory helps explain the technique of H.D.'s imagism, its illusion of immediacy and directness. Furthermore, it helps demonstrate a continuity between imagism and the later, Freudian poetry, where the ideogramic method of direct presentation is expanded into a hieroglyphic method presenting things of the unconscious. It may also help account for why H.D. declined to "furnish a meaning to philosophers," preferring that the poetry speak for itself. But Pound's emphasis on the ideogramic method should not distract the grammatologist from imagism's inscription of Neoplatonism. According to the poet herself, the lyric "Hermes of the Ways," which launched her writing career, marked the inauguration of "H.D.— Hermes—Hermeticism and all the rest of it."[63] Critic Zara Bruzzi insists that "many of [H.D.'s] early poems should be read as Neoplatonic accounts of human experience."[64]

Following the end of the war, the break-up of the imagist circle, and the traumatic jellyfish and writing-on-the-wall experiences, H.D. started writing prose, beginning with *Notes on Thought and Vision*, venturing farther with autobiography in an effort to reformulate a poetics that could accommodate these experiences.

## Auto-Bio-Graphic Complex

In *Her* (1927), the whirling of pine and sea around Oread's vortex of instantaneous perception is refigured as hysterical delirium. What Pound famously described as "an intellectual and emotional complex in an instant of time" becomes a symptomatic complex, signifying the absence of a subjective point of reference from which self can be distinguished from world[65]:

> Her Gart went round in circles. . . . she cried in her dementia, "I am Her, Her, Her." . . . She said, "I am Hermione Gart," but Her Gart was not that. She was nebulous, gazing into branches of liriodendron. . . . Her Gart peered far . . . tried to focus one leaf to hold her on to all leaves . . . She was nothing. . . . She tried to drag in personal infantile reflection. . . . Sylvania. I was born here. . . . Pennsylvania. I am part of Sylvania. Trees. Trees. Trees . . . liriodendron. . . . Pennsylvania whirled round her in cones of concentric color . . . concentric gelatinous substance that was her perception of trees grown closer, grown near . . . translucent like celluloid. The circles of the trees were tree-green; she wanted the inner lining of an Atlantic breaker. . . . She wanted the Point. She wanted to get to Point Pleasant. (*Her* 3–7)

Fenollosa's theory that "the moment we express subjective inclusions, poetry evaporates" no longer satisfies the autobiographical poet in search of self-clarification. This symptomatic retranscription of "Oread" is H.D.'s way of problematizing the imagist aesthetic, exposing the limitations of its science, and demonstrating that the "auto-graph" is no less vital to her writing than the "bio-graph," the "living picture" of the ideogram.

Her suffers from the lack of an adequate (self-)signifying practice and is consequently exposed to a world where there is insufficient differentiation between object and subject, self and other. From time to time she collapses into hysterical psychosis as represented by her shattered discourse. Salvation arrives in the form of a hieroglyph, a personal symbolic medium, which she forges in semiconsciousness; it provides the needed mediation without trapping her in alienating definitions of self or femininity or poetry, which are as disturbing as having no medium of (self-)signification at all.⁶⁶ *Her*, I believe, is the first expression of H.D.'s desire to formulate a "*her*metic definition" and to find affirmation for a poetic ego whose dissolution was the toll of war.

## Palimpsest and Cryptogram

Another postwar signpost of H.D.'s transition from ideogram to autograph is "Secret Name: Excavator's Egypt" (composed 1923), the last of three prose pieces collected under the title *Palimpsest* (published 1926).⁶⁷ "Secret Name" fictionalizes a trip she took with Bryher to Karnak and Thebes in 1923 at the time of the Tutankhamen excavations. Writing—or rather, recording, is the theme of this text, as indeed it is the theme of the entire book. The protaganist—translator, secretary, and archaeologist—applies her unique combination of textual skills to the excavation and transcription of an unrecorded other world:

> Her common or everyday eyes were recording the scene before her. The blacks and yellows, the inked-in shadows, the out of the way sifting of sun on sand. This common form of registering impressions was . . . most distasteful to her. (*P* 179–80)

> Tourists of every description, workers in various metiers, draughtsmen, reporters, cinema and plain cameramen. They saw the first wheel emerge. (181)

> She wanted to dive deep, deep, courageously down into some unexploited region of the consciousness, into some common deep sea of

unrecorded knowledge and bring, triumphant to the surface some treasure buried, lost, forgotten. (179)

Hired by a "famous Egyptologist" to record the excavation findings, Helen is more than just a recording secretary: she is a "high-class experiment" of Bodge-Grafton's, a scholar in her own right, a researcher and philologist specializing in Greco-Roman with her own angle on translating Egyptian (189). Unlike the draftsmen, reporters, and cameramen, who employ common, mechanical means to record uncommon objects, she also entertains the uncommon recording of ordinary things, their translation into the "hieratic" through the projective powers of her own, palimpsestic fantasy. She reads common objects as hieroglyphs, signs to dream by, entering into the spirit of things Egyptian and exploring the medium of what she calls "psycho-hysterical visionary sensations" (187).

In part, she is "hypnotized by this strange glamour" of Egypt (209), its tombs and statues and especially by its hieroglyphs, their "wild iridescent presences" (226). But her uncommon recording of things is also an effect of her frustrated desire; wishing for rapturous rapport of inspired company but forced to engage in mere pleasantry,[68] she finds substitute satisfaction in the fantasia of a personal sign language.[69] Hieroglyphs are the cue to subjective research in "Secret Name"; hypnosis, hallucination, "psycho-hysterical visionary sensations" are the desired effects of a charmed, exploratory perception. But what kind of writing medium is this?[70] Her hieroglyph, like Fenollosa's ideogramic Chinese, eludes "a wealth of erudition"; it is "unassailed by modern scholarship," and it "appeal[s] to emotions with the charm of direct impression, flashing through regions where the intellect can only grope" (*Chinese Written Character*, 5, 21).

Is it poetry or an allegory of writing (of recording and decoding) which constitutes the narrative of "Secret Name"? Lyrical passages mark the protagonist's absences from the scene of narrative action, suggesting alternation between realism and surrealism. But the surface level of narration, with generic voice, character, dialogue, and (marriage) plot, is so thin it barely conceals the author's primary interest in glyphs and grams. "Beneath" the discursive layer of the text, the subversive secretary excavates/transcribes another world of signs, cryptic and hieratic. In her translator's eyes, narrative characters suggest written characters, or characters resembling letters of Egyptian script. She perceives, for example, the decorous former army officer Rafton as camel-headed (174) like the statues or etchings

of ibis-headed Thoth and lion-headed Sekhmet, subverting his propriety and reserve, recasting his otherwise unbearably petty and
patronizing manner into otherworldly presence. Their charmed encounter among moonlit ruins climaxes in an embrace that literally
presses them into a wall of hieroglyphics (209, 216), "dehuman-
is[ing]" (209) the romance, privileging the script over dialogue, voice,
and personality.

"Secret Name" is a cryptonymy, a medium of name play. Bodge-
Grafton, for example, puns with the name of the "famous Egyptologist," the actual scholar E. A. Wallis Budge. Plots are encrypted in the
play of names. Bodge-Grafton employs Helen to "graft"/draft/graph
his recent findings "on" data he has unearthed and recorded. Grafton embodies Rafton, who signifies official and practical (Roman)
reality for Helen; he is the "raft on" which she stays afloat on the
semiotic stream of preconscious fantasy. The most secretive and
significant cryptonym is "Mrs. Thorpe-Wharton," in which the word
*mother* is anagramatically encrypted, an obvious reference to the
matronly role this Edith Wharton–like character performs in the
melodramatic text of the narrative, and a less obvious allusion to the
Egyptian mother goddess who enchants the symbolic subtext. The
secret name to which we are alerted in the story's epigram is Isis, the
name of Mother Egypt, whose decoding Helen has been unconsciously performing throughout.

This cryptonymic, hieroglyphic mother signals another textual
layer, the primal, marginal, maternal, subconscious level of the narrative palimpsest, or what Julia Kristeva calls the "semiotic," poetic
genotext, as opposed to the "symbolic," discursive, phenotext. Rachel Blau DuPlessis explains:

> The interplay of these two sides in H.D. has a particular name: palimp-
> sest. Meaning what it conventionally does in ancient scribal practice: an
> over-written page, a script under which is shadowed another script,
> another text. As H.D. defines this as epigraph to her novel called by that
> very name: one text "erased" but "imperfectly" to make "room for
> another" writing. Thematically, morally, textually in H.D. the erasure of
> the signs (mark, trace, index, imprint) of the "mother"—the text made
> marginal, by the signs of the "father"—the text of dominance. . . . Can
> see them as interactive. . . . could say lower one is original, therefore
> right. . . . Or, could as well place them together as the situation of
> writing. Could say, this palimpsest is the visual image of the situation of
> writing.[71]

Certainly in "Secret Name," H.D.'s representation of the hieroglyph is a "visual image of the situation of writing." Helen's predilection for cryptography leads her to the pharaoh's tomb, where, gazing
at the mummified thing that had been dead "four thousand years,"
which "had attained, by sheer permanence, a cryptic power," she
beholds "cloud-like dark images . . . emerg[ing], as from a darkened
crystal, small images from the past" (182). The crypt is a hieroglyph
par excellence, a sign signifying signs across a world's remove from
the natural operations of the ideogram.

Elsewhere, in *Tribute to Freud*, H. D. draws an analogy between
memory and the mummified Theban, occupants of the psyche's
living tomb. Her drawing is itself an excavation of memory, and what
she remembers is a memory of excavation, an instructive childhood
recollection of unearthing "things under things," uncovering

> white, wingless creatures. . . . The base of the log had been the roof of a
> series of little pockets or neat open graves, rather like Aztec or Egyptian
> burial-chambers. . . . These curled, white slugs were unborn things.
>
> There were things under things, as well as things inside things. (20–
> 21)

This is not the "thing" that imagism sought to treat directly but the
unborn thing, the thing buried alive in subconscious memory, accessible only to the cryptic translation of dreams. Like canopic jars,
which store the vital organs of the dead in anticipation of the afterlife,
the crypts of unconscious memory preserve semiotic matter until it is
(re)born into conscious signification through psychoanalytic decipherment.

This analogy brings us to H.D.'s Freudian writing, which attempts
to decrypt the word-thing, where "thing" is a lost, forgotten, buried
feeling for a love object whose memory is preserved in key words or
poetical phrases and hence recoverable if the right cue is given in
transference. The cryptography of H.D.'s analysis in *Tribute to Freud*
recalls the treatment of the Wolf Man, one of Freud's famous patients, for whom a unique method of symptom decoding called
"cryptonomy" had to be invented.[72] But unlike the Wolf Man, H.D.
does not consider herself to be a "case"; her cryptic words are eventually translatable into etymologies common to the whole human
race. It remains for her to recover the root(-word)s of her dreams and
to decode them in the psychopoetics of her future writing, since, as
she pronounces in her *Trilogy*,

> I know, I feel
> the meaning that words hide;
>
> they are anagrams, cryptograms,
> little boxes, conditioned
>
> to hatch butterflies
> > (WDNF 53)

and

> Psyche, the butterfly,
> out of the cocoon.
> > (TA 103)

H.D. applies psychoanalytic semiology in order to remember and extend her analysis with Freud. Near the end of her 1933 session, she found that she could give the Professor only a mere token of the appreciation she felt for his work and that "to express this adequately would be to delve too deep, to become involved in technicalities" (TF 63). Ten years later, she was able to signal a more adequate appreciation in Tribute to Freud, whose "technicalities" are the telltale signs of her appropriation of the techniques of free association, wordplay, and transference. These were the semiotic practices Freud used in her analysis; they are now the practices she adapts in writing her tribute, thereby making them, in some unique way, hers, and using them in turn to explore "Freud" or the "unexplored region" that his "hieroglyph of the unconscious" opens up.

### Free Association

Greek tear jars are props in the original scene of analysis:

Tendencies of thought and imagination . . . were not cut away, were not pruned even. My imagination wandered at will; my dreams were revealing, and many of them drew on classical or Biblical symbolism. Thoughts were things, to be collected, collated, analyzed, shelved, or resolved. Fragmentary ideas, apparently unrelated, were often found to be part of a special layer or stratum of thought and memory. . . . these were sometimes skillfully pieced together like the exquisite Greek tear-jars and iridescent glass bowls and vases that gleamed in the dusk from the shelves of the cabinet that faced me where I stretched, propped up on the couch in the room in Berggasse 19, Wien IX. (TF 14)

A figure of analytical reconstruction, the jars appear again in "The Master" as precisely that which Freud bequeaths, H.D., a sign of her Freudian legacy:

> I said good-bye
> and saw his old head
> as he turned,
> as he left the room
> leaving me alone
> with all his old trophies,
> the marbles, the vases, the stone Sphynx,
> the old, old jars from Egypt;
> he left me alone with these things.
>
> (CP 459)

"Greek tear-jars" and "the old, old jars of Egypt" cue the analysand's deep memory of childhood dreams and fantasies, prompting the play of transference and the free play of word association. To apply Freud in the absence of his charming presence, H.D. must recall and re-present his things. In *The Flowering of the Rod* (1944), jar is a key figure, a "crypt" of memory and a cryptography, whose piecing together and decoding through free association releases "Psyche," a revitalized spiritual presence intended to heal a discontented modernity.

*The Flowering of the Rod*, the third and final part of *Trilogy*, is introduced in *Tribute to the Angels* as "a tale of a Fisherman, / a tale of a jar or jars" (*TA* 105). Tracing the movement of a jar or jars that is/are repeatedly lost and found through the course of its narration, *The Flowering of the Rod* is not a "tale" so much as a collection, collation, analysis, shelving or resolving of "fragmentary ideas, apparently unrelated" but eventually "found to be part of a special layer or stratum of thought and memory" which we, the readers, are invited to piece together skilfully in collaboration with the writer.

The figure of the jar is structurally and symbolically complex. There is, first of all, the jar(s) in the text, which we can trace as Champollion traced the cartouche in deciphering the Rosetta stone. Recognizably ancient ("unguent jars, alabaster boxes of the . . . Hyksos," "charms" from "tombs" [*FR* 132]), they recall the jars on Freud's shelves, and they are inscribed with mysterious "sigils" (132) signaling the object of a Freudian hermeneutics. These are hieroglyphic containers whose unsealing (decoding) will release a forgotten presence; though hermetically sealed, they nonetheless signal the presence they are secreting ("the jars were sealed, / the fragrance got out somehow" [132]). In other words, they typically function like a Freudian dream symbol, revealing repressed content not by immediate disclosure but by signaling other jars bearing other memories and perceptions.

The figure of the jar also structures the narrative frame of the text. *The Flowering of the Rod* is a "tale" housed in a frame that hinges, as it were, on a door left a*jar* between two rooms, two symbolic realms, one darker or less known than the other (recalling the hieroglyph of "Secret Name" described as "a door, hinged, swinging . . . for the chosen, gifted spirit" [*P* 229]). One jar frames the "tale of a Fisherman," a rememoration and restoration of the story of Christ in apocryphal images and symbols. The other jar frames the narrative of Mary. As enigmatic as the jar of myrrh that she carries about with her ("it is not on record . . . how she found the alabaster jar" [129]), Mary's story is the unrecorded gospel, a tale from the crypt of scriptural memory which we have not yet opened. (H.D. hints at the contents of the Gospel of Mary (Magdalene), one of the gnostic gospels discovered in the nineteenth century and still exciting much scholarly discussion at the time she was writing; what is more, her story precedes by less than a year the spectacular unearthing of the Gospel of the Egyptians from the bottom of an earthenware jar in Upper Egypt in 1945.)[73]

The figure evolves: unsealing the jar of one story allows it to spill over into the other, creates an alchemical reaction, the distillation of which is a revitalized "Christos-image" (*WDNF* 27): a new spiritual essence that comes from the infusion of the forgotten presence of Mary, whose memory is induced by the word association "Mary-myrrh," into the deadened logos of Christ(ianity).[74]

The tale of a fisherman is familiar to modernist mythopoeia. There are the Fisher-King of *The Waste Land* and the Christian romance that we survivors of the wreck of modern civilization are intended to "shore against our ruins" as if we had salvaged a bottle with a saving message. H.D.'s supplementary "tale of a jar or jars" compounds the canonical tale by recovering "heretical" (*WDNF* 53) news of ancient "Magdala" (135), a "tower-town" of prelapsarian paradise. Scriptural rubble—heretical, apocryphal, canonical—this is the uncensored stuff of the primal dream, brought into the symbolic present of H.D.'s dream-poem and left, like shards of pottery or tablets of clay, for the reader to assemble into some manifest, messianic text.

Wordplay

Another technique of translation H.D. appropriates from analysis is wordplay: "We play hide-and-seek, hunt-the-slipper, and hunt-the-thimble and patiently and meticulously patch together odds and ends of our picture-puzzle. We spell words upside down and back-ward and crosswise, for our crossword puzzle" (TF 119). Application of this technique can best be seen in Trilogy. For example:

> Osiris equates O-sir-is or O-Sire-is
>
> Osiris,
> the star Sirius
>
> relates resurrection myth
> and resurrection reality
>
> through the ages.
> (WDNF 54)

H.D.'s play on the proper name Osiris does not deconstruct the word into pictorial representations of the operations of nature but instead decodes its ancient mystery. The end of The Walls Do Not Fall opens the quest for "spiritual reality" to the discovery of the all-father of prehistory, emphasizing the copula enclosed in the name as "proof" of his existence: Osiris "is." She forges anagrammatic and homo-phonic links between Osiris and Sirius as further "evidence" of an equation between this and other resurrection myths, Jesus and the Star of Bethlehem, Adonis and Venus, Star of the Sea.

Her lyrics reverse Fenollosa's imperative for translators of the ideo-gram to "avoid the 'is' "; moreover, they return mystique to language, collapsing the grammatologist's double question (what is the origin of writing and what is writing?) into one luminous "is." Freud, himself, may be the source of this figure, since it was he who once put a figurine of "the very Egyptian Osiris . . . into [her] hands, [saying] 'This is called the answerer.' (TF xiii). In the final analysis, H.D.'s word search translates Freud's wordplay into hermetic hermeneutics, the search for "the true-rune, the right-spell" and for the associated sound—"there is zrr-hiss / lightning in a not-known" (WDNF 58)—the sound the buzz bombs make as they fall on the ruins of London. This is Oz-zzr-hiss, the sign of the "Healer" (54) answering "the patient" in search of a cure for (her) war terror. Signaling the resurrection myth for the modern scribe to translate and record, Osiris answers those questions that inaugurated the poem: "we passed the flame: we wonder / what saved us? what for?" (4).

A more elaborate example of wordplay is to be found in *Tribute to the Angels*:

> Now polish the crucible
> and in the bowl distill
>
> a word most bitter, *marah*,
> a word bitterer still, *mar*,
>
> sea, brine, breaker, seducer,
> giver of life, giver of tears;
>
> Now polish the crucible
> and set the jet of flame
>
> under, till *marah-mar*
> are melted, fuse and join
>
> and change and alter,
> mer, mere, mère, mater, Maia, Mary,
>
> Star of the Sea,
> Mother.
>
> (*TA* 71)

Using foreign and ancient languages to arrive at a distillation of origins, H.D.'s Freudian philology demonstrates how Mary decodes an obscure desire to reclaim the mother from her "sea" of origins. The express purpose of this wordplay is to clear the name of Mary Magdalene, the marred and marginalized Mary of the Scriptures, and to reintegrate her image with that of the Virgin Mary at a deeper layer of memory/meaning than that from which the Judeo-Christian myths derive. The play continues in *Flowering of the Rod*, where Mary is equated with myrrh, a mnemic image of the olfactory order, which, according to Freud, is our most primitive sense, bound to our most primal memories:[75]

> I am Mary—O, there are Marys a-plenty,
> (though I am Mara, bitter), I shall be Mary-myrrh;
>
> . . . . .

*I am Mary, the incense flower of the incense-tree,*
*myself worshipping, weeping, shall be changed to myrrh.*

(FR 135, 138)

H.D.'s hermetic translation at once reveals and conceals the original meaning of Mary and the mysteries of Magdala, which antedate the patriarchal myth of Virgin birth. Wordplay *divines* the ritual sense (es-sense) of suffering and joy over birth and death which was originally Mary's; it invokes the origins of the cross, the tree on which effigies of Attis-Adonis-Tammuz were hung in worship of the all-mother of prehistory, the original Stabat Mater:

> I am that myrrh-tree of the gentiles,
>
> .  .  .  .  .
>
> who kneel before mutilated images
> and burn incense to the Mother of Mutilations,
> to Attis-Adonis-Tammuz and his mother who was myrhh;
>
> .  .  .  .  .
>
> I am Mary, I will weep bitterly,
> bitterly . . . bitterly.

(135)

This is Mary's cross; is this also her caduceus, the sign of an original faith in spiritual and psychic healing, whose derivation traces as far back as Thoth, to the Tau-cross of hermetic medicine? Tapping the root of a philological tree that is accessible only to the poet's dream, H.D. claims to have achieved with her Freudian word magic what no modern archaeological scholar could hope to accomplish, namely, the revitalization of modern Christianity with images of ritual prehistory.

### Transference

H.D. testifies that the mother transference was indeed enacted in her analysis with Freud: "The Professor's surroundings and interests seem to derive from my mother rather than from my father, and yet to say the 'transference' is to Freud as mother does not altogether satisfy me. He had said, 'And—I must tell you . . . I do *not* like to be the mother in transference. . .' I asked if others had what he called this mother-transference on him. He said ironically and I thought a little wistfully, 'O, *very* many'" (TF 146–47). But how does H.D.

transcribe that transference? Her collaborative reconstruction of the princess dream as the "projection" of a "repressed psychic urge" (37) that originates in the "family-complex" (14) reiterates Freud's first general exposition of transference based on the oedipal complex.[76] According to Freud, the subject in transference projects onto the physician one of her cultural "prototypes" or "imagos" (usually the father but also possibly the mother, brother, or someone else), and in transference, as Laplanche and Pontalis put it, "the subject's relationship to parental figures . . . is once again lived out" (*Language of Psycho-Analysis*, 458).

H.D. comments very little on the technique of transference in *Tribute to Freud*, although her explanation of the dream work displays the thinking which Freud later expanded upon to explain the mechanism of transference he had observed in analysis. She notes how unconscious dream thoughts are veiled by preconscious residues of the day before (72). Freud calls this mechanism displacement to account for his experiences in treatment as well as for the masking of the dream thought: "An unconscious idea is as such quite incapable of entering the preconscious and . . . it can only exercise any effect there by establishing a connection with an idea which already belongs to the preconscious, by transferring its intensity on to it and by getting itself 'covered' by it. Here we have the fact of 'transference,' which provides an explanation of so many striking phenomena" (*SE* 5:562–63). H.D.'s explanation of the dream censor reiterates Freud's discussion of the work of repression in dreams, which he later develops to account for the occurrence of resistance in analysis. She writes: "The sleeping mind was not one, not all equally sleeping; part of the unconscious mind would become conscious at a least expected moment; this part of the dreaming mind that laid traps or tricked the watcher or slammed the doors on the scene or the unravelling tapestry of the dream sequence he called the Censor" (72). Freud observed that transference onto the physician occurs at the moment when important content is in danger of being revealed, testifying to the proximity of an unconscious conflict and to a strong reaction against having that conflict exposed. Accordingly, transference is that area or arena where the patient's particular problems get played out with immediacy, where the patient confronts, as Laplanche and Pontalis say, "the permanence and the force of his unconscious wishes and phantasies" (*Language of Psycho-Analysis* 458).

As I mentioned earlier, H.D. testifies in her *Tribute* that she gave "signs" to Freud that she did not want to be analyzed, deciding to defer her analysis for some future time. Later, in Freud's absence, she sets the stage for a self-analysis in the context of her poetry. But (how) does self-analysis work? Can the dream symbols of self-analysis avoid becoming an idée fixe, idealized signs or symptoms of a self-signifying desire, unchallenged by a transference dialogue? Freud doubted the efficacy of self-analysis for want of an interpersonal relationship to mediate the play of self-reconstruction and to reinforce self-criticism positively (so say Laplanche and Pontalis, *Language of Psycho-Analysis* 460). Yet, H.D. believed she could set the transference (back) in motion while writing her tribute in the presence of Freud's memory. It is in this belief that she proceeded to conduct the dream-visions of *Trilogy*, *Helen in Egypt*, and *Hermetic Definition*.

**2**

# Autobiographical Fantasy: Cryptobiography, Cinematobiography, Otobiography

> There is a book . . . called *The Gift*. . . . It is autobiographi-
> cal, "almost." . . . There was a great deal more to be said
> than I could more than hint at, in the seven sections of the
> autobiographical fantasy. . . . Certainly [it] . . . synthesizes
> or harmonizes with the Sigmund Freud notes. I assembled
> *The Gift* during the early war years, but without the anal-
> ysis and the illuminating doctrine or philosophy of Sig-
> mund Freud, I would hardly have found the clue or the
> bridge between the child-life . . . and the orgy of destruc-
> tion . . . lived through in London. . . . But this was no
> mechanical intellectual trick of mind or memory, the Child
> actually returns to that world, she lives actually in those
> reconstructed scenes, or she watches them like a moving-
> picture.
>
> "H.D. by Delia Alton" (187, 188, 189, 192)

After surviving the trauma of World War I, H.D. began life-writing.[1] At first she limited herself to transcribing those haunting, visionary experiences that arose as aftereffects of the war during therapeutic visits to the Scilly Isles and to Greece. The result of this undertaking was the "ghosted" prose and "hallucinated writing" of *Hedylus* (1928) and other works that failed to satisfy her need to relive the war years in her own way (*TF* 148–49).[2] None of these works could claim to have the healing charisma of the later, (post-)Freudian writing: instead, they amounted to the sterile labor of an overworked and "detached intellect" (*TF* 149), to the symptomatic signature of a traumatized memory.

Freud assigned her to reconstruct the war years in writing and to do so without narratological "tricks" or poetic embellishment, "just a straight narrative." The result of this undertaking was the autobiographical *Bid Me to Live,* over two decades in the making.[3] As the title melodramatically suggests, this narrative is emphatically biographical; not just a writing of life, it is a writing to live, a reliving past life in one's own terms, thereby quelling the war terror for the present and obtaining the vision and technique to overcome it in the future war, which she would write her way through.

"For me, it was so important," Norman Holmes Pearson recalls H.D. as testifying, "it was so important, my own LEGEND. Yes, my own LEGEND. Then, to get well and re-create it" (*TF* v). The reverse also holds true for H.D.: to recreate it and get well thereby. By the time she was ready to compose *Hermetic Definition* (1960) while convalescing in the hospital a year before her death, writing to live became the therapeutic imperative of her post-Freudian muse: "She draws the veil aside, / unbinds my eyes, / commands, / write, write or die" (*HD* 7).

But though the stress clearly falls on the *bio* of her autobiography, it is not clear what emphasis falls on the *auto,* the writing self or subject. According to "H.D. by Delia Alton," itself a cryptic autograph,[4] the new, Freud-inspired life-writing in *The Gift* (1941) is the work of fantasy, particularly childhood fantasy. The writer of *The Gift* is the phantasmal subject, "the Child," and not the remembering or intellectualizing adult. This technique of recalling the phantasmal autobiographical subject through the medium of transference narrative marks her departure from the systematic, step-by-step reconstruction of the classical bildungsroman and even from the self-consciously evolving artistry of the künstlerroman.

H.D.'s figure of childhood fantasy and her technique of recall through the "trance" of simulated "transference" are the structuring nuclei of her Freudian life-writing. Her application of the term *fantasy* and related terms (daydreaming, psychic reality, primal fantasy, sexual fantasy, hysterical (bisexual) fantasy, childhood memory, screen memory, and telepathy or thought-transference), which Freud employs in his psychopathology of everyday life, are further telltale signs of an intricate intertextuality, they are especially telling in *The Gift,* where H.D. elaborates them in the Freud-like, explanatory and illustrative passages. But as the mystic amanuensis of H.D.'s memoir notes, the poet puts a decidedly occult accent on these Freudian terms of reference.[5]

Though Freud understood fantasy to be the product of both near-waking, preconscious activity (what he calls secondary revision or daydreaming) and the unconscious, H.D. emphasizes the unconscious, almost to the exclusion of the waking or living memory. Like Freud, she privileges fantasy as the medium or focal point of psychical reality/research, where we can see the transition from unconscious representation to conscious thought and, with it, the mechanisms of repression and the return of the repressed. But unlike Freud, she idealizes this medium as the site of actual return for the repressed and youthful subject of visionary, primal fantasy. The child of individual and racial prehistory occupies center stage of *The Gift* and H.D.'s subsequent life-writing. Her autobiographer is the female child who inhabits the womb of maternal memory, and the setting is as important to the scenography of revived fantasy as the subject herself.

*The Gift* records how H.D. finds and exploits the narratological medium best able to carry out and to further Freud's assignment of the writing cure: this is the medium of the dream work as reconstituted in imaginary transference (with "Freud" as mother). H.D. uses various techniques to set the scene for this transference, or "entrancement," of which I have identified three: the *crypto*biographical technique involves the raising of the dead child or mother(s), whose essential memory has been encrypted in hieroglyphic images and placed in reserve in the unconscious; the *oto*biographical technique involves reviving or bringing maternal memories back to presence in song recovered by developing an ear for Freud's transference cues; the *cinemato*biographical technique is the direct memory screening of childhood fantasy without the mediation of screen memory. It is another form of the living pictograph of imagism, a cinematograph animated and brought to life in cinemato-bio-graphy, which is none other than the "projection" of the archaic, animistic soul of prehistory.

These adapted or "occulted" techniques, together with the Freudian concepts of fantasy, projection, and the uncanny, are the figures of intertextual study in this chapter. But before entering into detailed discussion of the technicalities of H.D.'s adaptation, I should like to point out that her psycho-graphic technology derives most directly from her transcription of Freud's work, which she knew from analysis and which she read in his own autobiographical productions, such as *The Interpretation of Dreams*. I read H.D.'s autobiographical fantasy as a critical and occult supplement to Freud's *Autobiographical Study*, an inter*bio*textuality or an auto*duo*biography.[6]

## An Exchange of Lives

In a curious passage of *Tribute to Freud* (77–81), H.D. proposes to take Freud's place in reconstructing his autobiography:

> He had worked with the famous Dr. Charcot in Paris. There are other names that figure in the historical account given us by Professor Freud himself in his short *Autobiographical Study.* . . . But I [wanted to know] when and how the Professor happened on the idea that led to his linking up neurotic states of megalomania and aggrandizement with, in certain instances, fantasies of youth and childhood. . . . I wanted to know at what exact moment, and in what manner, there came that flash of inspiration, that thing that clicked, that sounded . . . in the inner Freud mind, heart, or soul, *this is it.* (76–77)

The passage develops into a speculative redramatization of the origins of psychoanalysis, which it attributes to the genius of Freud's megalomania. Fantasies of greatness enabled Freud to overcome the anti-Semitism troubled his boyhood and, later, his residence in Paris while training with Charcot, affording him the insight to recognize the delusional dramaturgy of the psychotic inmates of Saltpêtrière.

Her argument? That Freud is essentially a master of stagecraft who perceived in his own individual case a universal tendency to "act out" one's fantasies in real life. Freud saw the *world*, not just Charcot's observation theater, as a stage and saw life patterns as repeated performances of phantasmal production. The psychotic behind bars who claimed to be Caesar was simply acting the part to which he had aspired as a child and on which he had become regressively fixated as an adult. H.D.'s redramatization of Freud's dramatic breakthrough allows us to see the theatrical origins of psychoanalytic therapeutics. Having successfully acted upon his own fantasies of grand, historical achievement at critical moments in his life, Freud sets up a practice that is designed, in turn, to facilitate the therapeutic enactment of the delusional fantasies of his patients:

> There is Caesar behind bars—here is Hannibal, here am I, Sigmund Freud, watching Caesar behind bars. . . . I will conquer. I will. I, Hannibal—not Caesar. I, the despised Carthaginian, I, the enemy of Rome. I, Hannibal. So you see, I, Sigmund Freud, myself standing here, a favorite and gifted, admit it, student of Dr. Charcot, in no way to all appearances deranged or essentially peculiar, true to my own

orbit . . . my childhood fantasies of Hannibal, my identification with
Hannibal, the Carthaginian (Jew, not Roman)—I, Sigmund Freud, understand this Caesar. I, Hannibal! (*TF* 80)[7]

As H.D. sees it, Freud turns his "study" into a theater for reproducing and working through fantasies otherwise enacted under suppressive circumstances that condition a symptomatic fixation. As
stage manager he sets the scene in which the subject can verbalize
and thereby make conscious the repressed, unconscious desire ob-
sessively or hysterically acted out elsewhere. From this dramatic
reconstruction, H.D. recognizes her own megadesire to be a prophetess, no more (or less) delusory than Freud's wish to be a world-
conquering hero. Confirming this desire, she proceeds to fantasize
her future role in extending the newly established psychoanalytic
realm of healing.

H.D. admits that "this obviously is not an historical account of the
preliminary steps that led to the establishment of a new branch of
psychological research" (81), reiterating Freud's own testimony at
the beginning of his *Autobiographical Study*: "Since I must not contra-
dict myself and since I have no wish to repeat myself exactly, I must
endeavour to construct a narrative in which subjective and objective
attitudes, biographical and historical interests, are combined in a
new proportion."[8] Her narrative reconstruction of "Freud" is thus
somewhat justified; yet, she does not stop at adapting his life to
elaborate her own autobiography. A subtler retranscription is at play
in *Tribute to Freud*, where she exploits his part in mother and father
transference to "establish" crossing lines of descent in the genealogy
of H.D.-Freud.

By a "trick" of autobiographical fantasy, working freely in simulated transference, Freud refigures as H.D.'s parents. In her replay of
analysis, Freud conducts her to forgotten childhood memory and
then slips into the background while it acquires a life of its own,
evoking further memory from the transpersonal and transhistorical
unconscious. The image of Freud as doctor, onto which she initially
transfers memories of her father, is displaced by the image of Dr.
Charles Doolittle as it acquires affective priority. By a curious reversal
of imaginary facility, the childhood scene that transference had originally conjured forth now recalls Freud as if he were a distant kins-
man of the father:

Father? . . . He is New England, though he does not live there and was
not born there. He comes from those Puritan fathers . . . [who] fought

with Indians and burned witches. Their hats were like the hats
the doctors wore, in the only picture that was hanging in his study.
The original picture was by Rembrandt. . . . The half-naked man on the
table was dead so it did not hurt him when the doctors sliced his arm
with a knife or a pair of scissors. Is the picture called *A Lesson in Anatomy*?

It does not really matter what the picture is called. It is about doctors.
There is a doctor seated at the back of the couch on which I am lying. He
is a very famous doctor. He is called Sigmund Freud. (33–35)

H.D.'s picture of her father includes Freud, just as it includes the
physicians of Rembrandt's day: a figurative crossing over (chiasmus),
H.D.'s picture is a reflection of Freud's staging of transference with
props, paintings on the walls, archaeological treasures and old books
on the shelves. But the reflection acquires the mnemonic facility of
the original scene, opening memory to a re-view of forgotten details
concerning Freud. Her repicturing casts Freud and her father in the
same light of scientific objectivity represented in Rembrandt's cold-
blooded dissection. Moreover, it illuminates the puritanical ideology
of the Enlightenment to which these scientist-fathers subscribe and
with which they fight savagery and witchcraft. H.D.'s paternal memory is perhaps a subtle, critical reminder that Freud once turned to
the Inquisitors' handbook, *Malleus maleficorum* (*The Witches' Hammer*),
for research on treating female hysterics and that, in general, he
sought to exorcise the primitive, animistic mind that survives in the
delusional fantasies of neurotics.[9] Likewise, the Freud who plays the
part of the mother in transference is seen, by another trick of autobiographical fantasy and figure (again chiasmus) to acquire a distant
kinship to Helen Doolittle (née Wolle). Memories of her maternal
heritage, originally prompted by Freud, are seen, in turn, to recall his
own Moravian motherland:

My father's second wife was the daughter of a descendant of one of the
original groups of the early-eighteenth-century, mystical Protestant
order, called the Unitas Fratrum, the Bohemian or Moravian Brotherhood. Our mother's father was part mid-European by race, Polish I
believe the country called itself then, when his forefathers left it, though
it became German. . . . Livonia, Moravia, Bohemia—Count Zinzendorf,
the founder of the renewed Bohemian brotherhood, was an Austrian,
whose father was exiled or self-exiled to Upper Saxony, because of his
Protestant affiliations. The Professor himself was an Austrian, a Moravian actually by birth. (32–33)

This interweaving of genealogies is not a regular feature of Freud's therapy, but it figures in H.D.'s "delayed analysis" as especially efficacious: "The sea grows narrower, the gap in consciousness sometimes seems negligible; nevertheless there is a duality . . . but they are not one. So in me, two distinct racial or biological or psychological entities tend to grow nearer or to blend, even, as time heals old breaks in consciousness" (32). H.D. refers to the weaving or blending not only of maternal and paternal genealogies but also of parental and Freudian genealogies. A crossing over of Moravianism and Puritanism, scientism and Freudianism, H.D.'s autobiographical fantasy employs the figure of chiasmus to cast the illusion of a common, psychogenetic if not biogenetic descent (in modern genetics, coincidentally, *chiasma* refers to the crossing of chromosomal material in replicative meiosis). With this figure, she mythologizes her relation to Freud, signaling an autobiographical desire to be his inspirational offspring, the spiritual or psychic heir to Freud's legacy of psychoanalysis. Once the line of kinship is established, it is but a small leap of faith to equate Freud's medical unorthodoxy with Moravian protestantism: "From the actual family of Bethlehem, Pennsylvania, the scientific 'Pastor,' the part-German or Slavonic grandfather (as well as the scientific father who is yet in a way, 'from outside'), from a legend of a new way of life, a Brotherhood, dedicated to peace and universal understanding, it is not really such a far cry to Vienna and to Sigmund Freud" (DA 189).

H.D.'s picture of Freud as protestant outsider corresponds to Freud's own picture, and it reminds us that he opens his *Autobiographical Study* with the contention that psychoanalysis owes its origins/originality to his alienation from the intellectual community as a Jew, "for at an early age I was made familiar with the fate of being in the Opposition and of being put under the ban of the 'compact majority.' The foundations were thus laid for a certain degree of independence of judgement" (*SE* 20:9). Later on, he further contends that it was because of "official anathema against psycho-analysis . . . that the analysts . . . formed themselves . . . into an 'International Psycho-Analytical Association' " (*SE* 20:50).

H.D. prompts speculation concerning the role Freud's Jewish and Moravian background played in the history of psychoanalysis as a heterodox institution of heterological thought (a protesting "brotherhood" of independent thinkers). But why should she emphasize this "other" Freud? To what effect? The answer seems clear: in her autobiographical reversal, with Freud and Freudianism as the subjects of her analysis, the repressed "other" of psychoanalysis is called to the foreground, where its genius might be revealed and recognized. Affirmation of this heterodox Freud provides, in turn, affirmation for the heterodox poet, who has reason to believe that the source of her poetic gifts lies buried in her suppressed Moravian past, which goes back at least as far as the eighteenth century.

Just recently, cultural historians have pursued a similar line of thought: "There is relevance in examining Freud's connections to the Moravian Jewish tradition," Michel de Certeau observes in his comparative investigation of the critical traditions of psychoanalysis and European mysticism.[10] What they share, he discovers, is a radical critique of the standard epistemological unit of the age: the bourgeois individual. Psychoanalytic biography, he explains,

> dismantles—like the mysticism of the sixteenth and seventeenth centuries in the context of a *received* religious tradition—the historical and social figure that is the standard unit of the system within which Freudianism developed. Even if social pressures can lead it to encomiums in defense of the individual, psychoanalytic biography is in principle a form of self-critique, and its narrativity is an anti-mythic force. (15)

It is psychoanalytic *auto*biography that H.D. adapts and employs to demystify the myth of the universal, self-same, *male* individual which had come to dominate her and her culture's sense of identity, certainly the sense of poetic identity in the literary circles she (had) traveled in. The "other" that Freudian biography reveals and confirms for H.D. is the mother of her own mystical disposition, a personal reserve as yet unexploited in her modernist quest for both originality and tradition.

But whereas H.D. might attribute this radical reorientation of her (life-)writing to Freud, Freud's characterization must be attributed to her autobiographical fantasy; the Freud of the H.D. "LEGEND" is just that: legendary, not actual, a fetish figure whose "protestant" genealogy she draws to cover the "gaps" of individual, racial, historical, ideological differences between them, and within her own mixed origins. This is not to criticize H.D.: the purpose of analysis is precisely to bridge the abysses of consciousness and memory in the forging of healing connections. But in using Freud to expose one dominant and debilitating myth of culture, H.D. creates another, the myth of a visionary tradition that incorporates both Moravianism and Freudianism, a myth the reader should not mistake for history outside of H.D.'s life-writing.

Having said that, I should like to note that in another autobio-graphical study, "On the History of the Psycho-Analytic Movement" (1914), Freud reflects on the erotic origins of Moravian mysticism: "Dr. [Oskar] Pfister, a pastor in Zurich, has traced back the origin of religious fanaticism to perverse eroticism in his book on the piety of Count von Zinzendorf."[11] Did H.D. come across this reference in her readings or in her discussions with Freud? Was this the cue for her to make autobiography the site of psychic as well as genealogical re-search? At one point, she states outright: "I must have the absolutely pure, mystical Moravian pietism or poetism or hard-boiled Freudian facts," implying that poetism, the middle term of this either/or would be the medium of mediation between antithetical factions.[12] Who, then, would be better suited to this inquiry into erotic-mystic sources than she who would also derive therapeutic benefit in writ-ing out her fantasy of gifted otherness, restoring faith in her sup-pressed maternal heritage, and conjuring the charismatic return of the repressed mothers.

Before proceeding to discuss *The Gift*, the story or stories of H.D.'s recovery of the mothers as seen or sounded through childhood mem-ory, I should like to turn back to two earlier experiments in writing Freudian autobiography—to *Her* and to *Nights*. The clinical Freud to which H.D. alludes in *Her* is noticeably different from the later psy-choanalytic medium she discovers in *Tribute to Freud*, which com-bines medicine, art, and the occult. *Her* is not so much a prefiguration of *The Gift* and subsequent autobiography as a testament to the inadequacy of the narrative discourse of case history for the produc-tion and signification of visionary self-consciousness.

## *Her*: Studies in Hysteria

As I have suggested, we might read H.D.'s *Her* side by side with Freud and Josef Breuer's *Studies on Hysteria* and with related studies, such as Freud's "Dreams and Hysteria" and "Hysterical Phantasies and Their Relation to Bisexuality." But why should H.D. take up writing hysterical studies, and how does she adapt the language of psychoanalysis and the symptomatic "discourse" of hysteria to her specific needs and desires?

In the period between wars, H.D. was looking for the medium that would accommodate her need to clarify or even master the traumatic visionary experiences she outlines in *Tribute to Freud*. In "Secret

Name: Excavator's Egypt" (written two or three years before *Her*), she demonstrates a certain ability to host "psycho-hysterical visionary sensations" (*P* 187) at the prompting of a hieroglyph and to flip in and out of autohypnosis in a way that recalls Breuer's description of hysterical consciousness, "occurring with varying frequency and duration, and often alternating rapidly with normal waking states."[13] "Secret Name" reveals a desire to be the hysterical subject, to possess or to be possessed by the hysteric's alternative state of consciousness, to have "visions" that transcend ordinary perception and that present the "things" of unconscious fantasy directly, without the mediation of intellection, conscience, or discursive convention.

Had H.D. read *Studies on Hysteria*, particularly Breuer's case study of Anna O. (there is no hard evidence that she did), she would have discovered all the components of a hagiography: a possessed subject, a chronicle of visions, speaking in tongues, healing and transcendence. The "talking cure," for which Breuer's patient has been canonized in medical history, with its polyglot translations of hallucinogenic fantasies, could have struck H.D. as a radically other discourse attuned to the hieroglyphic operations of the unconscious beyond the realm presented by stream-of-consciousness narrative.

Whether or not she had *Studies* in mind when she composed *Her*, H.D. writes her autobiographical fiction in the genre of case history narrative. As a diagnostic study, the narrative fails, but its purpose is not to mime the concepts and procedures of clinical psychology. Reference to the case history seems instead to be aesthetic and heuristic and possibly also therapeutic. As the protagonist declares: " 'She was delirious. . . .' 'Delirious? She can throw herself into those sub-normal hysterical states at a moment's notice.' 'It wasn't hysterical. It was real' " (*Her* 191). The "hysteria" presented here, though seemingly histrionic, is actually very serious, "real" in its delirium, in its aesthetic/psychic sub[version of]normality, echoing Breuer's account of "true" delirium hystericum:

> First and foremost, of course, among hypnoid states are to be numbered true auto-hypnoses, which are distinguished from artificial hypnoses only by the fact of their originating spontaneously. . . . On account of the dream-like nature of their content, they often deserve the name of *"delirium hystericum."* (SE 2:216)

Frequent reference to psychoanalytic etiology (8, 15, 24, 33, 40, 191), ultimately yields no definitive term, "no word for her dementia" (3).

The search for a sign system, ambiguously symptomatic and artistic, analytic and hieratic, continues:

> How could I be hysterical? . . . Solid and visible form was what she had been seeking. I will put this into visible language, Amy Dennon will say you were harassed, disintegrated and disassociated by preliminary erotic longings, wakened as it were in sleep. . . . The dream in the dream should be put into stark language. Birds in traps, enemies in pitfalls, the Athenians in the pit at Syracuse. . . . At times she started into some trance, the dream was broken and a heavier state retook it. (210, 213)

What Her is "seeking" are the words to present or to signify her poetic vision in the most direct, true-to-self way; she envisions her recovery of words, or rather, of word-things, hieroglyphics that act as window to the soul:

> Things, a bird skimming across a window, were a sort of writing on a wall.
> "The Greeks made birdflight symbolic. . . . The sort of way the wing went against blue sky was, I suppose, a sort of pencil, a sort of stylus, engraving to the minds of augurers, signs, symbols that meant things. I see by that birdflight across an apparently black surface, that curves of wings meant actual things to Greeks, not just vague symbols but actual hieroglyphics . . . hieroglyphs." (125)

A hieroglyphic "language" that would mediate between things and flights of fantasy is the sought-for signifier, whose lack she suffers in the overwhelming immediacy of perception, experienced as a dissolution of boundaries between interior and exterior worlds:[14]

> She wanted to climb through walls of no visible dimension. Tree walls were visible, were to be extended to know reach of universe. Trees, no matter how elusive, in the end, walled one in. Trees were suffocation. "Claustrophobia" was a word that Her Gart had not yet assimilated.
> "Agoraphobia" rang some bell . . . with no wide door opening. Her Gart had no a, b, c Esperanto of world expression. (7–8)

Her seeks a *her*metic formula that would signal and signify her unformulated poetic thought and transport her beyond a stifling, undifferentiated world; she is without an adequate medium of mediation, certainly without an adequate language ("words beat and formed unformulated syllables" [25]), and thus without the means of self-projection. Having tested her options, she dismisses the symbolic systems of the sciences as far too abstract: "She had grappled with the biological definition, transferred to mathematics, found the whole thing untenable. . . . A biological-mathematical definition of the universe . . . had eluded her" (5–6).[15] But artistic media also elude her: "She realised precisely that people can not paint nor put such things [as she perceived] to music" (6). For the moment, delirium is her only substance of expression.

The scene of hysterical collapse which takes center stage over the last sixty pages of *Her* is particularly reminiscent of passages from *Studies on Hysteria*. Just as, according to Breuer's clinical narrative, Anna O. stages her own "private theatre" (*SE* 2:22), Her acts out her delirium with symptomatic "paraphasia" and mixing of languages. In both cases, the scene is attended by a nurse in whom the patient finds an audience and with whom she engages in monological disputes. But whatever the similarity, the *théâtre d'hystérie* that figures in *Her* facilitates the author's self-re-vision; it is not merely a clinical representation. The generic case history supplies H.D. with a narrative model for making her own untold story signifiable and for experimenting with discursive and symptomatic complexes that might afford her the most direct presentation of unconscious or preconscious self-signification.

The climactic sickbed scenes of *Her* compare with the most disturbed scenes of Anna O.'s case history, in which the hysteric's language is as visibly distorted (feverish) as her body. Breuer describes the "functional disorganization" of his patient's speech in detail:

> She was at a loss to find words, and this difficulty gradually increased. Later she lost her command of grammar and syntax; she no longer conjugated verbs, and eventually she used only infinitives, for the most part incorrectly formed from weak past participles; and she omitted both the definite and indefinite article. In the process of time she became almost completely deprived of words. She put them together laboriously out of four or five languages and became almost unintelligible. When she tried to write . . . she employed the same jargon. (25)

Consider the following passage from *Her*:

> A bird had done a trapeze-turn across a window like a bird on a string hung on the Christmas tree and I am the word Aum and I am Tree. I am Tree exactly. . . . Now she saw Tree and I am Tree and I am the word Aum and I am Her exactly. For the writing was what had started things

and the writing was the same writing. . . . I am the word AUM. I am Her. The word was with God. I am a fool in Shakespeare. . . . It was obvious that people should think before they call a place Sylvania. . . . It was heavy with trees, a sort of paradise of trees, trees, trees, trees; dogwood, liriodendron, you know, the tulip tree. (197–99)

Could this hysterical medium, if employed under aesthetically controlled conditions, prompt and articulate unconscious vision? Had H.D. made such a speculation, she could have found support in Breuer's assessment of Anna O.'s poetic generativity and genius: "She was markedly intelligent, with an astonishingly quick grasp of things and penetrating intuition. She possessed a powerful intellect which would have been capable of digesting solid mental pabulum and which stood in need of it. . . . She had great poetic and imaginative gifts." (21).[16] Another passage from *Her* appears almost to parody Anna O.'s talking cure, while pointing undecidably to Her's abnormal and "super-normal" facilities of unconscious (preconscious?) articulation:

The person who was Nurse Dennon dropped her sewing. . . . She came and stood by the bedside . . . like Ham, Shem and Japheth. Miss Dennon, it was obvious, stood on her own feet. "Are you a little tired of talking?" "No. I'm tired of not talking. It seems I have never talked. I want to talk and talk forever." . . . "I wish Miss Gart now you are getting better you would tell me what's upset you." The figure spoke as Ham, Shem and Japheth might speak if Ham, Shem and Japheth could speak. It made it interesting. (. . . if you happened to know its name was Ham, Shem and Japheth it would do anything for you. . . . Remove mountains. Its outer or world name is Amy Dennon. Its inner or occult name is Hamshem.) Hamshem went on sewing. (199–201)

But whereas Anna O. talks her way out of hysteria into lucid consciousness and normal speech, Her merely exhausts her hysterical capacity for talking-out. The talking cure is ultimately not the expressive medium she searches for, nor does she end her search for adequate self-signification in symptomatic speech. Instead, she fantasizes a medium of writing that is as direct and concrete as tracing figures in snow, which is precisely what she does to cool her fever and to extend her horizons at the end of the story:

Her feet went on making the path. Her feet were pencils tracing a path through a forest. The world had been razed, had been made clear for

this thing. The whole world had been made clear like [a] blackboard. . . .
Now the creator was Her's feet, narrow black crayon across the winter
whiteness. . . . She trailed feet across a space of immaculate clarity,
leaving her wavering hieroglyph as upon white parchment. . . . Then
her thought widened and the tension snapped as swiftly. (223–25)[17]

Sexuality, the truly psychoanalytic subject of hysterical case study,
is not omitted from H.D.'s study on hysteria; she speculates, as does
Freud in his essay "Hysterical Phantasies and their Relation to Bisexuality" (1908), on the bisexual locus of Her's visionary-erotic or "hysterical" experiences. In a plot that accompanies Her's search for an
appropriately esoteric medium of writing, *Her* narrates the search for
an appropriately otherworldly soulmate—in lovers of both sexes. It
is an intricate, complex plot that I will not attempt to disentangle
here, except to clarify what I believe to be a critical adaptation of
Freud's plotting out of the relation between bisexuality and hysteria.

According to Freud, hysterical fantasy reveals the subject's ambivalence toward the sexual orientation of her desire. Failing to decide
on a sexual identity, the hysterical subject entertains fantasies of
doubling that identity, playing both male and female parts in love.
Likewise, Her assumes both parts in the production of *Pygmalion* she
stages with her male and female lovers. Bewitched and perplexed by
her double role, Her finally admits she is at a loss to decide which sex
she is and to know which role, or object, would give her genuine
satisfaction. She sees her vacillation as contributing to the illness that
terminates both affairs. But she also regards her complex love as the
source of ecstatic, visionary reverie, pointing not only to an eroticism
capable of transcending the sexual norms of patriarchy but also to a
poetism capable of envisioning worlds beyond those formulated by
conventional discourse.

The bisexual component of H.D.'s case study is, however, not
sufficiently problematized or analyzed to be read as a critique of
Freud. In her delirium, Her denounces psychoanalytic interpretation
of love's variations: Fayne, her lover, "wanted to lend me some
books, psychoanalysis, German books . . . [which] caught one in a
mesh . . . if you translated it. . . . it was mother and father and
Oedipus complex . . . a black mesh" (203). She defiantly and simply
concludes that "there were people who loved . . . differently" and
"there were people with suppressions" (203). This observation is
neither effective nor convincing, though, and her search for a lover
reveals not a soul mate so much as a stalemate.

## *Nights*: Cryptobiography and Mysteria

Between *Her* (1926–27) and *The Gift* (1941), H.D. wrote *Nights* (1931, 1934), another autobiographical fantasy featuring another erotic triangle.[18] *Nights* covers roughly the span of years during which she experimented with cinematography while living with Bryher in Kenwin, her Bauhaus villa near Vevey.[19] *Nights* is even less clinical, more esoteric than *Her*, though it displays a similar affinity for/resistance to psychoanalytic terminology. Less clinical, more revisionary, *Nights* is above all theatrical. Like Her, Natalia occupies the narrative stage as a psychological (or psychic) spectacle. But unlike Her, whose *théâtre d'hystérie* displays the frustration of a woman dispossessed of language and the medium to express her desire, Nat conducts night after night of orgiastic carnival, fired by a passion beyond formulable pleasure, which she transcribes in her heretic's journal.

Although it casts vague allusions to the discourse in *Beyond the Pleasure Principle* on the metapsychology of life, love, and death, *Nights* is not clearly modeled on any particular Freudian text. A daring, heterodox adaptation of the dream work and the hieroglyph of the unconscious, *Nights* focuses its psychic research on the perverse eroticism of one woman's mystical ecstasy. The self-dramatizing subject is not a hysteric but, as I shall presently explain, a "mysteric" and a cryptobiographer.

*Nights* is composed of two parts: the first, "Prologue," is a pseudo-psychoanalytic pre-view of the text by the pseudonymous John Helforth (H.D.), and the second, "Nights," Natalia's journal, is the text under scrutiny.[20] The second half of *Nights* is presented to the reader, Helforth, who is himself a "half-and-half sort of person" (*N* 5), a scientist hampered by poetic reflections and a poet hampered by scientific reservations: "My psychological investigations were marred by my own imagination," he muses, "and when I wanted to let go and write a purely popular . . . tale or novel, my scientific training spoiled it" (5); the doubleness of the text clearly reveals H.D.'s own ambivalence toward her creative application of psychoanalysis.

The staging of *Nights* reads like a restaging of her presentation of the notes of her jellyfish experience to Havelock Ellis for psychological evaluation. Helforth, unlike Havelock, is not uninterested; he and Nat are of a mind, he being perhaps a little envious of her capacity for independent research:

I knew enough about Natalie, to know that her problems would have been my problems, but for my somewhat tantalising scientific habits. I had lost much and gained little, perhaps, in my explorations into the new doctrines of the unconscious. . . . Where I had the stimulating yet painful experience of psycho-analysis, (those hours I spent with Dr. Frank in Vienna), she had those perilous hours of fervid, analytic concentration on her papers. (6–7)

Avoiding a replay of Ellis's dismissal of her work, H.D. presents the manuscript of "Nights" to an ideal reader of female psychology. Helforth is willing to lay aside his catholic fears of unorthodox interpretation and daring enough to recognize the demonic element in her writing: "Every line seemed to bleed fire. . . . She was presenting truth . . . in some other medium" (21–22). He prefigures the "uncanonical" Freud of her *Tribute to Freud* (*TF* 15) who appreciates the psychic "medium of the mind, and the body, as affected by the mind's ecstasies or disorders" (*TF* 13). A fantastic substitute for the unappreciative Havelock, Helforth is even willing to consult his Freudian oracle about the occult substance of Nat's writing: "It would be an interesting incident, a little something to proffer Professor Frank, should I ever find time for another series of séances with him, in Vienna" (16).

The bipartite structure of *Nights* anticipates the final reconstruction of *Tribute to Freud*, the appended prelude, or "Advent," being a revision of the diary which H.D. kept during her analysis. It also compares with the structure of Freud's studies on literature, which begin with a speculative introduction, followed by textual passages for analytical scrutiny. (I am thinking specifically of "Delusions and Dreams in Jensen's *Gradiva*" [1907(1906)] and of "The Uncanny" [1919]. The allusive title of H.D.'s text, however, suggests Shakespeare's carnivalesque *Twelfth Night*, and indeed, there are twelve carnal entries in Nat's burlesque journal.

In content, "Nights" reads like the confessions of ecstatic mystics of the late Middle Ages, the most famous of whom is Saint Teresa of Avila:

She would be . . . Saint' Angelo. . . . Renne would say, father-fixation and religious mania. . . . She saw no force for it but death, and as the aura of radiant life sped through her, she saw that she was not so much healed as shocked back, re-vivified, for fresh suffering. Would she die sometime in some such shock-aura of pure light? And if so, would she be flung into a mediaeval hell, filled with the most hideous of refuse,

come to life, the horrors of the unconscious? Was her fervour, after all,
an illicit escape . . . ? (51–53)

Nat's express wish to be "Saint' Angelo" suggests a reference
to Angela of Foligno, who once wrote "The Word was made flesh
in order to make me God,"[21] and certain passages of "Nights"
call to mind the autobiography of Saint Thérèse de Liseux, *The Little Flower of Jesus*, a copy of which can be found in H.D.'s library.[22]
Nat transcribes mystical ecstasy as a figurative (transfiguring)
flowering:

> His lips would open her mouth, his eyes would drop their poison, she
> would drink the poison of the earth-flower that drew power from the
> earth-heart. . . . His lips would open her mouth, breathing the darkness
> that was sleep, that was oblivion; his rooted-stalk would push down.
> Those other lips would be penetrated by the slow poison of that beating
> earth-flower, down and down, into her drugged body. He would break
> anew a wound, work into a cauterized wound, to renew and re-create.
> He would work into her, fertilize, invoke that flower.
>   She had worshipped that dark bloom, he had brought fervour to it.
> (65–66)

This is not the delirium of hysteria[23] or the symptomatic fantasia of
bisexuality; it is, instead, the true confession of "mysteria," in which
sexual identity is resolved or dissolved into one sexless chord of
ecstasy: "She was sexless, being one chord, drawn out, waiting the
high-powered rush of the electric fervour" (51), there being "no
localization of force" in either body as the demonic, orgiastic power
"creeps into bones, dissolves personality, so that they lie, sex undifferentiated. . . . She . . . negative to his positive, dim ray" (102). A
fantastic resolution (dissolution) of hysteria brought on by the profound ambivalence of bisexuality, mysteria is also a radical revision of
Freud's metapsychology of love and death in *Beyond the Pleasure
Principle*. Natalia fantasizes and realizes a pleasure beyond the homeostatic nirvana (*SE* 18:56), a pleasure that Freud describes as the
reduction of unpleasure to zero excitation, to lifeless quiescence or to
an inorganic deathliness preceding life to which all life paradoxically
aspires. Although also an "atavism" (103) of a kind, Nat's ecstasy
exceeds Freud's nirvana in energy and intensity, forcing a mystifying
binding of pleasure and pain, of eros and death, which in Freud
figure as discrete metapsychological entities.
  "Nights" reads like a woman's response to the following passage of

*Beyond the Pleasure Principle*, in which where Freud admits the limitations of his science:

> Science has so little to tell us about the origin of sexuality that we can liken the problem to a darkness into which not so much as a ray of a hypothesis has penetrated. In quite a different region, it is true, we *do* meet with such a hypothesis; but it is of so fantastic a kind—a myth rather than a scientific explanation—. . . For it traces the origin of an instinct to *a need to restore an earlier state of things*. (*SE* 18:57)

Nat's sexuality *is* darkness, a dark bloom penetrated by a ray of sexual enlightenment; her orgiastic ecstasy is a ritual death, a "black," atavistic magic whose poison-medicine obliterates "white thoughts": "She believed that David's kiss was death because there was only blackness as she dropped . . . and it spread (when she stopped breathing) a black canopy over her head. . . . They were out of European, modern computation, white thoughts. Their thoughts were Egyptian, Indian, Hindoo, American Indian. They met in the Greater Arcana" (79).

Following Freud's practice of pursuing fantastic hypotheses, H.D. re-visions his nirvana principle, according to which "every unpleasure ought thus to coincide with a heightening, and every pleasure with a lowering, of mental tension due to stimulus."[24] "Nights" reads like her autobiographical elaboration on "feminine masochism," which is itself an elaboration—on an exception to the nirvana principle. According to Freud, feminine masochism is entirely based on a primary, erotogenic masochism (as opposed to a secondary, moral masochism), characterized by pleasure and pain and best exemplified by "the subject in a characteristically female situation; they signify, that is, being castrated, or copulated with, or giving birth to a baby" (*SE* 19:162). Nat's blissful description of her lover's lovemaking as reopening a wound—"he would . . . work into a cauterized wound"—illustrates Freud's description of erotogenic, feminine masochism—and more. She "blooms" to this wounding, feels the spread and surge of new "roots," is charged with the ecstasy of oblivion and the promise of rebirth.

Natalia describes what Luce Irigaray identifies as a mystic's, or *mystérique*'s, masochistic *jouissance*. "This is the place where consciousness is no longer master, where, to its extreme confusion, it sinks into a dark night that is also fire and flames . . . : *mysteria* . . . . Mystery, me-hysteria" ("*La Mysterique*," 191). According to Irigaray, mystic ecstasy is the delusional fantasy of blissful self-dissolution in the presence of a greater power; such fantasy is the symptomatic (hysterical, psychotic) expression of the dissolution or devolution of ego and sex, neither of which the subject felt she ever properly possessed. Instead, the *mystérique* feels possessed by the "God" of her orgasm, a mythified figure of the masochism that delivers her from the mundane insignificance of women's lot in a patriarchal world. "And if she does not feel raped by God, even in her fantasies of rape," Irigaray explains, "this is because He never restricts her orgasm, even it is hysterical. Since He understands all its violence" ("*La Mystérique*," 201).[25] The difference between Irigaray's description and Natalia's is that Natalia's violating, electrifying "deity" (*N* 51) is not, finally, masculine; the god of her dreams is (also?) a goddess, "pre-Ionic, gross, with large breasts" (56)—an atavistic Venus.

Leaving aside for later discussion the politics of the therapeutic efficacy of H.D.'s autobiographical fantasy, *Nights* can be read as an advance in research, which would, like *Studies on Hysteria*, root out the psychological/psychic sources of hallucinatory or visionary experiences. It is cryptic research in the sense that it describes erotic self-analysis as a descent into the underworld hell of the unconscious. "La mystérique: this is how one might refer to what, within a still theological onto-logical perspective is called mystic language or discourse. Consciousness still imposes such names to signify that other scene, off-stage, that it finds *cryptic*" ("*La Mysterique*," 91).[26] It is cryptic also in another sense: the author of the text that is presented to Helforth is dead. Natalia's journal is literally a tale from the tomb whose resurrection into the public domain of living letters depends solely on Helforth's judgment and that of his muse, Dr. Frank, Viennese clairvoyant, a mythic chimera of different, sometimes dissenting, psychoanalytic personae, Helforth's supreme authority.

"Frank" is not only a cryptonymic allusion to Freud; it is also an anagrammatic play on the two names Freud and (Otto) Rank. It is to Rank that H.D. turns for affirmation of her poetic appropriations of psychoanalysis before rediscovering it later in Freud. She notes in "Advent" that Freud referred her to Rank's *Mythus von der Geburt des Helden* (*Myth of the Birth of the Hero*) (*TF* 120), but it is his essay "The Play-Impulse and Aesthetic Pleasure," from *Art and Artist* (1932), which echoes in *Nights*. To appreciate all the sources of her autobiographical fantasy, I should like to turn briefly to this other member of Freud's circle.

Otto Rank was responsible for extending psychoanalysis to include the field of aesthetics. In *Art and Artist*, he calls for an elaboration of Freud's theory of creative production, which he criticized for confining the idea of play to wish-fulfilling hallucination, "stop[ping] short at the problem of will, and the particular character of wish-fulfilment which distinguishes hallucination from dreams, play, art and, indeed, religion."[27] Drawing upon Kant and Schiller, Rank constructs the notion of a will-to-art (91), whose function is to produce illusion and to generate "a surplus of pleasure" (108), which in turn shatters and disperses the neurotic ego trapped in "mortal fear" and solipsistic "immortality-symbolism" (101). Artists, accordingly, are they who are able to overcome this mortal fear of "unreality" and give up any investment they have in "reality" (100–101) so as to entertain and express fantasies that afford the "dissolution of their individuality in a greater whole" (110). He uses this idea of pleasure-generating play to distinguish the artist from her negative counterpart, the neurotic who cannot overcome her mortal fear of unreality or yield up her investment in bourgeois realism. Whereas "the neurotic must first learn to live playfully, illusorily, unreally, on some plane of illusion," Rank observes, "this is a gift which the artist . . . seems to possess from the outset" (108–9).

As aesthetic critic, H.D.'s Helforth-Frank is not so ideal a reader that he suspends all criticism of Natalia; he judges harshly, concluding that although her writing may be gifted (*N* 21), in Rank's sense of the word—that is, in its capacity to reflect the explosion of ego boundaries and the transcendence of mortal fear in ecstatic, erotic communion—it does not translate its generation of individual pleasure into a universal medium for communion with "a greater whole." "The trouble with Nat Saunderson," he decides, was "that she wouldn't project herself, materialise herself, for any sort of public" (24). Since Helforth is a pseudonym for H.D., we may regard this judgment as reflecting the critical dissatisfation of the author herself. Though just a beginning in the art of writing cryptobiography, *Nights* self-consciously fails to find a public medium, to mediate the psychical space between the private arena (hell) of her visions and the past and future history of the race.

## Introducing *The Gift*: "Art as Necromancer"

In *The Gift*, H.D. develops a biographical technique, a Freudian technique, a Freudian technique, that reveals the source and the meaning of the "miraculous gift that makes an artist," as Freud puts it in "The Goethe Prize" (*SE* 21:211). With this development, she implicitly challenges Freud's belief that "analysis . . . can do nothing towards elucidating the nature of the artistic gift, [or] . . . the means by which the artist works" (SE 20:65). Like *Nights, The Gift* is cryptobiographical: its pages are devoted to retracing and reviving the "psychical genealogy" (*SE* 2:281) of the poetic-erotic vision. They are also dedicated to the maternal ancestor(s) whose loving, living memory H.D. uncannily invokes:

To<br>
Helen<br>
who has<br>
*brought me home*<br>
for Bethlehem Pennsylvania 1741<br>
from Chelsea London 1941<br>
*L'amitié passe même le tombeau*

H.D. brings the dead to life not, as her psychic alter ego Delia Alton explains, by any "mechanical intellectual trick of memory or mind"; instead, she proceeds by a psychic application of psychoanalysis. Transference as the author of *The Gift* practices it is a necromancer's art, and the medium of writing is "the Child"—the audio-clairvoyant of childhood memory. Evoked by the transference of thoughts in writing, the Child has direct access to the adult Hilda's individual and racial prehistory. *The Gift* is the Child's "family-portrait or a series of family-portraits, but more particularly of the Child's mother and the grandmother" (DA 188). The Child is a necromancer to whom the mothers transmit secret memories: "In the fifth section, 'The Secret,' the grandmother tells the Child, in dream or half trance, of a memory of her own grandmother's or a fear based on the community memory" (DA 188). It is the Child who preserves and perceives the cryptic vision generated down the line of dreaming mystics:

> The Child, only half a "Moravian" and mystified by inscriptions on some of the oldest tombstones, perceives a strange affinity in the tiny, dark creature who is her mother's mother. . . .
>
> Through Mamalie, the Child traces back her connection with the *Jednota* [the first Moravian society] in Europe and with the vanished tribes of the Six Nations in America, with whom Zinzendorf had made a curious, unprecedented treaty. In fantasy or dream, the grandmother tells the story. (188–89)

Such idealization of the Child does not derive from Freud, though he privileges childhood fantasy-memory as the medium through which to observe the psychogenesis of individual and universal dreams. But Nietzsche has a chapter, "From the Souls of Artists and Writers," which contextualizes H.D.'s source of mystification:

> *Art as necromancer.*—Among the subsidiary duties of art is that of con-
> serving, and no doubt also of taking extinguished, faded ideas and
> restoring to them a little colour: when it performs this task it winds a
> band around different ages and makes the spirits that inform them
> return. It is only a phantom life that here arises, to be sure, such as
> appears about graves or like the return of the beloved dead in dreams;
> but the old emotions are again aroused . . . and the heart beats to a
> rhythm it had forgotten. . . . one must overlook it in the artist himself if
> he does not stand in the foremost ranks of the Enlightenment and the
> progressive *masculinization* of man: he has remained a child or a youth
> all his life, stuck at the point at which he was first assailed by his drive to
> artistic production; feelings belonging to the first stages of life are,
> however, admitted to be closer to those of earlier times than to those of
> the present century. Without his knowing it, his task becomes that of
> making mankind childlike; this is his glory and his limitation.[28]

In *The Gift*, the Child occasionally takes complete possession of the narrator's thoughts, though she expresses herself in the words of the adult, psychoanalytically informed writer. Here narration is a composite of memory, fantasy, critical re-vision, hieroglyphic method, and ideological (heterological) intervention into normative biographizing of life development. The focus of *The Gift* clearly falls on the narrative production, illustration, and exploration of fantasy as a protopoetic realm of repressed imagination belonging specifically to prepubertal girlhood, the subject of prohibitions imposed by patriarchy and puritanism.

The narrating I (or eye) of the Child is further compounded by that of visionary mothers for whom she acts as interlocutor, invoking and interpreting their dearest memories and fantasies. These memories-fantasies extend beyond prenatal dreams of intrauterine existence across the barrier that normally separates one generation of life from another to reveal the suppressed, unrecorded desires of her mother, of her mother's mother, and of her mother's mother's mother a century earlier. As cryptobiography or "auto-*thanato*-bio-graphy,"[29] *The Gift* translates clinical practice into necromancy, conducting the transference dialogue across the threshold of life/death.

The seven chapters of *The Gift* cover roughly the span of H.D.'s childhood from early school age (five or six) to pre-puberty (ten), and from chapter to chapter we witness a development that is figured less by empirical markers of growth than by changes in the scope and focus of childhood fantasy and imagination. In order, they are "Dark Room," "Fortune Teller," "The Dream," "Because One Is Happy," "The Secret," "What It Was," and "Morning Star."[30] The first six chapters are childhood reminiscences as recounted by a "middle-aged" Hilda, who appears in the narrative present of the seventh chapter. Each of these chapters is encapsulated in a space of narrative memory that is occasionally punctured by psychoanalytic commentary ("Dark Room" and "The Dream," most noticeably).

Like *Nights*, *The Gift* does not draw on just a single Freudian text; instead, the seven chapters evidence the influence of a constellation of texts that address the key subjects of dreams, fantasy, and autobiography, including "Dreams and Occultism" (1933 [1932]), "Creative Writers and Day-Dreaming" (1908 [1907]), "Childhood Memories and Screen Memories" (1901), "A Childhood Recollection from *Dichtung und Wahrheit*" (1917), and "The Uncanny" (1919). What Freud offers this necromantic art of cryptobiography is the technique of calling back to life dead memories, memories of the dead in the double scene/séance of transference. H.D.'s Child derives not only from her experience of analysis but also from Freud's description of childhood memory:

> Remembering in adults, as is well known, makes use of a variety of psychical material. Some people remember in visual images. . . . Other people can scarcely reproduce in their memory even the scantiest [visual] outlines of what they have experienced. Following Charcot's proposal, such people are called *auditifs* and *moteurs* in contrast to the *visuels*. In dreams these distinctions disappear: we all dream predominantly in visual images. . . . this development is similarly reversed in the case of childhood memories: they are plastically visual.[31]

H.D. develops both visual and auditory components of the dream memory. The adult Hilda who remembers the child Hilda is both *auditif* and *visuel*, though in *The Gift* the *visuel* is at first more active in remembering the earliest childhood memories. More precisely, H.D. develops these components into a psychic technology or what I earlier referred to as cinematobiography, which employs the technique/technology of projecting childhood memory, of visualizing memory behind the screen, and of letting the images flow like a moving picture or like the visions in a crystal ball; and otobiography, the technique/technology of developing an ear for the (m)other in Freud's voice as he engages in transference dialogue, of sounding the mother(s) and tuning in to their song, translating what one hears in cryptic lyrics into feeling and spirit.

## Cinematobiography: Camera Obscura or Dark Room Developments

The Child of H.D.'s childhood reminiscence is seen from both interior and exterior focal points by the observing, remembering, speculating, and re-visioning narrating subject. Like Freud's childhood memory, that which figures in "Dark Room" is primarily visual. "Visual memory," Freud writes,

> preserves the type of infantile memory. In my own case the earliest childhood memories are the only ones of a visual character: they are regular scenes worked out in plastic form, comparable only to representations on the stage. In these scenes of childhood, whether in fact they prove to be true or falsified, what one sees invariably includes oneself as a child, with a child's shape and clothes. This circumstance must cause surprise: in their recollections of later experiences adult *visuels* no longer see themselves. (*SE* 6:47)

But whereas Freud inevitably draws a distinction between memory and fantasy, the phenomenal status of H.D.'s recollection remains ambiguous, memory is undistinguished from fantasy. The interior space of her childhood memory often reflects the Child's exterior surroundings, and sometimes the demarcation between the two is unclear.

Though what she sees may be dark and cloudy, H.D.'s adult *visuel* is something of a visionary: she can see through screen memory to the actual infantile psychic presence, or so it seems. But according to Freud, the visual memory of infancy

> contradicts all that we have learnt to suppose that in his experiences a child's attention is directed to himself instead of exclusively to impressions from outside. One is thus forced . . . to suspect that in the so-called earliest childhood memories we possess not the genuine memory-trace but a later revision of it, a revision which may have been subjected to the influences of a variety of later psychical forces. Thus the "childhood

memories" of individuals come in general to acquire the significance of "screen memories." (*SE* 6:47–48)

That H.D.'s childhood memories do not distinguish between the Child's inner and outer worlds, that her adult *visuel* focuses as much on the psycho- or photogenesis of the Child as on her material surroundings, suggests that H.D.'s memories go back even earlier than Freud's, to before the division of inner from outer world or of subject from object as constituted or reproduced by the psychic mechanism of introjection and projection.

Understanding H.D.'s adaptation and application of Freud's term *projection*, a concept metaphor that he himself derives from cinematography, is the key to reading the psychopoetic intertext of *The Gift*.[32] According to Freud, projection and introjection are the primitive mechanisms at work in the psychogenesis of opposition between subject (ego) and object (world). "In so far as the objects which are presented to it are sources of pleasure, [the ego] takes them into itself, 'introjects' them . . . and, on the other hand, it expels whatever within itself becomes a cause of unpleasure (. . . the mechanism of projection)."[33] To emphasize the psychogenic origins of the syntactical subject and object, Freud refers to this process of introjection and projection as "the language of the . . . oral [instinct]."[34]

H.D.'s use of *projection* is not oppositional: it is not conditioned by a dialectic or an economics of pleasure, nor does it function against a counteroperation of introjection. Projection is the only mechanism that figures in her memory of childhood fantasy, the outer world of the Child being as ghostly and demonic as the inner. It is the "animism" of projection, its roots in mythology and religion, which especially interests H.D., although she basically uses the term in a sense that, like Freud's, is "comparable to the cinematographic one: the subject sends out into the external world an image of something that exists in him in an unconscious way" (Laplanche and Pontalis, *Language of Psycho-Analysis*, 354). Most important, the Child's dreams are to be viewed as projections, just as Freud says—"A dream is . . . among other things, a *projection*: an externalization of an internal process."[35]

"Dark Room" is the "psychical location" of the Child in childhood memory. It is the camera obscura of memory's photographic I/eye, which views the external space of the family room of the Wolle-Doolittle household at the same time that it envisions the mental picture of this space that the Child is developing. The external scene of memory is obscured by a simultaneous recollection of the internal process(ing).

The adult Hilda remembers the Child's struggle to visualize her "self" in the frame, literally, the picture frame, of the extended family. She performs increasingly complex acts of projection, enabling her to distinguish living relatives from the dead and the nuclear family from those more removed or who have mysteriously faded out of the picture, until she perceives a genealogical order and arrangement. As the chapter proceeds, the Child is transferred from family room to schoolroom to local auditorium. Each view of physic displacement is accompanied by a vision of the changes in her capacity to make a psychological accommodation: literally, a moving picture of early life. "Dark Room" refers to the site of childhood reminiscence, where memory figures as a developing negative or series of negatives. It also refers to the original site of the production of fantasy; as such, it is not just a "locality" or psychic *space* but also a "structuring action" or "phantasmatic" (see Laplanche and Pontalis, *Language of Psycho-Analysis*, 317).

*The Gift* represents child development as technological advance: the earliest memories are recalled as daguerreotypes (*G* 1), and the later memories, leading up to the memory of the present, are featured in Technicolor motion pictures. H.D. refers to the prephotographic device when she speaks of those *"coffres forts* or the *camera obscura* where our living inheritance is stored," those *"*boxes or cameras or 'safes,' where indeed the treasure of the individual life and of its racial and biological inheritance is . . . [preserved and projected]" (*G1* 70). In this "dark room" of the psyche archaic memory is mysteriously processed and protected from the forces of enlightenment, which would repress and replace the world of dreams with the reality principle of scientific positivism. Hence, "Dark Room" is also the site of a metaphysical or metapsychological debate with Freud and where the more speculative passages of his writings on fantasy are appropriated by H.D.

In the opening scene of "Dark Room," the Child gazes at "the daguerreotypes and old photographs" (*G* 1) of her mother and grandmother, of her mother's sisters and their children and husbands. As she looks, the Child acquires a picture of her maternal heritage which is only partly informed by the photographs. The photographs activate memories and fantasies beyond what they themselves represent, cuing further reminiscences like dream hieroglyphics. Hilda projects visions of other female relatives, other little girls, other selves, onto the faces of photographs, filling the gaps where missing persons have not been recorded in the family photo album. The opening scene then draws to a close.

There is a blank space in the text before the next scene appears, with an entirely new setting and with moving, speaking characters. The auditory focus turns to a conversation between Mama, the Child's mother, and Mamalie, her maternal grandmother, concerning another missing relative, Fanny, Mama's little sister, who died before Mama was cognizant of death and whose name signals an uncanny bridge of affection between the mothers (see Chapter 3). The scene lasts as long as it takes Hilda to display intuitive insight into this secret maternal communication and to transform her bewilderment into empathy and vision through an exercise of sympathetic magic, a projection of that spirit—"l'amitié passe même le tombeau"—which animates all the photographic memories of *The Gift*. The scene then fades out, followed by another ellipsis before a new scene fades back in.

H.D. follows Freud in presenting childhood memory as "plastically visual," and her commentary elaborates Freud's metaphor of "screening," speculating how in time technology might duplicate the camera of the mind, hence, reversing the order of vehicle and tenor of his figure. Freud views the psychological apparatus as analogous to the photographic apparatus—

> I shall remain upon psychological ground, and I propose simply to follow the suggestion that we should picture the instrument which carries out our mental functions as resembling a compound microscope or a photographic apparatus, or something of the kind. On that basis, psychical locality will correspond to a point inside the apparatus at which one of the preliminary stages of an image comes into being (SE 5:536).

Whereas H.D. views the photographic apparatus as analogous to the psychic/psychological apparatus:

> Because [childhood fantasy] once had been like that, it would be possible with time and with the curious chemical constituents of biological or psychic thought-processes—whatever thought is, nobody yet knows—to develop single photographs or to develop long strips of continuous photographs, stored in the dark-room of memory, and again to watch people enter a room, leave a room, to watch, not only those people enter and leave a room, but to watch the child watching them. (*G1* 69)

It is interesting that H.D. should favor the camera obscura as opposed to camera lucida to figure the mystifying process of memory-fantasy. The *Oxford English Dicitonary* distinguishes the terms as follows:

Camera obscura [L.; lit. "dark chamber."] *Optics*. A darkened chamber or box, into which light is admitted through a double convex lens, forming an image of external objects on paper, glass, etc., placed at the focus of the lens. Also *lit*. Dark room. Camera lucida [L.; lit. "light chamber."] *Optics*. An instrument by which the rays of light from an object are reflected by a prism, and produce an image on paper placed beneath the instrument which can be traced with a pencil.

In *Camera Lucida: Reflections on Photography*, Roland Barthes suggests that because camera lucida is the true progenitor of photography and because of its capacity to externalize the inner image completely, it could be seen as far more mysterious than the camera obscura:

It is a mistake to associate Photography, by reason of its technical origins, with the notion of a dark passage (*camera obscura*). It is *camera lucida* that we should say (such was the name of that apparatus, anterior to Photography, which permitted drawing an object through a prism, one eye on the model, the other on the paper); for, from the eye's view point, "the essence of the image is to be altogether outside, without intimacy, and yet more inaccessible and mysterious than the thought of the innermost being; without signification, yet summoning up the depth of any possible meaning."[36]

But H.D.'s camera obscura refers precisely to the "dark passage" of childhood memory and beyond, to memory of individual and racial prehistory, a passage that, as she sees it, is further revealed by the mechanical figure of projection, that is, by the projector at work in the dark room of the cinema. According to H.D., the precise technology of "projection" remains unknown, though the phenomenology may be revealed to the most "gifted" observer. The key to this knowledge is the secret of "letting flow" the unconscious store of images at the core of deep memory, mnemic images that have not yet been "screened" by secondary mechanisms of repression and intellection and thus remain rich with mystery:

All this is really very simple. The trouble is, the process of this letting loose or letting flow, continuous images like a moving-picture, is a secret one can not, with the best will in the world, impart. Because one

really does not quite know how it works, when it will work or how long
it will continue to work, once it is started. The store of images and
pictures is endless and is the common property of the whole race. But
one must, of necessity, begin with one's own private inheritance. (*G1*
69)

Clearly, this description mystifies Freud's technological rhetoric,
which at least one Freudian reader argues cannot be reduced to
metapsychology. Jacques Derrida contends that Freud's use of mechanical metaphors, particularly figures of optic and graphic machinery, to illustrate and explain the psychic system is of an entirely
different order from the "intrapsychic metaphor" he otherwise employs. Freud's discursive reliance on technological rhetoric is not,
Derrida says, just rhetorical; Freud points to a "technics" of recording
memory ("the historico-technical production of this [mechanistic]
metaphor"), to a frame of reference that lies outside of the "individual . . . psychical organization."[37]

In H.D.'s revision of Freud, the "intrapsychic metaphor" encompasses the mechanical ones.[38] "Dark Room" views the technology of
memory-fantasy just as a child or a primitive or a mystic might, with
the intention of taking Freud's insights farther afield, pursuing his
occult speculations. Consider this passage:

At times we are motivated by the primitive curiosity of the proverbial
tiresome child who "wants to see the wheels go round," yet even so. . . .
Someone must reveal secrets of thought which combine a new element;
science and art must beget a new creative medium. Medium? Yet we
must not step right over into the transcendental. . . . For the mechanism, the very complicated coils and wheels and springs that are brain
matter . . . can be unhinged by disassociation . . . [and] shock can scatter
the contents of this strange *camera obscura* . . . where our living inheritance is stored. . . . It does exist . . . an actual psychic entity. (*G1* 69–70)

H.D.'s medium, a pun on the photographic medium and the psychic medium, is another figure of the unconscious. Freud himself
figures the unconscious as a medium between physical and psychic
processes. Consider the following passage from "Dreams and Occultism" (1933 [1932]), where he attempts to demystify telepathy
with a psychoanalytic explanation:

The telepathic process is supposed to consist in a mental act in one
person instigating the same mental act in another person. What lies

between these two mental acts may easily be a physical process into which the mental one is transformed at one end and which is transformed back once more into the same mental one at the other end. The analogy with other transformations, such as occur in speaking and hearing by telephone, would then be unmistakable. . . . It would seem to me that psycho-analysis, by inserting the unconscious between what is physical and what was previously called "psychical," has paved the way for the assumption of such processes as telepathy. If only one accustoms oneself to the idea of telepathy, one can accomplish a great deal with it—for the time being, it is true, only in imagination.[39]

In "The Dream," the third chapter of *The Gift*, H.D. comments further on the psychocinematic nature of projection:

> The dream? . . . The dream-picture focussed and projected by the mind, may perhaps achieve something of the character of a magic-lantern slide and may "come true" in the projection. But to "come true," it must . . . photograph the very essence of life, of growth, of the process of growing. . . . The dream, the memory, the unexpected related memories must be allowed to sway backward and forward, as if the sheet or screen upon which they are projected, blows and is rippled in the wind of whatever emotion or idea is entering a door, left open. (*G3* 605–6)

The passage proceeds with a set of instructions to the autobiographer, as if she were operating a psychic movie camera or editing a strip of screen memories into psychic montage: "The wind blows through the door, from outside, through long, long corridors of personal memory, of biological and of race-memory. Shut the door and you have a neat flat picture. Leave all the doors open and you are almost out-of-doors, almost within the un-walled province of the fourth-dimensional" (*G3* 606).

Although H.D. began to explore the "fourth-dimensional" before her serious engagement with film, her use of the term may in part be informed by the new language of cinematography which she, along with Sergei Eisenstein and others who contributed to the avant-garde journal *Close-Up* were determined to forge.[40] In his essay "The Fourth Dimension in the Kino" (1930), Eisenstein outlines the "fourth dimension: of montage in a playfully cryptic language specifically constructed for the new art of cinema":

> Orthodox montage is montage according to *dominants*, i.e. joining together of the parts in accordance with their predominant character. Montage according to tempo. Montage according to the dominant infra-

cadre tendency. Montage according to the lengths (degrees of slowness) of the pieces and so forth. Montage according to foreground, or background. . . . This condition embraces all the stages of intensiveness of montage conjunction—of shock.[41]

Eisenstein's cryptic speech signals, moreover, a hieroglyphic method: "The cadre [frame, framework, scheme] never becomes a letter, but always remains a hieroglyph having a number of meanings" (187). Elsewhere, in a more readable passage from "Film Form," Eisenstein explains this hieroglyphic method of the fourth dimension: "The point is that the . . . combination of two hieroglyphs of the simplest series is to be regarded not as their sum, but as their product, i.e., as a value of another degree; each, separately, corresponds to an *object*, to a fact, but their combination corresponds to a *concept*. From separate hieroglyphs has been fused—the ideogram."[42]

Here we have precisely a cinematographic version of the ideogrammatic method outlined by Pound and Fenollosa. Pound once said that "the logical end of impressionist [imagist] art is the cinematograph."[43] For H.D., the fourth dimension of the cinematograph is the living hieroglyph of the unconscious, which some "shock" of memory can re-present and decode. As an auto-crypto-cinemato-bio-grapher, she seeks the imagistic formula that would unlock the secret of "these bone boxes, these *coffres forts* or the *camera obscura* where our living inheritance is stored" (G1 70). The combination of two key hieroglyphs, "two of these boxes or cameras or 'safes,'" could shock the memory into revealing past visions "hidden, buried under the accumulated rubble of prescribed thinking" (G1 70) so that, as she says, "I am for a moment (through a picture carved on a wall, tinted with just such bright colors as we had in our own paint-box) Egyptian; a little cell of my brain responds to a cell of someone's brain who died thousands of years ago" (G1 70). H.D.'s is surely a mixed *medium*, a Freudian-Fenollosan-Eisensteinian medium, an auto-bio-thanato-telepatho-cinemato-graph.

And that is not all. There is also the stagecrafting of childhood reminiscence to consider. Toward the end of "Dark Room," the narrative opens onto the local auditorium, where the Child beholds her first theatrical production. To the Child's eye, the play, in this case, an adaptation of Harriet Beecher Stowe's *Uncle Tom's Cabin*, is the moving equivalent of the photograph, but it is even more charming in its capacity to prompt her own inner flow of images and speculation.[44]

Hilda is particularly struck by little Eva, who "died, but . . . came back again in a long nightgown" (G 14). We are reminded of Freud's depiction of childhood memories as "representations on the stage," in which "what one sees invariably includes oneself as a child, with a child's shape and clothes" (SE 6:47). H.D.'s memories extend beyond Freud's, however, to the fourth dimension of psychic montage.

When the Child is out of the theater and in the lamplit street, she witnesses a transformation: the crowd of dispersing players suddenly becomes a spectacular procession of folk pageantry down through the Middle Ages and the glory of Rome (G 17–18). The scene is clearly intended to demonstrate the vital link between childhood memory and primitive or ancient artistic production and to display the mechanism of projection which in the Child operates the switch between ontogenetic and phylogenetic fantasy. It is also an adaptation of Freud's speculation in "Creative Writers and Day-Dreaming" that the origin of art may be found in child's play.[45] Whereas Freud argues that "the creative writer does the same as the child at play . . . creat[ing] a world of phantasy which he takes very seriously . . . while separating it sharply from reality" (SE 9:144), H.D. would agree instead with Nietzsche in privileging childhood play-fantasy over the age of Enlightenment and in viewing the task of the gifted artist as that of "making mankind childlike."

H.D.'s camera obscura might be said to "occult" Freud's writings on fantasy and childhood memory in the double sense of the term. The *Shorter Oxford English Dictionary* gives at least two meanings that are appropriate to consider here: "Of the nature of or pertaining to those sciences involving the knowledge or use of the supernatural (as magic, alchemy, astrology, theosophy, and the like); also *transf.* magical, mystical"; "To hide, conceal; to cut off from view by interposing some other body. Now chiefly in scientific or techn. use." *The Gift* may be said to occult Freud's body of writing on fantasy, memory, play, and projection by interposing H.D.'s writing on the same, deliberately obscuring his scientific speculations and technical descriptions with her psychic mediation.

H.D.'s application of projection, for instance, adapts and mystifies the most occult meaning that Freud himself lent to the term, namely, its operation in animism, mythology, and demonology. "I believe," Freud writes in "Determinism, Belief in Chance, and Superstition" (1901), "that a large part of the mythological view of the world, which extends a long way into the most modern religions, *is nothing but psychology projected into the external world. The obscure recognition . . .*

of psychical factors and relations in the unconscious is mirrored . . .
in the construction of a *supernatural reality*, which is destined to be
changed . . . into the *psychology of the unconscious*.[46]

My reading of H.D.'s mystification of the Freudian sense of projection agrees in part with the reading Adalaide Morris gives. According
to Morris, H.D. rehabilitates Freud's use of the term: H.D. "shuns the
psychoanalytic meaning and resuscitates the borderline so that it lies
not between the neurotic and the psychotic but between the neurotic
and the psychic."[47] Whereas Freud uses *projection* primarily to refer to
"defensive exteriorization of unconscious material," H.D., Morris
contends, "open[s] the boundaries of the self to another, higher
reality, not in order to deny its operations but in order to claim and be
claimed by them" (429). I cannot agree with Morris that H.D.'s projection signifies "a transcendence, a breakthrough into a new dimension" (429), but I do agree that H.D. believed in her own illusion, the
fantasy of transcendence which is an effect of her occultation of
Freud.

Why then does H.D. choose, consciously or unconsciously, to
obscure Freud's "illuminating doctrines," as she calls them? Is her
occultation of Freud a defense mechanism, just as psychoanalysis, in
its most clinical moments, claims projection to be? (Laplanche and
Pontalis, *Language of Psycho-Analysis*, 318). Might H.D.'s autobiographical fantasy be itself an elaborate screen memory, in which,
according to Laplanche and Pontalis, "defences are . . . bound up
with the primary function of phantasy, namely the *mise en scène* of
desire—a *mise en scène* [of] . . . what is *prohibited*" (*Language of Psycho-
Analysis*, 318), which defends in retrospect the self that was exposed
in analysis, namely, the self that harbored a "suppressed desire for
forbidden signs and wonders," a desire "to be a Prophetess"? In
"Advent" H.D. confesses her fear of self-dissolution (dis-illusion?)
under the anatomizing gaze of the father: "My father's telescope, my
grandfather's microscope. If I let go (I, this one drop, this one ego
under the microscope-telescope of Sigmund Freud) I fear to be dissolved utterly" (*TF* 116). And, in "Writing on the Wall," she perceives
that sometimes "the Professor's explanations were too illuminating. . . . my bat-like thought-wings would beat painfully in that
sudden searchlight" (*TF* 30). Does not writing *The Gift* afford her
further "self"-exposure behind the screen of mystery and mystical
obscurity? Does it not present a (w)rite of passage which constructs
self-affirming autobiographical defenses against the illuminating
forces of patriarchal enlightenment which would otherwise rob her
of her sense of creative power, of feminine otherness, of giftedness?

H.D. took it upon herself to add an illuminating chapter of her own to Freud's *Autobiographical Study* with her cinematobiography and its occult(ed) inquiry into the nature of the artistic gift. Here she takes to heart Freud's advice to "accustom oneself to the idea of telepathy" and other such psychic phenomena in order to "accomplish a great deal with it . . . [if] only in imagination" (*SE* 22:55).

## Transference, Telepathy, Otobiography

The adult *visuel* of H.D.'s childhood memories is also an *auditif*, but she does not develop her uncanny ability to sound and revive the song of past life on her own. It is through Freud, his medium of transference, that she acquires the technique of listening for the other, of becoming attuned to the mothers, now dead but living on in the song-lines of distant, affective memory. Freud remembers and evokes the muse/music of memory, encrypted in ancient lyrics and rhymes whose words and tunes she had forgotten. This audio-voyant and "master-musician" (*TF* 105) charms her ear into hearing that maternal *amitié* which traverses even the grave. It is his voice, "SIGMUND, the singing voice" (*TF* 88) for which she must listen in transference before she can revive the distant song of the mother:

> About the Professor, there was music certainly; there was music in every syllable he uttered and there was music implicit in his name, the *Sieg-mund*, the victorious voice or utterance. There had been music everywhere in Vienna . . . Beethoven . . . Mozart . . . Schumann . . . Schubert. . . . And here was the master-musician . . . who would harmonize the whole human spirit, who like Orpheus, would charm the very beasts of the unconscious or subconscious mind, and enliven the dead sticks and stones of buried thoughts and memories. (*TF* 105–06)

Here we have the full meaning of Freud's "charm," of his healing oracular charisma, or so H.D., in conformity with the *Shorter Oxford English Dictionary*, understands the meaning of the term. It derives the substantive from "(O) Fr. *charme*:—L. *carmen* song, verse, oracular response, incantation" and defines it as "1. *orig.* The chanting of a verse having magic power; incantation; hence a magic spell; a talisman; an amulet, etc. Also *fig.* (cf. *spell.*) 2. *fig.* That which fascinates or attracts, exciting love and admiration." To charm, from "(O)Fr. *charmer*" is "to act upon with or as with a charm or magic; to put a spell upon; to bewitch, enchant." Oracular, musical, magical, Freud charms H.D.'s ear, attuning it to the mother, who had spent her honeymoon in Vienna, where she—and also the child she may have been carrying, "a girl, that first child that lived such a very short time" (*TF* 16)—heard the songs H.D. was hearing now. "Why had I come to Vienna?" she asks herself. "The Professor had said in the very beginning that I had come to Vienna hoping to find my mother. Mother? Mama. But my mother was dead. I was dead; that is, the child in me that had called her mama was dead" (17). She had come to Wien IX, Berggrasse 19, to raise the dead.

How does this charismatic technique work outside the actual scene of transference in the delayed analysis of her otobiography? Delia Alton attests that "certainly *The Gift* synthesizes or harmonizes with the Sigmund Freud notes" (DA 192); but how does H.D. make the transition or transposition from the play to the page? She *writes*, and in the most general Freudian sense of that activity, she materializes maternal fantasy: "Writing was in its origin the voice of an absent person, and the dwelling-house was a substitute for the mother's womb, the first lodging, for which in all likelihood man still longs" (*SE* 21:91). *Tribute to Freud* dis-plays the particular techniques of her maternal transcription, starting with the recall of poetry. By recalling the lyricists Freud called upon, who resonated with significance for them both, bridging whatever personal, ethnic, linguistic gaps existed between them, sounding the depths of their respective motherlands, H.D. appropriates Freud's most effective medium of transference.

That it is Goethe's lyric *Kennst du das Land?* that translates the powerful, poetic connection between analyst and analysand and survives the passage of time and death is profoundly significant. An immediate sense of Freud's charming presence returns to H.D. as she transposes this line. But this lyrical transposition does not revive just the memory of analysis. Behind Freud's poet is also the imagist's: Goethe is the lyricist Pound calls upon to instruct aspiring poets in the art of *melopoeia*: "Let the candidate fill his mind with the finest cadences he can discover, preferably in a foreign language, so that the meaning of the words may be less likely to divert his attention from the movement. . . . Let him dissect the lyrics of Goethe coldly into their component sound values, syllables long and short, stressed and unstressed, into vowels and consonants."[48] H.D.'s translation of Goethe is not logocentric; it is Goethe's music (*melos*) that she recalls hearing in Freud's signs and gestures ("there was music in every syllable he uttered"). But neither is her translation a cold dissection of "component sound values." Her otobiographical ear resonates with an arousing love and admiration that she hears in the voice of her medium and in the passage to the womb of song.

Words, signs, sounds that pass between H.D. and Freud are channeled through the tunnels of the outer and inner ear to the most primitive sensor of the listening subject, the illiterate "mollusk" of the prehistoric psyche:

> They were there. They were singing. They went on singing like an echo of an echo in a shell—very far away yet very near—the very shell substance of my outer ear and the curled involuted or convoluted shell skull, and inside the skull, the curled, intricate, hermit-like mollusk, the brain-matter itself. Thoughts are things—sometimes they are songs. I did not have to recall the words, I had not written them. Another mollusk in a hard cap of bone or shell had projected these words. There was a song set to them. . . . a song we sang as school-children, [in] another setting . . . . *Kennst du das Land*? (*TF* 90)

More sensitive to the pulsations of song than to the logical, categorical, rational formations of thought, this mollusk seems attuned to what Freud in *Civilization and Its Discontents* describes as the "oceanic feeling" of prenatal memory.[49] But before pursuing this discussion, I should like to consider H.D.'s sources in the atavistic music of modernism.

In part, H.D. still hears with the ear she had trained in the music hall of modernism. Her sounding of the depths of Freudian poetics echoes what both Pound and Eliot were thinking and saying about poetry by the time of her analysis. In 1928 Pound revised his *melopoeia* to mean a "a force tending often to lull, or to distract the reader from the exact sense of the language. It is poetry on the borders of music and music is perhaps the bridge between consciousness and the unthinking sentient . . . universe" (*Literary Essays*, 26). Eliot alerts us to the primitive, prehistoric roots of music in poetry. "Poetry begins," he writes in 1933, "with a savage beating a drum in a jungle, and it retains that essential of percussion and rhthym."[50] The uncanny tympanum of the ear, he contends in *After Strange Gods* (1934), grounds the modern in the savage, accompanies the intellect in the making of modern poetry. Later, in *Four Quartets*, he associates rhythm with the "rustic" (l. 36), vitalist tradition of primitive society ("East Coker" ll. 26–44); and in the "murmuring shell of time" of "Dry Salvages" (l. 160) the uncanny ear reappears, resounding to the inarticulate "wailing" of "all sea voices," which are submerged in the matter and memory of an illiterate cosmos.

Like Pound's *melopoeia*, H.D.'s lies on the border between the conscious and the unconscious, the personal and the universal; but it also borders on Freud's unconscious at the site of transference. And whereas she, like Eliot, distinguishes between the *logopoeia* of higher culture and the musicality of primitive, transpersonal memory, unlike Eliot, she unequivocally privileges the "lower" orders of feeling and sentient being.

The play of transference between H.D. and Freud invokes another poetic tradition. The strictly patrilinear line of poetic descent which Pound and Eliot elect to retrace and revive is not the "line" H.D. takes with Freud. The singing she hears in Freud's psychic workshop is an orchestration of cryptic signs drawn from childhood reveries and drawn out in the play of transference so as to sound the song of the mysterious, depthless mother. "Mother? Father? . . . It is *she* who matters," H.D. testifies, "for she is laughing . . . with us or over us and around us. *She* has bound music folios and loose sheets on the top of our piano. About *her*, there is no question" (*TF* 33). It is she who matters because it is *mater* whose memory embodies H.D.'s song; it is she, not the cold, rationalist father, whom she quests without question, whom she would recover in the play of mother transference which dominates the scene of her analysis. Moreover, it is she who matters to H.D. who, in turn, would locate the artist whom the mother represses and whose gift she takes with her to the grave. "Did your mother sing to you?" Freud asks: "I said she had a resonant beautiful voice but that she had some sort of block or repression about singing. Our grandmother loved me to sing to her, old-fashioned hymns. . . . My older brother and I sang little nursery songs to our mother's accompaniment. . . . I told him again that my mother died in spring, at this very time" (*TF* 176). What mat(t)ers, what H.D. would *mater*ialize in transcribing, transposing her analysis into poetry, is the uncanny revival of her mother's song, a return of her lyrical (re)sources. It is the mother who matters also to Jacques Derrida, whose "otobiography" I find very useful in reading H.D. Derrida derives the notion from Nietzsche's autobiography and pedagogy (*Ecce Homo, Thus Spake Zarathustra, On the Future of Our Educational Institution*).[51] He celebrates in Nietzsche what he sees as a privileging of the ear (in place of the canonical phallus) as the organ or umbilicus that connects us to our maternal no less than to our paternal genealogy. "The ear is uncanny. Uncanny is what it is; double is what it can become; large or small is what it can make or let happen (as in laisser-faire, since the ear is the most tendered and most open organ, the one that, as Freud reminds us, the infant cannot close); large or small as well the manner in which one may offer or lend an ear" (*The Ear of the Other*, 16). Nietzsche's ear, Derrida says, is "uncanny," in the sense that it generates the line of a "tele-printer" (36) to dead fathers, whom it traces in the voices of ped-agogues as they speak dead languages of dead nations erected in the father's name. But this ear is also uncannily feminine, double, poten-tially duplicitous. Paraphrasing Nietzsche, Derrida writes:

> There, this is who I am, a certain masculine and a certain feminine. . . . You will not be able to hear and understand my name unless you hear it with an ear attuned to the name of the dead man and the living feminine—the double and divided name of the father who is dead and the mother who is living on, who will outlive me long enough to bury me. The mother is living on, and this living on is the name of the mother. This survival is my life whose shores she overflows. (16)[52]

It is "her—this ear" that Derrida would "feign to address" (33) as the uncanny ear of memory and learning. He paints "her" as a figure of introjection, of taking in, "invaginat[ing]" (36) the "living," tonal and emotional, qualities of language while expelling, projecting what Nietzsche calls the deadly "historico-scholastic method of teaching the mother-tongue," derived from the systematic teaching of classical philology (21). University scholars teach the rigid structures of gram-mar and logic "as if it were a dead language and as if one had no obligation to the present or the future of this language" (21), but the ear can otherwise be attuned to the *omphalos* (36) or primal mat(t)er of signification, to the colloquial or indigenous body of language which nourishes syntactic and semantic variability and is the body out of which the proper language is cut (21–22).

Nietzsche, Derrida says, puts his ear to the ground to listen for the generative semantics of a maternal syntax that the state institution would standardize and suppress. His figure of the *omphalos*, Derrida observes, resembles "both an ear and a mouth" (36), the orifices at either end of the uncanny umbilical cord through which the living feminine of the dead word is transmitted: "It has the invaginated folds and involuted orificiality of both. Its center preserves itself at the bottom of an invisible, restless cavity that is sensitive to all waves which . . . are always transmitted by this trajectory of obscure circum-volutions" (36). Derrida's recursive tracing of Nietzsche's *omphalos* is also an allusion to the figure that dominates the "Proteus" section of

*Ulysses,* the work of another modernist musician, James Joyce.[53] Here, the dead language of the father, as represented by Stephen Dedalus's scholarly Greek and Latin and by the imperial English that colonizes and represses Ireland's mother tongue, is transfused with the protean, preconscious flow—the "wavespeech" of maternal memory. As Dedalus walks along the strand, musing on news of his mother's death, he opens his ear to the "navel cord" of primal language spoken (projected) by the sea of subconsciousness:

> Creation from nothing. . . . A misbirth with a trailing navelcord. . . . Gaze in your omphalos. Hello. Kinch here. Put me on to Edenville. Aleph, alpha: nought, nought, one. . . . Tides, myriadislanded, within her, blood not mine, *oinopa ponton*, a winedark sea. . . . His lips lipped and mouthed fleshless lips of air: mouth to her womb. Oomb, allwombing tomb. His mouth moulded issuing breath, unspeeched: ooeeehah: roar of cataractic planets, globed, blazing, roaring wayawayawaya- wayawayaway. . . . Listen: a fourworded wavespeech: seesoo, hrss, rsseeiss, ooos. Vehement breath of waters and seasnakes, rearing horses, rocks. In cups of rocks it slops: flop, slop, slap: bounded in barrels. And, spent, its speech ceases.[54]

In his picture of the ear of the (m)other, however, Derrida traces the figure of woman's historiographical effacement. While it ever gives rise to new generations of language, this primal language of the living feminine remains, like the mother, unrepresented and urepresentable in the language of the nation and its public institutions. "Woman, if I have read correctly," he writes, "never appears at any point along the umbilical cord, either to study or to teach. . . . No woman or trace of woman . . . save the mother, that's understood. But this is part of the system. The mother is the faceless figure of a *figurant,* an extra. She gives rise to all the figures by losing herself in the background of the scene like an anonymous persona" (38).

H.D.'s ear is also uncanny and double: it is attuned to the dead father of psychoanalysis, recording his professorial discourse, his clinical diagnoses, his logic of interpretation. But it is more remarkably attuned to the mother, to the resonant mat(t)er of Freud's words. In the play of transference, she recovers her ear for *melopoeia,* which had been deafened or deadened by the psychological repercussions of war, and she recovers an acoustic image of the dead mother, who, H.D. testifies, had been "morbidly self-effacing" (*TF* 164). Unlike Derrida's-Nietzsche's otobiography, which resounds with the language of the living feminine but cannot give her a figure, H.D.'s would retrace and refigure the maternal autograph. Part of her purpose in writing is to bring the mother out of the dark, to draw the faceless "mollusk" out of its shell and into the range of vision and audition.

H.D. addresses "her—this ear" when she begins her maternal biography with this transcription:

> On desperate seas long wont to roam,
>     Thy hyacinth hair, thy classic face,
> Thy Naiad airs, have brought me home
>     To the glory that was Greece
> And the grandeur that was Rome.

with the following attribution:

> This is, of course, Edgar Allan Poe's much-quoted *Helen*, and my mother's name was Helen. (*TF* 44)

Here we have a *figure* of the return of the "wavespeech" of maternal subconsciousness as conducted through transference and sounded by the poet's lines. The mother survives in poetry; poetry names the living feminine: "the mother is living on, and this living on is the name of the mother."

The connection between H.D. and her mother is, moreover, transmitted across more than one line, one c(h)ord, of poetry. She recalls Poe by first recalling the lyrics of the *Chambered Nautilus*, by Oliver Wendell Holmes, a native northeastern American like herself and a favorite of her school years. She transposes: "*Till thou at length art free . . . Leaving thine out-grown shell by life's unresting sea! . . . Build thee more stately mansions, O my soul*" (43). In the acoustic figure of the *Chambered Nautilus* is the implied figure of the uncanny ear, "the very shell . . . of my outer ear and the curled involuted or convoluted shell skull and inside the skull, the curled, intricate, hermit-like mollusk" (*TF* 90). In the chambered nautilus of her psychic ear, H.D. hears the echoes of home in the verses of "Holmes," which sing of her beloved motherland ("they went on singing like an echo of an echo in a shell" [*TF* 90]). Home is also the re-creative space of analysis in which she and Freud "justify all the spiral-like meanderings of my mind and body" (44).

H.D. invokes her mother's name in the meters of Holmes and Poe, the lyrics of schoolgirl memory. What *face* the name recalls cannot be pinned down; no mother iconography reveals itself in Poe's "Naiad airs." Yet "Helen" names the very current of song, the musical impulse that runs deep in memory and links, like wave upon wave, the song-line of a lifetime and beyond—the "old-fashioned hymns" of her grandmother, and of her mother before her. Through the medium of simulated transference of her delayed analysis, H.D. tunes into the maternal wavelength, which travels the line of descent along a displaced genealogy, like a Bergsonian impulse of *élan vital*.

But H.D. is not content to inherit a faceless, "morbidly self-effacing" mother-muse. Her transposition of Poe's "Helen" merely marks the transition from imagism to Freudianism and beyond, to the "high-water mark of achievement" (43) of her mythopoeic modernism. Poe's "Helen" marks the oracular medium of a Freudian transition between the objectivized "Helen" (1924) of her imagist period and the subjectivized, self-dramatizing *Helen in Egypt* (1952–55), the "Cantos" of her maturity. These transpositions of "Helen" mark the process of bringing Helen home, giving life and face to the mother, her muse, and to Hellas, mother of the lyric.

## Maternal Fantasies, Uncanny Reminiscences, (M)other Gifts

The crypto-cinemato-oto-bio-graphical narrative of chapters 2 and 4 of *The Gift*, "Fortune Teller" and "The Secret," flow from maternal reserves of fantasy and imagination into the medium of childhood fantasy as viewed in retrospect from the interpretative frame of childhood memory. The psychic mechanisms that process this flow are projection and thought transference (telepathy), or so the narrator would have us believe. Mama and Mamalie enter the phenomenal field of the adult *visuel*, where they expose their mysterious "gifts," whose artistic nature eludes Freud's own (auto)biographical speculations.

*The Gift* performs an autobiography of recovery, in a double sense of the term. In retelling the story of her maternal descent, H.D. recovers a sense of being gifted, of regaining possession of the repressed and suppressed musical and psychical gifts of her mother(s). Conversely, she *recovers from* a sense of being dispossessed of these gifts, a sense that so painfully surfaced in her symptomatic writer's block. Analytic speculation in chapters 2 and 4 enact a desire to answer questions of loss of origin that punctuate her autobiographical narrative:

Mama gave all her music to Uncle Fred, that is what she did. That is why we hadn't the gift . . . she gave it away, she gave the gift to Uncle Fred, she should have waited and given the gift to us. But there were other gifts, it seemed. (12)

Well, where had Mamalie's gift gone then? (86)

The poet-genealogist takes her cue from Freud's own (auto)biographical studies, elaborating, in particular, his speculations on the maternal origins of Goethe's artistic gift:

If we now return to Goethe's childhood memory and put in the place it occupies in *Dichtung und Wahrheit* what we believe we have obtained through observations of other children, a perfectly valid train of thought emerges. . . . It would run thus: 'I was a child of fortune . . . I did not have to share my mother's love. . . .' The train of thought . . . then goes on to . . . the grandmother who lived like a quiet friendly spirit in another part of the house. . . .

   Goethe might well have given some such heading to his autobiography as: 'My strength has its roots in my relation to my mother.' (*SE* 17:155–56)

These chapters of *The Gift* are not merely adaptations of the scene of mother transference but explorations in the uncanny. The staging of "Fortune Teller" and "The Secret" is set not only for the re-production of childhood fantasy and memory but also for the retrieval of maternal fantasy and memory, which had been repressed and forgotten *by the mothers themselves*. Mystery inhabits these memories as well as the act of remembering; projection and telepathy are psychic (and not just psychological) mechanisms of uncanny reminiscence.

In what sense are these mechanisms and reminiscences uncanny? The psychoanalytic sense of the term is obscured by Freud's complex etymology and philology.[55] He traces many meanings and themes in his essay "The Uncanny" (1919) of which, I believe, H.D. appropriates and elaborates only certain ones in *The Gift*. H.D. herself uses the term explicitly throughout her work. It appears several times on one page of "Secret Name: Excavator's Egypt" in reference to the strangely familiar atmosphere of Egypt, the "home-like, very familiar" yet "uncanny" sphinxes, the "uncanny, skeleton-like trees . . . skeleton palms, lost in that space," and the "uncanny perceptions in the tomb" (*P* 203), which she later, uncannily refers to as a "birth-house" (214). She also uses the term in "Morning Star," the last chapter of *The Gift*, to describe the feelings generated by the "wave of memories and terrors repressed since the age of ten" which the shock of living and writing through the London blitz had opened like a floodgate: "My hands were cold with that freezing uncanny coldness that one associates with ghosts and ghost stories" (139). These uses of the term invite direct comparison with those employed by Freud in "The Uncanny." H.D. takes her cue, I believe, from Freud, who states at the outset of his study that to explore this subject, "the writer," that is, Freud, "must start by translating himself into that state of feeling, by awakening in himself the possibility of experiencing it."[56]

To begin with, H. D., like Freud, uses the term *homelike* (*heimlich*) to mean both "familiar" and "strange" (or unhomelike, unfamiliar, *un-heimlich*) (*SE* 17:226); she exploits the double capacity of the term to imply its opposite in a way that accords with what Freud elsewhere notes about the antithetical meaning of primitive Egyptian words, hence the appropriateness of its emblematic appearance in "Secret Name: Excavator's Egypt."[57] According to Freud, in consultation with Grimm's dictionary, *heimlich* invariably means *unheimlich*, signifying at once the "familiar, amicable, unreserved . . . *the idea of 'homelike,' 'belonging to the house' . . . withdrawn from the eyes of strangers, something concealed, secret . . . Heimlich* parts of the human body, *pudenda*. . . . [A] *heimlich* meaning, *mysticus, divinus, occultus, figuratus* . . . that which is obscure, inaccessible to knowledge" (225–26).[58]

For analytical purposes, however, Freud revises the ambiguity inherent in the term so as to accommodate a further, psychological sense of change over time, of development or regression. In his revaluation, the interchangeability of *heimlich* and *unheimlich* becomes the transition from *heimlich* to *unheimlich*; semantic ambiguity is supplemented by psychological ambivalence. "Thus," Freud concludes after a little etymological doctoring, "*heimlich* is a word the meaning of which develops in the direction of ambivalence until it finally coincides with its opposite, *unheimlich*" (226). The reason for the change, he explains, is the unveiling of "something which ought to have remained hidden" (241), so that what was once familiarly secret and concealed has become unfamiliarly exposed and revealed. The experience of the uncanny is the not wholly desirable effect of a failure of repression: "The uncanny [*unheimlich*] is something which is secretly familiar [*heimlich-heimisch*], which has undergone repression and then returned from it" (245).

*The Gift* exploits both the synchronic ambiguity and the developmental ambivalence of the Freudian meaning of *uncanny*. Moreover, like Freud, H. D. illustrates the uncanny with figures of the double, which give rise to feelings of horror and wonder. These figures include the coupling of death and life (the return of the "dead" mother(s) who have been mummified in memory), the coupling of death and birth (as in the figure of the Egyptian "birth-house/tomb" in "Secret Name"), or the coupling of death with life and birth (as in the mnemic image of "Miss Helen at school" teaching the Child about the Egyptians, who "built little houses to live in when they were dead" [G 5]).[59] There is also the figure of unconscious communication between individuals who are separated in time and space (or telepathy, as in the doubling of the self and/as mother or grandmother). Like Freud, H. D. emphasizes the feeling of being buried alive as the most uncanny feeling of all (SE 17:244), the feeling of being encrypted in a living tomb or dead womb, still waiting to be born. "Yes, I was 'Buried Alive,'" she testifies in "Advent" (139), alluding to the instructive pictures on Freud's office wall, "a bizarre print or engraving of some nightmare horror, a 'Buried Alive' or some such thing, done in Düreresque symbolic detail" (TF 61).

Ultimately, having illustrated his sense of "the uncanny" in a lengthy, convoluted reading of E. T. A. Hoffmann's "Sandman," Freud concludes that "an uncanny experience occurs either when infantile complexes which have been repressed are once more revived by some impression, or when primitive beliefs which have been surmounted seem once more to be confirmed" (249). In other words, an uncanny experience arises from sources in the repressed unconscious whose arousal may be attributed to memories of individual or racial prehistory, to the reliving of an eroticism or animism that once animated the world of the child or of the "primitive" mystic. The return of this earlier world view after it has been repressed or surmounted by the forces of growth and enlightenment of consciousness (including the "reality principle" of scientific posititivism) may be interpreted as a rebellion of the unconscious, breaking through the censors of reason. According to Freud, writers of fiction retain the power to solicit the uncanny which most people normally possess only as children and lose in the process of maturing, or which saints and prophets once possessed but have long since lost to the exorcisms of history. Yet, fascinated by "the possiblities of poetic license and the privileges enjoyed by story-writers in evoking or in excluding an uncanny feeling," Freud willingly concedes that "the storyteller has a *peculiarly* directive power over us" (251), compelling the audience with artistic gifts whose mysterious technique lies beyond the illuminating speculations of psychoanalysis.

The narrator of *The Gift* self-consciously employs "the poetic li-

cense and the privileges enjoyed by story-writers in evoking" a return of the repressed and surmounted memories of prehistory in a
way that gives rise to a feeling of profound, *heimlich-unheimlich* ambivalence, as Freud describes. "I had gone down," H.D. writes in the
retrospective present of the final chapter of her reminiscence, "been
submerged by the wave of memories and terrors repressed since the
age of ten and long before, but with the terrors, I had found the joys
too" (*G* 139). The cryptic phrase, "and long before," implies the
memories, terrors, and joys that had been repressed a generation or
more before, memories that her mystic Moravian mothers had repressed and perhaps surmounted since the age of modern science
came to dominate their households, making what was once homelike, unhomelike and then, in time, homelike again, before the Child
appears on the scene and sees through the spell of repression.

   *The Gift* rediscovers for the woman poet the gifts of artistic and
mystic expression which the mothers repressed and the fathers surmounted in the name of progressive enlightenment or, as Nietzsche
diagnosed, "the progressive *masulinization* of man." "Fortune Teller"
reads like an uncanny exhumation of the mother's buried eroticism,
just as "The Secret" recovers the grandmother's memory-fantasy of
mystical, burning rapture which "should have remained hidden"
and concealed.

### "Fortune Teller"

   Chapter 2 of *The Gift* represents the Child's pre-natal memory of a
reverie/revelation her mother entertains on a visit to a gypsy fortune-
teller on the wooded outskirts of her hometown of Bethlehem, Pennsylvania. The scene of rememory is uncanny in two senses. First, the
Child occupies the mother's unconscious as all-seeing, though she
herself is nowhere to be seen; she is a child in the womb of maternal
memory and fantasy, envisioning her mother's experience before she
was even conceived. In a return to pre-prenatal life, the Child relives
the adult's sense of being buried alive, making *heimlich* a feeling that
had become paralyzingly *unheimlich*, bringing Hilda "home" to
Helen, to Hellas, the other, sensual mother, who had been missing
all her life.[60] Second, the Child remembers scenes that have been
either consciously or preconsciously repressed (and therefore impressed upon the deep unconscious) or never consciously recorded
at all. By implication, the Child has become the mother's telepathic
double with the ability to receive the uncanny transmission of deeply

cherished, long-standing secrets that had never consciously passed between them.

Fantasy appears to be the medium of communication between narrating and narrated subjects. Scenes from Mama's early adult life seem to (e)merge directly into Hilda's consciousness. Childhood reminiscence dissolves any barriers set up by screen memories as well as any boundary between individual psyches, in an uncanny display of thought transference. In "Dreams and Occultism," Freud describes thought transference, or telepathy, as the phenomenon that claims "that mental processes in one person—ideas, emotional states, conative impulses—can be transferred to another person through empty space without employing the familiar methods of communication by means of words and signs (*SE* 22:39). To the spatial dimension of this definition, H.D. adds a temporal one: she communicates with or receives "ideas, emotional states, conative impulses" from her mother not only through "empty space" but also through "empty time." These ideas, feelings, and impulses traverse unrecorded history, spanning the gap between life and death, emerging in the "past" of present narrative reminiscence, and giving the impression of time transcended. I recall once again H.D.'s dedication to her mother: "l'amitié passe même le tombeau."

The narrator of "Fortune Teller" behaves like the author of "Dreams and Occultism," who beckons an (imaginary) audience of psychoanalysts to "have kindlier thoughts on the objective possibility of thought-transference" (*SE* 22:54) and who even goes so far as to suggest that it was "the original, archaic method of communication between individuals . . . in the course of phylogenetic evolution" (55). Just as Freud proceeds to illustrate his openness to thought transference with a story about a fortune-teller drawn from analytic experience (40), so also does H.D.'s narrative figure a fortune-teller whose actions open Mama's mind to occult possibilities, affording her a certain, psychic revelation.

Mama's fortune-teller is a gypsy, hailing from the Old World and employing Old World techniques to read her thoughts. Mama confronts her with ambivalent fascination. "This woman," she thinks, "belonged to the superstitions and magic of the old Indian legends. She belonged, did she, to the old, old wisdom, that had led the very Magi to a star. . . . this is . . . maybe sorcery, maybe witchcraft" (G2 38). Yet, though she hails from the Old World, the gypsy fortune-teller also employs New World techniques: she is a thought-reader of the analytical sort. Her verbal and gestural cues activate an unconscious association, bringing unconscious trains of ideas into (pre)conscious apprehension with the same effect as clinically monitored scenes of transference:

> "Carnations," said the gypsy and she made a great sweep of her arms above what Mama presumed was a heap of carnations on the table. This was thought-reading . . . thought Mama. . . . the woman's images and ideas seemed to pick up the thread of what she had been thinking, though even so, Mama would not have re-constructed her thoughts if the images of the gypsy had not recalled them to her. (37)

H.D.'s fortune-teller is cast in the same ambiguous light as Freud's, and it remains unclear whether she is, in truth, an agent in an occult event or something of an analyst.[61] In Freud's narrative, epistemological uncertainty is only rhetorically resolved. The fortune-teller's "prophecy" could, Freud says, be thought transference, a falsely remembered event, or an act of the unconscious, psychically intervening in the act of recollection. "If you . . . decide on the latter," he warns, "do not forget that it was only analysis that created the occult fact" (42).

It remains unclear in H.D.'s narrative whether the fortune teller is really a thought-reader or simply a fortuitous prompter of the repressed desire awaiting its cue to surface into consciousness. But what happens after the thought-readings have started to take effect is beyond the realm of the day dreaming imagination. Carnations recall Mama to the scene of her near seduction by a certain Mr. Fernandez, a Spanish student who courted her with carnations. Mama remembers their clandestine meetings at the summerhouse just outside the grounds of the seminary where she taught and lived under the strict, puritanical vigilance of her father, the principal. He "even once almost expelled one of the Lovatt [love-it?] girls from New York," she remembers, "because she lowered a little basket out of her window and one of the University boys put letters in it" (39). The word is the thought-reader's magic wand, the analyst's key signifier, an overdetermined word that arouses unconscious, irrepressible desire, just as it signals danger: "I was melted away. . . . His kisses were—but I must not think of his kisses because I thought it all out and I got him to go away and he sent me red carnations" (39). Taking her cue from the fortune teller, the Child breaks through Mama's resistances and presses home her thoughts.

The Child feels Mama's terror that "something dreadful might have happened" in a vaguely concealed, mythic image of "a girl who was raped away—raped, yes . . . by the darkness, by Dis, by Death" (40). It is a rape fantasy of sorts, though it is formulated in the familiar (*heimlich*) figures that she (Mama? Hilda?) knew from *Tanglewood Tales*. She then feels Mama lose consciousness to a sinking, submerged feeling, which the excited and terrified young woman fails to recognize as a plunge into the mystic-erotic passion of her maternal Moravian heritage. The word *carnations*, the Child mysteriously knows, is the magic, metonymical link to "a whole set of poetical and biological emotions that there were no names for" (40). Mama's carnations cue the recall of Mamalie's "black rose," the dream-hieroglyph of a mystical, masochistic *jouissance*:

> Suddenly, she knew it, she recognised it, it was the black-rose that Mimmie [Mamalie] would speak of, that black-rose of despair when one was happiest (that was it); if one were happy, swept quite, quite away, melted away so that even your name was forgotten . . . when someone sounded words from a deep-sea shell, in another language that sounded like the sound of the sea when you first heard it—Mama had never been to the sea—in a deep-sea shell. So far away, she had gone, the summer-house was wreathed in fragrant sea-weed and the jasmine-flowers were froth and pearls from the sea, and she was a mermaid, ageless, timeless. (40)

Generated along the umbilicus of the maternal unconscious, this heretical feeling lives on and resurges despite the teachings of orthodoxy: "She was a mermaid, ageless, timeless, with a whole set of poetical and biological emotions that there were no names for, that were things having to do with the Tree of the Knowledge of Good and Evil and that were not right" (40). The Child is a swimmer in the sea of the unconscious, in search of the mermaid mother, the *mère-maid*, the sexual imaginary of the maternal-feminine now become *unheimlich*, forbidden or perverse eroticism.

## "The Secret"

Chapter 4 features another maternal fantasy, recounted by maternal grandmother, as before, through the telepathic medium of the Child. The camera obscura is the dusk-darkened interior of the family house, whose inhabitants have withdrawn out-of-doors to enjoy the cool twilight of a hot summer day, except Mamalie and the child, Hilda. (The Child herself appears in this childhood reminiscence.) Between waking and sleeping consciousness, Hilda slips out of bed and encounters her grandmother on the staircase; she takes the unusual opportunity to approach this elderly, enigmatic figure, who, like the grandmother in Freud's description of Goethe's autobiography "lives like a quiet friendly spirit in another part of the house."[62] Though Mamalie's deafness ordinarily discourages Hilda from disturbing her, she observes that Mamalie "is hearing something all the same" and that "maybe she is hearing something now in the dark" (G 76). Hoping to discover whatever it is that she appears to be listening to, Hilda follows close behind. "If I stay in her room with her," she speculates, "I might hear something."

The dark room of childhood reminiscence becomes the cinema-theater of Mamalie's darkening bedroom. It darkens, Hilda observes, not only with approaching nightfall but also with the growing sense of mystery about her grandmother's person. Without warning, Mamalie lapses into one of her entranced states, "a dream or a sort of waking dream" (97), a penumbra of consciousness. Her curtains are drawn and her candle is lit, one candle in a saucer of water, so that the entire room is cast in the shadow of her mood.[63] As she sweeps in and out of wakefulness and dream-reverie, Mamalie mistakes Hilda for Hilda's mother (74), or for one of Hilda's aunts (Mamalie's daughters, Laura and Aggie [75, 77]), or for the Moravian sister, Lucy (89), who had seen Mamalie through a severe bout of fever many years ago and who Hilda knows is dead. This uncanny mix-up of names in turn prompts the Child to take up the play and recast the mise en scène of her grandmother's awakening unconscious.

Like Mama's encounter with the fortune-teller, Hilda's encounter with Mamalie is a double session; it is ambiguously cast as a scene of transference or as a séance with spirits of the past or both. The familiar home becomes something of a haunted house, an *unheimlich* house, in which Hilda senses the uncanny. "It was like listening in the dark, though we had the candle . . . about something that didn't happen at all, like the ghost story about the man who nailed his coat to a coffin and then screamed because he thought a skeleton hand had got him" (93). But she enters into the spirit of things as if she were at once entertaining a hypnotized patient and an entranced mystic.

The Child knows intuitively how to direct the play between them. Making herself invisible (like an analyst behind her couch) and acting the character her grandmother projects onto her, Hilda pushes her into very deep waters, asking leading questions with key verbal cues: "I say, 'Yes Mimmie,' because Mama and Aunt Aggie call her 'Mimmie.' I am afraid she will remember that I am only Hilda, so I crouch down under the cover so she will only half see me, so that she won't remember that I am only Hilda" (79). Mamalie responds to Hilda's gesture as if she had overheard the child's thinking; she translates Hilda's fear into her fear, a fear of exposure: " 'It wasn't that I was afraid,' she [Mamalie] said, 'though I was afraid. It wasn't only that they might burn us all up, but there were the papers. Christian had left the secret with me. I was afraid the secret would be lost" (79).[64]

The secret to which Mamalie refers is the existence of the "Hidden Church" of revolutionary mystics within the Moravian Brotherhood, alerting the Freudian reader once again to the uncanny themes of this chapter, since these are precisely the terms in which Freud speaks of the uncanny. "According to [Friedrich von Schelling]," Freud explains, "everything is *unheimlich* that ought to have remained secret and hidden but has come to light."

With Hilda's charmed and charming guidance, Mamalie gradually reveals the untold story of the *"Wunden Eiland* [Wounded Island] initiates," a small, elect band of "the chief medicine men" of Indian and Moravian "tribes" committed to the idea of world peace and mystic harmony and above all to "the Ritual of the Wounds," who held a clandestine meeting to draw up a secret pact and to exchange ceremonial gifts (86). Nearly one hundred years after this meeting took place, Mamalie's first husband, the never-before-mentioned Christian, discovered the deerskin parchment on which the dialogues, pledges, and songs of the initiates had been recorded in many languages. Identifying some scratchings as ancient Greek and Hebrew, he set out to decipher the whole text as if it were the Rosetta stone and he, Champollion. Mamalie contributed to the decoding by transposing the accents and rhythms of the text into living song; reading it with her ear, she was able to transmit the "spirit" that had been encrypted there for all eternity. In the process, she is uncannily transformed, inhabited, as it were, by the return of the repressed: "In trying over and putting together the indicated rhythms, she herself became one with the *Wunden Eiland* initiates and herself spoke with tongues—hymns of the spirits in the air—of spirits at sunrise and sunsetting, of the deer and the wild squirrel, the beaver, the otter, the kingfisher, and the hawk and eagle" (86–87).

Mamalie reveals her "gift" of speaking in tongues, of transcending language barriers by "singing with no words or with words of leaves rustling and rivers flowing and snow swirling in the wind . . . the breath of the Spirit" (88). But it is a gift that has to be concealed.

Though a hundred years had passesd since the signing of the treaty and the burning of Gnadenheutten (the original Moravian settlement) in the war that ensued between dissenters from both factions, Mamalie and Christian are forced to keep their discovery silent and, like the initiates themselves, to suppress their mystical zeal before "the stricter Brethren of the church [who] said it was witchcraft" (88).

Alarmed by Mamalie's revelation of what ought to have remained secret and hidden, overwhelmed by her astonishing transition from familiar homebody to unfamiliar fanatic, Hilda asks, "Is Mamalie a witch?" (88) But what troubles and bewilders Hilda *then* is what later stirs the adult *visuel* and the reawakened Child of mysticism, namely, the nature of the source of "the gift": "Well, where had Mamalie's gift gone then? I did not ask her, but I sense now that she burnt it all up in an hour or so of rapture" (86). In recalling the scene of ritual initiation, Mamalie burns with the rapture that burned the initiates. Any distinction between ecstatic vitality and tragic mortality eludes the Child, since she conflates Mamalie's description of the "burning" of Wunden Eiland's mystic passion with the destruction of Gnadenheutten by fire. And there are other confusing reports that Christian had "burnt himself up with zeal and devotion" (96) and that Mamalie herself had nearly died of fever (91–92, 95). As a child *then*, Hilda is unable to assimilate Mamalie's mystic erotism; but *now* as the Child she hosts a passionate return of religious understanding. It is this later, clairvoyant Child who beholds, in the graphic iconography of the Moravian Christ, a figure of the spirit of masochistic *jouissance*. With newfound conviction she speaks for the followers of her hidden church against the "stricter Brethren," who had decreed that "our saviour was not to be worshipped in a startling transparency which showed the wounds, wide and red and blood dripping, when a candle was pushed forward, back of the frame, in the dark" (96).

From grandmother to granddaughter, we witness a transfer of mystic-erotic-poetic feeling and the transmission of the visionary gift. We see that through the medium of childhood memory, the adult is afforded a glimpse into her own deeply repressed religious psychology. We also see that for the uncanny cryptobiographer, maternal fantasy is what matters; it is vitalistic, libidinal, spiritual, whereas paternal objectivity is puritanical, cerebral, and abstract. The difference is reflected in the hieroglyphic (iconographic) pictures that decorate the walls of the camera obscura of memory, the mother's feverishly bleeding Christ and the father's cold-blooded dissection— Rembrandt's *Lesson in Anatomy*.

"Morning Star"

The last chapter of *The Gift*, set in 1941 in H.D.'s Chelsea apartment during the bombardment of London, opens onto the narrative present. But when Hilda reenters the present light of day after dwelling so long in the twilight of distant memory, her room is dark: the windows have been blacked out against the air raids (132), and the poet's mind has gloomily withdrawn behind a weakening defense of reason ("I was tired of trying to understand things, I was tired of trying to explain things. . . . The mind, the body is not built to endure so much. . . . I could not be brave, I would not be philosophical" [136–37]). The psyche of the narrative present is located in another camera obscura, no less encapsulating than that of childhood reminiscence, yet more fragile—the outer shell of reason being not the "deep-sea shell" of primitive fantasy but a brittle facade of self-consciousness, increasingly exposed to the barrage of "shell shock" and exhausted by the strain of mortal fear. Hilda now describes herself as a "middle-aged woman, shattered by fears of tension and terror" (135), huddled in a chair and braced for the next explosion. "There is the roar outside that will, perhaps this time," she despairs, "shatter my head, shatter my brain, and all the little boxes that have been all the rooms I have lived in, have gone in and out of, will fall . . . fall . . ." (134).

"Morning Star" occults Freud's clinical concept of deferred action (*Nachtraglichkeit*): the revived and altered awareness of a past event that because of the subject's affective and sexual immaturity, could not be assimilated at the time of first perceiving and so was sunk into the obscurity of repressed, unconscious memory. A later, distantly related event activates the revival and revision (or what Freud also calls re-transcription) of the original event with efficacy or even "pathogenic force," as Laplanche and Pontalis explain (*Language of Psycho-Analysis*, 112–13). According to Freud, the nature of the first event, impressed upon memory without conscious significance, is sexual; only after puberty or after he or she is capable of being aroused will a second, related event recall the first with a revisionary, sometimes traumatic input of sexual fantasy and imagination. For the adult Hilda, the second event that spurs memory into (com)motion is the "orgy of destruction" (DA 192) of the London blitz, the first event being the child's prepubertal perception of love and war in an image transmitted through her grandmother.

Shattered walls, sinking floors, blazing fireworks set off by bombs exploding all about her Chelsea room are the external stimuli that blast through the psyche's defenses, scattering the contents of the tomb where the memory of the Moravian holocaust three centuries earlier had been preserved. The original event of Hilda's deferred revision is transpersonal and transhistorical; it is first communicated to the Child in the uncanny, double session with Mamalie. Mamalie's story comes back to the war-beseiged adult Hilda with all the heat and passion of mystical erotism which as a child she could neither assimilate nor appreciate. Mamalie's account is itself a deferred revision of a past event, the destruction by fire of Gnadenheutten, which either she conflates in the telling or Hilda in the listening with the feverish enactment of the "Ritual of Wounds" at Wunden Eiland. For the adult *visuel*, the "savage burning arrows of enemy tribes" are one and the same as the flaming dart of mystic desire, "the arrow that flieth by day" (96). For the middle-aged poet, struggling to survive the World War II, the erotic revival of this memory acts as a latent transfusion of "visionary power," transforming mortal fear into mystic, orgasmic joy and the prophetic will to live/write for tomorrow.

# 3

# Mourning, Mystery, and Melancholia:
# Life-Writing Therapy

> I cared about Fanny. And she died. . . . Mama cried (al-
> though I had seldom seen her cry) because Fanny died, so
> Mama had cried. I did not cry. The crying was frozen in
> me, but it was my own, it was my own crying.
>
> . . . I, the child was incarcerated as a nun might be, who for
> some sin—which I did not then understand—is walled up
> alive in her own cell. . . . I, the child, was still living, but I
> was not free.
>
> H.D., The Gift

> In what, now, does the work which mourning performs
> consist? . . . Reality-testing has shown that the loved-object
> no longer exists, and it proceeds to demand that all libido
> shall be withdrawn from its attachments to that object.
> Each single one of the memories and expectations in which
> the libido is bound to the object is brought up and hyper-
> cathected, and detachment of the libido is accomplished in
> respect of it. . . . When the work of mourning is completed
> the ego becomes free and uninhibited again.
>
> Freud, "Mourning and Melancholia"

In the same moment that it constructs an autobiographical fantasy,
adapting and revising Freudian narrative in the telling of a life story,
*The Gift* performs a work of mourning. In this chapter I focus on the
therapeutic strategies of *The Gift* and on some of their feminist implications.

H.D. confesses to having suffered a form of melancholia, to a past
inability to mourn ("the crying was frozen in me" [*G* 4]) connected
with erotic inhibition ("I, the child was incarcerated as a nun" [85])
and defensive frigidity ("to live I had to be frozen in myself" [85]).
But she also testifies to a triumphant, if delayed, recovery ("I was not
free . . . to express my understanding . . . until" [85]), implying that

this freedom is, as Freud describes it in "Mourning and Melancholia," the liberating effect ("the ego become free and uninhibited again")[1] of mourning, of finding the tears that were "frozen in me . . . my own crying" (G 4).

H.D. undertakes a (w)rite of passage from melancholia to mourning, from a frozen, incarcerated crying to a liberation of tears and, beyond that, to a revelation of what was originally lost—the gift. We know that H.D. cried during her analysis with Freud: "I cried too hard" begins the "Advent" to her "Writing on the Wall" (115). She knows that her healing is finally complete when she recovers, realizes, and puts to the reality test her "inherent, inherited" ability to read signs: "I was not in fact, completely free, until again there was the whistling of evil wings, the falling of poisonous arrows, the deadly signature of a sign of evil magic in the sky" (G 85).

According to Freud, mourning is normal, but melancholia is pathological: "Mourning is regularly the reaction to the loss of a loved person, or to the loss of some abstraction which has taken the place of one, such as one's country, liberty, an ideal, and so on. In some people the same influences produce melancholia instead of mourning and we consequently suspect them of a pathological disposition" (SE 14:243). The symptoms of melancholia are clear: "a profoundly painful dejection, cessation of interest in the outside world, loss of the capacity to love, inhibition of all activity, and a lowering of the self-regarding feelings" (244). It is this last symptom that distinguishes melancholia from mourning: "The disturbance of self-regard is absent in mourning; but otherwise the features are the same" (244). The clearest symptom of H.D.'s melancholia was her inability to cry, a certain emotional frigidity that she relates to "the wave of . . . repress[ion]" under which she had been "submerged . . . since the age of ten" (G 139). The Gift, I contend, is a work that mourns and heals this childhood melancholia, which carried through into H.D.'s womanhood and intensified with the horror and devastation brought on by the First World War.

The purpose of this chapter is to investigate and disclose the technicalities of this intertextual work of mourning, to determine which psychic mechanisms H.D. supposes to be operating in writing herself out of her melancholia. According to Freud's speculative etiology, the cause of the disease may include a problem of recognition:

In one set of cases it is evident that melancholia too [like mourning] may be the reaction to the loss of a loved object. Where the exciting causes are different one can recognize that there is a loss of a more ideal kind. The object has not perhaps actually died, but has been lost as an object of love (e.g. in the case of a betrothed girl who has been jilted). In yet other cases . . . a loss of this kind has occurred, but . . . the patient cannot consciously perceive what he has lost. . . . he knows *whom* he has lost but not *what* he has lost in him. This would suggest that melancholia is in some way related to an object-loss which is withdrawn from consciousness, in contradistinction to mourning, in which there is nothing about the loss that is unconscious. (245)

In H.D.'s case, the clearest cause of melancholia was precisely the one that Freud first elaborates: the loss, but not the actual death, of "an object of love," for example, by a betrothed girl who has been jilted." H.D. had once been involved with, "engaged to," Ezra Pound and had, in a way, been jilted;[2] she explores the complications and emotional aftereffects of the relationship in *Her* and in *End to Torment: A Memoir of Ezra Pound* (1958). She was more straightforwardly jilted by her husband, Richard Aldington, however, and eventually transcribed the story in another therapeutic autobiography, *Bid Me to Live* (1939, 1949)—work that Freud had originally assigned.

But another cause of H.D.'s melancholia was far more obscure than these jiltings, and she devotes *The Gift* to identifying, deciphering, and working through it. The first clue to this condition is the dead mother: "'My mother, my mother,' I cry," she noted of a dream, "'sob violently, tears, tears, tears'" (*TF* viii). But though it is clearly the dead mother *whom* she mourns, it is less clear *what in herself* this mother loss represents, the mystifying source of her melancholia. It emerges in the course of *The Gift* that it is not the actual death of her mother that H.D. finds so disturbing but, rather, her mother's "morbidly self-effacing" nature (*TF* 164). The repression and suppression of her mother's charismatic gifts, which had been repressed and suppressed in her mother before her, are inherited by the daughter as a sense of self-loss. What is frozen in the child is the expression of that gift: hence, her latent feelings of being stillborn or buried alive, a self-loss that she could represent to her consciousness only cryptically as the inability to weep for the dead little girl Fanny, her mother's first child, who died and was buried without having the chance to flower. Pertinent to these speculations is that H.D. herself, in the middle of her war trauma, gave birth to a stillborn daughter.

For H.D., melancholia is a dis-ease of the "self," a failure of self-projection, which Freud describes more clinically as a problem of narcissism. "The melancholic," he observes, "displays something

else besides which is lacking in mourning—an extraordinary diminu-
tion in his self-regard, an impoverishment of his ego on a grand
scale. In mourning it is the world which has become poor and empty;
in melancholia it is the ego itself" (246). Freud notes that melancholia
is often punctuated by an antithetical affliction of the ego, which he
calls mania: "The most remarkable characteristic of melancholia, and
the one in most need of explanation, is its tendency to change round
into mania—a state which is the opposite of it in its symptoms" (253).
Though he questions whether mania is in fact the pathological counterpart of melancholia and not a genuine expression of deliverance
from the disease, Freud notes that it can in any case be detected in
signs of "joy, exultation or triumph" (254), which wholly oppose the
symptoms of melancholia.

If melancholia is a problem of narcissism, then the counterpart
of the disease would more precisely be megalomania, the signs of
which Freud believed he could read in H.D.'s writing on the wall,
and which she herself registered as a sense of triumph or "victory."
But whether it is mania or a genuine liberation from melancholia,
H.D.'s writing of *The Gift* signifies a recovery of that lost object which
could not formally be identified. *The Gift* is a recovery and a working
through *in writing* which is in itself evidence of her charismatic power
to heal.

While I contend that *The Gift* is a therapeutic writing, a narrative
performance that revives and adapts a "life," I am not suggesting that
it should be read simply as applied psychoanalysis or even as a
continuation of the writing cure that Freud assigned H.D. in analysis. Indeed, I propose that *The Gift* may also be read as H.D.'s
preferred "cure" for the narrative blindness that troubles the Freudian text, particularly where she perceives the therapeutic potential of
psychoanalysis to be blocked by its own speculative inhibitions concerning female sexuality.

There is a certain hiatus in Freud's thesis about mourning and
melancholia. Freud himself does not find wholly believable the claim
that the subject's "principled" adherence to reality will overrule his
or her libidinal attachment to the lost love object and will dissolve the
"hallucinatory wishful psychosis" that could compensate for the loss
of satisfaction. He neither explains nor names the psychological force
which mobilizes this work of mourning and re-turns the ego to the
domain of eros. It is here that I see H.D. entering and altering Freud's
text. *The Gift* hypothesizes and illustrates a work of mourning that
mobilizes a "primary, feminine masochism," a painful pleasure or

pleasure *beyond* pleasure—what Leo Bersani in *The Freudian Body* refers to as "masochistic *jouissance*."[3] In her autobiographical revision of the psychoanalysis of mourning, H.D. entertains the obliteration of her mortal fears and the wall of repression which had protectively incarcerated her psyche for decades. With bombs exploding all about her, she withdraws inward to the depths of the unconscious; or rather, the unconscious surges into consciousness, breaking through ego fortifications in a wave of terror that also brings joy: "But with the terrors, I found the joys too" (*G* 139).

## A Woman's Work of Mourning

The narratives of fantasy and therapy are intricately inter-woven in *The Gift*. At the same time that it plots the onset of girlhood melancholia and its climactic dissolution, H.D.'s autobiography plots the symptomatic development of childhood sexual fantasy, revealed in the childhood reminscences of nightmare "speculations" concerning the taboo of virginity and the mysteries of defloration and orgasm. At another level, H.D. *plots* against the phallocentric psychoanalytic account of the psychological structuring of childhood sexuality and the developmental (fantasy) processes in girls, which Freud admitted to be inadequate.

*The Gift* outlines childhood development by staging the structuring action of fantasy. The subject of H.D.'s childhood reminiscence is between five and ten years old, an age at which, according to Freud, the child lives in the shadow of the castration complex, the "latency period" of childhood.[4] H.D.'s childhood, like Freud's latency period, is marked by intensive dreaming and fantasizing. Freud models the phantasmal stage of girlhood on the boy's "phallic organization" and "castration complex":

> Analytic observation enables us to recognize or guess connections be-
> tween the phallic organization, the Oedipus Complex, the threat of
> castration, the formation of the super-ego and the latency period. . . .
> the process which has been described refers . . . to male children only.
> How does the corresponding development take place in little girls?
>     At this point our material—for some incomprehensible reason—
> becomes far more obscure and full of gaps. The female sex, too, de-
> velops an Oedipus complex, a super-ego and a latency period. May we
> also attribute a phallic organization and a castration complex to it? The
> answer is in the affirmative. (*SE* 19.177–78)

H.D. however, proposes other phantasmal agencies, such as defloration and virginity. The fantasy of defloration is seen to derive in part from a primary feminine masochism, which the mothers express in their mystical "flower-language" (Mamalie's black rose of joy and despair; Mama's tabooed red carnations).

The ear, not the phallus, is the child Hilda's primary organ of pleasure. An organ of memory embedded in song, an organ of remote communication, the ear presents an uncanny conduit to the mothers; it is attuned to their private language and their subconscious thoughts, translating their cryptic musings into affective understanding. The ear is what receives the maternal gift of female self-expression. Freud also speaks about the little girl's gift, but only in terms of a phallic, libidinal economy. For Freud, the gift is the baby of fantasy which the little girl wishes her father to give her in compensation for her lack of a male organ. "Her Oedipus complex culminates in a desire, which is long retained, to receive a baby from her father as a gift—to bear him a child" (*SE* 19:179).

In Freud's scheme of things, only the boy comes into possession of the phallus, the symbolic potency or potential to signify his membership in the patriarchal economy. He enters the oedipal complex and proceeds to its dissolution through symbolic castration and the sacrifice of his desire for the mother, guided by the incest taboos to which he unconsciously subscribes in the name of the father. He is compensated for his pains with a paternal self-signifying power of his own through which he gains a respectable place and position in the larger, patriarchal family of the community and nation. Marked by his maleness as one of the initiated, he gains access to the institutional hierarchies that organize and structure themselves in the totemic order of fathers and sons. Conversely, by virtue of her femaleness, the girl is disqualified from this ritual initiation. Though she too may go through the oedipal complex, she does not stand to inherit the phallus since she has no organ, no signifier of desire, to sacrifice to patriarchal taboos. The most she is expected to inherit from her mother is a sense of female insufficiency, and for the "loss" of pleasure she suffers after making the oedipal break, she receives no real or symbolic compensation. Instead, she is left with only the delusory hope that her father will give her a phallic substitute, a male child.

H.D.'s childhood reminiscence shows Hilda gradually awakening to the gift of expression which is her rightful maternal inheritance before it is forbidden or expropriated by a variety of institutional factors, a censorious sex education, a patriarchal market economy, a puritanical morality, an Enlightenment (witch-burning) ideology, as well as by a morbid, maternal self-effacement and childhood sexual trauma. Given these genealogical obtrusions, H.D.'s therapeutic fantasy might be previewed as follows: the adult *visuel* of childhood reminiscence must retrace and make good her losses through a rememorative process, thus restoring the "gift economy" of her foremothers.[5]

The primary concern of the narrator as she plots her autobiography is to expose and dissolve her paramount fear of suffering a permanent loss of erotic-poetic expression. She fears what Ernest Jones called *aphanisis*, or the fading out of the self in critical moments of development. Ernest Jones coined the term while conducting research on female sexual development, which he, unlike Freud, believed to have "its own aims and activity from the outset," according to Laplanche and Pontalis (*Language of Psycho-Analysis*, 40). H.D.'s childhood reminiscences are visualized from the perspective of this faded subject, who has inherited a sense of self-effacement in the process of becoming feminine. Her fantasies are projected from the "dark room" of her repressed sexual imagination like the haunting visions of an anchoress in her cell or like the shadowy reflections of a prisoner in a cave. The symptomatic figure of aphanisis is eventually displaced by a therapeutic figure of anamnesis, a psychoanalytic recall of inherent or inherited memory which dispels the darkness and brings the maternal eros to light.

The immediate "cause" of Hilda's aphanisis is disclosed in narrative passages that bear resemblance to detective fiction. "The Secret" offers a clue or two: "The 'thing' that was to happen, happened . . . before Christmas . . . but I cannot date the time of the thing that happened, that happened to me personally, because I forgot it. I mean it was walled over and I was buried with it . . . so great was the shock to my mind when I found my father wounded" (G 85). The next chapter, "What It Was," proceeds to unveil "the thing" from the child's alarmed and arousing daydream. Two traumatic events are gradually disclosed: a memory of discovering her father, concussed and bleeding after a railroad accident (G 105–28), and a more obscure memory of unsolicited sexual exposure. The shock of the first event is reinforced and compounded by the second, whose telling follows so closely on the narration of the first event as to suggest that memory has conflated the two. In the second event, she accepts a ride from a man driving a milk cart as she is walking home from school. When they approach the top of Black Horse Hill, the memory turns into a nightmare: "The cart jerked and the horse began to run. I looked at the man and I saw he was . . . he had . . . and he said . . . but I said, 'I get out here, I live here,' but I did not live at the Fetters' Farm" (G 128). The ellipses signify Hilda's shock at the milkman's exhibitionism and the lack (not just the loss) of words to name and articulate her experience.

"The 'thing' which happened to me," is, it seems, a "phallic" thing, though not precisely castration. Hilda is traumatized by the sight of the paternal body; that her father bleeds, loses consciousness and self-possession, is as shocking to her as the milkman's exhibitionism. The "laying bare" of the body behind paternal sobriety and authority is especially shocking since it is a "possessed" body, a "wild" body ("the cart jerked and the horse began to run"), a body out of control ("was this a drunk man?" [106]). Hilda fails to assimilate the experience in part because her puritan fantasy of paternal omniscience and benevolence has been violated. She unconsciously responds to this wounding of her ego ideal by seeking sanctuary behind the imaginary walls of her interior church, becoming a "nun" in girlhood and displaying all the symptoms of melancholic withdrawal and paranoiac self-defense as Freud describes them in "Mourning and Melancholia": "An object-choice, an attachment of the libido to a particular person, had at one time existed; then, owing to a real slight or disappointment coming from this loved person, the object-relationship was shattered. The result was not the normal one of a withdrawal of the libido from this object and a displacement of it on to a new one, but . . . withdraw[al] into the ego" (SE 14:248–49).

What "frees" Hilda from her defensive enclosure, her melancholic frigidity, is the memory and resurgence of a maternal, masochistic jouissance. Only later, forty-five years later, in England during the Second World War when she inhabits a "wounded island" that recalls the Wunden Eiland of Mamalie's reverie ("was that this island, England, pock-marked with formidable craters, with Death stalking one at every corner?" [G 140]), only when she inhabits this wounded, burning land-body, can she feel and understand what Mamalie felt when she told her story of the Wunden Eiland initiates and their fierce eros, whose passion became even further inflamed in the massacre and burning of the Moravian settlement of Gnadenheutten. Only when "again there was the whistling of evil wings the falling of poisonous arrows" is Hilda's "mortal fear (personal fear)" dispelled, her psyche liberated and revitalized by the war's "orgy of destruction" (DA 192).

But the plot digresses. "What It Was" discloses the immediate cause of Hilda's nunlike anesthesia, but it does not account for the most troubling symptom of all, girlhood and maternal amnesia, Mamalie's forgetting of her hidden church, Mama's forgetting of her musical gifts, and Hilda's forgetting that she was to have been a gifted child: "Yet I remember the strange gap in consciousness, the sort of emptiness there, which I soon covered over with my childish philosophy or logic, when [Mama] said, '. . . the fortune-teller told me . . . I would have a child who was in some way especially gifted'" (21). Hilda's confinement in mortal fear and frigidity after her traumas is a secondary development or aggravation of an already-existing melancholia. From the beginning, mother, grandmother, and Hilda display symptoms of an enforced dispossession of their gifts. Had Hilda inherited her mothers' song of mystic, mournful joy, and had she been initiated into the female mysteries of life, love, and death, instead of becoming an object of cultural and libidinal suppression, she would have been psychologically able to accommodate a trauma like her father's accident, understanding it in the full context of mystic passion which, in retrospect, she knows to be much more accommodating than the enlightened or puritan frame of mind.

Neither "The Secret" nor "What It Was" interrogates the keeper of the asylum, the warden of the church cell, to discover "where . . . Mamalie's gift [had] gone" (G 86) and why Mama gave the gift away: how does the history of witch burning and Indian fighting relate to the suppression of Moravian mysticism and to the colonization of women's sexual imagination? There is a subplot in *The Gift* that recasts the history of the little girl's feminization as the cause of melancholia.

## A Very Black Sexuality

Luce Irigaray's close, critical reading of Freud in *Speculum of the Other Woman* uncovers a strong analogy between melancholia and femininity in Freudian discourse, which offers much to further my reading of H.D.'s work of mourning.[6] Unlike Marie Bonaparte, whose *Female Sexuality* (1949) promotes and perpetuates a conventional, Freudian belief that morbidity, masochism, and frigidity derive from woman's recognition of her "biological inferiority," Irigaray sees too many gaps in Freud's phallocentric picture of female sexuality to be convinced that woman "naturally" fosters a negative self-image and that analysis does not intervene in woman's sexual self-reflection to ensure such an image.[7] Like H.D., Irigaray rewrites Freud, though she employs a different parodic style. Adopting an attitude of radical irony, Irigaray enters the play Freud stages in his mock lecture "Femininity"; as one of the imaginary women in his audience, she records the scheming logic of his speculations, exposing their ludic(rous) antifeminism.

"If," Irigaray writes, "all the implications of Freud's discourse were followed through, after the little girl discovers her own castration and that of her mother—her 'object,' the narcissistic representative of all her instincts—she would have no recourse other than melancholia" (66). She repeats her point, emphasizing the textual rather than the anatomical construction of Freud's "female sexuality": "If you reread 'Mourning and Melancholia' . . . you will be struck by the way the libidinal economy of the little girl, after she finds out that both she and her mother are castrated, crosschecks with the symptoms of melancholia" (66).[8]

As Irigaray sees it, Freud's figure of "the little girl" is "de-narcissized" in his story of her entry into the Oedipus complex. She alludes to the passage in "Femininity" where Freud passes a death-sentence on the girl's (auto-)erotism: "the little girl . . . has been able to get pleasure by the excitation of her clitoris and has brought this activity into relation with her sexual wishes directed towards her mother . . . now, owing to the influence of her penis-envy, she loses her enjoyment. . . . Her self-love is mortified" (SE 22:126). When the little girl "discovers" her castration (the little boy only "fears" the threat of castration, a threat made real when he gazes upon the "castrated" body of woman), she withdraws her love for her mother and for her "self" and cultivates an abject coldness towards the female sex in general. She observes that whereas Freud's "little girl" feels severely alienated from her body-ego because of this discovery of her "lack," his little boy, even after his castration crisis, is at home in his body; moreover, he is "narcissized" (68) by his penis. The threat of castration severs him only from the once-desired mother with whom he no longer identifies (as "phallic mother") since he sees that she is castrated, mutilated, inferior. He identifies instead with his own precious organ, which has been saved from castration, and he reveres the father for his possession of a larger organ, one which he knows he himself will come to possess and which will bring with it its own paternal power of familial and cultural authority, including the right to possess a mother substitute.

For the Freudian woman as Irigaray re-presents her, femininity is a narcissistic "wound" (70); it is a "setback she cannot mourn," since the loss of her dearest object, her first love, mother-love, cannot be represented. The boy in Freud's oedipal narrative represents the relationship to his mother as phallic not only because the phallus refers to that part of his body which is most visibly, tangibly aroused while he entertains incestuous fantasies but also because it is the symbol afforded him by his culture. The little girl in Freud's discourse is doubly disadvantaged; not only can she not see that corresponding part of her which gives her pleasure, but she also cannot symbolize it or come into conscious possession of it through symbolization. The boy can proceed upon the dissolution of his Oedipus complex to represent his repression of incestuous desire as symbolic castration; he can signify his social contract by presenting himself as the possessor or administrator of the law of the phallus/father and by referring or subscribing to the codification of culture and society entirely in patrilinear, patriarchal terms. The girl, however, inherits no "phallic" equivalent; instead, she inherits a gap, a hole in the symbolic, libidinal economy. As Irigaray reads it, the Freudian woman lacks not the phallus/penis but a signifier of her own; the "lack" is not in her but in Freudian representations of femininity and in cultural representations that psychoanalysis un-self-critically reflects (67–71).

H.D.'s cryptobiography figures a little girl whose self-image is mortified. The Child enters the stage of H.D.'s reminiscence at the age of five, the beginning in Freud's oedipal scheme of the latency period after "castration," the time in Freudian girlhood which Irigaray marks as the advent of incurable melancholia. *The Gift* opens onto a grave scene: the memory of a girl who was burned alive in her flammable crinoline (1–2). This memory sparks related memories of a host of dead little girls: Aunt Agnes's "little girl," Hilda's little sister Alice, the Lady's (Papa's first wife's) "little Edith," and Mamalie's Fanny, who was also Mama's little sister: "[Of] Aunt Agnes' children . . . five grew up. There had been a little girl; and in our own plot at Nisky Hill, there was a little girl who was our own sister and another little girl who had been the child of the Lady who had been Papa's first wife. But the girl in the crinoline wasn't a relation, she was just one of the many girls at the seminary . . . and she screamed" (1–2).

Hilda's vision extends from "our own plot" to the town's mortuary ("dead-house") where "one of the [Moravian] Sisters was lying" (5): she sees an extensive, family "plot." Among the dead (g)hosted by

Hilda's girlhood memory, female family members are clearly more numerous. Unlike the dead Civil War soldiers who occupy graves on Nisky Hill, the dead girls and women represent mysterious premature deaths: the figure of the Unknown Sister replaces the Unknown Soldier in this history. "Why was it always a girl who had died?" Hilda wonders. Early death, she suspects, is a fact of her maternal genealogy which she must simply accommodate as part of her female self-image: "I seemed to have inherited that. I was the inheritor . . . . I inherited Fanny from Mama, from Mamalie, if you will, but I inherited Fanny. . . . Why was it always a girl who had died? Why did Alice die and not Alfred? Why did Edith die and not Gilbert? I did not cry because Fanny died, but I had inherited Fanny" (4). Hilda's morbid sense of maternity-femininity at the outset of her childhood reminiscence appears to say what Irigaray says about Freud's account of the dawning of the little girl's sexual self-consciousness: "that *in the beginning was the end of her story*" (43).

But unlike Irigaray's rereading of Freud, which stays rigorously close to the text of "Femininity," H.D.'s autobiographical prose strays into the realm of fiction, including the more speculative medium of Freud's writing on "the uncanny" in creative writing. Whereas Irigaray sees that for the Freudian woman femininity is "a setback she cannot mourn," H.D. sees that for the Freudian autobiographer another world of female fantasy has yet to be researched/remembered. She sees the little girl's "comeback" begin with her discovery of literature, when Hilda beholds Harriet Beecher Stowe's little Eva return from the dead: "Little Eva died . . . we saw her die. It was a stage. . . . this was our first time at the theater. . . . Little Eva died and it was just as if she had died, but then she came back again in a long nightgown. Little Eva was not really dead at all" (14).

H.D. adapts and contests Freud's grave picture of femininity by recasting it as uncanny rather than as lacking. Her work of mourning charts the little girl's rediscovery of her female sexuality, which must first be disinterred from the tomb of maternal memory and then researched in the double light of Moravian mysticism and psychoanalytic theory. The process of re-remembering requires at once both fantasy and critical revision. Literature itself is seen to be her medium of intervention into Freud's story of mortified girlhood; it prompts Hilda's childhood speculation that behind the deaths of so many little girls is a demonic father. "I can not say," Hilda darkly muses,

that a story called *Bluebeard* that Ida read us from one of the fairy tales, actually linked up in thought—how could it?—with our kind father.

There was a man called *Bluebeard,* and he murdered his wives. How was it that Edith and Alice and the Lady (the mother of Alfred and Eric) all belonged to Papa and were there in the graveyard? No, of course, I did not actually put this two-and-two together. . . .

Papa had a black beard. . . . There was a man with a black beard and a dead wife or dead wives and there was Edith and there was Alice and there was the Lady whose name, written on stone, was, Ida told us . . . Martha. The name Martha was written on a stone and Alice was written and Edith. My name was Hilda; Papa found the name. (7–8)

This is, as Hilda sees it, the writing on the wall: her name is next on Papa-Bluebeard's list of victims. Such speculation is in keeping with Freud's view of childhood theorizing as characteristically animistic. But her demonic Bluebeard is also an adaptation of the Sandman, who haunts the fantasy of the boy hero in E. T. A. Hoffman's short story, which Freud regards as an exemplary text of the uncanny (*SE* 17:227–33). For Freud, the figure of the Sandman represents the boy's fear of castration, whereas, for H.D.'s Hilda, Bluebeard represents the little girl's fear of paternal gynocide.

The child recalls Hilda to a diabolical plot; but what the child attributes to a mythic Bluebeard, the adult realistically attributes to patriarchal suppression. Hilda fears not castration but paternal intervention that effectively cuts her off from her mothers' whole story, so that a significant part of herself remains forever missing. Hers is a fear of being silenced and suppressed like the wife (or wives) and the mother (or mothers) who inhabit the father's house as if it were a "dead-house," their song, their passion, having been gravely prohibited (or inhibited). Hilda's fear culminates in the fear of slipping into an unspeakable obscurity like the unnamable "other" little girl and the unknown Lady, Papa's first wife and child.

In response to these fears, Hilda fantasizes a maternal counterplot; she initiates her "comeback" by retelling from memory Mama's half-told story of her secret visit to a fortune teller and of her premarital encounters with a romantic Spanish student. Her retelling stresses Mama's ecstatic or erotic feelings, which had been censored from the original telling with paternal prohibition in mind: "Of course we never told Papa," Mama says to Hilda (23). As raconteur, Hilda exploits childhood memory/fantasy in order to reclaim her mother's story, though it appears as if the child, herself, were the storyteller and setter of the stage. In "Fortune Teller," Mama's untold fantasies are projected by Hilda's telepathic, necromantic memory. Moreover, Mama's morbid self-effacement is rehabilitated in the process. Hilda's remembrance injects a masochistic *jouissance* into Mama's secondary (or moral) masochism, suffered as occupant of a subordinate, feminine position in a patriarchal household and workplace (the seminary Papalie administers). As the familial Mama fades out of the picture, an image of the other woman emerges. Hilda beholds a highly gifted musician with irrepressible, sensual charm:

> When Madame Rinaldo [Mama's singing instructor] singled her out from among all the girls, for the timbre and quality of her rich low-toned contralto voice, she thought it must be another joke; she did not really register the fact at all, that Madame Rinaldo considered her, as it were, a gift from heaven. . . . Mama, of course, did not know that she was beautiful, so when the Spanish Student followed her . . . and caught her in the dark . . . she was not so much surprised as stricken, as if she must explain to the poor boy that he had made a mistake. . . . "Why, Mr. Fernandez,' she might have said, disentangling herself from the wild embraces, '. . . I am—I am the Principal's daughter.' (G2 27–28)

Hilda's symptomatic narrative clearly exposes the paternal origin of Mama's inhibition and the "mortification" of her gift. Mama's sexual self-consciousness is seen as so paternally policed that she is compelled to deny the Spaniard's attraction to her. Aided by Mama's romantic mnemic images of Madame Rinaldo and Mr. Fernandez, Hilda is able to figure (as in prosopopoeia) the vital gift that the puritan father attempts to efface. The clearest depiction of the patriarchal economy is Papalie's channeling of Mama's innate musical abilities into the teaching of Uncle Fred, so that the libidinal energy she could have (re)generated in the cultivation or sublimation of her expressive powers is spent, wasted, and exhausted on the less-gifted son for the sake of upholding a canonical and exclusively masculine musical tradition (G 11–12; G1 76). We see the most wounding blow to Mama's narcissism is delivered when, in a thoughtless outburst, Papalie attacks her singing so that she "never sang any more, not even in church" (G 21).

Mamalie, Hilda rediscovers, has also been silenced by the prohibitions imposed on her gifts, her song which celebrates life with erotic, intoxicating, and irreverent joy, offending the "stricter Brethren." With its "hymns of the spirits in the air—of spirits at sunrise and sunsetting, of the deer and the wild squirrel, the beaver, the otter, the kingfisher, and the hawk and eagle" (87), its passionate delivery at ritual "love feasts," Mamalie's song recalls the love song of Solomon, his Song of Songs, whose intense communication of erotic joy has, according to at least one observer, never been surpassed: "The scent of apples, the laden vines, the flowing milk, the brimming honey and wine; young animals leaping with new life, roe, deer, singing birds, bursting pomegranates, swelling figs, mandrake . . . the imagery of fertility accumulates until the reader is himself spellbound by its sensuality.[9] Marina Warner tells us that Solomon's Song met with opposition from orthodox Jewish fathers in the first century but was translated into allegory by Christian mystics (126). Mamalie's song would seem to derive from this mystic tradition that perhaps goes back as far as the cults of Orpheus-Dionysus. The mothers' musical capacity is a hidden church, a rich, libidinal source of artistic, religious, sensual, and charismatic expression, which has been sealed and buried like an archaeological treasure in the family tomb: "The gift was there," observes Hilda, "but the expression of the gift was somewhere else. It lay buried in the ground" (G 4).

It is this burial, this family plot, and not the plot of castration, which Hilda fears and over which she grieves. But the therapeutic autobiographer projects beyond the symptoms of mourning and melancholia, beyond the exposure of patriarchally conditioned masochism in little girls and women, to a primary, female imagination.

## Girlhood Nightmares or Primary Female Fantasies

A crucial, critical aspect of H.D.'s work of mourning is her narrative re-presentation of Freud's primal fantasy. Through the medium of girlhood reminiscence, H.D. uncovers a vital (re)source of female creativity which has not been suppressed or expropriated by the fathers of the church, the oedipal fathers, or the fathers of the Enlightenment. In chapter 5, "Because One Is Happy," H.D. reconstructs two nightmarish visions of childhood. One is an actual dream and the other a photographic illustration of the "scientific idea" of a nightmare, which, though only a reproduction, is able to conjure demonic images into consciousness from the depths of the unconsious. In both of these nightmare reconstructions, the reader is invited to enter with Hilda into the dark room of girlhood imagination to witness the projection of what we might call the all-powerful mother of prehistory, a grotesque personification of an erotic counterforce projected by H.D.'s desire to dispel the effects of her feminine melancholia.

Hilda's childhood reminiscence reveals that Mama wilfully attempted to censor her daughter's sexual curiosity in complicity with the ruling orthodoxy of the puritanical paterfamilias. But what Mama attempts to cut out of Hilda's actual field of vision leaves a lasting impression: "There was [a] book with a picture; Mama cut it out. Because Mama cut it out, it was there always" (G 50). What is censored from consciousness impresses itself more deeply in the little girl's fantasy, where it links with images in the maternal unconscious, the camera obscura of individual prehistory. Mama literally applies her scissors to a copy of *Simple Science*, excising a photographic illustration titled *Nightmare*, whose features Hilda knows only through a much-revised memory. But the little girl's curiosity persists:

> What I wanted to know was, what was a nightmare, was the nightmare real?
> It was . . . like an old witch . . . on a broomstick, it was a horrible old woman with her hair streaming out and she was riding on a stick, it was a witch on a broomstick. She was going to stick the little girl right through with her long pointed stick and that was what would happen in the night if you went to sleep and had a bad dream . . . a nightmare (51, 59–60).

Hilda's "nightmare" is, in fact, a redoubled re-vision, an adult re-presentation of a childhood memory/fantasy based on a scientific editor's interpretation and reproduction of the "idea" of nightmare, "corrupted" by Mama's radical editing of the text. Her photographic memory is not a "simple science" but is compounded by at least four interventions in the presentation of its real content. Since, as Hilda recalls, *Simple Science* had been given to her as a suitable, school-age replacement for the more "infantile" collection of Grimm's fairy tales which had been her childhood "bible," she was led to regard the former text as the proper truth, a scientific realism replacing "unreal" fantasy.

But childhood reminiscence has its irony. As remembered, the pictorial *Nightmare* from *Simple Science* displays a "witch on a broomstick . . . a horrible old woman . . . riding on a stick . . . straight at the girl who was asleep" (51): science conjures forth an awesome and uncanny spectacle of defloration, complete with witch-incubus, more grim than Grimm, or so Hilda reflects: "It seemed a funny thing to put in the book . . . but the book was science, they said it was to explain real things. Then a witch was real; in Grimm it was a fairy tale but a witch in a book called *Simple Science* . . . must be real" (51). Childhood memory calls paternal as well as scientific "reality" into question since, as Hilda notes, both her father and grandfather were scientists:

"Papa and Papalie were working at real things, called science; the old witch was riding straight at the girl who was asleep" (51). Moreover, this memory subverts Mama's complicity with enlightened, paternal powers by raising girlhood fantasy to the level of preconscious speculation, appalling Hilda with thoughts of virginity, defloration, and the "science" of witchcraft.

Hilda's nightmarish memories are recalled in stages that suggest periods or phases in the speculative sexuality of girlhood. The first nightmare appears in the opening scenes of "Dark Room" with its photographs and daguerreotypes of dead little girls:

> The picture was a girl lying on her back, she was asleep, she might be dead but no . . . she was asleep. She had a white dress on like the dress the baby wore in the photograph Aunt Rosa sent Mama, that Mama tried to hide from us, of Aunt Rosa's baby in a long white dress in a box, lying on a pillow. The baby looked as if she were asleep, the girl in the picture looked as if she were dead, but the baby was dead and the girl was asleep and the picture was called *Nightmare*. (50)

Once again, another dead little girl enters the dark room of Hilda's childhood memory, only this time death is metonymically and homonymically associated with virginity and defloration: Aunt Rosa = Rose = Flower = Aunt Flower = Auntie = Anti-Flower = Defloration = Wound = Death. The full picture of this nightmare is not given until the next chapter when the relationship between Mama and Hilda appears to have changed along with the character of girlhood fantasy; in the later scene, Hilda behaves aggressively toward her censorious mother and, as if in retaliation, recovers a vicious, grotesque, imaginary reproduction of the missing object of conflict:

> I have not forgotten that she has cut out the picture. . . .
>     "Why did you cut it out, Mama?"
>     "Oh—I—I—thought you would forget."
> Listen[10]—it was a picture of—it was a picture of a nightmare. It was a picture of a little girl who was not married, lying on a bed, and a horrible creature that was like an old witch with snarling face, was riding on a stick, like a witch rides on a broomstick. She was going to stick the little girl right through with her long pointed stick and that was what would happen in the night if you went to sleep and had a bad dream which the *Simple Science* . . . calls a nightmare. (59–60)

This grotesque elaboration of the missing picture links unconsciously with a "real" nightmare that Hilda dreams between the time she first sets eyes on the photograph and the time she attempts to fill in the gap left by Mama. This dreamt nightmare is also re-presented in parts or stages, each of which suggests a re-vision of Freudian primal fantasy. Having uncovered in analysis those typical fantasies comprised in the family romance, Freud proceeded to hypothesize the existence of unconscious formations that originate in racial pre-history and hence transcend individual experience. In "The Archaic Features and Infantilism of Dreams" (1916–1917 [1915–1917]), he observes that "the prehistory into which the dream-work leads us back is of two kinds—on the one hand, into the individual's prehistory, his childhood, and on the other, in so far as each individual somehow recapitulates in an abbreviated form the entire development of the human race, into phylogenetic prehistory too" (*SE* 15: 199).

According to Freud, primal fantasies act as collective myths that serve the child's naïve inquiry into the enigmas of sexuality. The fantasies that facilitate this inquiry are thus foundational to the history of the structuring action, the fantasmatic, of the individual's imaginary life as a whole. Hence his term, *primal fantasies*, which he further categorizes into fantasies of the "primal scene" (where parental intercourse, generally interpreted "as an act of violence on the part of the father," according to Laplance and Pontalis [*Language of Psychoanalysis*, 335], is first observed), of "seduction" (where sexual feelings are first aroused), and of "castration" (where the difference between the sexes is revealed).

The first part of H.D.'s reminiscence of the nightmare recalls and revises Freud's primal scene:

> The serpent has great teeth, he crawled on Papa-and-Mama's bed and he was drinking water out of a kitchen tumbler. . . . His great head is as wide as the tumbler but he drinks carefully and does not spill the water. . . . The thing is, there is another snake on the floor, he may want water out of a glass, too; there is nothing very horrible about this until the snake on the floor rears up like a thick terrible length of fire hose around the legs of the bed. Then he strikes at me. (56)

The reminiscence then shifts its focus from the parental bed with its phallic "thing" to a scene from *Arabian Nights* which screens (in a double sense) the dreamer's "castration anxiety": "We spread out the *Arabian Nights* on Mama-and-Papa's bed and I said, 'This is a girl,' but Gilbert [her brother] said, Aladdin was a boy. Was he? He wears a dress, he has long hair in a braid. . . . . Is it only a boy who may rub the wishing-lamp? . . . The snake has sprung at me" (56–57). The final scene of reminiscence is a radically revised fantasy of seduction, featuring a "kiss of death" from a nightmare snake that has taken on prehistoric proportions:

> I shout through the snake-face, that is fastened at the side of my mouth, "Gilbert; Mama, Mama, Mama."
> The snake falls off. His great head, as he falls away, is close to my eyes and his teeth are strong, like the teeth of a horse. He has bitten the side of my mouth. I will never get well, I will die soon of the poison of this horrible snake. (57)

The first scene of this reminiscence allegorizes Freud's description of primal fantasy as a primitive form of sexual theory. The two snakes that figure along with the parental bed suggest the double aspect of Hilda's sexual curiosity: the one with "the great head" who drinks water from a tumbler suggests the child's thirst for knowledge, while the other which coils around the legs of the bed "like a thick terrible length of fire hose" before striking the dreamer, suggests the "organ" of law, a ruling measure of sexual imagination, which puts a damper on her burning wish for forbidden knowledge. When the primal scene fades out a scene of castration comes into view; behind the screen of infantile bibliophilia, the dreamer inquires about Aladdin's gender, about sexual difference and sexual privilege. When she protests against the information offered by her elder brother, that her sex lacks the right to foresee/fulfill destinies, she is violently struck by the "snake." It is then that the nightmare reveals a prehistoric character that exceeds the childhood memory of the individual. It is as if the snake in the dream has poisoned the memory of the narrator with a venomous narcotic so that the nightmare expands:

> The monster has a face like a sick horrible woman; no, it is not a woman. It is a snake-face and the teeth are pointed and foul with slime. The face has touched my face, the teeth have bitten into my mouth. Mary, pray for us. . . . This is the vilest python whom Apollo, the light, slew with his burning arrows.
> This is the python. Can one look into the jaws of the python and live? Can one be stung on the mouth by the python and utter words other than poisonous? Long ago, a girl was called the Pythoness; she was a virgin. (58)

In spite of screen memories and dream censors, a more primal fantasy erupts into narrative consciousness. Behind the veil of classical enlightenment (the dream symbol of Olympian Apollo) there emerges the cult figure of the serpent goddess/priestess, which anthropologists associate with the mantic female mysteries and the orgies of Orpheus and Dionysus.[11] We know from *Tribute to Freud* that Delphic Apollo's pythia and the Cretan serpent goddess had figured in H.D.'s transference dialogue, but *The Gift* would lead us to believe that they originate in her dreams unmediated by acquired archaeological knowledge. Or else they originate in a prior dialogue between herself and her childhood nurse, Ida, whose name triggers a chain of word associations: Ida = Mountain Ida (in Crete) = Cretan serpent goddess = Delphic pythoness = prehistoric Apollo = prehistoric Greece, Hellas = Helle = hell, underworld; or Hellas = Helen = Mother of ontogenetic and phylogenetic prehistory. "This is Ida, this is that mountain, this is Greece, this is Greek, this is Ida; Helen? Helen, Hellas, Helle, Helios, you are too bright . . . you are sitting in the darkened parlor . . . you who are rival to Helios, to Helle, to Phoebus the sun" (57–58).

Attached to the same string of associations which brings the pythoness into consciousness is another figure of prehistory: "I pull at Ida's apron but it is not Ida, it is our much-beloved, later, dark Mary" (57). Hilda had mentioned this "later, dark Mary" earlier, in her description of a picture whose brooding, menacing, iconographic figure occupies the house of scientist fathers as an uncanny spirit: "We were not all alone, there was Mama, there was Ida. . . . On the stair wall were some . . . photographs . . . ; there was a lady too, lying on the ground with a big book open and a skull (like Papa's Indian skull on his bookcase); she was someone in the Bible, Mary-someone in a cave with long hair" (38). Like the pythoness, dark Mary hails from an unrecorded savage or pagan prehistory; she suggests a demonic version of Saint Anne, mother of Mary, who taught the Virgin to read. She is, we gather, a priestess of the maternal mysteries, a pythia in her cave, reading from her sybilline letters.[12]

In the dark room of personal memory, Hilda projects nightmare images that belong to the race that since the advent of so-called classical history, patriarchal culture has attempted to suppress and surmount. She attests to the psychic reality of these reminiscences with the conviction of a scientist who has just discovered a new substance to add to the elemental chart: "It is so real that I would almost say an elemental had been conjured up, that by some unconscious process my dream had left open a door, not to my memories alone, but to memories of the race" (58). Yet, rather than directly redress patriarchal history with her findings, Hilda/H.D. instead chooses the intermediate medium of revision. She re-researches and re-visions Freud's anthropological and archaeological speculations, which are clearly cast in the light of a patriarchal bias.

As dream work that re-presents a primal fantasy of "castration," H.D.'s serpent nightmare reads like a radical re-vision of Freud's view in "Medusa's Head" (1940 [1922]). Here Freud contends that the snakes that replace hair on Medusa's head in many artistic renderings "replace the penis" and that the horror she inspires is none other than the "terror of castration."[13] Like Freud's Medusa, H.D.'s pythia inspires terror, but it is the terror of "virginity" rather than castration. Virginity inspires complex feelings in the girl-dreamer; the nightmare snakes arouse not only the horror of being struck (corresponding to Freud's view of the child's view of the "violence" done to the mother in the primal scene) but also the more deadly, more uncanny horror of being "stung" by the pythoness: "The monster with a face like a sick horrible woman . . . a snake-face." And yet this memory of poisonous horror comes with its own antidote: the figure of "dark Mary, who is enormous and very kind," dispels the mortifying effects of the sting and urges the dreamer to drink a medicinal draught of milk: "I pull at Ida's apron but it is not Ida, it is our much-beloved, later, dark Mary. She looks at the scar on my mouth. How ugly my mouth is with a scar, and the side of my face seems stung to death. But no, 'You are not stung to death,' says dark Mary, who is enormous and very kind. 'You must drink milk,' she says" (57). Dark Mary's imperative signifies the dreamer's unconscious desire to be nursed—but on whose milk, mother Mary's? or, the snake's own milk-venom? Dark Mary's instructions to drink milk might be a cryptic allusion to the ritual practice of the prophetess of the snake goddess: her orgiastic snake-dance invited the bite whose poison was supposed to have induced oracular visions.[14] At a deeper level of the female unconscious, Hilda's nightmare symbolizes a maternal fantasy of the source of the dream itself, of the origin of mantic or charismatic vision—the visionary gift. In another chapter of *The Gift*, Hilda recalls Mama explaining: "*Gift?* That was the German for poison" (*G2* 31).

Hilda's witch-incubus signals further Freudian re-vision. Her nightmare reminiscence of the "horrible old woman . . . who was going to stick the little girl right through with her long pointed stick" recalls Freud's theory in "The Taboo of Virginity" of how "primitive" peoples designate old women to deflower virgins.[15] Freud explains this custom as a result of men's desire to avert the "horror of blood," the "fear of first occurrences," and a "generalized dread of women," especially the danger of woman's fierce hostility following "the first occasion of sexual intercourse" (*SE* 9:198). As he sees it, the first penetration and the rupturing of the hymen is a brutal act of violation that administers an unforgivable injury to the woman's ego (200–208).

To illustrate his explanation, Freud alludes to Ludwig Anzengruber's play *Das Jungferngift* (Virgin's venom), whose title, he observes, "reminds us of the habit of snake-charmers, who make poisonous snakes first bite a piece of cloth in order to handle them afterwards without danger" (206). Freud implies that virgins must be handled like poisonous snakes by prospective snake-charming husbands who are advised to substitute a "piece of cloth" (the old woman's stick) for the virgin to "bite" so that her "venom" (the hostility she feels at being treated so injuriously) is spent elsewhere than on the body of the man into whose possession ("handling") she has come. In a revision of this observation, Hilda's nightmare features a primal fear of virginity which is charmed away by a maternal figure of prehistory. There is no accompanying hostility toward the husband because there is no husband in the girl's primal scene.

H.D.'s girlhood reminiscence redramatizes Freud's dramatic illustration of primitive customs and taboos concerning defloration; her witch-incubus suggests what Freud would explain as an uncanny return of "surmounted," animistic superstition into the child's "primitive," dreaming mind. But Hilda's witch is not seen as performing a ritual defloration for a prospective husband, as recollected by the adult *visuel*:

> "What is a virgin, Mama?"
> "A virgin is—is a—is a girl who isn't married."
> "Am I a virgin, Mama?"
> "Yes, all little girls are virgins."
> All little girls are not virgins. The python took shape. (58–59)

Since Hilda clearly does not derive her understanding of virginity from family education, this "primitive" notion of virginity apparently hails from the dream of an archaic culture that existed before the establishment of patriarchal economics. According to Sir James Frazer,

> The word *parthenos* . . . applied to Artemis, which we commonly translate Virgin, means no more than an unmarried woman, and in early days the two things were by no means the same. . . . there was no public

worship of Artemis the Chaste; so far as her sacred titles bear on the relation of the sexes, they show that, on the contrary, she was, like Diana of Italy, especially concerned with the loss of virginity and with child-bearing. . . . Nothing, however, sets the true character of Artemis as a goddess of fecundity though not of wedlock in a clearer light than her constant identification with the unmarried, but not chaste, Asiatic goddesses of love and fertility, who were worshipped with rites of notorious profligacy at their popular sanctuaries."[16]

Hilda's defiant "all little girls are not virgins" also suggests an understanding of the term *virgin* that hails from the era of the late Middle Ages, when witches were thought to be persons of the female sex who conducted liaisons with the devil. Her virgin is a "witch" demonically possessed: "It is terrible to be a virgin because a virgin has a baby with God" (60). More precisely, she is a virgin-witch, a double figure, oxymoronic and uncanny, charismatic and terrible. A figure of woman's power of horror, Hilda's bewitching incubus is, at once, *heimlich* (the familiar broomstick figure) and *unheimlich* (the unfamiliar pythia). She is the figure of "evil magic" which Hilda at last remembers to invoke in her war zone and which gives her the power to transfigure her surroundings from a scene of devastation into "an orgy of destruction." A talisman of primal female fantasy, she comes to Hilda's rescue at the height of her narcissitic crisis, displacing her self-effacing self-image of frigid passivity and giving her the imaginative strength to reframe her sense of bombardment.

As I read them, H.D.'s nightmare reminiscences stage a subtle protest in the name of the mothers' hidden church, which, though it finds sanctuary in Moravian mysticism, hails from as far back as matriarchal prehistory. She aims her protest at the orthodox fathers of cultural as well as familial history, at the fathers of the Inquisition and the Enlightenment, as well as at the oedipal fathers of the paterfamilias. Perhaps she found support in Ernest Jones's study *On the Nightmare*, which contends that the specifically feminine, masochistic content of nightmares had its origins in the morbid misogyny of the orthodox church:

> . . . repression of the feminine, masochistic component of the sexual instinct rather than that of the masculine is apt to engender the typical Nightmare. . . .
> . . . *the Witch belief represents in the main an exteriorization of the repressed sexual conflicts of women, especially those relating to the feminine counterpart of the infantile Oedipus situation.*

Probably all religions, and notably the Christian religion, represent solutions of the masculine Oedipus complex and are worked out by men with this unconscious end in view, the problems of women being a secondary matter. . . . the conflict between son and father is dealt with by dividing the figure of the latter into two, God the good father and the Devil the bad father. To diminish this conflict as far as possible it was important to diminish the significance of feminine charms and desires. The one thing that would be more intolerable than anything else would be indications of sexual desires on the part of women and . . . this is what fornication with the Devil really represented. . . . The behaviour of the Church in ascribing all manner of unworthy traits to women, and even debating whether she had a soul at all or was merely a beast, was without question due to its degrading attitude toward sexuality in general . . . a manifestation of a morbid misogynous revulsion produced by extreme repression.[17]

H.D.'s "nightmare" represents the attempt of a single author to confront the history of woman's sexual suppression by subverting, in fantasy and imagination, prohibitive, canonical configurations of femininity (virginity) with heretical visions of maternal prehistory.

Her subliminal protest against the church fathers also extends to the father of psychoanalysis, who, in "Femininity," debates whether or not woman has a sex (a sexual psyche, soul) and draws his con- clusion "in conformity" with "convention" and with "Nature": "It would not be surprising if it were to turn out that each sexuality had its own special libido appropriated to it. . . . But nothing of the kind is true. There is only one libido [and] . . . following the conventional equation of activity and masculinity, we are inclined to describe it as masculine" (SE 22:131).

How then, do these nightmare narratives contribute to a work of mourning? First, by doubling the signifying potential of the master symbol of her dream (the snake or python), H.D.'s girlhood fantasy deconstructs the Freudian convention of representing two sexualities through one phallic sign. To the one phallic "thing" H.D. adds a mantic signifier associated with a primary, female imaginary. To determine whether H.D.'s innovative semiotics is genuinely rehabili- tative or, rather, symptomatically advanced, I recall Irigaray's diag- nosis of Freudian femininity:

The little girl has then no *consciousness* of her sexual impulses, of her libidinal economy and, more particularly, of her original desire and her desire for origin. In more ways than one, it is really a question for her of a "loss" that radically escapes any representation. Whence the impossibility of "mourning" it. . . . The non-symbolization of her desire for origin, of her relationship to her mother, and of her libido acts as a constant appeal to polymorphic regressions (be they melancholic, maniacal, schizophrenic, paranoiac . . . ). She functions as a *hole* . . . in the elaboration of imaginary and symbolic processes. But this fault, this deficiency, this "hole," inevitably affords woman too few figurations, images, or representations by which to represent herself. It is not that she lacks some "master signifier" or that none is imposed upon her, but rather that access to a signifying economy, to the coining of signifiers, is difficult or even impossible for her because she remains an outsider, herself (a) subject to their norms. (68–71)

Though uncannily doubled, H.D.'s phallic signifier is a figure of undecidable efficacy, signaling at once a woman's escape from a patriarchal assignment to the unsignifiable gap of femininity *and* entrapment in regressive fantasy, however maniacal. That H.D. reads the signs of her dreams as transcendentally healing is implied in her symbol of the double snake, the symbol of the Hippocratic seal.

Hilda's nightmare re-visions punctuate and puncture the narrative of childhood reminiscence like a wound, but it is a wound that is seen to shatter the boundaries of identity, to expand rather than compromise the little girl's/woman's narcissism. The narrating "I" sinks into the abyss, the "hell-hole" or "snake-pit" opened up by fantasy, abandoning self-possession to the demon of dreams, the "python" and his deadly "animism." H.D. stagecrafts her autobiographical fantasy to cast the illusion that it is the narrator, herself, who drinks the narcotic venom of girlhood dreams and who thereby relinquishes authorial mastery to unconscious memory, submerging her writer's ego in a deeper, expanding range of vision.

And clearly it is a healing vision this narrative narcosis proceeds to induce. The end of "Because One Is Happy" stages a therapeutic mise en scène that transposes the child-dreamer from the dark room of morbid self-reflection into the pythia's nightmare cave, where she is encouraged to take a draught of the serpent's bitter venom. The effect is one of blissful transport; the reminiscing "I" is carried from nightmarish darkness out into the daydream of ecstatic reverie under the brilliant light of a summer's day, and from closed, dark interiors to the wild out-of-doors, to a lake in a wood abundantly alive with small animals (67–72). Signifying the return of animism and totemism in childhood, the reminiscence that follows Hilda's nightmare memories illustrates how the pythia mediates a vital recovery of her capacity for self-projection.

In striking contrast to the demon psychosis, which, according to Freud, haunts and eventually destroys the overwrought hero of E. T. A. Hoffmann's "Sandman," H.D.'s narcotic nightmare represents a healing form of delusional fantasy.[18] Her efficacious nightmare might also be read as a striking contrast to the Wolf Man's fantasy-phobia, which Freud attributes to unresolved castration anxiety derived from his originary vision of the primal scene.[19] Dark Mary's cure is the unlikely treatment of unpleasure with a greater unpleasure; the poison-medicine of self-dissolution brought on by fantasies of primary feminine masochism. Hilda's dreams inflict a far greater injury to the ego than that entertained by Freud's boy-heroes, but in the end they afford a greater pleasure and a greater capacity to endure trauma.

The final scene of "Because One Is Happy" may be read as a fantasy of sexual fulfillment; the dominant figure of this passage dilation, expanding and deepening conscious arousal toward an outer world of boundless life and toward an inner, animating eros. In this scene, Hilda is located in a boat on a lake that she scans for its fabulous and mysterious white water lily (71–72). It is perhaps a recasting of the sublime setting of Mallarmé's prose poem "The White Water-Lily," if not of the lake setting of the "Fifth Walk" of Rousseau's *Reveries*. The scene draws to a climax when Hilda's boat finally contacts her subliminal object of desire, the submerged "white rose." Following the outline of the flower into its watery depths, her gaze is seen to dilate, encompassing the whole psychic field while displacing and diffusing her focus. What she sees instead of the object itself is an image of her own scope of erotic fantasy and of her inherent capacity to recall mystic depths beyond the surface of consciousness. A limpid allusion to Narcissus, the child's submerged water lily signals the unconscious recovery of her maternal inheritance, of Mamalie's black rose of joy and despair:

> Then I saw what it was we had come to see. It spread back and it was bigger than a white rose. . . . not just one water lily there on the water. . . .
>     They were not at first there, but as the boat turned round and shoved against the bulrushes and then the bulrushes got thinner and you could see through them . . . you saw what was there, you knew that something was reminded of something. That something remembered something. (71–72)

Like Narcissus, the child Hilda gazes into the pool that reflects her own (sexual) self-image; but she does not see the Medusa's head that, according to Freud, the boy sees when he gazes upon the body of a woman. Instead, she sees a watery, multifoliate rose that "poisons" any mnemic trace of phallic imagination and drowns her mortal fear in a wave of ego-dissolving bliss.

### Uncanny Fanny—*Mise en Abyme*

Freud exploits autobiography as a medium for his speculations about "distressing experiences" and their "mastery." By juxtaposing *The Gift* to those passages in which Freud employs autobiographical narrative in the theorization of the death drive, I can show more clearly how H.D.'s autobiographical narrative adapts and revises Freud's literary innovations to perform a woman's work of mourning. Two passages in particular come to mind: the short essay "A Childhood Recollection from *Dictung und Wahrheit*" and the much-celebrated *fort:da* passage of *Beyond the Pleasure Principle*—both of which entertain narrative speculations on early boyhood's sadistic mastery of severe disappointment.

Between "A Childhood Recollection" and *Beyond the Pleasure Principle*, Freud wrote "The Uncanny," in which he reveals a desire to possess the artist's control over "the uncanny in life" and particularly in our deeply ambivalent relation to death.[20] If mastery over death in art and theory is the implicit desire of Freud's narrative, then how does the literary artist H.D. adapt Freudian narrative to represent woman's relation to death, her "mastery" of the uncanny, and of her melancholia, without inscribing or subscribing to his desire? How does H.D.'s autobiographical re-vision intervene in Freud's representation of the masculine desire to master death or to master the uncanny feminine in life?

In "A Childhood Recollection," Freud juxtaposes the death work of the mother to the death wish of the son (Goethe), the artist-to-be. Freud notes that Goethe records only two recollections of early childhood. The first, which Freud does not pursue, is Goethe's uncanny memory of having been born "as though dead" and of having been brought back to life "only after great efforts" (*SE* 17:147). The second recalls a scene of destruction, wherein Goethe, then a little boy, takes extreme delight in hurling and smashing the household crockery. It is not the joy afforded by destruction which intrigues Freud but that the event should have remained intact in memory for so long and that Goethe should have used it to open his autobiography. "A mischievous trick, with damaging effects on the household economy, carried out under the spur of outside encouragement, is," he muses, "certainly no fitting headpiece for all that Goethe has to tell us of his richly filled life" (149).

Freud treats this recollection as a screen memory, behind which he discovers the "cause" of this violent outburst: the birth of a sibling and the shattering loss of the unrivaled possession of his mother's love. In response to this "narcissistic injury," the boy retaliates, Freud tells us, by hurling and shattering the housewares—"a symbolic action, or, to put it more correctly, a *magic* action, by which the child . . . gave violent expression to his wish to get rid of a disturbing intruder" (152). To reinforce his telling of the "true story" behind the screen, Freud relates another story, drawn from psychoanalytic experience, which tells of a boy ("little Erich") who reacts to his mother's pregnancy by hurling housewares out the window and threatening to assault the maternal body (154). As Freud retells it, this event of Goethe's boyhood is a display of infantile sadism which compensates for his narcissistic injury and prepares the injured party emotionally for the death of the same sibling he had wished away. "*Goethe . . . as a little boy,*" Freud underlines, "*saw a younger brother die without regret*" (151).

Freud proposes the hypothesis that infantile sadism is a primitive form of mastery over life's—that is, over maternity's—unforeseen events. Concerned to supply us with a reading of a recollection that could hardly serve as a fitting headpiece for the life story of a great artist, he neglects to explain that this sadism is primarily aimed at the mother—the mother who gave him such a difficult birth, who introduced another baby onto the scene, depriving him of his "exclusive possession" of her and thereby rupturing the insular, imaginary world of his "primary pleasure-ego": in short, the uncanny, "duplicitous" mother who gives life and love and then threatens to withdraw them. Freud's silence on the subject of the (boy's) sadistic mastery of "uncanny" maternity implies his approval of the severe taboos placed on woman's sexuality by patriarchal civilization described elsewhere in "The Taboo of Virginity" and *Civilization and Its Discontents*.

In another autobiographical study, the *fort:da* passage of *Beyond the Pleasure Principle* (SE 18:14–17), Freud narrates the story of how his grandson, Ernst, invented a game of "departure/return" to symbolize and thereby master the otherwise distressing situation of his mother's "going away." The game, Freud recollects, involved a reel of string that Ernst flung out of sight before pulling it back. The first part of this game, the flinging away, signifying departure, was accompanied by the child's interjection, *fort!* "gone" and the second, the reeling it back in, signifying return, by *da!* "there". To Freud's mind, the game marks a breakthrough, the infantile equivalent of a cultural achievement, the staging of a play that sees the child take control of his circumstances, transforming his helpless passivity into masterful activity. But while he undoubtedly affords himself great delight, the boy does not necessarily, Freud speculates, perform this mastering action in the service of the pleasure principle. Such action, he speculates, could be the aggressive expression of an altogether different order, the death drive:

> At the outset he was in a *passive* situation—he was overpowered by the experience; but, by repeating it, unpleasurable though it was, as a game, he took on an *active* part. These efforts might be put down to an instinct for mastery that was acting independently of whether the memory was in itself pleasurable or not. . . . Throwing away the object so that it was "gone" might satisfy an impulse of the child's, which was suppressed in his actual life, to revenge himself on his mother for going away from him. In that case it would have a defiant meaning: "All right, then, go away! I don't need you. I'm sending you away myself." (16)[21]

The *fort:da* passage recalls Freud's account of Goethe's childhood reminiscence with its mischievous enactment of sadistic fantasy, a play that enables the boy to master not only his immediate situation but also distressing situations of the future: the boy, Goethe, Freud observes, goes on to see "a younger brother die without regret." Similarly, a footnote to the *fort:da* passage adds that, "when this child [Ernst] was five and three-quarters, his mother died. Now that she was really 'gone,' the little boy showed no signs of grief" (16).

Before comparing these passages with H.D.'s autobiographical exploration of the little girl's response to death and other distressing situations, I should like to relate what Freud says here about the boy's cultural achievement—his translation of passivity into activity, his mastering of his mother's "turning away from him" by symbolically throwing her away—to what he says in "Female Sexuality" about the girl's turning away from the mother in her preoedipal crisis. In response to her discovery of her own and her mother's "castration," the little girl, Freud contends, turns away in dark despair without attempting to compensate for the narcissistic injury sustained. Far from being an act of masterful retaliation and self-possession, this turning away marks a turning point in the little girl's/woman's life history which she will never re-turn. Unlike the little boy who overcomes his woundedness by sadistic, symbolic action, the little girl is said to magnify her loss by repressing her active sexual trends even to the point of inflicting permanent injury (frigidity): "The turning-away from her mother is an extremely important step in the course of a little girl's development. . . . there is to be observed a marked lowering of the active sexual impulses and a rise of the passive ones. . . . often enough when the small girl represses her previous masculinity a considerable portion of her sexual trends in general is permanently injured too."[22]

How, then, does H.D.'s autobiography adapt and revise this fatal story of feminization? Like Goethe's, H.D.'s first childhood recollections open onto a grave, uncanny scene. Her first self-image is negative, ghostly. She recalls having been born not "as though dead" but as though among many dead little girls and the maternal shades of her mother and grandmother. Even in her infancy, Hilda knew her mothers as women, ominously repressed, robbed of their vital gift of sexual self-expression.

Whereas the speculating psychobiographer of "A Childhood Recollection" and *Beyond the Pleasure Principle* seems to identify with the boy subject who ingeniously triumphs over the injury unwittingly inflicted by his mother, the author of *The Gift* identifies, instead, with the mother and the grandmother, with their mortal loss of a little girl. Jacques Derrida perceptively traces the autobiographical desire mobilizing the *fort/da* passage:

> *Beyond [the Pleasure Principle]* . . . writes autobiography . . . . the word *beyond* . . . imprints a prescription upon the *fort:da*, that of the overlapping by means of which proximity distances itself in *abyme* . . . .
> [Freud] recalls to himself that Ernst recalls (to himself) his mother: he recalls Sophie. He recalls to himself that Ernst recalls his daughter to himself in recalling his mother to himself. . . . [Freud] recalls that Sophie is dead: the daughter (mother) recalled by the child died soon after. . . . This cadence might lead one to believe that a dead woman is more easily preserved. . . . Sophie, then, daughter there, mother here, is dead, taken from and returned to every "exclusive possession." Freud can have the desire to recall (her) (to himself) and to undertake all the necessary work for her mourning. In order to speak of this one could mobilize the entire analysis of *Mourning and Melancholia*. ("Freud's Legacy," 322–27)

In her adaptation of Freud's autobiographical *mise en abyme*, the reminiscing Hilda identifies with the dead little girl whose life (story) has been prematurely cut off.

Hilda identifies with Fanny, Mamalie's dead little girl and Mama's dead little sister, whose story has become a taboo subject. When spoken, the name Fanny prompts frigid silence in Mamalie, automatic weeping in Mama, and a synthesis of the two in Hilda: "Mamalie did not seem to think of Fanny. . . . Mama cried (although I had seldom seen her cry) because Fanny died, so Mama had cried. I did not cry. The crying was frozen in me" (3–4). Fanny signifies a narcissistic wound, not one that has been inflicted by the intrusion of a new brother onto the scene of a perfectly happy, anaclitic relationship such as the one Freud supposes to have existed between the boy, Goethe, and his mothers (mother and grandmother) but one that has been inflicted by the vacancy of little girls—"sisters"—in the haunted house of unaccommodating (matricidal? infanticidal?) fathers. To Hilda, Fanny signifies a gap in the generation of feeling between mothers and daughters, a void in her own self-definition, a dead end to her autobiography for which the only explanation, it first appears, is a mystifying fatalism:

> Why was it always a girl who had died? . . . there was Alice—my own half-sister, Edith—my own sister, and I was the third of this trio, these three Fates, or maybe Fanny was the third. The gift was there, but the expression of the gift was somewhere else
> It lay buried in the ground . . . in the old graveyard. (4)[23]

But like the crockery-shattering scene in Freud's account of Goethe's childhood memory, the Fanny scenario in H.D.'s reminiscence is a screen memory for another, darker story. Fanny signifies more than the loss of Mamalie's little girl: a cultural, as well as familial, "plot," the mortification of girlhood, and the taboo of female sexuality. Fanny represents what is lost, effaced, expropriated, and repressed of Hilda's maternal genealogy, what Mama excises with her scissors as she carries on the tradition of female self-censorship and ex-matriation. Mamalie loses her ability to feel for Fanny; Hilda loses her expression of Fanny-feelings. As Hilda (later) sees it, the mothers submit to the pressures of civilization and perform a *grave* operation, the affective equivalent of a clitoridectomy, a taboo operation that can be neither named nor made comprehensible to the little girl/woman whose sexual normalization is at stake.

Also like Freud's (auto)biographical speculations, H.D.'s autofantasy stages a comeback, a return after the departure and the injury to one's ego: "Was I indeed Frances come back?" The critical passage from "Femininity" which relates the psychological process by which the little girl's "self-love is mortified" (*SE* 22:126) is, it seems to me, the grim subject of H.D.'s radical revision. The double definition of *fanny* supplied by *The Collins English Dictionary* helps reveal the critical play between these two passages: "Taboo. . . . the female pudendum" or "pet name for Frances." The pun on the word *fanny* is a display of the wish-fulfilling fantasy behind H.D.'s autobiographical restaging of the little girl's/woman's sexual history. She would have "Fanny" back, brought home, returned, made *heimlich* after having, through severe repression, been made unfamiliar, homely, *unheimlich*, mortifying. In her dream of Fanny's return, Hilda would see Fanny returned to Frances, to her proper name, a translation from the diminutive (fanny = female pudendum = clitoris = little penis). She would see Fanny returned to her proper name, just as she would see her property, her inheritance of the gift, restored. As Fanny come back, as Frances, Hilda would retrieve her buried treasure from the grave and thus repossess that of which she had been disinherited.

I read this Fanny passage not just as a mise-en-scène[24] but also as a *mise en abyme*, a staging of a scene of recovery which reflects the staging of the work of mourning performed over the course of the narrative as a whole. I also read it as a *mise en abîme*, as a recovery of female sexuality and expressivity out of the abyss of cultural and discursive (non)representation afforded women and out of the abysmal story Freud tells of the little girl's/woman's oedipalization.

"Fanny" is also a one-act play performed by the mothers before the speculating audience of child-dreamer and the reminiscing adult, Hilda/H.D. Like Freud's Goethe and Freud's grandson, the mothers invent a play or a game that allows them to symbolize a distressing situation (the loss of Fanny) and thereby overcome it. They do not, however, employ the same sadistic processes of self-mastery Freud's little boy is seen to enact. The mothers do not undertake to master disturbing thoughts by enacting in play a fantasy of destroying the wounding object, in other words, by performing a symbolic display of self-reassuring (omni)potency; instead, they dispel disturbing thoughts by engaging in a communal joke at the expense of the wounded ego.

In the beginning, the mothers find the pronunciation of Fanny's name to be painful, but over time and after countless repetitions of their one-act play, Fanny's name becomes the cue to pleasure, even mirth. Initiated before Hilda was born, this play consists of a curious exchange between Mama and Mamalie. Upon hearing Fanny's name, Mama would cry; Mamalie, who was not so easily moved, would then ask Mama why she was crying; Mama would say it was because Fanny died. Mamalie thinks it "funny" (odd, strange) that Mama should weep for a sister she was too young to know; Hilda thinks it "funny" (odd, strange) that Mamalie should not mourn the death of her own little girl. Over the years, as this "dialogue" is played and replayed, "Fanny" becomes a laughing matter, even though her memory surfaces whenever the family makes its visit to the graveyard:

> And then there was Fanny, difficult to find in the crowded plot where Mamalie's and Aunt Agnes' other children were. There was Elizabeth Caroline for instance. . . . But Fanny, among them all, had become a myth; she was a family by-word. "Why so sad, Helen?" Mamalie might say. Then Mama would answer, perhaps too suddenly, too swiftly, forcing the expected "Mimmie, of course, you know why. I'm crying because Fanny died." And they would both laugh. (3–4)

As in Freud's staging of the game of departure/return, the mothers repeat an act that is unpleasurable or only eventually pleasing, and is thus indicative of a primary aggression, of an impulse to injure the injury. In H.D.'s staging of the game, however, what the mothers "throw away" is not a symbolic representation of the injuring object but a symbolic representation of the wounded, maternal subject: once a signifier of maternal (re)production and loss, Fanny becomes a laughing mat(t)er. The mothers display a painfully pleasurable capacity for coping with mortal injury. That is, they find a formula to resolve a problem in the economics of libido. To restore the loss of psychic property, they invest a substantial portion of their remaining resources in feminine masochism, a primary masochism that rediscovers pleasure in pain and that affords a "hypercathexis" necessary to accomplish the work of mourning (this hypercathexis being a rebonding of libidinal energy released in the affective detachment from the lost love object onto the ludic byword "Fanny" has become).

Hilda's recollection of the mothers' play also reads like an allegorical restaging of the "first stage" in the psychogenesis of jokes, with its primary emphasis on repetition and the rediscovery of the familiar. "Play," Freud writes in *Jokes and Their Relation to the Unconscious*, "appears in children while they are learning to make use of words and to put thoughts together. This play probably obeys one of the instincts which compel children to practise their capacities. . . . In doing so they come across pleasurable effects, which arise from a repetition of what is similar, a rediscovery of what is familiar . . . and which are to be explained as unsuspected economies in psychical expenditure."[25] Freud takes up this theme of repetition in the *fort:da* passage, where he implicitly ascribes the play instinct to the death instinct and where he discloses the "unsuspected [libidinal] economy" as sadistic. In H.D.'s narrative, the mothers are seen to repeat their scene of mourning (and mutual misunderstanding) until the original meaning of Fanny's death is rendered nonsensical and excessively "funny." Pleasure is released with the destruction of thoughts and feelings of reverence, propriety, any sense of the proper or personal, in short, with the destruction of any binding allegiance to the father, in whose name the family is registered, the children are enumerated, their losses and gifts accredited.

From the ludic perspective, the mother's play is therapeutic. It seems to the child-joker that the mothers stage an elaborate pun, translating the unfamiliar and estranged "Fanny" into a canny, "family by-word." In the eyes of the adult artist, the mothers prompt a change of mood, transforming morbidity into hilarity, somber sobriety into intoxicating high spirits, and division into communion: "they would both laugh." In making an analogy between the efficacy of jokes and drugs, Freud contends that "a change in mood is the most precious thing that alcohol achieves for mankind, and on that account this 'poison' is not equally indispensable for everyone. A cheerful mood, whether it is produced endogenously or toxically, reduces the inhibiting forces, criticism among them, and makes accessible once again sources of pleasure which were under the weight of suppression" (*SE* 8:127). The staging of uncanny Fanny momentarily displaces a history of suppressive, patriarchal criticism; it also dis-plays women's production of pleasure at the expense of self-interest and even self-loss. Against grave, narcissistic injury, laughter is seen to be the "best medicine," or the best "poison," the "gift" of a maternal counterplot to transcend mortal fear.

## Mo(u)rning Star

H.D.'s work of mourning is accomplished when the first, uncanny recollection of "the girl who was burnt to death" is finally "brought home" (made *heimlich*) in the last chapter, following a break in the narrative which signifies the crying frozen in Hilda for nearly forty-five years.[26] Between "Morning Star" and "What It Was," there is an ellipsis that separates childhood reminiscence from middle-aged reality and from the healing revelation that throws a new light on the preceding narrative. In place of symptoms of affective anesthesia and mortified self-love, H.D. presents signs of a triumphant recovery. Projections of a morbid self-image onto images of mortified little girls are transfigured by an epiphanic memory of the Wunden Eiland initiates, of their burning passion.

The image of the burning girl with which H.D. opens her childhood recollection gathers emblematic, if not prophetic, significance by the end of the narrative. In "A Childhood Recollection from *Dichtung und Wahrheit*," Freud writes that "in every psycho-analytic investigation of a life-history . . . it usually happens that the very recollection to which the patient gives precedence, which he relates first, with which he introduces the story of his life, proves to be the most important, the very one that holds the key to the secret pages of his mind" (*SE* 17:149). Having said this, Freud curiously neglects Goethe's very first recollection of being born "as though dead," overlooking a theme he treats extensively in his essay on the uncanny—namely, the theme of being buried alive, the infantile fantasy of intrauterine existence. That Freud does not concern himself with the significance of this recollection contradicts his own biographical imperative to explain "the meaning of the earliest childhood memories" by analyzing the one "the patient . . . relates first" (149) and furthermore reflects his failure to explain the uncanny. He chooses to bypass this apparently unaccountable first memory and to subject the second one instead to speculative analysis. This second event (of crockery smashing), is made accountable as a scene of sadistic mastery; as a boy Goethe learns to overcome the trauma of narcissistic injury by a symbolic enactment of a fantasy of destruction. Conversely, H.D.'s narrative shows that it is not egoistic aggression that best serves the subject in its attempt to accommodate the traumatic flux of life, death, and love but, rather, an expansion of the ego, through fantasy and imagination, so that this flux may be absorbed by a less-centered, less-individuated or alienated self-image. This is what she relearns through her mothers: the therapeutic efficacy of masochistic *jouissance*.

Working through her childhood recollections, Hilda acquires an "uncanny familiarity" with the wisdom of the dead, which has a beneficial retroactive effect on those first, initiating memories. Consider the memory of the burning girl. At first, this catastrophic female figure bears no other relation to Hilda's self-sense than the perception of early mortality shared by numerous little girls in her family:

"The girl in the crinoline wasn't a relation, she was just one of the many girls at the seminary" (2). By the end of the story, she commands attention as something mysteriously akin to the burning, charismatic figure that dominates Mamalie's memory.

Rachel Blau DuPlessis suggests that H. D.'s fire images might themselves be read as figurative applications of the gift, a duplicitous, feminine treatment, at once medicinal and poisononous, of memory's morbid and melancholic character:

> Burning is the most ambiguous and potent recurrent image [in *The Gift*]; from the stunning opening recalling a young girl, caught aflame in her own crinolines, burning to death at her grandfather's seminary, burning is often . . . associated with the vunerability and preciousness of girls as symbols of life and sacrifices to it. . . . Mamalie's whispered vision exposing the child to a rich mystical heritage is illuminated by a shadowy small candle floating in water. The child's monumental fear that a shooting star will fall on their family in fact predicts the terrors of war that occasioned this work. Fire tempers, tests, illuminates; it consumes, tortures, destroys. This work is, then, fire to fight fire: female fire, poet's fire, fires of outcasts, fires of vision to counter Blitz fires and the explosions of war.[27]

To pursue this burning figure a little farther: Hilda's discovery of Mamalie's rediscovery of the untold story of the Wunden Eiland initiates recovers the memory of Anna von Pahlen. It was she who inspired the birth of the hidden church, offering herself to the Indians in exchange for Morning Star, who gave herself to the Moravians in a ritual ceremony of peace (88, 99).[28] By the end of Hilda's reminiscence, the epiphanic image of Anna–Morning Star burning ecstatically in the circle of flaming huts is superimposed on the image of the girl who was burned to death in the flaming hoop of her crinoline. Re-projected in the mystic light of Hilda's inherited dark room of memory, the opening recollection loses its horrifying morbidness. It is not death that ultimately figures here but the death of "mortified self-love" in the all-consuming flames of a communal passion. The burning figure arises in memory to blast through the erotic anesthesia and maternal amnesia that marked the end of girlhood, at the same time subverting the frigid figure that emblematizes Freud's story of the little girl's "feminization."

Anna–Morning Star signifies the late arrival/return of a figure, image, or mnemonic trace of the value of woman's eros outside a patriarchal or capitalist economy. She is an expression of the value of the gift that "lay buried in the ground" with dead girls and women. The true worth of her gift is to be appreciated only in other, "older countries," with "altars [on which] flowers had lain, wild pansies, mountain laurel, roses" (4), where defloration is understood not as an irreparable wound or an inconsolable loss of self-love but as a ritual passage, an opening into a communal ego or libido, where death is understood not solely in terms of individual mortality but as an individual's participation in the "seasonal," cosmic play of life and death. Morning Star signifies the imaginary return of a ritual frame of reference, of a form of mourning which celebrates death as a power of eros.

The recovery of the memory of Anna–Morning Star emblematizes the recovery of woman. She represents the resurgence of an "older world," whose gift economy and whose communion rites reflect a primary, feminine masochism—in other words, an other order that recognizes and values what women recognize and value as the basis of human community. She also represents a real historical possibility. That she, Anna–Morning Star, was an acutal historical personage and not just a mythical pythoness or witch, that she was once an actual prophetess-princess and is an actual ancestress, reinforces H.D.'s autobiographical fantasy with material reality. As Irigaray observes, mysticism is the only place in the history of the West in which woman speaks and acts so publicly (*Speculum*, 191).

Hilda's rediscovery of her ancestral power of mystical self-expression is preceded by her rediscovery of her inherited power of musical expression. Both gifts derive from a primary maternal fantasy, as can be seen in "The Secret" and at the climactic end of the final chapter, where the adult Hilda explicitly equates the mystical and the musical. In the "Notes" to "Dark Room," H.D. explains:

> Jedediah's [Mamalie's father's] mighty bass and the "surge and thunder" of his trombone had not stilled in her a delicate Celtic lyric that ran alongside the mighty torrent of German classic tradition.
>
> It had threaded its way into her heart and into mine; it was an unspoken tradition, breathless, almost voiceless; this was something we understood together and perhaps we two only. If Jedediah gave Uncle Fred the whole ocean of musical-consciousness called Haydn or called Bach, well, it was something over which we had no control, we could not argue about it. . . . But . . . this song did make a furrow or runnel in my emotional or spiritual being that later let through a stream-of-consciousness that, in retrospect, is more precious to me than the St. Matthew Passion and the Mass in B Minor. For it was my own interpretation of the *Gift*. (*G1* 76)

This genealogical re-vision subverts the classical patrilineal picture of the transmission and cultivation of hereditary gifts. Moreover, it undermines the dominant phallomorphic figure of cultural achievement. Jedediah's booming trumpet does not stifle Mama's delicate lyric; the song of her hidden church prevails, though not so perceptibly as her father's "canon." It is the heterodox "passion" of her Celtic twilight and not the "surge and thunder" of his *Sturm und Drang* tradition which Hilda hears and transposes into her lyrical stream of consciousness. Mamalie reaches her grandaughter through female passages ("this song did make a furrow or a runnel in my emotional or spiritual being"); she pierces Hilda to her "core" of feeling, not like a witch with a pointed stick but like an Orphic mystic with an enchanted song, tunneling through the canals of the uncanny ear and opening channels to the sea of unconscious memory.

Anna, however, does not chant a Celtic lyric in the climactic last pages of *The Gift*; she jubilantly wails a "litany of the wounds":

> Wound of Christ,
> Wound of God,
> Wound of Beauty,
> Wound of Blessing,
> Wound of Poverty,
> Wound of Peace.
>                    (G 141)

With her "gifted" vision Hilda "hears" a "great choir of . . . voices" above the harrowing sirens, crashing walls, and exploding bombs; she hears "strange voices that speak in a . . . staccato rhythm" and in "Indian dialects" she does not understand (142). This is song that uncannily transcends the logocentrism of words, breaking the sound barriers of national languages and dissolving ethnic as well as personal enmities. She hears a more primal, maternal lingua franca, which, like the poison-medicine of jokes, shatters the inhibitory, paranoiac self, affording a primitive, regressive sensation of communion-consummation.[29]

The figure of repetition, which is foregrounded in this litany, is a crucial component of the figure of masochistic *jouissance* which dominates the tropological character of *The Gift*. Repetition is one of the formal means that H.D. uses to transfigure the negative photographic images of girls and women which dominate the opening pages into a vitalistic, acoustic image: primal drumbeats, or hoofbeats, since the image of "Philippus, Lover-of-horses" (142), the Moravian Hippo-crates (from the Greek *hippos*, "horse") is the final, triumphant figure to arise from the wave of Hilda's climactic epiphany. What might otherwise horrify the phallogocentric reading eye, whose focus is trained on the heroic ego, may also, through a transfer of textual attention, caress and arouse the lyrical ear that is attuned to cosmic rhythms. I read the opening paragraphs, in light of these last pages, as a victory of H.D.'s uncanny ear over the conventional, specularizing eye:

> There was a girl who was burnt to death. . . . the girl who was burnt to death, was burnt to death in a crinoline. . . . the girl's . . . ribbons caught fire and she was in a great hoop.
> The other girls stand round. . . . There had been a little girl. . . . there was a little girl . . . and another little girl. . . . But the girl in the crinoline . . . was just one of the many girls . . . and she screamed and Papalie rushed . . . and Papalie wrapped . . . but she is shrieking . . . because of the hoop. (1–2)

The sounding of the mothers in this last chapter of *The Gift* alerts us to the figure of repetition at work throughout, instructing the reader (how) to rediscover and appreciate the uncanny feminine in H.D.'s charismatic prose.

## Mystic (Re)Vitalism, Freudian Revisionism

Poetism is the medium of mediation between H.D.'s Moravianism and Freudianism. As she put it, "I must have the absolutely pure, mystical Moravian pietism or poetism or hard-boiled Freudian facts" (*Herself Defined*, 9).Through the poetism of *The Gift*, she projects her autobiographical fantasy with therapeutic efficacy, restoring her "vision of power and of peace" (G 135) and affording her the transition from imagistic cameo to prophetic verse: "*The Gift* was assembled before the Sigmund Freud 'Writing,' and during those years, I returned again to poetry," Delia Alton testifies. "*The Walls Do Not Fall* is, in a sense, like certain passages of *The Gift*, runic, divinatory. This is not the 'crystalline' poetry that my early critics would insist on" (DA 192–93). *The Gift* marks an exchange of media, from "crystalline" to "crystal-gazing ball" (G1 70). In the medium of life-writing, the object of perception becomes the object of the visionary: fantasies, reveries, memories—these are what outlive death, what survive the breakup of relationships, what cope with the dissolution of literary circles, and moreover, what neutralize and charm the repercussions of war.

Whether a survival technique, a defense mechanism, a play impulse, a megalomania, "a hidden desire to 'found a new religion,'" or "merely an extension of the artist's mind . . . projected from within" (*TF* 51), H.D.'s critical recovery of "vision" also implies a critical revision of Freud. The spirit with which she animates "Morning Star" and revitalizes a war-weary world view with a prophecy of spiritual renewal also reviews and re-visions the work of the Professor, particularly his writings on eros and civilization.

As H.D. sees it, Count von Zinzendorf's Moravian pietism is a communal sublimation of masochistic *jouissance* or what Freud calls "perverse eroticism" (SE 14:37). Moravian love feasts, passion plays, ecstatic trances, speaking in tongues, burning raptures are represented in *The Gift* as the acting out of erotic fantasies, whose effect is the exploding of individual ego boundaries and the shattering of barriers erected between nations. Those initiates who partake in the ritual of wounds achieve communion with the world spirit, an all-embracing pantheism that sings without words. A cosmic ego, this primitive communalism is devoted to the animism of the muses, in striking contrast to the fascist allegiance to a *Supermensch*, to the father (or fuhrer) of ego idealism.

According to Freud in *Civilization and Its Discontents*, religion fails to offer a realistic program for the human community since, at best, it can only frustrate rather than satisfy basic human instincts. Eros, Freud says, mobilizes human communality by bringing together "single human individuals, and after that families, then races, peoples and nations, into one great unity, the unity of mankind" (*SE* 21:122). But this drive toward community is severely undermined by the "instinct of aggression," or the death drive. This counterdrive is, accordingly, "an original, self-subsisting instinctual disposition in man," best seen in "sadism, where [it] twists the erotic aim in its own sense and yet at the same time fully satisfies the erotic urge" (*SE* 21:121).

The eros of community is further undermined by individual egoism, which, though it pursues "happiness" and the "programme of the pleasure principle," contradicts the communal pursuit of the same through "altruism": "In the process of individual development . . . the main accent falls mostly on the egoistic urge (. . . towards happiness); while the other urge . . . a "cultural" one, is usually content with the role of imposing restrictions. . . . The two processes of individual and of cultural development must stand in hostile opposition to each other" (140–41). Not absolutely pessimistic, Freud proceeds to say that this "is a dispute within the economics of the libido . . . and it does admit of an eventual accommodation" (141). Yet he sees little reason for optimism, noting how very few persons, and even fewer communities, possess the intellectual and artistic gifts to achieve satisfaction through libidinal sublimation (80). In any case, art, he tells us, is nothing but an illusory satisfaction ("a mild narcosis"), religion but a "mass-delusion," and science simply beyond the reach of the majority (81).

H.D. offers a revisionary view of the erotic, artistic, and mystic mobilization of world unity. Her revived memory of the Moravian Brotherhood, of its vision of Unitas Fratrum, projects a cultural form of communion that is clearly employed in the service of eros and bound to the purpose of creating the greatest happiness. The Child observes that Mamalie laughed when she recalled her feeling of becoming "one with the *Wunden Eiland* initiates" and concludes that "she and Christian . . . must have been very happy" (G 86–87).

Freud does not deny that the desire for happiness may be satisfied through religious love, but he believes that such satisfaction is "altruistic" or "aim-inhibited." People who are capable of this sort of satisfaction, Freud speculates "bring about in themselves . . . a state of evenly suspended, steadfast, affectionate feeling, which has little external resemblance . . . to the stormy agitations of genital love, from which it is nevertheless derived" (102). He suggests that Saint Francis of Assisi "went furthest in . . . exploiting love for the benefit of an inner feeling of happiness" in this altruistic sense (102). But Mamalie's "Christian," following Count von Zinzendorf's heresy of ecstasy, went farther than the "stricter Brethren," including "Brother Francis," in his all-consuming pietism and devotional happiness (G 95–97).

If by "perverse" we mean simply "extra-genital satisfactions" (SE 21:104), then H.D.'s fantasy of ecstasy is indeed a form of "perverse eroticism": it is closer to the body, less sublimated than the satisfaction brought about by intellectual abstraction. But from her perspective of revived religiosity, Zinzendorf's "fanaticism" is neither merely illusory nor altruistic; it is visionary and erotic. Moreover, it is savagely egoistic and aggressively masochistic; precisely the combination of human instincts which Freud considered antithetical to culture and community. But the pantheistic spirit that animates Mamalie's memory is none other than the return of totemism or anim-

ism, which supposedly only children, primitives, and severe neurotics entertain. In the case of the Moravian mystic, this animism, or
primary narcissism, is accompanied by a primary, feminine masochism, graphically represented by their wounded, bleeding Christ.
This is the "passion" that Mamalie's (love for) "Christian" embodies.

H.D, synthesizes even more unlikely, though also more efficacious, alloys of egoism and communal mysticism, of masochism and
eros, than does Freud with his antithetical alloys of egoism and
altruism, sadism and eros, which, nevertheless, he hypothesizes to
be the universal formula of human nature. H.D.'s formula envisions
a solution, however unlikely, to the economic problems of libido. As
she sees it, the critical ingredient for cultural rehabilitation and communal happiness is the masochistic component that Freud entirely
overlooks in formulating *Civilization and Its Discontents*. Yet elsewhere, in his case study of the Wolf Man, he celebrates precisely the
healing "work of religion," which channeled his patient's paranoiac
animism and "masochistic impulsion" into "an incomparable sublimation, without much renunciation," and which brought him satisfaction "in the story of the Passion of Christ" as well as "access to
social relationships."[30]

When pressed to explain the rapturous, communal, "oceanic feeling" that the religious testify to experiencing, Freud refers to a "primary ego-feeling" or to a "pure pleasure-ego" that supposedly ante-
dates a truly religious feeling, which can be accommodated by only
the ego of historical self-consciousness:

> Originally the ego includes everything, later it separates off an external
> world from itself. Our present ego-feeling is, therefore, only a shrunken
> residue of a much more inclusive—indeed, an all-embracing—feeling
> which corresponded to a more intimate bond between the ego and the
> world about it. If . . . this primary ego-feeling has persisted . . . it would
> exist in them side by side with the narrower and more sharply demar-
> cated ego-feeling of maturity, like a kind of counter-part to it. (*SE* 21:68)

But according to Freud's Enlightenment dialectic, this primitive, undifferentiated, cosmic ego is eventually and necessarily supplanted
by a higher prototheological wish for an omnipotent father, so that
"the part played by the oceanic feeling, which might seek something
like the restoration of limitless narcissism, is ousted from a place in
the foreground" (72). What is clear to Freud is that the origin of the
properly religious attitude derives from the primal need for a paternal deity. "There may be something further behind that," he adds,
"but for the present it is wrapped in obscurity" (72).

This "something further" behind or beyond the field of the unconscious illuminated by psychoanalysis is precisely what H.D.'s psychic
research in the "runic, divinatory" passages of *The Gift* and in her later
poetism proposes to reveal. But to take psychoanalysis farther she
must occult Freud. Her crypto-cinemato-oto-biography occults his
technique of recalling memory in transference so that she can re-enter
the strange camera obscura or womb/tomb of the animistic mind,
whose hieroglyphic projections give birth to charismatic vision. She
occults his technique of listening for the (m)other in transference
dialogue so that she can sound the wave rhythm of the "deep-sea
shell" of the cosmic *omphalos*, primal muse of all culture. According to
H.D., the oceanic feeling lives on in the name of the mother, which
present civilization would do well to place back in the foreground.

It is this primal mother that Freud remarkably forgets (suppresses
or represses) in his shortsighted and dissatisfying account of Genesis, as H.D. subtly notes in *Tribute*:

> It was so . . . conventionally Mosaic. As he ran over [his grandchil-
> dren's] names and the names of their parents, one felt the old impa-
> tience, a sort of intellectual eye-strain, the old boredom of looking out
> historical, genealogical references in a small-print school or Sunday-
> school Bible. It was Genesis but not the very beginning. Not the exciting
> verses about the birds and the reptiles, the trees, the sun and the moon,
> those greater and lesser lights. . . . it seemed the eternal life he visu-
> alized was in the old Judaic tradition. He would live forever like Abra-
> ham, Isaac, and Jacob, in his children's children. . . . That is how . . . ,
> faced with the blank wall of danger, of physical annihilation, his mind
> would work. (62–63)

Faced with the blank wall of annihilation, Freud projects his fantasy of surviving onto the dead name of his fathers and onto the
transmission of the fathers' seed: a conventionally patriarchal response. But H.D.'s creative "womb-brain" works by another mechanism; when she also is faced with annihilation she reads the writing
on the wall transcribed there by hieroglyphic mothers whose spirit
lives on in the animism, the totemism, the primitive rhythm, the
chromatism and tonalism, the shocking, erotic synesthesia of maternal fantasy which her post-Freudian poetism would embody.

The woman poet's occulting of Freud reads like an obscure critique
of Freud's decision to abandon the (m)other realm, the nature and
culture of female sexuality, to obscurity. Against his emphasis on
paternal genealogies and the father of prehistory, the author of *The
Gift* anticipates a pursuit of the mother in her future poetry.

The necessary, therapeutic byway through autobiography to a sense of her own erotic-poetic potential is, however esoteric, not unique to H.D, Nor can Freud claim to be the original cartographer. Rather, it is the necessary, therapeutic route of women's cultural history, as Virginia Woolf observed back in 1929. In H.D,'s individual history of life writing, we may glimpse the literary history of women in general: "In the early nineteenth century, women's novels were largely autobiographical. One of the motives that led them to write was the desire to expose their own suffering, to plead their own cause. Now that this desire is no longer so urgent, women are beginning to explore their own sex, to write of women as women have never been written before."[31]

# 4

# Helen's Pharmacy: Figures
# and Structures of Treatment
# in H.D.'s Palinode to Helen

Treatment. [TREAT v. + -MENT.] 1.Conduct, behaviour; action or behaviour towards a person, etc.; usage. 2. = TREAT
3. Management in the application of remedies; medical or
surgical application or service. 4. Subjection to the action
of a chemical agent. 5. Action or manner of dealing with
something in literature or art; literary or artistic handling
esp. in ref. to style.

Shorter Oxford English Dictionary

H.D. subjects the corpus of Western literature and the maligned,
malignant figures of (female) sexuality it embodies to a radical treatment. She begins with the classical texts of the ancient Greeks which
incubated and delivered the logos of Western thought, and specifically with the first histories and heroic epics that gave birth to the
notion of Man as subject, ego, heroic individual, and historical agent.
She begins here, having perceived that with the birth of Man came
the repression of woman, the violent forgetting of women as signifiers of an erotic power beyond the newfound mastery of epic
grammar, Platonic logic, and historical narrative. With the birth of
Man came the love of man for Man and the maligning of woman as
love's anathematized other, a double event whose cosmic meaning
the (male) poets have been singing and celebrating since Homer, or
so H.D. observes in her ironic, lyrical paraphrase of *The Iliad*, which
foregrounds both sides of the story:

> so they fought, forgetting women,
> hero to hero, sworn brother and lover,
> and cursing Helen through eternity.
> (HE 4)

With the militant forgetting of women (the severest form of forgetting, Freud has taught us, is repression), comes the fear and hatred of

women, the terror and horror of her "return" as figured in the haunting characters of Clytemnestra and Medea and the oedipal mother, Jocasta. Since for H.D. it is Helen who is the object of the revolutionary forgetting and reactive cursing that institutes Western mankind's masculinist and paranoid self-conception, it is Helen who becomes the "lost object" in her quest for cultural healing.

H.D.'s "Helen hated of all Greece" (2) can be traced to numerous sources in classical literature, notably the tragedies. The chorus in the *Agamemnon* curses Helen's memory:

> Alas, Helen, wild heart
> for the multitudes, for the thousand lives
> you killed under Troy's shadow,
> you alone, to shine in man's memory
> as blood flower never to be washed out. Surely a demon
> then of death . . . men's agony.[1]

The chorus denounces Helen on behalf of women themselves in Euripides' *Orestes*:

> Every woman
> loathes and despises the name of Helen, the woman
> who disgraced her sex.

The most outspoken of them all is Electra:

> *Murder!*
> *Butcher!*
> *Kill!*
> Thrust your twin swords home!
> Slash, now slash again!
> Run the traitress through,
> Kill the whore who killed
> so many brave young men.[2]

Iphigenia, in Euripides' *Iphigenia in Aulis*, supports her father's decision to sacrifice her to the gods, proclaiming that Helen has devalued the lives of all women along with her own:

> is it right
> For this man [Paris] to make war upon all the Greeks
> For one woman's sake and surely die?
> Rather in war is it far better that

> Many women go to their death, if this
> keep one man only facing the light
> And alive.[3]

In his didactic comedy *Helen,* Euripides has the woman herself denounce her own cursed image:

> Because of me, beside the waters of Scamander, lives
> were lost in numbers; and . . . I
> am cursed by all and thought to have betrayed my lord
> and for the Hellenes lit the flame of a great war.[4]

H.D.'s treatment of classical literature is not historical, though she traces Helen through literary history. In any case, history as a classical science, begins with the dismissal of the *myth* of Helen of Troy. In recording and establishing mankind's achievements, Herodotus is one step ahead of Homer in advancing the "forgetting" of women.[5] His *Histories* begin by proposing to demystify the (Persian, not Greek) belief that the abduction and rape of Helen was *the* cause of the Trojan War; the object of his history is to deny and repress the Homeric story that is already a denial and repression of woman.[6]

H.D. proposes that the best way to treat Helen is to treat literary language and history with a heterodox source study, one that looks beyond Greek roots and origins and derives, instead, from Freud's subversive etymology and philology. It is not the woman, Helen (if there ever was such a person), whom her palinode proposes to rehabilitate, but the palimpsest, the tracing and retracing of the Helen myths and legends that compose the literary canon. "Helen" is no more than the effect of a long process of repression. There being no original Helen outside the poetry and history that represses her memory, "Helen" *is* the repressed, who makes her symptomatic return in the obsessive fantasies of male authors who, together with the scholarly guardians of the canon, must repeatedly deny and denounce her haunting power.[7] To recover and re-present the "original" Helen requires a research technique that could trace beyond record, beyond literary history.

In *Trilogy,* H.D. had voiced a poet's uncertain desire to subject the canonical palimpsest to "alchemical" treatment: "your stylus is dipped in corrosive sublimate, / how can you scratch out / indelible ink of the palimpsest / of past misadventure?" (6). The later *Helen in Egypt* proceeds to allegorize such projected treatment: the long poem itself figures as a quest for the traces of Helen buried beneath this palimpsest and its odyssey of misadventure. What her alchemistry uncovers is that the original traces (or should I say originary, since memory and fantasy cannot be distinguished from the primal and the real in this project?) are not Greek but Egyptian. The earliest traces of Helen are undecipherable hieroglyphic characters. The originary Helen is, according to H.D.'s research, not an archetype of Helens but an arche-trace of primitive pictoideographic writing, "the hieroglyphs of Egypt" (82), in need of analysis and interpretation.

H.D.'s re-presentation of an Egyptian subtext shakes the edifice of Greek thinking which figures in *Helen in Egypt* as its most stable structure. Her research among Egyptian ruins/runes promises to have a destabilizing effect on all Western civilization, whose foundations were erected in the name of Hellas. "Beneath" the metaphysical structure of the unifying logos, the word of reason, the idea and institution of definitive speculation,[8] she uncovers a different form of thinking, perceiving, feeling, and communalizing which cannot be translated into readerly discourse, cannot be intellectually absorbed without a radical reconfiguration of mind. And she discovers, this radical difference is all in the writing.

H.D. imagines an originary trace of Helen which acts as a charismatic writing with the power to dissolve and displace the "indelible ink" of a reductive tracing-over of the Egyptian by the Greek. In her most "primal" guise, Helen reveals herself to be a charming cartouche of hieroglyphic characters whose meaning cannot be divined through the use of any lexicon. Instead of the legendary *figure* of Helen of Troy, "H-E-L-E-N-A" (95) appears, signifying the deconstruction of the proper name that has had to bear the full weight and value of a misogynous history.

"Helen" is a figure of astounding complexity. She is a written character, a proper name, a generic symbol of eros and female sexuality, a fantasy, a curse, a cue to remember, a signal to forget, a legend, a myth, a palimpsest of portraits of the classic femme fatale which can be traced from Homer and Euripides down to Marlowe, Shakespeare, Goethe, and Pound. And though she is, at bottom, Egyptian, her Greek character cannot be denied; it is her Greek *consciousness* that encompasses the dramatic and graphic scenes of *Helen in Egypt*, and whose memory "*she and we*" piece together in the "reconstruct[ion] [of] the legend" (11).

Helen is both the object of a quest for origins and the subject of a radical rereading. She is the Greek Helen who, after having (nearly?) died in the holocaust of the Trojan War,[9] is magically transported to the underworld of Egypt. There she walks among the tombs, translating hieroglyphs from the Book of the Dead, which she remembers with uncanny vitality. The subject of reading is also subject to analysis, an occult *psycho*analysis that conducts research beyond the bounds of its orthodox practice. Helen's enigmatic entry into Egypt allegorizes the depth psychology of an autohypnotic subject who dreams/remembers scenes and images in the hieroglyphic symbols of her repressed prehistory.

H.D.'s treatment of the classical Greek text is at once a translation and an analysis. Just as treatment is a complex figure, so also is translation. She does not perform an actual translation, at least not in the linguistic sense, nor does she transcribe actual Greek and Egyptian characters as Pound transcribes Chinese ideograms into his *Cantos*. Yet the poem displays the processes and effects of a double translation, of "Greek" into "Egyptian" and "Egyptian" into "Greek," which is more precisely to be understood as an allegory of translation.

H.D. "s "translation" of Greek into Egyptian entails the decentering and displacement of Greek philosophy, history, epic, and dramatic poetry, that is, the deconstruction of the logos and *heros* of Greek culture by a recovery and re-presentation of Egyptian hieroglyphs whose pictoideographic character is not reducible to phonological elements of a certain ascribable semantic value. The effect of this translation is a liberation of meaning from the stronghold of the logic of binary opposition, the logic of difference which negates and represses one of the terms of antithesis (such as "woman" in the antithesis "man/woman"). Since Egyptian writing consists of compound "words" (hieroglyphic composites) that *produce* rather than *reduce* antithetical meaning, it does not represent an "idea" of sexual difference but instead presents a compound "glyph" of sexual ambiguity. In Greek, the single word "Helen" refers to the solitary woman, the cursed, subordinated and repressed term of the binary oppositions proper/common (man/woman, masculine subject/female object) and proper/improper (hero/whore, Penelope/Helen). In Egypt(ian), "Helen" is never an isolated character but always a compound such as Helen-Achilles, or Helen-Paris or Helen-Thetis as transcribed in the hieroglyphs designating the names of indigenous deities (Isis, Osiris, Thoth).

Since what this translation entails is a descriptive or figurative exchange between ancient languages, represented entirely in English, it might more precisely be regarded as an analysis. In fact, it is both. The "translation" of Greek into Egyptian restores what Jacques

Derrida (after Plato) calls the *pharmakon* of writing, the condensation of compound, irreducible meaning in pictoideographic symbols: that is, it performs a radical analysis of the idealized (phonological) components of a language. The poem dramatizes this translation as Helen's ecstatic, analytic absorption with dream symbols, which Freud teaches us to consider as the "hieroglyphic" representations of the primitive psychic processes of condensation and displacement.[10]

Helen's slip from Greek consciousness into the Egyptian unconscious is a radical translation/analysis, but it is only half of the process. She proceeds to "read" these hieroglyphic symbols and to bring her repressed, Egyptian unconscious into her Greek consciousness, allowing her to articulate other possible meanings of her Hellenic sense of self. Throughout her trancelike meditation on the Trojan War, Egyptian characters surface unconsciously and symptomatically into her Greek memory, shattering and decentering the heroic narration of the event. H.D. *treats* the Greek text of Helen's story as a "secondary revision," a censorious text that reduces the rich, antithetical writing of her dream text to the logos of difference, organizing signifying power around the phallus, categorizing the sexes hierarchically, and defining mankind against female sexuality.

Textual treatment in H.D.'s *Helen* attempts to positivize the dream substance or the Egyptian content of analysis and translation: "the potion is not poison" (3), the treatment is medicinal, though the charismatic cue to dream and to remember is anathema to the Greek mind. Helen resists the urge to appropriate dialectical reason: "must I summon Hellenic thought / to counter an argument?" (37). Yet the alternative "thinking" that she self-consciously employs still affords a transvaluation of values. The primary processes of dreaming are ultimately seen to facilitate thinking even more than the rational secondary processes whose categories and abstractions are the object of dissolution and transformation. "Egypt" and its hieroglyphic (dream) writing are ultimately "resurrected" and restored.

Finally, I read *Helen in Egypt* as a critical, poetic treatment of *Civilization and Its Discontents* and a radical reapplication of terms that Freud attempts to define in *Beyond the Pleasure Principle* (that is, eros, thanatos, death drive, life instinct, quiescence, destructiveness). In making this suggestion, I am aware of aligning H.D. with such poststructuralist readers of Freud's sexuality/textuality as Hélène Cixous and Leo Bersani, without detracting from H.D.'s originality in having translated this critical subtext into a poem, which she offers to the world as a charm, a cue to dream and to convalesce within its charismatic healing powers.

## Palinodes, Palimpsests, and the
## *Pharmakon* of Writing

*Helen in Egypt* is a treatment of the phallogocentric structures and
figures of classical literature; it is also a literary structure and figure of
hermetic treatment.[11] Part 1 of H.D.'s tripartite long poem is a "later,
little understood" (1) form of palinode (*"a defence, explanation or apology"* [1]) which treats the classical genre to serious restructuring:
unlike the palinodes of Stesichorus and Euripides, H.D.'s gives
Helen center stage to present her own defense. This center stage is,
moreover, the site of H.D.'s undoing of the Greek conception of
Helen, of woman. Here, Helen cites and recites her case, resting her
defense or an "interminable analysis" of the transcript of her memory
of the Trojan War for which she has been popularly damned.

The transcript of her memory is a palimpsest, a structural figure of
memory and literary history, a memory text, whose fullest "reading"
requires treatment, a reversal of the treatment to which it was first
subjected when the Greek poets and historians erased at least one
version of the story to make room for another.[12] H.D.'s palinode
figures the erasure of an erasure to make imaginable the recovery of
an "originary" transcript of Helen's story. The figure of double erasure is a figure of writing which both remedies and poisons the
palimpsest of Helen's Greek memory. H.D.'s palinode" is also a
*pharmakon* of writing, a metaphorical drug or therapy that possesses
the double, "hieroglyphic" capacity to signify both pain and relief,
beneficence and harm.

At the outset of *Helen in Egypt*, H.D. announces her departure from
the tradition of writing palinodes to Helen, hinting that what is now
"little understood" about the "later" production will eventually give
way to a "restoration of sight" far beyond the Hellenized field of
vision: *"Stesichorus was said to have been struck blind because of his
invective against Helen, but later was restored to sight, when he reinstated
her in his* Pallinode. *Euripides, notably in* The Trojan Women, *reviles her,
but he also is 'restored to sight.' The later, little understood* Helen in Egypt,
*is again a* Pallinode, *a defence, explanation, or apology"* (1). She alludes to
the scholarly attribution of the origin of the palinode to the sixth-
century lyricist Stesichorus, suggesting that he recovered the less
well known story of Helen's detour from Troy (or Greece): *"We all
know the story of Helen of Troy but few of us have followed her to Egypt. How
did she get there? Stesichorus of Sicily in his* Pallinode *was the first to tell
us. Some centuries later, Euripides repeats the story"* (1).

Her research agrees with that of Greek scholar and translator

Richmond Lattimore, who recalls that Stesichorus "had said certain hard things about Helen, and as a result he lost his sight, which returned only after he had composed his Palinode, or Apology, from which we have his lines

> That story is not true.
> You never went away in the benched ships.
> You never reached the citadel of Troy."[13]

Stesichorus's story differs from "that story," the "standard version as told by Homer" (261), in referring to a "phantom" that went to Troy in place of Helen herself (261). H.D. supposes that Stesichorus knew "how Helen got to Egypt" and that he is the source of the variant, whereas Lattimore claims Egypt to be the source: "We do not know where Stesichorus (and Hesiod) said that Helen did go, if not to Troy. . . . But Herodotus . . . told a different story, which he claimed to have heard from the priests of Hephaestus in Memphis, Egypt" (261).

   That Herodotus should recover and record the story of Helen's detour from Troy to Egypt is consistent with the historian's desire to discount the significance of the part played by Helen in the Trojan War, and thus in the making of the Greek nation. In any case, his research does not extend to pre-Hel(l)enic sources of the story, nor does it attempt to reconcile the discrepancy between the Homeric and Egyptian versions: he is content to accept and emphasize that, as he would suggest a decade later, the Greeks fought merely for a phantom or phantasm of Helen and not for any true or real female object.[14]

   Euripides' *Helen* follows Stesichorus in allowing that Helen did not go to Troy, while it also specifies the agent and site of diversion. According to Euripides, the winged Olympian, Hermes, carried her out of the arms of her abductor into the sanctuary of pharaoh while an unperceiving Paris made for home with a phantom-idol.[15] Following this formula for palinodes to Helen, H.D. places Helen in Egypt. But the god she invokes as the agent of transfer is not Euripides' heavenly Hermes Argeiphontes but Hermes Psychopompos, god of an older, demonic order, who delivers dead souls to the underworld, who is also god of sleep and dreams, akin to Hermes Trismegistos, "the name . . . given by the Neoplatonists . . . and the devotees of mysticism and alchemy to the Egyptian god Thoth."[16] In H.D.'s palinode, Hermes-Thoth delivers Helen to Egypt, thus personifying a translation from the world of waking life to the underworld of dreams, a hermetic translation: "*According to the* Pallinode, *Helen . . . had been transposed or translated from Greece into Egypt*" (1).

Inquiry into the character of this compound deity should reveal the nature of the kind of treatment H.D.'s "later, little understood" palinode administers in the recuperation of Helen. In addition to being the messenger god of the Greeks, Hermes is also god of magic and medicine; Thoth is the secretary of the Egyptian gods, inventor of the charmed and sacred hieroglyphic script.[17] H.D.'s Hermes-Thoth is a trans-cultural scribe, a translator-physician whose occult powers enable him to raise the dead to life or to capture the spirit of his subject in the dead letter. Her Helen is the subject of a charismatic transcription from the text of the Greek (the dead language of the ancients) into the "Book of Thoth" (66).

The opening lyrics of *Helen in Egypt* figure verses from Thoth's book spoken by Helen, in keeping with the Egyptian custom of writing hieroglyphic inscriptions from the Book of the Dead on tombs and sarcophagi for the dead to read, ensuring their charmed conduct into afterlife.[18] They evoke a charming (acoustic, visual, and graphic) image of Helen's transposition into afterlife:

> Do not despair, the hosts
> surging beneath the Walls,
> (no more than I) are ghosts;
>
> .   .   .   .   .
>
> with reed of the papyrus;
> Amen (or Zeus we call him)
> brought me here;
>
> .   .   .   .   .
>
> the old enchantment holds,
> here there is peace
> for Helena, Helen hated of all Greece.
>
> (1–2)

At the stroke of Hermes' magic wand or of Thoth's reed, Helen is retranscribed into the hermetic Book of the Dead, where she out-lives her Greek legend and begins to acquire a character of enchantment, like that of the hieroglyphic script on the walls in which she is entombed. According to the famed British Egyptologist E. A. Wallis Budge, whose English translation of Thoth's *Book of the Dead* H.D. possessed,[19] "certain religious texts were thought to possess special virtue when written in hieroglyphs, and the chapters and sections of books that were considered to have been composed by Thoth himself were believed to possess very great power, and to be of the utmost benefit to the dead when they were written out for them in hiero-glyphs" (*Literature of the Ancient Egyptians*, 1). Given this added, charismatic ingredient, H.D.'s cryptic formula presents itself as im-measurably more potent a palinode than the classical formula sup-plied by Stesichorus and Euripides who confine their compositions to the power of the Greek logos and mythos.

Helen in Egypt "reeds" (reads like) an occult adaptation of Eu-ripides' *Helen*, though Euripides' text is no less self-conscious of its written, hence adaptable, erasable, transfigurable character. Near the opening of his play, when, just after she has been informed of her hateful reputation among the Greeks, Helen, the supposedly *real* Helen, in Egypt, who never accompanied Paris to Troy, allegorizes her predicament in a metaphor of painting, another figure of the palimpsest: "I wish that like a picture I had been rubbed out and done again, made plain, without this loveliness, for so the Greeks would never have been aware of all those misfortunes that now are mine. So I would keep what was not bad, as now they keep the bad of me" (201–2). Euripides' *Helen* is a censorious text: it treats the Homeric version of Helen like a bad impression whose extravagant beauty and corruptive power should be blanked out and replaced with a plain, less compelling female figure. Euripides chooses to present such textual reflexivity in the voice of his character, thereby casting the illusion that it is the woman herself who seeks correction by self-erasure and rehabilitative self-abnegation. It is at this point in the tradition of writing palinodes to Helen that H.D. intervenes. Playing on *Helen*'s palimpsestic metaphor, *Helen in Egypt* recovers the corrupt version and proceeds not by erasure but by exposure of deeper narrative layers, tracing Helen's genealogy back to pre-Hel(l)enic sources and undermining the Greek original (the Greek claim of origins, of originality). Instead of purging the text, *Helen in Egypt* allows further corruption, not simply by allowing the attractive fe-male figure of Helen of Troy to remain as mystifyingly potent as ever but by compounding canonical interpretations and contaminating the purely Greek text with foreign, Egyptian sources. The images that have been rubbed out or written over in the canonical canon are precisely those that surface hermetically in *Helen in Egypt*, where they haunt the Greek text with their hieroglyphic character.

To make a sudden shift from the ancient to the modern *pharmacia*: the structural allegory that H.D. employs in her writing of *Helen in*

*Egypt* seems to derive less from Euripides' metaphorical palimpsest than from Freud's "mystic writing-pad," which he uses to conceptualize the psych(olog)ical tracing of memory and perception.[20] Unlike Euripides' "painting," which, once erased, presents a clean surface for painting afresh, Freud's writing pad retains, at deeper levels, traces that were erased from the surface, so that even though the surface may be clear for receiving new impressions, other layers have been more indelibly inscribed:

> The surface of the Mystic Pad is clear of writing and once more capable of receiving impressions. But it is easy to discover that the permanent trace of what was written is retained upon the wax slab itself and is legible in suitable lights. Thus the Pad provides not only a receptive surface that can be used over and over again, like a slate, but also permanent traces of what has been written, like an ordinary paper pad. . . . this is precisely the way in which . . . our mental apparatus performs its perceptual function. The layer which receives the stimuli—the system *Pcpt.-Cs.* forms no permanent traces; the foundations of memory come about in other, adjoining [unconscious], systems. (*SE* 19:230)

Euripides' *Helen* foregrounds the repressive erasure and conscientious retracing and disfiguring of Helen's charming figure by an idealizing censor, but H.D.'s *Helen in Egypt* compounds this repressed and troubling phantom image of Helen with a psychic reality derived from depth psychology. Retrieving mnemic-images from the Western unconscious into the light of modern science, H.D. exposes the subject of her palinode to a new, psycho-/archaeo-logical analysis extending beyond the Greek. Her Egypt is the domain of Hermes Psychopompos and Hermes-Thoth, a poeticized version of the topographical and technical description of the psyche afforded by the mystic writing pad: in other words, an occult hyperbole or metaphysical conceit that elaborates and extends Freud's textual metaphor. In Egypt, Helen finds herself in the deepest substrata of memory, where she perceives the earliest traces of her consciousness preserved in cryptic script.

Here, in Egypt, a draught of Lethe dissolves the effects of the Euripidean censor and charms buried and forgotten memory into consciousness at the same time that it plunges living memory into the death of oblivion. Helen inhabits this "crypt of memory" in a double state of wakeful forgetfulness and sleep-enveloped memory, of conscious amnesia and deep, unconscious reminiscence, refusing to choose between the phantom and the real, which have been falsely opposed by the Greeks: *"Lethe . . . is the river of forgetfulness for the shadows, passing from life to death. But Helen, mysteriously transposed to Egypt, does not want to forget. She is both phantom and reality"* (3).

*Helen in Egypt* is itself a mnemonic device, a mystic writing that retranscribes and makes conscious the repressed, unconscious archetraces of memory no longer accessible to modern thought or translatable into modern language. In a sense, H.D.'s palimpsestic metaphor reverses the dynamic outlined in Freud's "Mystic Writing-Pad": whereas Freud uses the image of the mystic pad to explain perception as a work of repression (the clearing of the receptive surface), H.D. uses the image of cryptic writing to figure memory as a work of hypnosis, as a surfacing of deep memory traces (rather than as a clearing of the surface), and as a productive, metonymic flow of unconsciously generated images (rather than as a receptive reproduction of external impressions).

Helen's charmed consciousness appears to tap the very source of dream-memory, to dip into the flow of primary-process "thinking" and "representation." Lethe figures as the dream source or "medium" of free-flowing hieroglyphic images not yet translatable or definable in the logic and syntax of Greek. A dose of Lethe's potion is not lethal but reviving: "The potion is not poison, / it is not Lethe and forgetfulness / but everlasting memory" (3). The potion is metaphorical draft/draught of pictoideographic writing that intoxicates and enchants the dream reader, a mnemonic device that at once restores and falsifies (reconstructs) memory, a *pharmakon* of writing that, as Jacques Derrida says, "is good for *hypomnesis* (re-memoration, recollection, consignation) and not for the *mneme* (living, knowing memory)."[21]

*Helen in Egypt* expands Euripides' metaphor of the text, turning it into an archive or crypt, a "book of the dead," which exhumes the memory of Helen encrypted in hieroglyphs of ancient Egypt, supplementing and decentering the Greek classic and its supposed archetype of Helen with a psychoanalytic palimpsest. But H.D. also doctors the Freudian text. Freud's scientistic point of view prompts him to think of the mystic pad as a memory machine, stressing the double mechanism of inscription/erasure (though, as Derrida points out, the term *repression* exceeds the explanatory capacity of the mechanical metaphor, pointing to the political and the ideological.) In contrast, H.D. stresses the organic and the mystical operations of memory by dramatizing the "mysticism" of hypomnesia. Helen is the "living ghost" who (re)traces the origins of her "self," her primary thoughts and representations, buried alive in the crypt of memory. But H.D. stays within the realm (however expanded) of psychoanalysis.[22] A Freudian translation of a Freudian trope, H.D.'s mysticism adds the element of fantasy to the mystic writing pad, a fantasy of origins mobilized by the desire for presence, a fantasy of the *other* woman whom Helen/H.D. desires to know in all her potent immediacy.

Finally, H.D.'s treatment of Euripides' *Helen* reads like an antidote to patriarchy. In Helen's pharmacy, memory is allowed free play among the sites of preoedipal or pre-Hel(l)enic fantasy, corrupting the Greek idealization of "femininity" which Euripides' text attempts to define and illustrate. Though posing as a palinode to Helen, Euripides' comedy actually redresses the sexually independent woman, superimposing a picture of domestic perfection on a figure of autonomous, active female desire. Euripides' *Helen* is an iconography of "civilized" femininity dedicated to erasing older, "barbaric" traces of Helen and to neutralizing the charm of a powerfully erotic, war-inspiring, demonic female figure (known to Shakespeare and to Marlowe as "the face that launched a thousand ships") so as to impress the consciousness of Greek men with a figure of passive, featureless, and domesticated femininity.

Euripides makes no attempt to conceal the psychological and political repression that his recording of Helen entails and he overtly reinforces this repression with metaphysical antinomies.[23] In his "Greek" view, the good, true, and real Helen is she who remains unquestioningly, quiescently faithful to her lord and master, Menelaus, while the bad, false, and unreal Helen is she who willfully entertains desires of her own, abandoning the paterfamilias for forbidden pleasures. In his retracing of the legend, the good Helen is whisked away to pharaoh's paternal sanctuary while Menelaus goes warring after bewitching phantoms. With a trick of rhetoric (hysteron proteron), Euripides reverses the order of origin, re-presenting the "bad" Helen as a fake copy, a corrupt imitation or phantom image of the ideal original (191, 192, 193, 213, 214); it is a metaphysical rhetoric that finds support in Plato's attack on mimesis. The moment Menelaus rediscovers the "truth" is charged with as much power as is the moment that Oedipus discovers his "crime." The phantom Helen, whom Menelaus has retrieved from Troy and imprisoned in a cave, evaporates into thin air when the real Helen is brought into the light of day (216). Against this Euripidean reduction, H.D.'s Helen figures as both phantom and reality, undermining the philosophical opposition Euripides' Helen represents and giving subversive priority to the expression of the repressed, other woman.

## This Anodyne of Egypt

H.D. treats the palimpsest of legendary Helens with a *pharmakon* of writing. It is instructive to read this figure of writing, Helen's potion-poison, in light of Jacques Derrida's reading of Plato's "pharmacy." Compare the following passages from *Helen in Egypt*,

> The potion is not poison,
> it is not Lethe and forgetfulness
> but everlasting memory,
>
> .  .  .  .  .
>
> *O Helen, Helen, Daemon that*
> *thou art,*
> *we will be done forever*
> *with this charm, this evil philtre,*
> *this curse of Aphrodite . . .*
>
>                               (3–4)

with those from Derrida's "Plato's Pharmacy,"

> Writing is no more valuable, says Plato, as a remedy than as a poison. (99)

> This *pharmakon*, this "medicine," this philter, which acts as both remedy and poison, already introduces itself into the body of the discourse with all its ambivalence. This charm, this spellbinding virtue, this power of fascination, can be—alternately or simultaneously—beneficent or maleficent. The *pharmakon* would be a *substance*—with . . . occult virtues, cryptic depths refusing to submit their ambivalence to analysis, already paving the way for alchemy. (70)

As in Plato's text, the *pharmakon*-philter functions in H.D.'s text in multiple ways: as a theme or leitmotif (like the love-potion/poison theme in *Tristan and Isolde*);[24] as a charm, a poetic substance of undecidable meaning which fascinates the reader; as a metaphor of writing, the *pharmakon* of writing, which possesses the capacity of the Egyptian hieroglyph to signify irreducible ambivalence and thus subvert the authority of the word, the reductive logos of discourse; as a cue to dream, to fantasize, to enter into the flow of the primary processes of perception which symbolize the crosscurrents of life-forces in the service of pleasure; as as a mnemonics, a cue to ecstatic, hypnoid memory or *hypomnesia* facilitating the recovery of the deepest traces of memory while poisoning this memory with the substance or content of its charm; and as a therapeutics for the Western imagination, especially modern consciousness, so immobilized in logical and categorical abstraction, so alienated from the vital, mobilizing source of representation. *Helen in Egypt* serves in particular the modern *woman* poet, supplying a healing anodyne[25] for an imagination oppressed by the effects of a reductive translation of "femininity" by the institutions and ideologies of Western patriarchal culture and by the dominance of male fantasy since the time of the Greeks.

The most potent semiotic function of this psychopoetic anodyne is its deconstruction of metaphysical antinomies. "Helen" is herself an Egyptian "character," a deconstruction of the Greek anthropomorphic or mimetic (idea of) character, with the power of the *pharmakon* to transcribe antithetical meaning. She is both phantom and reality; she is and she is not Helen of Troy; she is the philter of Aphrodite which signifies both love and death. "She herself is the writing," Helen repeats (*HE* 22, 91), whenever she perceives an ontological ambiguity in the traces of her memory.

We might read "Helen" as a synecdoche of the poem as a whole: *Helen in Egypt* is a *pharmakon* of writing, a poetic deconstruction of the Greek idealization of Helen. In another sense, *Helen in Egypt* is H.D.'s pharmacy or fantasy, wherein "Helen" acts as *pharmakon* (or *pharmakeus*). More precisely, she acts just like the hieroglyphs of dreams as understood by Freud and as he had hoped to understand through reference to Egyptology. In his comparative research on symbolization in dream and "primitive languages," Freud turns to the German philologist, Karl Abel, quoting him in his essay "The Antithetical Meaning of Primal Words":

In the Egyptian language, this sole relic of a primitive world, there are a fair number of words with two meanings, one of which is the exact opposite of the other. . . . [Also] in this extraordinary language there are not only words meaning equally 'strong' or 'weak' and 'command' or 'obey'; but there are also compounds like 'old-young', 'far-near', 'bind-sever', 'outside-inside' . . . combining the extremes of difference. (*SE* 11:156–57)

Freud emphasizes that "according to Abel it is in the 'oldest roots' that antithetical double meanings are found to occur," that "in the subsequent course of the language's development this ambiguity disappeared," and that "all the intermediate stages can be followed, down to the unambiguousness of modern vocabularies" (158). While he shares Abel's Enlightenment view that the unambiguousness of modern languages is a sign of cultural evolution, Freud nonetheless stresses the need for modern healers to be able to translate these primitive languages and the repressed ambivalence of the archaic (infantile, neurotic) psychological material which the hysterical symptom or dream symbol represents:

> In the correspondence between the peculiarity of the dream-work . . . and the practice discovered by philology . . . we may see a confirmation of the view we have formed about the regressive, archaic character of the expression of thoughts in dreams. And we psychiatrists cannot escape the suspicion that we should be better at understanding and translating the language of dreams if we knew more about the development of language. (161)

Just as Freud advocates the understanding and translation of hieroglyphic dream language for psychiatric therapeutics, so does H.D. champion the writing and reading of hieroglyphic poetry as a cultural cure. Her treatment, like Freud's, is translation, and like Freud's translation it is complex, envisioning, in the first instance, the translation from modern, civilized language, from the socialized or normativized symbolic order, into the hieroglyphic symbols of the primary processes of the dream and, in the second instance, translation from the dream into a revitalized, less discursive and more poetic Greek, or German or English. The first instance of this translation, the translation from the Western mind based on the logos of the Greek into the script of Egypt is the privileged moment of H.D.'s translation; it is the moment of the initiation of treatment, of administering the cure for the modern imagination, stifled by overly categorical thinking and being.

This reverse translation from the "civilized" to the "primitive" functions as a radical analysis, a lifting of the repression of the primary processes imposed by the laws of syntax and the rules of exchange in social discourse. The dissolution of categorical thinking reverses the translation accomplished by the Greeks when they officially anathematized the reading and writing of "barbaric" Egyptian and when they formally subjected the semantic ambiguity they found in the vestiges of myth inhabiting their own discourses to a logical reduction. "All translations into languages that are the heirs and depositories of Western metaphysics," Derrida explains (providing a clue for reading H.D.'s "Egyptian" translation), "produce on the *pharmakon* an *effect of analysis* that violently destroys it, reduces it to one of its simplest elements by interpreting it. . . . Such an interpretative translation is . . . as violent as it is impotent: it destroys the *pharmakon* but at the same time forbids itself access to it, leaving it untouched in its reserve" ("Plato's Pharmacy," 99).

H.D. recovers this semiotic reserve and applies it to classical literature and Western literary history, chiefly to restore the symbolic power of "woman," of the *pharmakon* of "femininity," which has been violently, if impotently, reduced to a sign of patriarchal desire and ultimately to a symptom or to an entire history of female sexual repression.[26] Her "Helen" functions potently and charismatically as a signal to dream, to remember forbidden desires (for the mother, the all-powerful chimeric Isis), owing her charm to her undecidable meaning: is she life or death (eros-thanatos), love or strife (eros-*eris*), active or passive (man-woman)? Throughout *Helen in Egypt*, these semantic ambiguities arise, troubling the too Greek-minded, too defensive Achilles but satisfying the dream desiring, memory-thirsting, pleasure-seeking Egypto-Greek Helen.

That H.D. should champion the primitive dream-processes over the "civilized" rational and normative symbolic order as a cure for modern "uptight" culture is not terribly original, in light of the surrealists' discovery and exploitation of psychoanalysis in the early part of this century; but what does seem to be original about this long poem is its attempt to cure a very specific culture: that which Freud outlines in *Civilization and Its Discontents*. In other words, *Helen in Egypt* proposes to cure psychoanalysis, the Freudian text, of a gloomy, prophetic pessimism that issues from a chronic adherence to an enlightenment teleology that insists on the "economic necessity" of the suppression of eros and woman, however grave that economy.

Freud reasons that civilization is doomed to a progress that requires the increased repression (suppression, exploitation, alienation) of the vital processes, of sexuality and especially women's sexuality:

Women soon come into opposition to civilization . . . those very women who, in the beginning, laid the foundations of civilization by the claims of their love. Women represent the interests of . . . sexual life. The work of civilization has become increasingly the business of men, it confronts them with ever more difficult tasks and compels them to carry out instinctual sublimations of which women are little capable. . . . What [man] employs for cultural aims he to a great extent withdraws from women and sexual life. His constant association with men, and his dependence on his relations with them, even estrange him from his duties as a husband and father. Thus the woman finds herself forced into the background by the claims of civilization. . . . In this respect civilization behaves towards sexuality as a people or a stratum of its population does which has subjected another one to its exploitation. Fear of a revolt by the suppressed elements drives it to stricter precautionary measures. A high-water mark in such a development has been reached in our Western European civilization. (*SE* 21:103–4)

Despite the circularity of his argument, (born of women's love, civilization progresses to antilove, antiwoman, and ultimately, anti-civilization), Freud theorizes no way out of this death drive of progress. His figure of civilization as strictly reserved for men and male bonding reappears in H.D.'s poetry as the armada of Greek warlords who "fought, forgetting women, / hero to hero, sworn brother and lover, / and cursing Helen through eternity"; his figure of eros reappears as "the evil philtre of Aphrodite," the power of love and female sexuality to divert men from their civilizing death drive. But in H.D.'s re-presentation of forces, civilization and eros, man and woman are not so oppositional, nor is culture doomed to such grave repression/sublimation of vital forces.

Contrary to Freud's vision, H.D. saw liberation in one of mankind's most primitive forms of sublimation, poetry, and the most primitive form at that, lyrical, imagistic, hermetic (versus epic) poetry. Moreover, she saw the deeply repressed female imagination as the potent (p)reserve of the *pharmakon*. In the hieroglyphic figure of Helen, she demonstrates how she intends to charm, translate, and cure the death-driven patriarchal machine of Greece/modern civilization into the thriving, artistic-erotic, mystery cult of Egypt.

## Helen, *Pharmakeus*

"In Egypt," in her "pharmacy" of incantatory lyrics, imagist mnemonics, and primal fantasies, Helen acts the part of *pharmakeus*, bewitching the categorical "Greek" with hieroglyphic antithesis, disarming Greek idealism of the misogynous brother-love it so aggressively opposes to "the evil . . . Aphrodite." Derrida elaborates upon the function of the *pharmakeus*:

> . . . *pharmakeus*. That is the name given by Diotima to Eros. . . . A being that no "logic" can confine within a noncontradictory definition, an individual of the demonic species, neither god nor man, neither immortal nor mortal, neither living nor dead, he forms "the medium of the prophetic arts, of the priestly rites of sacrifice, initiation, and incantation, of divination and of sorcery (*thusias—teletas—epodas—manteian*)" ([*Symposium*] 202e). ("Plato's Pharmacy," 117)

As *pharmakeus*, Helen mixes and dispenses a potion of erotic ingredients which undermines man's egological and ideological defenses, undoes his narrative discourse of heroism and conquest, and dispels his horror and hatred of woman.

H.D. allegorizes her radical critique of the Greek domestication (sublimation and repression) of eros in a violent meeting between Helen and Achilles, that exemplary *"héros fatal"* (26). The agon between them embodies and personifies the clash between a (postoedipal) Greek and a (preoedipal) Egyptian cultivation of love. Achilles champions a Greek ethos that privileges manly pursuits and homoeroticism while denying female desire and sexuality. When he recognizes Helen to be that "woman of pleasure" (15), the erotic force that drove the Achaeans to war at the expense of the Greek nation, he attacks with the intent to suppress her forever (15–17). But Helen sees through his limited Greek consciousness and invokes a reminiscence of mother-love, no less shattering than the reminiscence of war, yet potent enough to break through the warrior's defenses and to open onto the ecstasy of communion (15–17).

The moment of their clash is climactic and repeatedly referred to throughout the palinode as the turning point in the history of the recording of the Helen legend. Dramatizing the revelation of a different kind of erotic "power," this climax suggests not only the essence of Helen's apologia but also the essence of H.D.'s defense of eros, as defined against the domestic love of patriarchal marriage and seduction: *"Achilles attacked her, certainly. But Helen returns again and again "to [it]." We may surmise that this "attack" meant more to her than the approaches of her husband, Menelaus, or the seduction of her lover, Paris. (Provided of course, that Helen had ever been lured from Sparta to Troy)"* (39).

Achilles enters Helen's Egypt as a phantasm of memory, dream and myth. In one sense, he is himself a figure of translation or intertextuality, as is Helen, "transposed or translated from Greece into Egypt" (1), from Homer's *Iliad* into *The Book of the Dead*. Once again, the metaphorical transporter is Hermes-Thoth, god of occult medicine and writing, Helen's muse of translation. That Achilles should make his appearance in the palimpsest of Helen legends is not a sign of H.D.'s originality: we find literary antecedents in W. S. Landor's *Imaginary Conversations* and in Goethe's *Faust*, whose figure of Helen as both phantom and reality, as "both in Ilium and in Egypt," as phantasmal object of Achilles' "burning passion," suggests a powerful and likely source for H.D.'s hermetic Helen.[27]

Where H.D. displays her originality, I would argue, is in her allegorical adaptation of Freud's attempt to theorize the conflict between eros and death first outlined in the biological and ontological terms of "pleasure" and "reality" in *Beyond the Pleasure Principle*. The agonistic meeting between Helen and Achilles dramatizes the agonistic description of forces—eros versus thanatos (life instinct versus death drive) (*SE* 21:118–22), ego and aggression versus eros and world community (143–45), civilization versus eros and women's sexuality (103–4)—which Freud formulates and reformulates in *Civilization and Its Discontents*. Though his purpose is to identify and define the primary force that mobilizes civilization and to clarify the effects of the repression or sublimation of that force, Freud never really reaches more than a rhetorical conclusion. At one point, he "concludes" that the progressive work of civilization is man's work, mobilized by ego-libido and the inhibitory/aggressive death drive that forces him to bind with other men and to separate from and repress eros and women (*SE* 21:99–106). Farther on, following labyrinthine disputation that fails to advance the argument and to which he himself refers as discursive *détours* (134), Freud makes the paradoxical claim that the true mobilizing force of civilization is eros, "whose purpose is to combine single human individuals, and after that families, then races, peoples and nations, into one great unity, the unity of mankind" (122). Freud's paradoxes and detours are, we may suppose, the irrepressible effect of the *pharmakon* of writing, which the theorist attempts to subdue but which the poet, *pharmakeus*, would, contrarily, dispense freely.

What is subversive about H.D.'s allegory is that it does not represent these terms as essentially or dialectically oppositional; in her palinode to pre-Hel(l)enic eroticism, these antithetical metaphysical terms are not reduced, as they eventually are in Freud's discourse, to a teleology of oppositions where one term is repressed in favor of the other. The contest between Helen and Achilles violently explodes metaphysical stalemates, eroticizes the death drive, and disarms the warrior-hero of misogynous ego defenses and paranoiac fear of heterogeneity.

I am suggesting, then, that this agon between Helen and Achilles may also be read as a contest between H.D. and Freud, between poet and theorist, in a poeticized reproduction of the scene that was hosted in Vienna in 1933–1934. Achilles is an appropriate figure for Freud since, like Freud, he defers to a rationalist metaphysic though he has a background in "Egyptian" or hermetic medicine. (H.D. alludes to this occult aspect of Achilles' character in her image of him as a charmed child in Chiron's cave [279, 284].) Also, like Freudian discourse, Achilles displays a great inconsistency of character, a certain bisexuality beneath his phallic charade, an uncontrollable passion beneath an exterior of exemplary discipline, and an anarchic rebelliousness, a refusal to subscribe to patriarchal closure (to "the command" of Menelaus, Agamemnon, and Odysseus, to the scholars and administrators of medical orthodoxy).

The agon begins with a challenge to Freud's conception of creative writing as essentially heroic, as a projection of the wish-fulfilling fantasies of "His Majesty the Ego, the hero alike of every day-dream and of every story."[28] Achilles, *héros fatal* (26), enters pharaoh's "kingdom," Helen's dream setting, where the ego has no majesty but is peacefully "at home" diffused among Egyptian characters and other dream symbols that fail to point to a single, positive identity or to fix the position of the dreamer. This decentering of the subject recalls Freud's description of the symbolic plasticity and "multiplicity of the ego" in the most primal formations of dreams and fantasies.[29]

The psychoanalytic allegory does not end here; it unfolds in more elaborate figures. In addition to being the arch-hero of *The Iliad* and, by implication, the majestic ego of Homer's day dream (or of Freud's aesthetic theory), Achilles is a classical embodiment of the Greek cultivation of manhood and an example of the developmental fortification of the ego as Freud describes it in *Beyond the Pleasure Principle* (26–27). Achilles appears before Helen in defensive layers, carrying the "protective shield"[30] of psychological armor, figuring the phallocratic (autocratic [HE 15]) culmination of a process of self-fortification guaranteed to withstand (the signs of) her ego-threatening erotism.

Desiring above all else to win a place among the immortals; enjoying the sadistic annihilation of women, boys, foreign cities; drawing "death from life" (HE 34), Achilles personifies Freud's "ego-libido" and its "component instincts" of "self-preservation, of self-assertion and of mastery . . . whose function it is to assure that the organism shall . . . die only in its own fashion" and to ward off any lure to digress from this aim by the foils of "the true life instincts" of sexuality, of eros (*SE* 18:39–40). Freud poetically refers to these "component instincts" as the "myrmidons of death" (39). It is, of course, the Myrmidons who form a death cult of hero worship around Achilles (*HE* 6, 9, 51) and whom Achilles places in the service of Agamemnon's war machine, in the name of the father (Helen's father, Tyndareus):[31] "*This is the Achilles of legend, Lord of the Myrmidons, indisputable dictator with his select body-guard. . . . he shares the Command . . . with Helen's discredited husband, Menelaus and with Agamemnon, the husband of her sister. There is also, Odysseus, with whom . . . there has been some plot. . . . If Odysseus succeeds in his designs, Achilles will be given Helen and world-leadership*" (51). With these Myrmidons he makes a pact of brotherhood, celebrating masculine mastery and conquest, dismissing women from his self-determined route to death and immortality, "cursing Helen for all eternity" for having interfered.

Achilles arrives in Egypt in ruins from having been "shipwrecked" (15) (recalling the shipwrecked Menelaus in Euripides' *Helen* (207)) but resists Helen's help with open hostility; requested to take her "potion" of Lethe, he accepts with a lash of invective, calling her in sequence "a witch . . . a vulture, a hieroglyph" (17). His vocal outburst represents as much the Greek anathema on Egyptian writing (22) as the anathema on Helen (5), and it dramatizes the violence of Greek translation, reducing the *pharmakon* to one of its simplest terms, to "poison" (from its antithetical meaning, poison-medicine), and the *pharmakeus* to "witch" (from poisoner-healer). The vulture suggests not only a mnemic image of the battlefield where he prematurely lost his life in Helen's war but also Isis, who sometimes took the vulture form to symbolize her compound mysteries of life-death.[32] He identifies Helen with Isis, the Egyptian Aphrodite, and he resists what he perceives to be her emasculating female charm, her hieroglyphic, aphrodisiac power to undermine his phallic self-preservation. Helen responds not by denying but by allowing his denunciations and by confirming her desire to undermine his heroic egoism, his aggression and militant defensiveness: "Perhaps he was right / to call me Hecate and a witch; / I do not care for separate / might and grandeur, / I do not want to hear of Agamemnon / and the Trojan Walls, / I do not want to recall shield, helmet, greaves, / though he wore them, / . . . he was in any case, / defeated" (18–19).

When Helen informs Achilles that "the potion is not poison" (3), she is not reiterating the reduction of the *pharmakon* in reverse; she is stressing the most reassuring aspect of a painful remedy.[33] Just as

Lethe brings on forgetfulness that allows for the deepest rememoration, so too does the potion poison Greek consciousness so that it can heal the alienated body of a repressed unconscious. Achilles' meeting with Helen is painful; it involves a shattering reunion and re-initiation into the mysteries of life and death which they experience together as ecstatically therapeutic. To repeat the lesson Derrida/Plato learned from Thoth: "There is no such thing as a harmless remedy. The *pharmakon* can never be simply beneficial" (99).

The *pharmakon* is the potent substance or "latent content" of the dream, which H.D., like Freud, represents as a primitive, spellbinding script. Absorbed by Helen's lyrical incantation and projected flow of mnemic images, Achilles succumbs to the power of the dream to dissolve the agon between them and to defer recourse to conscious memory, reason, or historical narrative. Her role as *pharmakeus* recalls that of Homer's Helen, who, in *The Odyssey*, slips a "powerful anodyne" into wine that Menelaus and Telemachus had been drinking in order to dissolve their embittered, man-to-man talk of war and misogynous diatribe, and to cast a dreamlike aura for an enchanting round of storytelling:[34]

> Helen, meanwhile . . . had had a happy thought. Into the bowl in which their wine was mixed, she slipped a drug that had the power of robbing grief and anger of their sting and banishing all painful memories. . . . This powerful anodyne was one of many useful drugs which had been given to the daughter of Zeus by an Egyptian lady, Polydamna. . . . For the fertile soil of Egypt is most rich in herbs, many of which are wholesome in solution, though many are poisonous. And in medical knowledge the Egyptian leaves the rest of the world behind. He is a true son of Paeon the Healer. (70)

Once under Helen's hypnotic spell, Achilles recalls scenes from his past, scenes that have never been recorded in the epic or dramatic narratives of classical Greece ("I tell and re-tell the story" [84]). He begins by evoking the scene of his arrival in Egypt and proceeds, regressively, through the scenes of Troy, of Greece, back to the scenes of his childhood, with his mother, Thetis, and his enchanting tutor, Chiron, in the reverse order of temporality and with the same distortion of reconstructed memory found in analysis. Helen, *pharmakeus*, analyst, sets the scene of transference that allows Achilles to recover his (pre)oedipal, "Hel(l)enic" relation to his mother, whose forbidden memory is revealed to him in cryptic Egyptian.

Achilles first recalls the scene of his arrival in Egypt from across the waters of the dead in the caravel of Osiris (26–27; 57–58), repeating the opening scene of Helen's hermetic transposition/translation into Egypt and a dream condensation of Achilles-Osiris. Recollection is, as in analysis, a collaborative production; Helen supplies the mnemonic techniques and devices, hypnosis, free association, transference, and when Achilles' memory meets with resistance, she also supplies her reconstruction and interpretation. Her function as analyst coincides with the function of Isis in the Isis-Osiris mysteries, where Isis collects and reassembles the shattered body of Osiris, and brings him back to life and potency. Achilles gradually welcomes Helen's "Isis-magic," submitting more and more to her reconstructions, helping her to piece together the shattered body of his memory text.

But Helen is not scholarly or "hieratic" in her interpretations (22); she helps Achilles re-member everything, including primal fantasies of maternal desire ("recalling, remembering, invoking / his sea-mother" 14), without the structural agency of the phallus, which, according to the Osiris myth, is lost.[35] The missing phallus, or signifier, is reflected in Achilles' interminable analysis of remembering, repeating, working through without the logic, linearity, or identity of epic or narrative discourse. Helen's radical analysis accomplishes the dissolution of Achilles' (Greece's) inhibitory sexual regime as well as its occupation of language. Conversely, in a positive sense, the displacement of the phallus facilitates Achilles' recovery of oedipal and preoedipal eroticism and his wholehearted conversion to the maternal mysteries, his and his civilization's cure.

## Hieroglyphs of Eros: Love-Death, Man-Woman

Although there is no ending, there is a climax to Achilles' analysis. With the aid of Helen's hypnotic lyricism, Achilles remembers/fantasizes his last scenes of battle, when from the field he scans Helen's figure on the ramparts, pacing between the turrets, gesturing with a wrist, a footfall, a veil (56). He recalls the enchantment that overcame him as he was fastening the greave at his ankle, how he followed her with his gaze as if scanning a poem or as if spellbound by her hieroglyphic image traced along the wall: "I began to count / and measure her foot-fall / from turret to turret; / if I remember the veil, / I remember the Power / that swayed Achilles" (56). His recollection breaks off at the moment he was struck and shattered by Paris's arrow, but Helen, in her Isis role, re-members (for) him:

some say a bowman from the Walls
let fly the dart, some say it was Apollo,
but I, Helena, know it was Love's
arrow.

(83)

This reconstruction of the scene is a radical transcription of the Homeric representation of Achilles' death: here, it is Helen's "power" to induce desire that deprives the invincible hero of his self-possession, makes him fumble with his armor, thus leaving his heel exposed to Paris's deadly, poison-tipped arrow. Here, Helen's sexual charm has the power to disarm and dispel heroic aspiration in an ironic reversal that displaces armor with *amour* and translates the enemy's arrow into Cupid's missile. Here, Achilles is subjected to Helen's *pharmakon* of love-death whose compound hieroglyph H.D. represents in a pun: "*the ultimate experience*, La Mort, L'Amour" (288).

This reconstruction is also a reinterpretation of Freud's conclusion that eros and death (woman's sexuality and man's death drive) are mutually exclusive, antagonistic forces whose opposition civilization must strive to neutralize and domesticate either by repressing eros and privileging the inhibitory structures of the patriarchal superego or by repressing death and "aggression" and privileging world community. As H.D. observes in *Tribute to Freud*, "Eros and *Death*, those two were the chief subjects, the only subjects—of the Professor's eternal preoccupation. They are still gripped, struggling in the deadlock" (103). But in *Helen in Egypt*, eros is eros-death, a *pharmakon* of eros whose double meaning cannot be repressed/reduced by one or the other of civilization's supposed causes. Here, love is ecstatic, orgiastic death, ego shattering and more powerful than the dream of heroic death which Achilles now perceives to be the stasis and impotence of immortality, the immobilization of eros which he and his Myrmidons were commanded to desire more than life: "We were an iron-ring / whom Death made stronger, / but when the arrow pierced my heel" (55).

This reconstruction alludes moreover to the restorative power of transference-love: Achilles' spellbound recollection of his "death," so overwhelming that he cannot speak (about) its climax, is a repetition of the climactic, agonistic meeting with Helen, when he first entered her (analytic) scene. The first scene is recollected by Helen who also cannot speak (about) its climax, which the text represents with an ellipsis, a blanking out:

I prayed, as he clutched my throat

with his fingers' remorseless steel,
*let me go out, let me forget,*
*let me be lost.* . . . . . .

*O Thetis, O sea-mother,* I prayed under his cloak,
*let me remember, let me remember,*
*forever, this Star in the night.*

(17)

In other words, Achilles' memory/fantasy/desire has been effectively treated by Helen's *pharmakon*; his desire to repeat the scene of his "death," to commune with the erotic Helen rather than to denounce and attack the whorish "witch" suggests that his (mis)understanding and maligning of woman's love has been radically doctored and cured.

But Helen's "analysis" of love (and) death does not end with Achilles, nor does it bring the revaluation of her (case) history to a close: *"Helen seems concerned not only with the mystery of their reconciliation but with the problem of why he had, in the first instance, attacked her. There seems this latent hostility; with her love, there is fear . . . and defiance not only of Achilles, but of the whole powerful war-faction"* (18). She is concerned to subject Greek mankind as a whole to her radical treatment, to heal civilization of its deathly, paranoiac misogyny. In interpreting the death scene that she and Achilles reconstruct in analysis, Helen realizes that *"here, values are reversed"* (9), that here, contrary to the ethos of Greek culture, not death but eros is the prime mover of civilized life, though she wonders what this means. Her subsequent speculation both mimes and undoes the philosophical questioning that Freud carries on in the labyrinthine discourses of *Beyond the Pleasure Principle* and in *Civilization and Its Discontents*. "A mortal after death may have immortality conferred upon him," she muses. *"But Achilles in life, in legend, is already immortal—in life, he is invincible, the hero-god. What is left for him after death?"* (9). Her cryptic, condensed answer, *"the Achilles-heel"* (9), defers immediate translation and puts it to the dreamer and her reader to pursue further interpretations.

*"The Achilles-heel"* is a cue to redream and dissolve the iconic figure of the hero in classical literature. It is also a veiled and subtle cue to read H.D.'s palinode as a subversive, poetic translation of Freud's teleological discourse on death and eros. In Freud's account of the

maturing ego (to paraphrase *Beyond the Pleasure Principle* and the highly derivative *Civilization and Its Discontents*), the inhibitory, self-protective death drive takes precedence over life-forces; it is the death drive that fortifies the reality ego, its structures of defense as well as the secondary processes of logical and rational thinking. It is the death drive that compels the ego to separate itself from the heterogeneous world, to secure a self-definition, and to form protective, paranoid alliances in the name of the same (sex, creed, nation, father, king, command). Patriarchal civilization, with its brother bonding, its masculine hegemonies and hierarchies, is the product of the death drive and, as such, is in conflict with life-forces and with eros. The heroic figure of Achilles in H.D.'s poem is emblematic of the death drive: "We were an iron-ring / whom Death made stronger," Achilles recalls, referring to the *"purely masculine"* circle of Myrmidons (55). But the figure of the Achilles' heel is a deconstruction of the theoretical opposition between death and eros, ego and world, male and female, death and life. It is a hieroglyph of dream-memory conjured up in analysis, which at one textual level is the radical analysis of Achilles and at another is H.D.'s radical analysis of the Freudian text.

In analysis Achilles rediscovers the mysteries of love-death which he had experienced in his brief, ecstatic encounter with Helen on the battlefield but which he had repressed in conformity with the reality of heroic consciousness. Whereas the hero cult makes a death pact to bind together in the name of a manly idealism whose aim is to exploit and express each man's death wish to attain immortal glory (55), analysis reinitiates Achilles in the mysteries of love-death, enabling him to rediscover and to value a sense of ecstatic communion with a foreign element, to enjoy a pleasure that has the power to shatter defensive structures and ego boundaries. Love's arrow finds a gap in the heroic surface; eros reveals the hero's Achilles' heel, penetrating and blasting through all the vestiges of militant resistance, destroying the hierarchy of categorical thinking and deidealizing heroic death. It is the full, pleasure value of life, of blissful death-in-life, of love that exceeds and shatters ego boundaries, disarming and de-mystifying its limiting egoistic aim, which Helen helps Achilles to see:

> This was the token, his mortality;
> immortality and victory
> were dissolved;

*I am no more immortal,*
*I am a man among the millions,*
*no hero-god among the Myrmidons;*

some said a bowman from the Walls
let fly the dart, some said it was Apollo,
but I, Helena, know it was Love's arrow;

the body honoured
by the Grecian host
was but an iron casement.

(9)

These phrases—"I am no more immortal," "I am a man among the
millions," "no hero-god among the Myrmidons"—are also tokens of
a cure for a mystified civilization obsessed with man's drive to make
his eternal, phallic mark: the ego deidealized and disseminated
among the others instead of bound and protected by the compound
instincts of self-preservation, self-assertion, and mastery, Freud's
"myrmidons of death." In place of a transcendental ego, a mortal
body; instead of psychological armor and defense, a penetrable,
shatterable ego; instead of the homeostatic pleasure principle of the
immortals, the blissful destructiveness of a "masochistic *jouissance*."[36]
Achilles dies, but not the death of a hero. Having enjoyed the "bliss
of the end" of erotic ecstasy, of the "flame-tipped . . . searing . . .
tearing . . . burning, destructible fury . . . destroying arrow of Eros"
(183), whose memory Helen helps revive, he "dies" into revitalized
or resurrected life, a life after love-death, a life of mystery and communion.

In other words, what survives of Achilles in this hermetic translation of the Greek story of the war that supposedly founded Western
civilization is the figure of an erotic destructiveness that is the basis of
human sexuality and communality. It remains for Helen to divine the
meaning of this war, which is primarily a war (an agon) between the
sexes and a war of sexual liberation. "It was God's plan" she perceives, "to melt the icy fortress of the soul, / and free the man" (10).
Sexual destructiveness liberates the man from paranoiac structures of
his ego; it also liberates the woman from culture's repression of her as
the other, the enemy or the booty of civilization.

Moreover, the hermetic translation of the war reverses and confuses the signs of sexual difference which have been made normative,

liberating sexuality from an immobilizing, categorical opposition: it is Achilles the man who is penetrated by the arrow of Helen's love, and it is Helen the woman who takes ecstatic delight in the fantasy of removing it, leaving a gap, a bodily wound: "Still I feel the tightening muscles, / the taut sinews quiver, / as if I, Helen, had withdrawn / from the bruised and swollen flesh, / the arrow from its wound" (8).[37] This wound, while it is clearly a "narcissistic wound" (the phrase Freud uses to describe symbolic castration and separation from the mother), nonetheless signifies an oedipal or preoedipal fantasy of a self-shattering, over-stimulating, yet binding, loving maternal presence. Helen, in any case, speculatively ascribes the power of erotic communion between herself and Achilles to a mutual knowledge of the primal mother: "How did we know each other? / was it the sea-enchantment in his eyes / of Thetis, his sea-mother?" (7).

Helen's invocation of Thetis/Isis delivers maternal desire from the crypt of Achilles' repressed unconscious, where civilization intended it to be dead and buried. But as Helen and psychoanalysis know, this desire is recoverable, not dead but mummified; it is vital, primal love made inaccessible but untouched in its (p)reserve: "*For from the depth of her racial inheritance, she invokes . . . the symbol or the 'letter' that represents or recalls the protective mother-goddess. This is no death-symbol but a life-symbol . . . Isis or . . . Thetis* (13).

H.D. uses "Thetis" as a Greek cognate for Isis (as well as for Aphrodite), though the different names of these deities do not signify one and the same primal *magna mater* so much as they signify the different elements, forces, or qualities of a primitive fantasy of maternal desire and presence. Isis is the least differentiated symbol and embodies almost all the palinode's antithetical meanings, hence suggesting that she is the most primitive or primal of the goddess glyphs. Thetis, however, is distinguished as a sea symbol: it is she that we sense in the mesmerizing flood of sea images, including incantatory, acoustic images that mime the rhythm of the waves (see especially 35–36, 93). It is the sea that carries Achilles to Helen in Egypt; it is sea talk that Helen uses as a hypnotic, mnemonic device to lure Achilles into deep memory and fantasy.

Thetis is also, I would argue, a hermetic symbol of what Freud dismissively refers to in the opening pages of *Civilization and Its Discontents* as the oceanic feeling of world communion which religious persons sometimes feel (*SE* 21:64–73). Freud sees no reason to accept this feeling as counterevidence for his thesis that civilization is principally mobilized by the death drive; he rejects the notion that religiosity has any libido of its own and considers it being only an affective "consolation" for the sexuality that we restrict in the name of the father (the incest taboo) and of brotherly love. H.D.'s poem, however, subjects this oceanic feeling and Freud's theorization of it to a radical analysis. In the figure of Helen, she discovers that this feeling arises from maternal fantasy, and far from being a fascistic mystification of the incest taboo and the patriarchal superego, it figures as the most effective antidote for such mystification.

In her analysis, the oceanic feeling that her poem strives to re-produce is seen to embody a deeper layer of feeling full of turbulence and destructiveness: it is masochistic *jouissance* rather than brotherly love that ignites communion between the "sea-enchanted" lovers, signifying the resurgence of an originary force or presence rather than a secondary construction or "consolation."[38] That force is at-tributed to a primal fantasy of the mother, to an atemporal and irrepressible eroticism, at once self-shattering and narcissistically satisfying, hence able to produce the sensation of the subject's hav-ing become one with cosmic primal mat(t)er and thus omnipotent. Like Leo Bersani, one of Freud's more recent (and contentious) readers, H.D. re-presents "the maternally derived traumatic model of sexuality" which can be found in Freud.[39]

H.D.'s poem may be read not only as an analysis but also as a sublimation of that primitive, undifferentiated sexuality that her anal-ysis rediscovers. The hieroglyphic representation of eros as love-death, man-woman, masochism-narcissism, pleasure-unpleasure, and other antithetical compounds symbolically reembodies that un-differentiated sexuality. A dream work, an artwork, her poem dem-onstrates how sexuality may be the impetus of cultural production, contradicting Freud's thesis that cultural work is the product of a desexualized libido. Moreover, it performs the cultural work of de-mystifying Freud and his civilization, disabusing them of the notion that civilization and sexuality (especially female sexuality) are cate-gorically opposed, and that the former must and will advance at the expense of the latter even if, in the end, it means the annihilation of the species.

In marked contrast to the dismal ending of *Civilization and Its Discontents*, H.D.'s palinode to Helen is repeatedly marked with signs of a new enlightenment. She and Achilles have both survived the *"holocaust of the Greeks"* (5), and together, in their recovery of a greater power than the impulse to war, they devote themselves to the creation of a new cultural organization. Or so the dream goes: *"They are both occupied with the thought of reconstruction"* (63). *"She would re-establish the Egyptian Mysteries in Greece, she would pledge herself anew to Achilles's work, 'to keep and maintain the Pharos,' and to the 'sea-enchantment in his eyes' "* (89).[40] Achilles has been not only translated from the Greek but also converted and resurrected from the grave of Western civilization into the bloom of Egyptian culture:

> Achilles said, he had work to do,
> to reclaim the coast,
> to keep and maintain the Pharos,
>
> a light and a light-house for ships,
> for others like ourselves,
> who are not shadows nor shades,
>
> but entities, living a life
> unfulfilled in Greece:
> can we take our treasure,
>
> the wisdom of Amen and Thoth
> back to the islands,
> that enchantment may find a place
>
> where desolation ruled,
> and a warrior race,
> Agamemnon and Menelaus?
>
> (89–90)

## Freud, Woman, and the Last Enlightenment

In her portrait of Freud, H.D. variably figures the Professor as Socrates (*TF* 84) and as Eros (103), with herself as priestess of love whose analysis has been an apprenticeship in metaphysical wizardry. "He is midwife to the soul," she muses at one point (116); "perhaps I will be treated with psychic drug, will take away a nameless precious phial from his cavern. Perhaps I will learn the secret, be priestess with power over life and death" (117). This charmed and charming re-presentation of Freud, whose philosophical features had become notably and increasingly grave in actuality, is not unlike Diotima's portrait of Socrates in Plato's dialogues:

> . . . behind the portrait of Eros, one cannot fail to recognize the features
> of Socrates, as though Diotima, in looking at him, were proposing to
> Socrates the portrait of Socrates (*Symposium*, 203 *c, d, e*). Eros . . . spends
> his life philosophizing (*philosophon dia pantos tou biou*); he is a fearsome
> sorcerer (*deinos goes*), magician (*pharmakeus*), and sophist (*sophistes*).
> (Derrida, "Plato's Pharmacy," 117)

But what sorcery, what treatment is being enacted, in turn, upon
philosophy to give it such a charming face? What mediation, beneficial and harmful, do these women perform on the features of philosophers to whom they play sorcerer's apprentice? (How) Do they see
through the mask of philosophical enlightenment to the sophistry of
Eros? What cure do they profer when they administered to philosophy a dose of its own repressed eroticism, its hidden medicine?

What did H.D. "take away" from her analysis with Freud? What
"psychic drug"? What "precious phial," philter, potion? What psychoanalytic "secret" would give her power "over life and death"? (*TF*
116, 117). Clearly not the grave, philosophical conclusions to the
metaphysical questions posed in *Civilization and Its Discontents*, to
which H.D. does not subscribe. "Perhaps" in her analysis with Freud
the physician and in her analysis of Freud the theorist, "perhaps" in
the transcription of her analysis in *Tribute to Freud*, and in her translation of Freud into the nondiscursive medium of poetry, she discovered the other Freud. "Perhaps" she rediscovered the sorcerer
and magician who attempted to mix such disparate, metaphysical
elements as life and death, as masculine and feminine, as eros and
ego, with the alchemical intention of concocting a cure for modern
neuroses, an intention that ran counter to the idealistic and positiv-
istic strains of Enlightenment philosophy which dominated Freud's
thinking. In transcribing and translating Freud's textuality, H.D.
brought to light the more radical impulse "secreted" there, in the
gaps and flaws of theory. "Perhaps" she found the magic formula, the
healing combination of terms: eros, masochism, ego, destruction,
oceanic feeling, community: love-death.

The secret of Freud's textuality is that its sexuality ultimately escapes definition and closure, mobilizing the production of hieroglyphic signs that constitute unresolvable but fruitful paradoxes,
riddles, repetitions, and new, irreducible antitheses, which explode
discursive unity and coherence. H.D. discovers that in spite of
Freud's desire for closure (for death), his representation of eros exceeds his attempt to define it as that countercultural, biologistic

female instinct that seeks pleasure in the discharge of sexual union, subject to the prohibitions and repressions of masculine civilization. Whether consciously or not, "the Professor himself proclaimed the Herculean power of Eros" (*TF* 103).

H.D. is not the only intense reader of Freud to have discovered his subversive sexual subtext. Leo Bersani is especially aware of Freud's masochistic *jouissance* in the papers on metapsychology.[41] But she is one of the first artists to have divined a cure for civilization's discontents in this alchemistry of metaphysical terms and to have attempted to administer it through the medium of poetry. In doing so, she acts as Freud's divining "scribe," as his "secret-ary,"[42] and once again we are in the domain of Hermes-Thoth, transposing the soul of Freudian thought from the realm of hermeneutics—of exposition, interpretation, explanation, and reduction—to the hermetic, the undecidable, and the riddling. It is this fully, poetically restored *pharmakon* of textuality, the symbolic secretion of an undifferentiated eros-death, which keeps psychoanalysis alive by repeatedly destroying its theoretical closure and sedimentation.

Does it matter that H.D. is a woman? Why does being a woman allow her, like Diotima, to perceive eros behind Socrates, or behind Freud and the "death-mask" of his grave philosophy? Perhaps because, as a woman, H.D. has less authoritative credibility to risk than the "father of psychoanalysis" and is therefore freer to explore and expand his less discursive, less theoretical or enlightened, more occult and poetic side. But also because she is committed to finding a cure for her own immobilization (she suffered from writer's block) in a culture that, as she had long since recognized, denied women the authority to speak (of) her own desire. With Freud, she discovers that to find a cure for herself would mean finding a cure for his civilization, for its paranoia and suppression of female sexuality, of the enigmatic, antithetical compounds of love, life, and death which female sexuality embodies.

Could she see eros behind the Socratic philosopher whose authoritative tracts on femininity ("Femininity" was published in English in the first year of H.D.'s analysis with Freud) appeal self-consciously to a misogynous metaphysics to solve otherwise unanswerable questions? Could she detect from those questions how much Freud wanted to know as well as how unknowing, how at a loss, he was on the matter of female sexuality? Was it his erotic curiosity (but not his epistemophilia, a symptomatic urge to master the unknown) which she recognized, appreciated, and appropriated for her own, healing art?

Why did H.D. come to believe that she *had* come into possession of the secret, the *pharmakon*, the psychoanalytic cure for inhibitory, deathly, categorical thinking? Partly, I suspect, because she felt privileged by Freud in their "work together" (*TF* 108) as his collaborator in analysis ("We have only just begun our researches, our 'studies,' the old Professor and I" [*TF* 100]). Partly because they shared a common interest in archaeology, Egyptology, and the occult.[43] Partly because, as a creative writer, she dreamed of entering the dark room full of archaeological treasures at the back of Freud's office and of being initiated into the Egyptian mysteries of life and death. Finally, because Freud invited her to think that she was gifted with psychoanalytic ability when he commented, "You discovered for yourself what I discovered for the race" (*TF* 18). So when he attempts to tell her that "my discoveries are not primarily a heal-all. My discoveries are the basis for a very grave philosophy. There are very few who understand this, *there are very few who are capable of understanding this*" (*TF* 18), she assumes the analytical authority to read between his lines, to understand and establish the basis for a healing that he so pessimistically, even symptomatically, denies.

Chief among the civilized neuroses that H.D. proposes to cure is the neurosis of psychoanalysis and its symptomatic failure to respond to the woman who seeks treatment for her estranged sexuality, that is, for her immobilizing, self-alienating desire for the phallus.[44] What prevents psychoanalysis from intervening in woman's repression of her own sexuality and from challenging her introjection of culture's patriarchal superego is its own philosophical subscription to the idea that in the natural course of sexual development woman will necessarily desire what she cannot have—the power to be a man: "The repudiation of femininity can be nothing else than a biological fact, a part of the great riddle of sex" (*SE* 23:252). When H.D. goes to Freud to be cured of her writing block, he tells her that "women did not creatively amount to anything or amount to much, unless they had a male counter-part or a male companion from whom they drew their inspiration" (*TF* 149). Yet, Freud contradicts himself ("you discovered for yourself what I discovered for the race"). And in the same essay that admits therapeutic impotence before the woman wishing to know and possess sexual difference, he confesses that he appeals to "the Witch-Metapsychology" whenever knowledge eludes him in the analytic process (*SE* 23:225). Like Achilles before his treatment in H.D.'s palinode, Freud suffers from a metaphysical horror of woman's heterogeneity, a witch fantasy.

H.D.'s palinode is a cryptic, healing response to the metapsychological Freud who wrote "Femininity," "Analysis Terminable and Interminable," and *Civilization and Its Discontents*; it is an explanation and an apology written in defense of psychoanalysis, its occult capacity to reveal and free the repressed power of woman. It is also a postponed "imaginary conversation" with the Freud who presented his theoretical defenses to her directly in their sessions. That this conversation is represented in the interactions of mythic figures and hieroglyphic characters is not surprising. Judging from the overdetermined symbolism that forms the manifest text of *Tribute to Freud*, and given (H.D.'s report of) Freud's resistance to a more flexible conceptualization of femininity, it is probable that much of the dialogue in her analysis was conducted in veiled terms, principally in terms of literary and mythical allusion: *Helen in Egypt* is a mimesis of that dialogue, though its content has been expanded to include the antithetical terms of Freud's metaphysical writings.

What is most therapeutic about H. D.'s palinode in feminist terms is the place and power of subjectivity which H.D. gives to her "female" protagonist. Helen is (mostly) "in Egypt," in that other realm, the preoedipal, pre-Hel(l)enic realm that Freud's psychoanalysis had only just discovered but had not yet dreamed of exploring, and to which Luce Irigarary draws our attention:

> As Freud admits, the beginnings of sexual life for a girl child are so "obscure," so "faded with time," that one would have to dig down very deep indeed to discover beneath the traces of this civilization, of this history, the vestiges of a more archaic civilization that might give some clue to woman's sexuality. That extremely ancient civilization would undoubtedly have a different alphabet, a different language. . . . Woman's desire would not be expected to speak the same language as man's; woman's desire has doubtless been submerged by the logic that has dominated the West since the time of the Greeks. [45]

From this other realm, which is at once a fantasy of psychoanalysis and of woman, H.D. attempts to write an originary language of desire and to bring into the stifled, modern consciousness of man, a more primitive, a more potent representation of our sexuality. Why might we call this a "woman's" language? Because women's entry into language and discourse as authoritative speakers with the same power as men to be self-signifying has been repressed ever since the Greeks, along with our expression of our sexuality. Have women through the ages of Western history not unconsciously and perhaps hysterically been "speaking" a more primitive, a more hieroglyphic language, a repressed language onto which an equally repressed sexuality has been cathected? And if it were verbalized, brought into consciousness, where it could activate new referential functions— what curative effects then?

H.D.'s palinode offers Freud's civilization a *pharmakon* of writing to cure a cultural memory alienated from the vital forces of life and eros and immobilized by a masterfully ambitious death drive. The *pharmakon* comes from that forgotten, maligned, and dismissed "other" world, the world before the Greeks, the world of women, the maternal world of ontogenetic and phylogenetic prehistory which H.D. symbolizes as *"this ancient Child Egypt"* (80). She presents it to the world in the form of a very long and not very readable poem ("little understood") as conceived by a woman who has a translator's sense of woman's otherness. Whether or not her researches lead to the discovery of a finite set of hieroglyphics that, in their irreducible antithesis or heterogeneity, represent a specifically female sexuality remains to be seen.

Only just now is classical archaeology freeing itself from the yoke of German romanticism, from its belief in the myth that all European civilization derives from the same Greek origin, from the reductive term *pre-Hellenic* that inadequately names the radical heterogeneity of cultures that gave rise to "Greece." (I am thinking especially of Martin Bernal's *Black Athena: The Afroasiatic Roots of Western Civilization*). And only just now is psychoanalysis, often in the form of artistic-critical inquiry, researching the so-called preoedipal realm that Freud's German ideology prevented him from conceiving as radically other. *Helen in Egypt* does not presume to go so far as to represent a woman's language, but it does answer affirmatively and foresightedly the question it repeatedly poses to the (Freudian) reader in the voice of a very ancient, very misunderstood woman: "Is the last enlightenment that of the woman Helen?" (262).

## Bewitching the Witch Metapsychology

The figure of the witch-*pharmakeus* who doctors Achilles' dreams and enchants the ghosts of his legions derives, at least in part, from the fantasies of psychoanalytic metapsychology. She is a dose of Freud's own medicine, the double enchantment of a reflection on a reflection, an antidote to poison. What she treats, as the foregoing sections of this chapter have attempted to show, is the long literary tradition from which she hails, including the literature of Freud, his *Civilization*. But that is not all: she is a figure of the post-Enlightenment, a countersign to the signs of Freud's failure to work through the animistic residues of his science, his own fantasies and projections, which he discreetly veils behind the language of philosophers, who do not always know what they are saying but who justify their conventional biases with a natural teleology. Hence, H.D.'s witchery signals a profound irony: she dis-plays the play of fantasy-speculation which is foundational to the theories of psychoanalysis, and particularly to the theories of femininity. For it is in the metapsychology and treatment of "woman" that Freud founders, in turn calling upon his witch (*Hexe*): "We can only say: "So muss denn doch die Hexe dran!" [We must call on the Witch to our help after all!]—the Witch Metapsychology. Without metapsychological speculation and theorizing—I had almost said phantasying—we shall not get another step forward" (*SE* 23:225).

Helen is not the only witch in H.D.'s oeuvre. She or her equivalent—heretic, Sapphic, ecstatic, mystic, fortune-teller, prophetess, forest dweller—figures throughout the writing that has featured in my discussion so far. This last section of the chapter launches an inquiry into the subversiveness of this intertextual figure. I return to *Studies on Hysteria*, to see where and how the witch emerges in Freud's writings, and where she enters H.D.'s writing as some form of critical response and elaboration. The figure reflected in H.D.'s writing is not simple, not simply oppositional; her witch is a figure of excessive mystification whose potential therapeutic effects are both beneficial and harmful.

Freud appeals to the witch metapsychology when he is baffled by the "enigma of woman," even though he claims to be concerned with "observed facts, almost without any speculative additions," as he does in "Femininity" (*SE* 22:113). Facts do little to illuminate this subject, which he introduces with dramatic exasperation:

> Throughout history people have knocked their heads against the riddle of the nature of femininity—
>
> *Häupter in Hieroglyphenmützen,*
> *Häupter in Turban und schwarzem Barett,*
> *Perückenhäupter und tausend andre*
> *Arme, schwitzende Menschenhäupter.*
> (113)[46]

Where Oedipus fails to enlighten him, the witch-sphinx answers his riddles, deciphering the hieroglyphs in which reason and observation are encrypted. With a speculative satisfaction curious to find in a conscientious scientist, Freud accepts what natural philosophy has to say on the nature of male domination: "To speak teleologically—Nature takes less careful account of [that (feminine) function's] demands than in the case of masculinity. And the reason for this may lie—thinking once again teleologically—in the fact that the accomplishment of the aim of biology has been entrusted to the aggressiveness of men and has been made to some extent independent of women's consent" (*SE* 22:131).

Just as dramatically, he calls upon the witch in "The Taboo of Virginity" (1918 [1917]) to explain otherwise inexplicable "rules of avoidance" universally applied among primitive people to menopausal or menstruating women. What she reveals is a "generalized dread of women," "the fact that woman is different from man, for ever incomprehensible and mysterious, strange and therefore apparently hostile. The man is afraid of being weakened by the woman, infected with her femininity" (*SE* 11:198). The bewitchery of facts does not stop here but continues to inform *Civilization and Its Discontents*, in which men's dread of women is formulated in reverse, as women's hostility to mankind. Since Freud unquestioningly regards civilization as the business of men and since civilization demands that men estrange the female sex and exploit it for "higher" purposes, "the woman finds herself forced into the background . . . [where] she adopts a hostile attitude" (*SE* 21:104).

As if spellbound by the explanatory powers of his (men's) defensive projections, Freud addresses his witch with perplexing horrors that he subsequently, un-self-critically, attributes to woman herself. We could read his famous theory of penis envy in this light, as a figure of female self-disenchantment serving as antidote for a fantastical castration anxiety, which is the reading Sarah Kofman, Luce Irigaray, Hélène Cixous, and Shoshana Felman give it.[47]

When Freud addresses the subject of feminine uncanniness in creative writing, his fantasies and projections are more exposed. In "The Uncanny," he attributes "the most uncanny thing of all," the "terrifying phantasy" of "being buried alive," to the transformation of another fantasy, not so terrifying "but qualified by a certain lasciviousness—the phantasy . . . of intra-uterine existence" (*SE* 17:244). To demystify this *unheimlich* (emasculating) return of the maternal body, psychoanalysis would see it domesticated, "qualified," by a certain "lasciviousness." Elsewhere, in "The Theme of the Three Caskets," Freud discloses the essence behind the figure of mythopoeic femininity, attributing her power of horror to woman's actual primeval character:

> If what we were concerned with were a dream, it would occur to us at once that caskets are also women, symbols of what is essential in woman, and therefore of a woman herself—like coffers, boxes, cases, baskets, and so on. If we boldly assume that there are symbolic substitutions of [this] kind in myths, as well, then . . . we see that the theme is a human one, *a man's choice between three women* . . . the tri-form Artemis-Hecate . . . The great Mother-goddesses . . . of life and fertility and . . . death . . . the woman who bears him, the woman who is his mate, and the woman who destroys him. (*SE* 12:292, 299, 301)

Woman, especially the mother, is Freud's "nightmare," in Ernest Jones's sense of the term: that is, the horrifying specter of a projected misogyny, which church fathers, humanists, and scientists alike have felt compelled to exorcise in the name of enlightenment.

Between the time when he wrote *Studies on Hysteria* (1893–1895) and 1900, when he wrote *The Interpretation of Dreams*, Freud was shifting the basis of psychoanalysis from empirical to phantasmal biography; he dreamed of outlining an etiology of neurosis rooted in a "devil religion." "The idea of bringing in witches is gaining strength," he writes in a letter to Wilhelm Fliess (24 January 1897):

> Their "flying" is explained; the broomstick they ride probably is the great Lord Penis. The secret gatherings, with dancing and entertainment, can be seen any day in the streets where children play. . . . I have ordered the *Malleus maleficarum* ["The Witches' Hammer"], and . . . I am beginning to grasp an idea: it is as though in the perversions, of which hysteria is the negative, we have before us a remnant of a primeval sexual cult, which was once—perhaps still is—a religion in the Semitic East (Moloch, Astarte). Imagine, I obtained a scene about the circumcision of a girl. . . .
>
> I dream, therefore, of a primeval devil religion with rites that are carried on secretly, and understand the harsh therapy of the witches' judges. . . . there is a class of people who to this very day tell stories like those of the witches.[48]

In another piece of correspondence he tells Fliess that "the mediaeval theory of possession, held by the ecclesiastical courts, was identical with our theory of a foreign body and a splitting of consciousness." It is perfectly clear that Freud saw the new science of psychoanalysis as a descendant of the old art of exorcising witches.[49]

In *Studies on Hysteria*, Freud writes of administering treatment as if he were a "father confessor who gives absolution . . . after the confession has been made" (*SE* 2:82). His techniques entail a milder form of exorcism and enlightenment than *The Witches' Hammer*, but in principle they are the same. "The pressure technique," for example, is used to extract and dispel the demon of repressed desire; the physician recalls the "patient's field of vision" (280) from unconscious memory, where the disturbing fantasy has lodged itself, and then presses for a verbal description, causing the patient to get rid of it, "like a ghost that has been laid" (281), "*by turning it into words*" (280).

Despite his subscription to the manuals of exorcism, Freud continues to appeal to the witch metapsychology while remaining blind to the paradoxes of ideology. Consequently, some critics of twentieth-century intellectual culture read Freud as a militant of scientific positivism, whose witch-hunt to end all subjective self-deception leads inevitably to the end of self-criticism. This is the reading of Freud which Theodor Adorno and Max Horkheimer present in their *Dialectic of Enlightenment* (1944). Written at the end of the Second World War, when disenchantment with the so-called progress of civilization was at its peak among European intellectuals, this book loudly denounces the intentions of the Enlightenment as nothing more than a misguided plot of world domination. Observing a continuity between modern technocracy and primitive magic as practiced by chauvinist shamans throughout history, the authors declare: "What men want to learn from nature is how to use it in order wholly to dominate it and other men. That is [Enlightenment's] only aim."[50] Their basic premise is that with each technological advance over superstition and belief, the culture of the Englightenment falls victim to its own mythology:

> The "unshakable confidence in the possibility of world domination" [*Totem and Taboo*], which Freud anachronistically ascribes to magic, corresponds to realistic world domination only in terms of a more skilled science. The replacement of the milieu-bound practices of the medicine man by all-inclusive industrial technology required first of all the autonomy of ideas in regard to objects that was achieved in the reality-adjusted ego. . . . Mythology itself set off the unending process of enlightenment in which ever and again, with the inevitability of necessity, every specific theoretic view succumbs to the destructive criticism that it is only a belief—until even the very notions of spirit, of truth and, indeed, enlightenment itself, have become animistic magic. (11)

When men's self-domination becomes the reality principle of history, then, say the authors, "imagination atrophies"; thought is impoverished and resigned. The aim of the Enlightenment is not just the "disenchantment of the world" but precisely "the extirpation of animism." "There is to be no mystery—which means, too, no wish to reveal mystery" (5). As I read it, Freud's sense of enlightment is not "dialectical" so much as contradictory. Depending on the subject of investigation, he may or may not propose analytic demystification. He reserves the mystery of the artistic gift for the poets, for instance. But, when the subject is femininity, it is enlightenment in Adorno's and Horkheimer's sense which Freud demands: here his desire is to abolish the enigma, master the uncanny, and thoroughly domesticate the riddling sphinx. Though admitting the incompleteness of his researches, he forecloses his essay "Femininity" with a dismissive refusal to "sweat" (schwitzen) any more over woman's hieroglyphics: "That is all I had to say to you about femininity. It is certainly incomplete and fragmentary and does not always sound friendly. . . . If you want to know more about femininity, enquire from your own experiences of life, or turn to the poets, or wait until science can give you deeper and more coherent information" (SE 22:135). He has given up further inquiry, but in the final analysis, science will have the last word.

Conversely, Freud allows his animistic imagination free reign when he turns his focus onto the lives of artists as illustrated in "A Seventeenth-Century Demonological Neurosis" (1923 [1922]) and Leonardo Da Vinci and a Memory of His Childhood (1910). Freud attributes the uncanny and mysterious power of the Mona Lisa to the artist's maternal fantasy, which he embellishes with narrative speculation of his own. In his reconstruction of Leonardo's early life, Freud forges spurious links among (1) the painter's early childhood memory of being struck by a vulture in the cradle and (2) a later memory of having read "in a book on natural history . . . that all vultures were females and could reproduce their kind without any assistance from a male" (90) and (3) the fact that Leonardo "had a mother, but no father" (90), was "illegitimate" (91), and (4) the speculation that Leonardo had been "seduced" by his mother ("like all unsatisfied mothers, she took her little son in place of her husband, and by the too early maturing of his erotism robbed him of a part of his masculinity" [117]), and (5) a remote thought of Freud's about the Egyptian mother goddess Mut, her hieroglyphic representation as a vulture (SE 11:82–90).[51] Though Freud confesses to a serious anach-

ronism—"have we any right to expect Leonardo to know [Egyptian],
seeing that the first man who succeeded in reading hieroglyphics
was François Champollion (1790–1832)?"—he insists on his mythic
etymology: "Can the similarity [of the Egyptian pronunciation of the
mother goddess's name Mut] to the sound of our word *Mutter*,
"mother," be merely a coincidence?" (88) Such farfetched, admittedly
unfounded inference betrays a desire to translate a maternal fantasy
of his own, to dispel his uncanny dread of the prehistoric omnipo-
tence of the mother.

Attuned to Freud's mysteries, H.D. draws on their figures precisely to demystify his program of disenchantment. Her Helen com-
prises all the elements of Freud's uncanny femininity; she enters
men's dreams not riding a stick but wielding it—the wand of her not-
so-anachronistic black magic:

> I drew out a blackened stick,
> but he snatched it,
> he flung it back,
>
> "what sort of enchantment is this
> what art will you wield with a fagot?
> are you Hecate? are you a witch?
>
> a vulture, a hieroglyph,
> the sign or the name of a goddess?
> what sort of goddess is this?"
>
> (*HE* 16)

Here is Freud's witch, death-goddess Hecate, Leonardo's Mut-
Mutter, the hieroglyphic vulture, and the primeval magic, condensed into a single dream image. She is also an ironic exposure of
patriarchal terror of matriarchal power projected onto woman since
at least the Greek enlightenment.

H.D. is not the only Freudian woman reader to address the demonological psychoanalytic treatment of women. She anticipates the
feminist psychoanalyst Catherine Clément, who underlines the exorcist's techniques in the analytical treatment of hysteria:

Conquering, forcing, adopting other measures, insisting: the work of
those two cathartics Breuer and Freud has still not left the magic circle.
Freud calls these practices "a little technical device": "I inform my
patient that in a moment, I am going to put pressure on her forehead,
and I assure her that, while I am pressing, a memory will arise as an
image or else an idea will come to mind. . . . I successfully distract the

pateint's [sic] attention from his search and conscious reflections, in short from everything that might translate his will; all of this recalls what happens when one stares at a crystal ball, etc."[52]

Just as Father Lactance, "the exorcist of Loudun" (16), "jumps on the body of Mother Jeanne des Anges, Freud presses the hysteric's forehead" (16). "Abreaction" is the term the cathartics use for the abracadabra of their treatment:

> At the center of this theater of catharsis unreels the process that Freud and Breuer called "abreaction": "Emotional discharge through which the subject liberates himself from the affect connected to the memory of a traumatic event, thus permitting it to not become or remain pathogenic." Wrested by a physical threat, the confession that one is possessed is a process of abreaction, in the same way that emotional discharge is in the cure: *it comes out*. (15–16)

H.D.'s response to psychoanalytic sorcery is, in part, to remystify the process abreaction "unreels," which, as she sees it, is essentially mysterious:

> The trouble is, this process of this letting loose or letting flow, continuous images . . . is a secret one can not, with the best will in the world, impart. . . . But one must, of necessity, begin with one's own private inheritance; there, already the measure is *pressed down and shaken together, and running over*. . . . there is no single formula that will fit. . . . it is not just glimpsed in a crystal-gazing ball. (*G1* 69–70)

Her intent is to *literalize* the figure of Freudian witchcraft and to make real the "unreeling" of her story or storage of mnemic images through the crystal ball of analysis. However doubtful a move it seems, this "taking the relay" from Freud's anachronistic speculations, it may be the most effective way to ensure that historical and cultural evolution takes place. Clément explains:

> If women begin to want their turn at telling this history . . . it will necessarily be . . . a history arranged the way tale-telling women tell it. And from the standpoint of conveying the mythic models that powerfully structure the Imaginary (masculine and feminine, complex and varied), this history will be true. On the level of fantasy, it will be fantastically true: It is still acting on us. In telling it, in developing it, even in plotting it, I seek to undo it, to overturn it, to reveal it, to *expose* it. (6)

H.D. takes the relay from Freud in telling her story, the story of woman, "developing it," "plotting it," to "reveal" and to "overturn" it.[53] But she also reveals, perhaps unintentionally, the danger of becoming beguiled by and trapped in the specular arena of this applied bewitchery. Making herself into an autobiographical spectacle, as hysteric, mysteric, and prophetess, in order to enlighten an audience of analysts blinded by their own scientific project(ion)s, perhaps reinforces her/their sense of female otherness, driving prejudices even deeper, forcing her to withdraw to the margins of society on the outskirts of literary circles and into the asylum of the clinic, or worse, into the asylum of the mind.[54]

H.D. did not, however, always go along with Freud's pressure technique, noting one occasion in analysis when the retelling of her story did not conform to his natural philosophy: "When I told the Professor that I had been infatuated with Frances Josepha and might have been happy with her, he said, 'No—biologically, no.' For some reason, though I had been so happy with the Professor (Freud— Freude), my head hurt and I felt unnerved" (TF 152). At the price of diminishing the joy (Freude) of their established rapport, she signals the telltale sign of her resistance, or so Freud would call it: "It is quite common for the patient to complain of a headache when we start on the pressure procedure; for her new motive for resistance remains as a rule unconscious and is expressed by the production of a new hysterical symptom. The headache indicates her dislike of allowing herself to be influenced" (SE 2:302).

H.D. would enter Freud's "magic circle" but not to be confirmed into his male "mysteries" (CP 455), or to recognize the "biological" theory of sexual preference. She is forewarned by Freud himself in his footnotes to his case history of Dora, where he admits not only to failing to realize his own countertransference in his overzealous role as father-confessor but also of overlooking her "gynaecophilia"—"it seems to me that the fault in my technique lay in this omission: I failed to discover in time and to inform the patient that her homosexual (gynaecophilic) love for Frau K. was the strongest unconscious current in her mental life."[55] In treating what he takes to be the reactivation of a diabolical pact or family seduction, Freud shows that he is not always prepared to subject his enlightened prejudices to critical scrutiny. He then leaves it to the patient, in this case H.D., to put up her "wordless challenge" (TF 99) whenever "the Professor's explanations were too illuminating" (30).

It is not H.D.'s lesbianism I wish to pursue here but rather the figure of bewitchery it strategically assumes.[56] In *Her*, she (Hermione Gart) entertains a forbidden romance with Frances Josepha (Fayne Rabb) in defiance of the father, who controls the domestic scene like an "Old Testament . . . God" (*Her* 100) and in defiance of her chauvinist lover (Ezra Pound/George Lowndes), who declares they should "be burnt for witchcraft" (165). In H.D.'s retelling, the more the family romance is impressed upon Her, the more she presents hysterical (ambivalent) resistance, culminating in a vision of anarchic annihilation:

> "You ought to marry George Lowndes." "Yes, mama." "This girl—she's all wrong . . . *most* unwholesome." "Yes, mama." . . . Yes, yes and no, no. Yes and no. No and yes. I will say yes, I will say no. . . . I will throw yes and no and no and yes like the shafts of a Pythian goddess. I will slay and kill and burn and break and slay and kill and burn. I will and I won't be taken in by all their vile antics. (176)[57]

*Nights* transforms the family arena into an erotic cinerama, just as the witch, according to Clément, "converts the unlivable space of a stifling Christianity" into pagan orgy (*Newly Born Woman*, 5). With this text, H.D. would persuade the Freudian reader, Helforth, to swallow the medicine prescribed by her narrative seduction, intiating *him* into the mysteries of (her) sex. She would have him "drink the poison" and "worship that dark bloom" (*N* 65–66) of her mandragora of free love. To deliver herself from the consecrated confines of the paterfamilias, H.D. dispenses a narcotic of ecstatic poetism: oblivious to the reality principle dictated by the oedipal father, Natalia acts out her burning desires in the boudoir of sexual fantasy. She proceeds with her witchcraft even though she knows that for transgressing the social contract upheld by psychoanalysis she would "be flung into a mediaeval hell, filled with the most hideous of refuse, come to life, the horrors of the unconscious" (53).[58] Just as the hysteric "unties familiar bonds, introduces disorder into the well-regulated unfolding of everyday life," Clément explains, the sorceress "heals, against the Church's canon . . . favors nonconjugal love" in the burning liberation of her passion (*Newly Born Woman*, 5).

From hysteric to mysteric, H.D. reveals and inverts the oppressive history of woman, the history of the suppression of her power to fantasize. As Clément observes, the hysteric

> resumes and assumes the memories of [the witch]: that was Michelet's hypothesis in *The Sorceress*; it was Freud's in *Studies on Hysteria*. Both

thought that the repressed past survives in woman; woman, more than anyone else, is dedicated to reminiscence. The sorceress, who in the end is able to dream Nature and therefore conceive it, incarnates the reinscription of the traces of paganism that triumphant Christianity repressed. The hysteric, whose body is transformed into a theater for forgotten scenes, relives the past, bearing witness to a lost childhood that survives in suffering. (5)

Recognizing, in *The Walls Do Not Fall* that "we have had too much consecration / too little affirmation," H.D. proceeds to develop this figure even if "this, this, this / has been proved heretical" (53). *Tribute to the Angels* reaffirms the heresy of Venus, whose name "we saw . . . desecrated" in a moment of patriarchal history (74). In the mortar and pestle of pharmaceutical fantasy, in the crucible of her passion for "the true rune, the right spell," she concocts a bewitching formula guaranteed to heal the ruinous image of woman's sexuality:

> O swiftly, re-light the flame
> before the substance cool,
>
> for suddenly we saw your name
> desecrated; knaves and fools
>
> have done you impious wrong,
> Venus, for venery stands for impurity
>
> and Venus as desire
> is venereous, lascivious,
>
> while the very root of the word shrieks
> like a mandrake when foul witches pull
>
> its stem at midnight,
> and rare mandragora itself
>
> is full, they say, of poison,
> food for the witches' den.
>
> Swiftly re-light the flame,
> Aphrodite, holy name, . . .
>
> return, O holiest one,
> Venus whose name is kin

to venerate,
venerator.

(74–75)

To make the transition from the solipsistic heresy of *Nights* to wordplay on the world stage of (pre)history, H.D. must recover the sorceress of her own psychical genealogy. She does so primarily in the figure of the heretical grandmother who bewitches childhood memory. As she retells it, the Child's schooled response—"The stricter Brethren of the church said it was witchcraft. What exactly is witchcraft? You can be burnt for being a witch. Is Mamalie a witch?" (*G* 88)—must be demystified. When Mamalie returns at the end of her story, what Hilda beholds is no witch but instead an oracle who has the gift of speaking in tongues, the charisma to fire communal imagination, and the passion to meet God in the conflagration of war. In the visionary's "illuminism of lucid madness" (Clément, *Newly Born Woman*, 54), she is enlightenment itself, or so Hilda reminisces/ foresees: "She had called me Agnes, and she had called me Lucy. I was Lucy, I was that Lux or Light" (*G* 135). Seen from the outside of the church canon, Mamalie (pre)figures what Clément calls "the apotheosis of woman" (*Newly Born Woman*, 31): no she-Gehenna, but the virtual embodiment of *Sanctus Spiritus* (*G* 135), recalling Michelet's *Sorceress*: "Woman at the witches' sabbat is all-fulfilling. She is priest and altar and she is the host with which all the people take communion. Basically, is she not God?" (quoted by Clément, *Newly Born Woman*, 31).

Following the command of her heretical muse, H.D.'s reminiscence "draws the veil aside, / unbinds [her] eyes" (*HD* 7) so that in place of the nightmarish old hag aiming her broomstick at a virgin in the service of patriarchy, the Child-*sauvage* recalls the redeeming figure of dark Mary. This is not the dark Mary who so impressed Walter Pater in his haunting revision of *La Gioconda*, or the vampire-vulture who, in turn, so impressed Freud in his reading of Leonardo's mother (*SE* 11:110).[59] She is a prepatriarchal, prehistorical figure of Aphrodite, personifying the wisdom and sanctity of female sexual fantasy. From here, it is only a small leap of faith to that other healing figure, Helen *pharmakeus*, antidote to a virulent misogyny that infects the uncanny canon of literary history.

On the subject of history, the question still remains, says Catherine Clément:

Do the abnormal ones—madmen, deviants, neurotics, women . . .
anticipate the culture to come, repeat the past culture, or express a
constantly present utopia? Michelet himself does not hesitate: it is
because the sorceress is the bearer of the past that she is invested with a
challenging power. Freud sees the power of the repressed working in
the same way: anachronism has a specific power, one of shifting, disturbance, and change, limited to imaginary displacements. (*Newly Born
Woman*, 9)

Does it make sense to address the limits of "imaginary displacements" if an entire literary tradition is being overturned? Whatever
the personal, psychological cost, is H.D.'s utopian nostalgia for the
archaic cult of Mary or the cult of Helen not therapeutically invalu-
able to a culture still mesmerized by the nightmare of (maternal)
femininity as first perpetrated by the universal reception of Goethe's
reminiscences and perpetuated in this century by a triumvirate of
patriarchal mythographers, James Frazer, Robert Briffault, and Sigmund Freud?[60]

How do we judge H.D.'s fantasizing, which derives as much from
delirium as from deliberated criticism, borrowing from Freud, yet
healing, making *heimlich*, through the poetics of psychoanalysis?
Once again, Clément offers food for thought:

At stake—the whole evaluation of psychoanalysis as a therapeutic
function. Is a disturbed, disturbing order reestablished by making the
symptom disappear, or does it definitively annul the innovating force
that is contained in the past but has become strange, foreign, other in
the present? That is how the hysteric, reputed to be incurable, sometimes—and more and more often—took the role of resistant heroine:
the one whom psychoanalytic treatment would never be able to *reduce*.
The one who roused Freud's passion through the spectacle of femininity in crisis, and the one, the only one, who knew how to escape him. (9)

H.D. roused Freud's passion, prompting his plea: 'The trouble is—
I am an old man—*you do not think it worth your while to love me*" (*TF* 16).
He appeals, that is, to her love in spite of concluding in "The Theme
of the Three Caskets" that "it is in vain that an old man yearns for the
love of woman as he had it first from his mother; the third of the Fates
alone, the silent Goddess of Death, will take him into her arms" (*SE*
12:301). That love conquers both wisdom and the horrors of enlightenment is H.D.'s uncanonical answer to uncanny Freud. More than
just a resisting heroine, knowing both the power of his influence and

the blind spots of his theory, she risks a prediction: "only I, / I will escape" ("The Master," *CP* 458). It is a prediction that predicates the transformation from self-dramatizing hysteric to posthistoric visionary. The woman, Clément writes, "has loosed herself from the ties that bound her to those showmen of she-bears: Simon Magus, Jean Bodin, Charcot, a certain Freud . . . all the masters. She, like the sorceress, is going to fly away. But this time, one will know what she becomes" (*Newly Born Woman*, 57). In the end is the beginning of her story: her "Hermetic Definition."

# Postscript: H.D.'s Dream
# of a Common Language

> The picture-writing, the hieroglyph of the dream, was the
> common property of the whole race; in the dream, man, as
> at the beginning of time, spoke a universal language, and
> man, meeting in the universal understanding of the un-
> conscious or the subconscious, would forgo barriers of
> time and space, and man, understanding man, would save
> mankind.
>
> H.D., *Tribute to Freud*

In the crucible of her poetism, H.D. mixes the hieroglyphs of her
dreams and revises the Freudian vision. Her treatment is personally
*and* culturally healing because it offers linguistic and conceptual
emancipation from the categories of thought which shackle the Western mind.[1] She privileges not the secondary revision of the dream, its
submission to "reality testing" or translation into the discourses of
"enlightenment," but its primary language, which, with its riddling
imagism and charismatic flow of picture writing, opens the doors of
speculation, imagination, and communication.

What she proposes is a revolutionary redistribution of signify-
ing/visionary power. The hieroglyph of the dream belongs to the
people; however varied its individual and racial genealogy, its etymological roots arise from a common myth, transcending or subverting the defensive superstructures of personal and national ego. Just
as Freud delivered dream interpretation from an elite of oneirocritics
to an open method of free association and lexicography, H.D. would
deliver Freud's dream work from the high priests of psychoanalysis
to the open field of poetry.[2]

It is precisely the future fortune of his dream work which she
addresses in the opening pages of *Tribute to Freud*. Knowing she
cannot compete with J. J. van der Leeuw, the Oxford-educated
scholar and wealthy, influential businessman who is the perfect embodiment of every kind of symbolic authority and who met with

Freud the hour before her session to discuss the future of the psychoanalytic empire, she entertains her worst fear: the transfer of Freud's
legacy to some unassailable heir. When van der Leeuw is killed a year
later in a plane crash over Africa, she returns to Vienna with the half-
conscious intention, as Freud recognized, to "take his place" (*TF* 6).

We might read H.D.'s role of prophetess as a claim to be Freud's
spiritual or psychic equal, an egalitarian rather than an elitist claim.
She knows the scope of cultural possibility behind his observation
that the dream work entails a "complete 'transvaluation of all psychical values' " (*SE* 4:330) because she shares his revolutionary insights.[3]
It is her claim to be *equal* that makes her his true heir: to claim to be
anything less would be to condone the hierarchization of his new
science into contending factions of an increasingly immobilizing institutional orthodoxy. Like every woman, she has access to the dream
hieroglyph, but she lays no claim on the hieratic:

> I was not interested,
> I was not instructed,
> nor guessed the inner sense of the heiratic [*sic*].
>                                    (*HE* 22)[4]

Her criticisms of the institutionalization of psychoanalysis anticipate
a recent grammatological critique of the historical process by which a
self-elected "secretariat" comes to be established as the "natural"
ruling class of the word. I quote Jacques Derrida: "Naturally destined
to serve the communication of laws and the order of the city trans-
parently, a writing becomes the instrument of an abusive power, of a
caste of 'intellectuals,' that is, thus ensuring hegemony, whether its
own or that of special interests: the violence of a secretariat, a discriminating reserve, an effect of scribble and scrypt."[5] Along with
high priests, H.D. exposes and discredits false prophets and petty
pretenders who capitalize on the vulnerabilities of their clients, turning a revolutionary resource into an oil field of psychological rack-
eteering. As she sees it, the generation after Freud features all the
riggings and trappings of what once was an original theory and
practice, now transformed into a system of mechanical procedure
guaranteed to make some men rich:

> We visualize stark uprights and skeleton-like steel cages, like unfin-
> ished Eiffel Towers. And there are many, I have reason to know, who
> think of the whole method or system of psychoanalysis in some such
> terms, a cage, some mechanical construction set up in an arid desert, to

trap the unwary, and if there is "oil" to be inferred, the "oil" goes to someone else; there are astute doctors who "squeeze you dry" with their exorbitant fees for prolonged and expensive treatments. A tiresome subject at best—have nothing to do with it—it's worn out, dated; true, it was fashionable enough among the young intellectuals after the First World War but they turned out a dreary lot and who, after all, has heard of any of them since? (*TF* 83)

In saying this, H.D. anticipates Catherine Clément's cynical exposé, *The Weary Sons of Freud* (1978), about those she calls "the nouveaux riches of the intelligentsia" and whom she charges with neglecting the original purpose of psychoanalysis in favor of the publishing business:

They exchange work against money, like everyone else. They work harder than you think . . . [but] [t]hey don't "treat" anymore. . . . Curing is for psychiatrists, for psychologists, for doctors, not for them, no thanks. . . . Nevertheless, make no mistake, that's where, once upon a time, they started out from. The point really was to cure, when long ago, like Moses and his Levites, they left the Egyptian tyranny of coercive psychiatry for the uncertain shores of the Promised Word, for a land full of possibilities. . . .

What have they become now that they won't accept their curative function any more? . . . they have begun to take a very real place in the world where publication is produced.[6]

Clément's criticisms of the current state of psychoanalysis discloses an optimistic rejoinder that we also find in H.D., namely, the entry of innovative women onto the scene:

If I didn't truthfully think psychoanalysis was a fundamental social activity whose history and evolution have an impact on our culture, on its developments and the politics that reflect them and that sometimes influence them, what would I care about making these criticisms? I wouldn't care at all.

But strangely enough, I have a feeling I'm not writing alone. Still more strangely, the people who advocate this kind of criticism and keep it alive are female psychoanalysts rather than male psychoanalysts . . . . instead of serving us up an elitist and literary image of [psychoanalysis], [these women have] lived up to what it *does*. That is, healing; that is, changing life; that is, giving us the individual and thus the collective means to live better. (30)

In her uncommon dream of a common language, H.D. foresees a field of speculation and healing to which women lend their vision: men and women, understanding together, will save the world from masculinist illusions of enlightenment.

But Freud *did* welcome women to contribute to his clinical and cultural practice, did he not? Like the gnostic cults that opened their doors after the church fathers had closed theirs, Freud admitted and encouraged the initiation of women analysts; they figured prominently in the developing stages of Freud's new science. Had H.D. chosen to enter the practice, she might have met with the same success as Marie Bonaparte, Freud's French translator, who devoted her career to extending his work on literature and female sexuality. Of Bonaparte, whose classic study of Poe was published in the first year of her analysis (1933), H.D. confesses that she wishes "to be another equal factor or have equal power of benefiting and protecting the Professor" (*TF* 43). Yet she chooses to engage from outside the institution, from the place of least advantage, neither in league with Freud's female disciples nor aligned with his feminist dissenters. Why? What kept her from joining forces? What feminism did she manage to negotiate? What does her "hieroglyph of the dream" offer the feminist Freudian reader, or any reader looking for an effective marriage of critical world views? To answer these questions, we should first consider Freud's treatment of his most promising female colleagues.

Upon being notified of the completion of a manuscript, Freud saw it fitting to commend the author, Lou Andreas-Salomé: "There could be no better news than that you have sent a little book on our psychoanalysis ('Gescholten viel und viel bewundert, Helena') to the printer. Allow me to say how much I look forward to reading it. Your excellent essay 'Anal and Sexual' is already in the compositor's hands."[7] That he should signal his praise in words he adapts from Goethe—"Much abused and much admired, Helena" ("Bewundert viel und viel gescholten, Helena" [*Faust* 2.8488]) especially befits a writer who sometimes turned to poetry to illustrate the complexities of psychoanalysis. But there is more here than meets the eye. Freud's Faustian reference, though ostensibly pointing to the extremely mixed reception of psychoanalysis in the medical and intellectual worlds, makes a less visible sympathetic allusion to an earlier work of Andreas-Salomé's, an essay on female sexuality. "Der Mensch als Weib" (1899) argues that "woman is . . . the antithesis of Faustian man; she does not pursue the unattainable, the infinite. Why should she, being herself the goal, *das Ewig-Weibliche*?"[8] Does Freud, then, speak from the place of "Faustian man" to psychoanalytic woman, praising her contribution to his genius? Suspicions of a patronizing intent, masquerading behind a show of collegial recognition, are borne out in Freud's final words to her. In his commemorative note of 1937, Frau Andreas-Salomé is honored for her dedication to analysis and, moreover, for not letting her "feminine frailties" or her "poetical and literary works" obscure her primary value of supporting and supplementing his work:

> For the last 25 years of her life this remarkable woman was attached to psycho-analysis, to which she contributed valuable writings and which she practised as well. I am not saying too much if I acknowledge that we all felt it as an honour when she joined the ranks of our collaborators and comrades in arms, and at the same time as a fresh guarantee of the truth of the theories of analysis. . . . She never spoke of her own poetical and literary works. She clearly knew where the true values in life are to be looked for. Those who were closer to her . . . could discover with astonishment that all feminine frailties . . . were foreign to her or had been conquered by her in the course of her life.[9]

Freud reserves any mention of her feminine strengths, though he applauds her devotion to strong men, including "an intense friendship with Friedrich Nietzsche, founded upon her deep understanding of the philosopher's bold ideas," and her attachment to "the great poet" Rainer Maria Rilke, to whom she had "acted alike as Muse and protecting mother" (297).

What he admires in Andreas-Salomé appears to be precisely what he admires in his own daughter, Anna, namely, an Antigone-like loyalty to an aging and vulnerable father-prophet. He invokes Anna to end his eulogy: "It was in Vienna that long ago the most moving episode of her feminine fortunes had been played out. In 1912 she returned to Vienna in order to be initiated into psycho-analysis. My daughter, who was her close friend, once heard her regret that she had not known psycho-analysis in her youth. But, after all, in those days there was no such thing" (297–98). It is not Goethe but Oedipus who speaks here, proclaiming that the most moving episode in the life of this dedicated woman was the sacrifice of any creative intiative of her own in order to benefit and protect the father, his life work. Furthermore, it is not only Antigone he commemorates but also Athena, the "comrade in arms" who springs from the head of the all-inspiring *pater* "as a fresh guarantee of the truth of the theories of of analysis."

But was he right or does he add a little poetic license of his own? Perhaps Andreas-Salomé did tell Anna that life had not begun until she discovered analysis; indeed, she says as much in *Mein Dank an Freud* (1931). But what she tells Freud about Anna is precisely what Freud neglects to recognize, namely, the daughter's poetical-feminine innovation: "I am sorry that I did not get to know your youngest daughter in 1912/13—I was about to do so on one occasion, but, alas, she escaped me. Perhaps she has become a poet-translator from foreign tongues? Or perhaps a poetess on her own account? That would be the finest translation of her father's psycho-analysis into a feminine medium."[10] Coming from a woman who in later years transformed herself into a poet-translator of psychoanalysis, this speculation discloses more about her own potential prospects than Anna's. A self-fulfilling prophecy, it confirms the "feminine" or childlike, animistic side of Freud which will inform the uncanny genre of her writing. In the same year that he completed his "Seventeenth-Century Demonological Neurosis" (1922), she wrote *Der Teufel und sein Grossmutter* (*The Devil and His Grandmother*), a dream play about the devil's return to his primal mother, marking, Ernst Pfeiffer notes, "not only her psychological gifts and intuitive understanding which . . . attained their full flowering through psycho-analysis, but . . . her creative gift."[11]

Where, then, does H.D. fit into this story? Is she not, like Lou Andreas-Salomé, a poet-translator of psychoanalysis, "a poetess on her own account," posing as a medium of femininity, extending the father's researches? She also inscribes a *Dank an Freud*, wishing to "translat[e] [her] admiration for what he stood for" (*TF* 63); but whereas Andreas-Salomé defers to Freud's superior powers of expression, declining any opportunity to elaborate his inquiries with innovations of her own and offering no more than a humble, simple "thanks," H.D. defers her thanks and makes no show of humility.[12]

H.D. could not at first find the words to express her gratitude to Freud, since to do so "would be to delve too deep, to become involved in technicalities" (*TF* 63). But these are the technicalities of intertextual appropriation, application, and in some cases, subversion of the father of psychoanalysis. She is no "scribbling" devotee like Marie Bonaparte and Hanns Sachs, she intimates to Walter Schmideberg (*TF* 15), and she is more outspoken on this point in "The Master":

> they will travel far and wide,
> they will discuss all his written words,
> his pen will be sacred
> they will build a temple
> and keep all his sacred writings safe,
> and men will come
> and men will quarrel
> but he will be safe;
> they will found temples in his name,
> his fame
> will be so great
> that anyone who has known him
> will also be hailed as master,
> seer,
> interpreter;
>
> only I,
> I will escape.
>
> (CP 457–58)

Are we, then, to read her (post-)Freudian poetics as a form of escapism, a refusal to negotiate the real, material conditions of this world, including its political (sexist) ideologies? Or, given her clearly stated departure from the ranks of psychoanalytic orthodoxy, should we not look for a dialectic of dedicated confrontation and elaboration? After all, she appeals to the transformative powers of the/Freud's "pen" in *The Walls Do Not Fall*:

> Let us . . .
>
> re-dedicate our gifts
> to spiritual realism,
>
> scrape a palette,
> point pen or brush,
>
> prepare papyrus or parchment
> offer incense to Thoth. . . .
>
> now is the time to re-value.
>
> (48–49)

After Freud's death, when she can be thoroughly emancipated from any deferential feelings she may have harbored, is "the time" for rededicating her poetic gift to a radical critique and extension of psychoanalysis. But what she proposes to perform does not violate so much as pursue Freud's thinking when he called on Nietzsche to proclaim the "complete 'transvaluation of all psychical values' ": the revolutionary return to the primary dream, which lives on in artists, children, and women.[13]

Only after Freud died could she proceed, in good faith, with her " 'delayed' analysis" unhampered by fears of her capitulation to the indomitable, paternal countertransference that drove Dora away and conspired to quell all feminist criticism. Certainly pressure had been placed on her to conform to his ideal of daughterly submission, as Estelle Roith points out in a highly suggestive passage at the end of *The Riddle of Freud*:

> I conclude this study of Freud and the origins of his attitudes to women with the observation of a small but telling detail. The poet H.D., who was in analysis with Freud, tells us that his favourite out of his large collection of antiquities was his statuette of Pallas Athené. . . . This statuette was his talisman. In 1938 Freud sent it on ahead with Marie Bonaparte for safe-keeping in his final exile. Athené, of course, is born not of a woman but out of her father Zeus's forehead. Zeus has thus appropriated motherhood. . . . In Aeschylus's *Oresteia*, it is the chaste Athené, her father's favourite child, who is chosen by Apollo to "oversee" justice when Orestes is tried for the murder of his mother. "She is one of us," Aeschylus has Apollo say . . . and there is a curious analogy here with Freud and his own illlustrious daughter Anna: his "Anna-Antigone," another protectress and guardian of aged heroes. . . . Freud himself saw in Orestes' acquittal . . . "echoes" of the revolution by means of which civilization succeeded from the matriarchal to the patriarchal order [*Moses and Monotheism* (1939), *SE* 23:114]. With this daughter, who was the one finally elected to carry his mission for him into the promised land, Freud was able to assure himself of the success of his own lifelong revolution.[14]

Roith does not speculate on the outcome of patriarchal intervention in the case of H.D., but we have it from the poet herself that Freud beckoned her to the Promised Land (*TF* 109–11). Near the end of her analysis, Freud presented her with the branch of an orange tree, another symbolic gesture that she interprets with the help of Goethe: "*Kennst du das Land, wo die Zitronen bluhn?* 'Do you know the land where the orange-tree blossoms?' It was on a winter day that the Professor handed me a branch from an orange-tree with dark laurel-like leaves" (*TF* 109). This is, as she reads it, not the telltale sign of a father's desire to seduce the daughter away from her own creative following but the sign of his recognition of her as the poet laureate who will take him beyond the grave into the dark continent of unexplored regions.

This is the affirmation she needs to take the relay from Freud and to carry it farther, striving to bring new life to his name, to his work, on the frontiers of femininity. She promises to guide blind Oedipus into an afterlife of which he never dreamed, but neither as mother-muse, like Lou Andreas-Salomé, nor as daughter-protector, like Anna-Antigone, nor even as "our Princess," Marie Bonaparte, who was exemplary in both roles. "I wanted to give the Professor something different," she announces.

> Princess George of Greece had been consistently helpful and used her influence in the general interests of the Psycho-Analytical Association. She was "our Princess" in that, as Marie Bonaparte, she had translated the Professor's difficult German into French and was ready to stand by him now that the Nazi peril was already threatening Vienna. She was "our Princess" in the world, devoted and influential. But is it possible that I sensed another world, another Princess? Is it possible that I (leaping over every sort of intellectual impediment and obstacle) not wished only, but *knew*, the Professor would be born again? (*TF* 39)

Into the maternal mysteries of Eleusis and Egypt, of vast preoedipal regions, she takes him; the sibyl bearing the orange branch, the mythical golden bough (90), is that other princess of Greece (39): the *"later, little understood"* Helen (*HE* 1), embodiment of all that is mysterious, contentious, and above all, promising about the future of psychoanalysis—"Gescholten viel und viel bewundert, Helena."

In another medium H.D. ensures that Freud lives on, exploring maternal prehistory, which became the special field of Freud's least dutiful daughter, Melanie Klein.[15] No outright dissenter, H.D. carries on these explorations, believing that she carries on his legacy, refusing to lose the hard-won affirmation she needs to proceed on her own without the support of an institution. But here is another story to tell, for according to Roith, Freud's suppression of Klein traces back to his Egyptology.

During the time that he was compiling the final notes to *Moses and Monotheism*, Klein, Roith says, "(who insisted throughout her life that she was dedicated to extending and developing Freud's work) was successfully established in England as the leader of what the aged and suffering Freud and his daughter, Anna, on whom he was now quite dependent, considered to be a dissenting school of psychoanalysis" (173).[16] Was he conscious of suppressing all mention of Karl Abraham, Klein's analyst and author of a celebrated study of Akhenaten which attributes the dawn of enlightenment not to the pharaoh but to the pharaoh's *mother*? Roith assembles the facts:

> Freud drew on a wide range of sources for his study of Akhenaten. He used many of his own psychoanalytic writings and he also drew on his disciple Otto Rank's *The Myth of the Birth of the Hero*. But, in omitting Abraham's essay, he omitted the most detailed psychoanalytic study of this topic: it was a celebrated one that he was intimately acquainted with entitled, "Amenhotep IV: A Psycho-Analytical Contribution Towards the Understanding of His Personality and of the Monotheistic Cult of Aton," which was published in 1912 preceding his own study by twenty-seven years. . . . Abraham credits the king's mother, Queen Tiy, with being not merely her son's guiding influence but the actual instigator of the Egyptian reform. . . . For Abraham, as for Freud, this king is the precursor to Moses but he grew up to devote his own considerable talents and energies to continuing *his mother's* work erasing his father's gods and with them, his name, from the length and breadth of Egypt. . . . Freud did not forget Abraham in other contexts. (171–72)[17]

The facts, as Roith sees them, call for a feminist interpretation. Freud, she argues, regarded Abraham's Queen Tiy as the supreme negation of his conception of femininity; his belief that monotheistic enlightenment was the creation of a masculine hero was so great that he tried to "erase Abraham's thesis altogether" (172):

> In not noticing Abraham's essay on Akhenaten, Freud could continue to avoid the intolerable fact of a woman's initiative in what he considered to be civilization's most important advance as well as the fact that this woman's influence over her son was rooted not merely in her physical or sexual image but in an intellectual and spiritual capacity of exceptional nobility. He was also able to omit all memory of Abraham's troublesome analysand and successor whose work had by that time succeeded in emphasizing the general power and influence of the mothering figure. (174)

Since H.D.'s last series of sessions with Freud took place in the year he began publishing *Moses and Monotheism*, we might assume that his anxiety concerning the fate of this work and of psychoanalysis, whose future he was in the process of establishing, could not have escaped her. She, we remember, had engaged him in discussions on the subject of Cretan archaeology and had wanted, in spite of his incredulity, to procure a serpent goddess for his collection (*TF* 175): was this for Athené, one token for another? But she does not press her point beyond subtle implication, too subtle to disturb his confidence in her, a thing she cherishes. Though sometimes angry, she also feels sorry for "the old man" (*CP* 454) aware of his grave danger in the face of failing health, the Nazi threat, and another European war looming on the horizon. Perhaps *because* of Klein's ascent, as visible as Freud's decline, H.D. feels no need to join his feminist critics, not then or, overtly, ever.

Through whose eyes, then, does H.D. see this revisionary, Egyptian, maternally inspired Helena? Through Freud's? Goethe's? Through her mother's, Helen Doolittle's? Through Homer's blind eyes, or the blinded eyes of Stesichorus, whose vision was said to he restored after he wrote his palinode? If she herself is Helen, then is it Helen's vision she proposes to cure or that of the men in whose fantasies she arises? What, then, is she if not a figure of supplementary specularity, another illusion of mythopoeia to add to the canonical conjurings of modernism and Freudianism?

Caught in the *abyme* of the cultural imaginary, the feminist reader of H.D. must inevitably pose the question: what is the therapeutic or political value of illusion? Do we not pull the proverbial wool over our eyes when we celebrate this legendary writing (of) self which evades the hard facts of oppression and avoids the hard work of a materialist critique of cultural history?

To end with what could not be clarified at the beginning of this book for want of demonstration of the workings of H.D.'s intertextual fantasies, I turn for help to Elizabeth Hirsh, who considers what femininsts have to gain, and lose, in the play of the imaginary. In her reading of *Helen in Egypt*, she underlines H.D.'s strategic reliance on Goethe as a trompe l'oeil:

> H.D.'s conception for *Helen* was partly derived from the second part of Goethe's *Faust*, in which Mephistopheles calls up the ghost of Helen of Troy at Faust's bidding, because he, Faust, wishes to marry the most beautiful woman in the world, even if only in a kind of make-believe. . . . The effect of this bizarre scene is wonderfully pathetic, a triumph and an allegory of art in which we *feel* for Helen even though we know she exists only as a figment of the Imagination, that is, doesn't exist. A triumph, then, like Mephistopheles', of *trompe l'oeil*.[18]

H.D.'s *Helen*, Hirsh suggests, presents yet another variation of the legend by uniting Helen, "who may or may not be dead" (7), with the ghost of Achilles and placing them in Egypt where together they recall archaic memories. "The progress of Helen's anamnesis . . . parallels that of her leading man, which culminates in the recovery, in effect the unveiling, of a certain *eidolon*, the memory of an image . . . [of] Achilles' mother" (7). That the mother should be recovered and revalued in the eyes of the greatest hero of all literary history is a significant rejoinder to the study of the archetypal hero in *Moses and Monotheism*. Moreover, if "His Majesty the Ego, the hero alike of every day-dream and of every story,"[19] could recognize the primal source of all his imaginings, then we would have come a long way in revaluing womankind, in seeing beyond the fetish veil of phallic self-centeredness. That H.D. should focus so centrally on the imaginary does not detract from the weight of her critique; instead she reinforces the efforts of poets, who, ever since the romantics, have attempted to transform the shape of history through the mediations of a symbolic imagination. Hirsh concludes that "feminist discourse should analyse but cannot purge itself of Imaginary effects because feminism depends on Imaginary effects for its putative existence and perpetually reinscribes them" (8).

To answer my own question: it is Freud's vision, the vision of the culture he hoped to enlighten, which H.D. intends to cure. She does so strategically, by having "him" see, through the altered conjurings of the poet he most respected, the primary, *maternal* imaginary he overlooked in his study of Moses and neglected altogether in his pessimistic prognosis of *Civilization and Its Discontents*. Given the material and symbolic means of articulation, it is this woman's imaginary that would dispel the witch metapsychology and surmount the nightmare matriarch who haunts his dreams. It is not woman's or the mother's imaginary that informs Freud's psychic genealogy; he draws his female figures from the reactive imagination of Goethe and poets of the masculine uncanny. Goethe's fear of the mothers, together with Rider Haggard's horrifying "She" (*SE* 5:453–54), infects all his writings on femininity, including the most "scientific" among them. If the imaginary can be so effective as to launch not only "a thousand ships" but also the witch-hunts of the early Renaissance, resulting in the very real deaths of hundreds of thousands of women,[20] whose residual potency we witness in anti-feminist backlashes of today, then the most effective antidote will be the imaginary

one promoted by H.D. But in the words of the poet who writes in her
wake, there is a whole "half-world" still awaiting translation:

> and we still have to reckon with . . .
> Goethe's dread of the Mothers . . .
> and the ghosts—their hands clasped for centuries—
> of artists dying in childbirth, wise-women charred at the stake,
> centuries of books unwritten piled behind these shelves;
> and we still have to stare into the absence
> of men who would not, women who could not, speak
> to our life—this still unexcavated hole
> called civilization, this act of translation, this half-world.[21]

# Notes

## Introduction

1. For critical works that have contributed to the study of the relationship between H.D. and Freud see Norman N. Holland, "H.D. and the 'Blameless Physician,'" *Contemporary Literature* 10.4 (1969): 474–506; Susan Stanford Friedman, *Psyche Reborn: The Emergence of H.D.* (Bloomington, Ind., 1981); Friedman, "A Most Luscious *Vers Libre* Relationship: H.D. and Freud," *Annual of Psychoanalysis* 14 (1986): 319–41; Friedman, "Against Discipleship: Collaboration and Intimacy in the Relationship of H.D. and Freud," *Literature and Psychology* 33.3/4 (1987): 89–108; Friedman, "The Writing Cure: Transference and Resistance in a Dialogic Analysis," *H.D. Newsletter* 2.2 (1988): 25–35; Joseph Riddel, "H.D.'s Scene of Writing: Poetry as (and) Analysis," *Studies in the Literary Imagination* 12.1 (1979): 41–59; Marylin B. Arthur, "Psychomythology: The Case of H.D.," *Bucknell Review* 28.2 (1983): 65–79; Peggy A. Knapp, "Women's Freud(e): H.D.'s *Tribute to Freud* and Gladys Schmitt's *Sonnets for an Analyst*," *Massachussetts Review* 24.2 (1983): 338–52; Janice S. Robinson, "What's in a Box? Psychoanalytic Concept and Literary Technique in H.D.," in *H.D.: Woman and Poet*, ed. Michael King (Orono, Me., 1986), 237–57; Evelyn M. Roming, "An Achievement of H.D. and Theodore Roethke: Psychoanalysis and the Poetics of Teaching," *Literature and Psychology* 28.3/4 (1978): 105–11; Claire Buck, "Freud and H.D.: Bisexuality and a Feminist Discourse," *m/f* 8 (1983): 53–66; Elizabeth A. Hirsh, "'New Eyes': H.D., Modernism, and the Psychoanalysis of Seeing," *Literature and Psychology* 32.3 (1986): 1–10.

2. Shoshana Felman, ed. *Literature and Psychoanalysis: The Question of Reading: Otherwise* (1977; Baltimore, 1982), 8–9.

3. Adrienne Rich's concept of "re-vision"—"of seeing with new eyes"—is especially applicable here, since it presupposes "the challenge and prom-

ise of a whole new psychic geography to be explored" for the woman writer. See "When We Dead Awaken: Writing as Re-vision," in *On Lies, Secrets, and Silence: Selected Prose, 1966–1978* (New York, Norton 1984), 33–49, 35. My study of intertextual revision differs methodologically but not politically from other feminist studies of H.D.'s revisionism. See Friedman, *Psyche Reborn*, esp. chap. 8; Hirsh, " 'New Eyes,' " Melody Zajdel, " 'I See Her Differently': H.D.'s *Trilogy* as Feminist Response to Masculine Modernism," *Sagetrieb* 5.1 (1986): 7–15; Rose Lucas, "Re(reading)-Writing the Palimpsest of Myth," *Southern Review* 21 (1988): 43–57; Rachel Blau DuPlessis, *H.D.: The Career of That Struggle* (Brighton, 1986), esp. 26–30 and 137 n. 48.

4. As Abel writes: "*Virginia Woolf and the Fictions of Psychoanalysis* examines and contextualizes [the] exchange within the historical moment Woolf shared with Sigmund Freud and Melanie Klein. . . . the book is less concerned with influence than with intertextuality. Woolf, as we will see, was familiar with the debates unfolding within British psychoanalysis, but rather than addressing them specifically, she engages in her novels the set of terms that generated the debates. Reading across the discourses illuminates them both. By alerting us to certain recurrent but submerged narrative tensions in Woolf's texts, psychoanalysis helps make us the discerning readers she desired. Woolf's fiction, in turn, de-authorizes psychoanalysis, clarifying the narrative choices it makes, disclosing its fictionality." Elizabeth Abel, *Virginia Woolf and the Fictions of Psychoanalysis* (Chicago, 1989), xvi.

5. Lisa Ruddick, "William James and the Modernism of Gertrude Stein," in *Modernism Reconsidered*, ed. Robert Kiely (Cambridge, Mass., 1983), 63.

6. Friedman, *Psyche Reborn*, 137.

7. H.D.'s Freudian autobiography may be seen as a subversive and therapeutic recovery of the "self" that had been misrepresented in the romans à clef of her masculinist colleagues. By reconstructing and working through her life story from prehistorical beginnings, she displaces the "Hilda" who emerges in "Hilda's Book" by Ezra Pound, her onetime lover/mentor, who, she never forgets, had said "You are a poem, though your poem's naught" (*ET* 12). Likewise, she recasts (or casts aside) her reappearance as the lusty "maenad, bassarid," in one of his *Pisan Cantos* ("God keep us from Canto LXXIX" [17]), as the frigid neurotic in Richard Aldington's *Death of a Hero*, as the extravagant beauty of John Cournos's *Miranda Masters*, and as the Isis figure of D. H. Lawrence's *Man Who Died*.

8. See Barbara Guest, *Herself Defined: The Poet H.D. and Her World* (London, 1985), esp. chaps. 23 and 27.

9. Julia Kristeva, *Black Sun: Depression and Melancholia*, trans. Leon S. Roudiez (1987; New York, 1989). According to Kristeva, the "disinherited poet" Gérard de Nerval manages to write himself out of his melancholia. "Creating prosody and an undecidable polyphony with symbols centered in the 'black spot' or 'black sun' of melancholia thus provided an antidote to depression, a temporary salvation" (170). Conversely, "there is nothing like

that in Duras. Death and pain are the spider's web of the text, and woe to the conniving readers who yield to its spell: they might remain there for good. . . . Lacking catharsis, such a literature encounters, recognizes, but also spreads the pain that summons it. It is the reverse of clinical discourse." (229).

10. Deborah Kelly Kloepfer, *The Unspeakable Mother: Forbidden Discourse in Jean Rhys and H.D.* (Ithaca, N.Y., 1989). "As a structuring device for this work," Kloepfer writes, "I offer a particular 'trope': the censored, repressed, or absent mother, a figure missing, not surprisingly so, when we acknowledge that text constitutes itself on the premise of her absence. . . . Although language constitutes itself at her expense, depends on her absence . . . the maternally connoted semiotic surfaces as a register to discourse, a memory, an intonational 'instinctual' breakthrough" (2, 11).

11. Friedman makes similar claims about H.D.'s revisionary Freudianism. She argues that like "later admirers and interpreters of Freud," including Herbert Marcuse, Norman O. Brown, and Geza Roheim, H.D. perceived the "more radical implications of Freud's work," particularly the "liberating and inspirational potential of a recovered unconscious." *Psyche Reborn*, 119.

12. Riddel, "H.D.'s Scene of Writing," 52.

13. Sigmund Freud, "Femininity" (1933 [1932]), *SE* 22:113.

14. Riddel, "H.D.'s Scene," 52.

15. Gayatri Chakravorty Spivak, "Displacement and the Discourse of Woman," in *Derrida: Displacement and After*, ed. Mark Krupnick (Bloomington, Ind. 1983), 171.

## 1. Telltale Signs of Intertextuality

1. Alicia Ostriker reads H.D.'s writing in light of Charles Olson's "Projective Verse," although unlike my emphasis on H.D.'s Olson-like critique of the "Egotistical Sublime," Ostriker's focus is on the prosody of "open form." See her article, "No Rule of Procedure: The Open Poetics of H.D.," *Agenda* 25.3/4 (1987–88): 145–54.

2. The first quotation from *Tribute to Freud* is taken from the section titled "Writing on the Wall," the second from the following section, "Advent." The first publication of "Writing on the Wall" was in book form as *Tribute to Freud*. H.D. explains in her prefatory note that " 'Writing on the Wall,' to Sigmund Freud, blameless physician, was written in London in autumn of 1944, with no reference to the Vienna notebooks of spring 1933," which she kept over the course of her first sessions with Freud. " 'Writing on the Wall' appeared in *Life and Letters Today*, London, 1945–46. 'Advent,' the continuation of 'Writing on the Wall,' or its prelude was taken direct from the old notebooks of 1933, though it was not assembled until December 1948, Lausanne" (*TF* xiv).

3. Julia Kristeva, *Desire in Language: A Semiotic Approach to Literature and Art*, ed. Leon S. Roudiez, trans. Thomas Gora, Alice Jardine, and Roudiez (New York, 1980), 36, hereafter cited in the text.

4. Cyrena Pondrom uses Kristeva's critical concept of intertextuality to discuss the poetics of *Trilogy*, although it is the transformative interweaving with Eliot's (not Freud's) texts that she demonstrates. See her article "*Trilogy* and *Four Quartets*: Contrapuntal Visions of Spiritual Quest," *Agenda* 25.3/4 (1987–88): 155–65.

5. Friedman argues in *Psyche Reborn* that Freud's "theories on the epistemology and language of the unconscious and his methods for translation" had tremendous influence on H.D. (51) and, in effect, shaped her transition from imagism to modernism (55). H.D., she says, paid her tribute to Freud by stating that he was "the first to draw the 'shapes, lines, graphs, the *hieroglyph of the unconscious*'" (50–51), but she does not claim that H.D.'s art of translation simultaneously re-visions Freud's epistemology and methods of translation. Further references to *Psyche Reborn* will appear in the text.

6. Janice S. Robinson proposes a much more straightforward reading of the work of translation between Freud and H.D. Instead of developing an intertextual practice, she explains, H.D. exploits an impressionistic understanding of Freudian concepts. "In *Advent*, . . . what Freud presented in theoretical terms, H.D. translated into visual terms" ("What's in a Box?" 238). "In her memoir *Thorn Thicket*, H.D. employs the literary technique of free association to convey the flavor of the psychoanalytic experience" (243). The theoretical terms Robinson reads "in translation" include displacement (238), repression (242), free association (243), working through (248), and regression (256).

7. Avital Ronell speculates on the debt psychoanalysis owes to Goethe and on the difficulty in tracing that debt since it is largely of the "fantasmatic order." Her speculations cast light on similar, though less explicit speculations by H.D. "Psychoanalysis was born along similar lines of delay and deferral, somewhat like the Mignon of *Wilhelm Meister*, without a proper name or genre and as an androgynous body of uncertain harmony sharing the genetic makeup of art and science. . . . If Goethe occupies a place of honor in the genesis and history of psychoanalysis, then Freud's testimony to this effect could be reasonably expected to suggest the specific terms of Goethe's membership in his large organization. Since the authority that Goethe exercises in Freud is largely of a fantasmatic order, however, it is very likely that any testimony Freud could give on this subject has been altered through secret negotiations he had had with himself, thus making it rather doubtful that what he has to say is strictly on the level." Avital Ronell, "*Goethezeit*," in *Taking Chances: Derrida, Psychoanalysis, and Literature*, ed. Joseph H. Smith and William Kerrigan (Baltimore, 1984), 146–47.

8. See especially Jean Laplanche and Jean-Bernard Pontalis, *The Language of Psycho-Analysis*, trans. Donald Nicholson-Smith (1967; London, 1973),

hereafter cited in the text. See also John Forrester, *Language and the Origins of Psychoanalysis* (London, Macmillan, 1980), also hereafter cited in the text.

9. As Rachel Blau Duplessis puts it, *"Tribute to Freud* is also a palinode, a defense of the one unassimilable symptom: the writing on the wall. . . . The strategy . . .—aggressive humility—is to claim that she would not, on her own, without the Professor's covering sanction, have initiated these intricate associations." "Language Acquisition," *Iowa Review* 16.3 (1986): 273.

10. *Tribute to Freud* clearly reads as a defense of Freud despite Freud's injunction that H.D. *not* defend him: " 'Please, never—I mean, never at any time, in any circumstance, endeavour to defend me, if and when you hear abusive remarks about me and my work.' . . . You will drive the hatred or the fear or the prejudice in deeper" (*TF* 86). Jacqueline Rose points out the double bind: "But there is something outrageous in Freud's demand that psychoanalysis cannot be defended . . . , since it snatches from the opponent the very rationality by which a critique, no less than a defence, of psycho-analysis should take place. This disarming of Freud of his own woman patient draws psychoanalysis back fiercely into its own practice and leaves her with an impasse which H.D. will then resolve—more or less and in her own way—through literary writing, memoirs, and finally, a tribute." She implies that H.D. reads Freud on her own terms—"in her own way"—and in the most strategic way, with "a tribute . . . perhaps the only possible re-sponse, to the laying down of the law." Jacqueline Rose, "Feminism and the Psychic," in *Sexuality in the Field of Vision* (London, 1986), 1–2.

11. She rejects Lawrence's assessment of Freud: "I was particularly an-noyed by his supercilious references to psychoanalysis and, by implication or inference, to the Professor himself. . . . He did not accept Sigmund Freud, or implied it in his essay" (*TF* 134). Her criticism is something of an under-statement. The "essay" of which she speaks is the vitriolic *Psychoanalysis and the Unconscious*, in which Lawrence denounces Freudianism for degrading the human spirit by replacing a creative, organic world view with a sterile, cerebral, and mechanistic one. According to Lawrence, Freud's "complex theory" reduces the "passional soul" to "a supreme machine-principle," and man to an "engine-driver" who "has invented his own automatic principles, and [who] works himself according to them, like any little mechanic inside the works" (211). He moreover accuses Freud of capitalizing on the sale of lewd dreams: "Freud disappear[ed] into the cavern of darkness, which is sleep and unconsciousness. . . . He came back with dreams to sell. But, sweet heaven, what merchandise! . . . Nothing but a huge slimy serpent of sex, and heaps of excrement, and a myriad repulsive little horrors spawned between sex and excrement" (203). D.H. Lawrence, *Fantasia of the Unconscious / Psycho-analysis and the Unconscious* (1922/1921; Harmondsworth, Eng., 1981). She also resists Pound, who addressed her Freudianism with patronizing disap-proval: "Have felt yr/vile Freud all bunk . . . you got into the wrong pig stye, ma chère. But not too late to climb out" (*TF* xii).

12. These daily sessions took place in Vienna from 1 March to 12 June 1933 and in the following year from 31 Oct. to 2 Dec. 1934.

13. "While there is no evidence that H.D. pursued this early interest in Freud during the imagist heyday in London," Friedman continues, "her exposure to psychoanalysis was renewed during the postwar years and greatly expanded as the twenties progressed. . . . By the late twenties, H.D. could hardly have escaped almost daily involvement with psychoanalysis; Bryher's enthusiasm was leading her to plan a future as an analyst, and the two women were attending many lectures on psychoanalysis and anthropology in Berlin. . . . During the year before H.D. actually saw Freud, she began 'intensive reading' of psychoanalytic journals and books, including many works by Freud" (*Psyche Reborn* 17–19).

14. See, for instance, Helmut Junker, "On the Difficulties of Retranslating Freud into English," *International Review of Psycho-Analysis* 14 (July 1987): 317–20.

15. Her close friendship with Bryher would have been particularly influential. As Friedman notes, "Bryher was an early advocate, even financial supporter, of psychoanalysis, and subscribed regularly to the *Psychoanalytic Journal*. . . . Determined to 'try out the theories,' Bryher began her analysis in 1928 with Hanns Sachs, one of the 'original Seven' around Freud. She regarded herself and her fellow analysands as 'pioneers' engaged in making early 'discoveries on the seas of the human mind' " (*Psyche Reborn*, 18). See Bryher, *The Heart to Artemis* (London, 1963), 242–46, 252–59.

16. In *An Outline of Psycho-Analysis* (1940 [1938]), Freud observes that there are two mental attitudes to be found in all psychoses, "one, the normal one which takes account of reality, and another which under the influence of the instincts detaches the ego from reality" (*SE* 22:202). It is the second attitude that finds expression in the production of a new delusional reality. H.D.'s doubled, detached, and englobed ego suggests such a reality in embryo.

17. "I had spoken of my disappointment in Havelock Ellis. He had not been interested in my experience in the Scilly Isles. . . . It had really been a great shock to me as I had visualized Dr. Ellis, during the time of writing my *Notes on Thought and Vision*, as a saint as well as a savant" (*NTV* 147–48).

18. I am indebted to Susan Stanford Friedman for pointing this out to me.

19. For a discussion of H.D.'s representation of Eleusinian landscape in her poetry, see Zara Bruzzi, " 'The Fiery Moment': H.D. and the Eleusinian Landscape of English Modernism," *Agenda* 25.3/4 (1987–88): 97–112.

20. "The ka was a term for the creative and preserving power of life. In ancient times it referred particularly to male potency, . . . but it had soon come to mean intellectual and spiritual power. . . . The *ka* was born with a person. . . . The *ka* accompanied a person like a kind of double, but when the person died the *ka* lived on. 'To go to one's *ka*' meant 'to die,' since the *ka* then left its mortal house and returned to its divine origin." Manfred Lurker, *The Gods and Symbols of Ancient Egypt*, trans. Barbara Cummings (1974; London, 1980), 73.

21. This "primordial Three-in-One," Demeter-Persephone-Dionysos, is not H.D.'s invention but one of the versions of the godhead thought to preside over the Mysteries of Eleusis. See Carl Kerenyi, "Kore," in Carl G. Jung and C. Kerenyi, *Science of Mythology: Essays on the Myth of the Divine Child and the Mysteries of Eleusis* (1949; rpt. London, 1985), esp. 126, 148.

22. Gary Burnett, *H.D. between Image and Epic: The Mysteries of Her Poetics* (Ann Arbor, Mich., 1990), 144, hereafter cited in the text.

23. Albert Gelpi comments on H.D.'s hermetic translation of Freud: "Though she did not argue with the Professor at the time, H.D. insisted that the art of healing went beyond the terms he set. After all, Hermes was called 'Psychopompos,' mediator of the underworld, where psyche and Spirit met, where human shades mingled with deities. As psychopomp Hermes was affiliated with the artist; by devising the lyre he made possible Apollo's song. His Egyptian predecessor Thoth was also the god of learning who invented all the arts and sciences: not only doctor and healer, mathematician and astronomer, but musician and writer—in fact, specifically the creator of the hieroglyphs and the scribe of the gods. Long before her sessions with Freud, Pound and Aldington and Lawrence, sibling-poets, had introduced her to the hermetic world." Albert Gelpi, "Re-membering the Mother: A Reading of H.D.'s *Trilogy*," in *H.D.*, ed. King, 179.

24. Gregory Ulmer, *Applied Grammatology: Post(e)-Pedagogy from Jacques Derrida to Joseph Beuys* (Baltimore, 1985), 138.

25. Riddel, "H.D.'s Scene of Writing," 45, hereafter cited in the text.

26. "In *Trilogy*," she adds, "H.D. begins to throw her rather considerable weight as daughter and poet as she leaves behind the conventional script, abandons Orestes, and takes off after the mother." Kloepfer, *The Unspeakable Mother*, 140.

27. H.D.'s critics, notably Susan Stanford Freidman and Adalaide Morris, have paid particular attention to this writing-on-the-wall passage in *Tribute to Freud*. Freidman argues that the collaborative translation of this writing "reinforced Freud's belief in [H.D.'s] hidden desire for an important destiny" (*Psyche Reborn* 73). Morris, however, takes up H.D.'s own questions regarding the nature of this uncanny script: "What creates these slides or magic transparencies? Where do they come from? The answer given in *Tribute to Freud* is ambiguous. . . . Images as signs and warnings from her own subconscious, images as signs and wonders from another world: the artist as moving-picture machine, the artist as psychic, the artist as message-transmitter." Adalaide Morris, "The Concept of Projection: H.D.'s Visionary Powers," *Contemporary Literature* 25.4 (1984): 412.

28. Sigmund Freud, *Studies on Hysteria* (1895), SE 2:276–78. Knowing that what he had to deal with were allegories, Freud inquired of his patient for interpretations, only to discover that she was a member of the Theosophical Society and had been reading its publications, including, most recently, a translation from the Sanskrit (278).

29. R. W. Hutchinson, *Prehistoric Crete* (Harmondsworth, Eng., 1962), 129. Hutchinson writes that "Minoan art is not only unlike its predecessors; it is also unlike all its successors, with the exception of arts directly influenced by it such as those of Mycenae and the Cyclades" (129). He goes on to mention that the idea of eidetic vision was also a useful tool for understanding the "peculiarities" of the "late Palaeolithic art of Spain and France" and the Bushman paintings of Rhodesia (129).

30. H.D. differentiates among types of dreams based on their intensity and luminosity (what she sometimes refers to as reality or actuality, their capacity to radiate with profound allegorical allusiveness): "With the Professor, I discussed a few real dreams, some intermediate dreams that contained real imagery or whose "hieroglyph" linked with authentic images, and some quaint, trivial, mocking dreams that danced, as it were, like masquerade[s]. . . . But the most luminous . . . while I was with the Professor was the dream of the Princess" (36).

31. This is perhaps the most discussed and widely disputed scene in all H.D.'s scenography. For masculinist interpretations and their feminist responses see Holland, "H.D. and the 'Blameless Physician,'" esp. 485–86; Joseph N. Riddel, "H.D. and the Poetics of 'Spiritual Realism,'" *Contemporary Literature* 10.4 (1969): 447–73; Friedman, *Psyche Reborn*, 81–82; Rachel Blau DuPlessis and Susan Stanford Friedman, "'Woman Is Perfect': H.D.'s Debate with Freud," *Feminist Studies* 7.3 (1981): 417–30; Estelle Roith, *The Riddle of Freud: Jewish Influences on His Theory of Female Sexuality* (London, 1987), 174–75.

32. This is perhaps an allusion to Freud's sketch "A Disturbance of Memory on the Acropolis" (1936), *SE* 22:239–48.

33. Friedman argues that H.D.'s hermeticism enabled her "to develop some of the striking similarities between Freud's psychoanalysis and esoteric traditions" (*Psyche Reborn* 189). For support she quotes David Bakan, *Sigmund Freud and the Jewish Mystical Tradition* (Princeton, 1958), which claims that Freud wrote out of a "generalized awareness of the basic tenets of Jewish mysticism, particularly the Kabbalah" (190). She also refers to one of H.D.'s most cherished sources of reference, Denis de Rougemont, *Love in the Western World*, which claims "parallels between Freud's concept of disguise and the various myths associated with the submerged mystical tradition" (191).

34. Freud (1890), quoted in Forrester, *Language and the Origins of Psychoanalysis*, 212.

35. H.D.'s copy of the revised edition (London: George Allen and Unwin, 1932) contains her pencil annotations as well as her inscription: "H.D. 8th February 1933." See Virginia Smyers, "H.D.'s Books in the Bryher Library," *H.D. Newsletter* 1.2 (1987): 18–25.

36. Freud, *The Interpretation of Dreams* (1900), *SE* 4:97.

37. See esp. "The Material and Sources of Dreams" and "The Dream-Work," *SE* 4:163–338.

38. A cartouche is an oval ring used in hieroglyphic writing to set off the characters of a royal name. It was the cartouche of a foreign (Greek) name, Ptolemy, which alerted the earliest investigators of the Rosetta stone to the idea that the name must be written phonetically rather than pictographically. Their efforts to isolate and identify the name's phonetic elements in the demotic text were continued by Champollion who worked on deciphering all the proper names, leading to the discovery that phonetic signs were used for Egyptian names as well. This discovery—that hieroglyphs were not only pic-toideographic but also phonographic—was the key to deciphering the Rosetta stone. See John T. Irwin, *American Hieroglyphics: The Symbol of the Egyptian Hieroglyphics in the American Renaissance* (New Haven, 1980), 20–21. Also E. A. Wallis Budge, *The Rossetta Stone* (1929; New York, 1989), esp. chap. 6.

A character-by-character transcription of these dream symbols into a cartouche of hieroglyphs would take the following form:

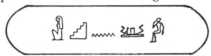

I derive the characters from E. A. Wallis Budge, *A Hieroglyphic Vocabulary to the Theban Recension of the Book of the Dead* (London, 1911), the edition that H.D. used as a reference. (See chap. 4, n. 19.)

39. "The construction of the dream-thoughts via the method of free association and the discernment of the meaning of the dream-element are two processes that go hand in hand," according to Forrester, *Language and the Origins of Psychoanalysis*, 71. The method of free association is privileged in post-structuralist readings of Freud (and H.D.); see, for example, Samuel Weber, *The Legend of Freud* (Minneapolis, 1982), esp. 11–12.

40. Forrester, *Language and the Origins of Psychoanalysis*, 126–27.

41. Sigmund Freud, "Constructions in Analysis" (1937), *SE* 23:260; Freud, *Inhibitions, Symptoms and Anxiety* (1926 [1925]), *SE* 20:171.

42. "We overcame the error of supposing that the forgetting we are familiar with signified a destruction of the memory-trace . . .—that is, annihilation. . . . Let us try to grasp what this [new] assumption involves by taking an analogy from another field. We will choose as our example the history of the Eternal City. . . . may perhaps be able to trace . . . the *Roma Quadrata*. Now let us, by a flight of imagination, suppose that Rome is not a human habitation but a psychical entity" (*SE* 21:69–70).

43. The only critical works I know that seriously examine H.D.'s transcendentalism in light of mystic sources are Friedman, *Psyche Reborn*, chap. 9 (on Kabbalah); and Andrew Howdle, "Feminine Hermeticism in H.D.'s *Trilogy*," *Studies in Mystical Literature* 4.1 (1984): 26–44, which refers to alchemy, Hermetica and Homerica. Works that examine her roots in romanticism, symbolism, and spiritualism include Cassandra Laity, "H.D.'s Romantic Landscapes: The Sexual Politics of the Garden," *Sagetreib* 6.2 (1987): 57–75;

Heather Rosario Sievert, "H.D.: A Symbolist Perspective," *Comparative Literature Studies* 16.1 (1979): 48–57; Dawn Kolokithas, "The Pursuit of Spirituality in the Poetry of H.D.," *San Jose Studies* 13.3 (1987): 66–76.

44. She makes no reference to Emerson but she did possess a copy of *The Heart of Emerson's Journals*, ed. Bliss Perry (New York: Houghton Mifflin, 1926), a late edition, possibly indicating a revival of her interest in (his) transcendentalism after the war.

45. On Poe's hieroglyphics, see Irwin, *American Hieroglyphics*, 43–235.

46. "*La Nature est un temple ou de vivants piliers / Laissent parfois sortir de confuses paroles; / L'homme y passe à travers des forêts de symboles / Qui l'observent avec des regards familiers.*" Charles Baudelaire, *Les fleurs du mal* (London, 1982), 194.

47. Ralph Waldo Emerson and Percy Bysshe Shelley, quoted in Irwin, *American Hieroglyphics*, 11.

48. Ralph Waldo Emerson, *Selections from Ralph Waldo Emerson*, ed. Stephen E. Whicher (Boston, 1957), 227, hereafter cited in the text.

49. Note that I have omitted from this citation the Wordsworthian echoes (ringing especially with the Preface to *Lyrical Ballads*) that privilege "the idioms of all languages," the "dependence of language upon nature . . . which gives that piquancy to the conversation of a strong-natured farmer or back-woodsman," and "the simplicity of . . . character" (33).

50. Henry David Thoreau, *Walden*, ed. J. Lyndon Shanley (Princeton, N.J., 1971), 309, hereafter cited in the text.

51. Walt Whitman, *Leaves of Grass*, vol. 7 of *The Collected Writings of Walt Whitman*, ed. Gay Wilson Allen, Scully Bradley, et al., 13 vols. (New York, 1961–), 34, 544, hereafter cited in the text.

52. "Now and then, rarely, comes a stout man like Luther, Montaigne, Pascal, Herbert, who utters a thought or feeling in a virile manner, and it is unforgettable. Then follow any number of spiritual eunuchs and women, who talk about that thought, imply it, in pages and volumes. . . . Great bands of female souls who only receive the spermatic *aura* and brood on the same but add nothing." Emerson, "From Journals," *Selections*, 376.

53. Irwin claims that the image of the leaf "as a basic, all-pervading natural form," which we find in both Thoreau and Whitman, derives from the central idea in Goethe's *Die Metamorphose der Pflanzen* (1790) as transmitted through Emerson, whom he quotes: "Goethe suggested . . . that a leaf or the eye of a leaf is the unit of botany, and that every part of a plant is only a transformed leaf to meet a new condition." As Irwin sees it, Goethe's sense of a "single basic form beneath the multiplicity of forms" is an "analogue" of Emerson's atomistic hieroglyph (*American Hieroglyphics*, 15).

54. See Jacques Derrida, *Of Grammatology*, trans. Gayatri Chakravorty Spivak (Baltimore, 1976), hereafter, cited in the text. "Derrida does not claim grammatology as his invention," Gregory Ulmer explains; "rather, he intervenes in a tradition of scholarship . . . [by] providing a theory for a mode of

research that up until now has produced almost exclusively (at least among its modern representatives) histories of writing. The historians of writing . . . have made available a considerable knowledge of the evolution of writing" (*Applied Grammatology*, 5–6). See esp. André Leori-Goruhan, *Le geste et la parole* (Paris, 1964); and Ignace J. Gelb, *A Study of Writing: The Foundations of Grammatology* (Chicago, 1952).

55. Ezra Pound, *Gaudier-Brzeska: A Memoir* (New York, 1970), 83–85, hereafter cited in the text. "Imagism is not symbolism," Pound writes. "The symbolists dealt in 'association,' that is, in a sort of allusion, almost of allegory. They degraded the symbol to the status of a word. They made it a form of metonymy. One can be grossly 'symbolic,' for example, by using the term 'cross' to mean 'trial.' The symbolist's *symbols* have a fixed value, like numbers in arithmetic, like 1, 2, and 7. The imagiste's images have a variable significance, like the signs *a*, *b*, and *x* in algebra. Moreover, one does not want to be called a symbolist, because symbolism has usually been associated with mushy technique." Pound outlines the "science" of imagism and its "ideogrammic method" in the first chapter of his *ABC of Reading* (1934; New York, 1960), 18–22, hereafter cited in the text.

56. See also Ezra Pound, "Affirmations: As for Imagisme," in *Selected Prose, 1909–1965*, ed. William Cookson (London, 1973), 344–47.

57. For a discussion of the originality of H.D.'s contribution to imagism and to the history of literary modernism, see Cyrena N. Pondrom, "H.D. and the Origins of Imagism," *Sagetrieb* 4.1 (1985): 73–100.

58. Ernest Fenollosa, *The Chinese Written Character as a Medium for Poetry*, ed. Ezra Pound (1918, San Francisco, 1936), 8, hereafter cited in the text.

59. Fenollosa offers other examples: " 'Rice-field' plus 'struggle' = male" and " 'Boat' plus 'water' = boat-water, a ripple" (10).

60. Derrida quotes Fenollosa's example: "For example, our sentence, 'Reading promotes writing' would be expressed in Chinese by three full verbs. Such a form is the equivalent of three expanded clauses. . . . One . . . is, 'If one reads it teaches him how to write.' Another is, 'One who reads becomes one who writes.' But in the first condensed form a Chinese would write, 'Read promote write.' " (*Of Grammatology*, 334–35 n. 44)

61. Derrida applauds Pound for his "break-through" work on Fenollosa, which grammatology now carries on. He notes that Fenollosa's "influence upon Ezra Pound and his poetics is well-known: this irreducibly graphic poetics was, with that of Mallarmé, the first break in the most entrenched Western tradition. The fascination that the Chinese ideogram exercised on Pound's writing may thus be given all its historical significance" (*Of Grammatology*, 92).

62. Pound's asterisk at the end of this sentence signals us to read this statement as the essence of his "principle of Primary apparition" formulated in his *Spirit of Romance* (New York, 1952).

63. "I was 21 when Ezra left [for Europe]," H.D. recalls, "and it was some

years later that he scratched 'H.D. Imagiste,' in London, in the [British] Museum tea room, at the bottom of a typed sheet, now slashed with his creative pencil, 'Cut this out, shorten this line.' H.D.—Hermes—Hermeticism and all the rest of it" (*ET* 40).

64. Bruzzi notes the frequent failure of critics to underline modernism's "habitual interweaving" of the classical with contemporary occultism. Only just recently has modernist criticism begun, for instance, "to explore Pound's early interest in Greek and Renaissance Neoplatonism, and the influence of theosophy on the vorticists." She especially notes that "H.D. shows knowledge of Neoplatonism from the inception of her career as a writer" (" 'The Fiery Moment,' " 98).

65. In his most celebrated formulation of the image, Pound explains that he uses "the term 'complex' rather in the technical sense employed by the newer psychologists, such as Hart. . . . It is the presentation of such a 'complex' instantaneously which gives that sense of sudden liberation; that sense of freedom from time limits and space limits; that sense of sudden growth, which we experience in the presence of the greatest works of art." Ezra Pound, "A Few Don't's" (1913), *Literary Essays of Ezra Pound*, ed. T. S. Eliot (London, 1985), 4.

66. For further discussion of the mediating powers of H.D.'s hieroglyph in *Her* and elsewhere, see Lucas, "Re(reading)-Writing," esp. 53; DuPlessis, "Language Acquisition," esp. 265–67. I shall return to this discussion in Chapter 2.

67. *Palimpsest* was one of the books that Freud ordered "as an introduction to making [H.D.'s] personal acquaintance." See Freud to Mrs. Aldington, 18 Dec. 1932 (*TF* 190).

68. "She could not say . . . of old, old sincerity, some atavistic inheritance, 'but here, but here—' What words would come to her over-stimulated brain should she begin to utter one shadow of the burning, furious love, the furious burning that was in her?" (188)

69. Autohypnotic or entranced states of consciousness and the hieroglyphic translation of common objects into "signs" that charm this state into being are found in the palm-dove passage (177–78), the cobra passage (174), the crescent-of-the-moon passage (176), the anemones passage (178), the scarab-beetle passage (210), the orgasmic jasmine-flower passage (187), the uncanny sphinx (203) and birth-tomb passages (216–17), among many others.

70. Robert McAlmon's "Forewarned as regards H.D.'s Prose" (an appendix to the 1926 edition) offers this "glittering blurb" to describe the medium of her writing: "A hysteria of submarine revelation; the subconscious in vibration, tyrannized by intellect having a classical spasm" (*P* 241).

71. DuPlessis, "Language Acquisition," 255. DuPlessis notes that *Her* also reads like a palimpsest, with its generative layer (or what Kristeva would call "genotext") of mysterious, cryptic signs, which irrupts into the narrative layer from the space of dreams (265–66).

72. Gregory Ulmer discusses the Wolf Man's psychotic language and how analysts Nicolas Abraham and Maria Torok undertook to decode it. "Sealed in the Wolf Man's psychic vault, then, is a word-thing, a word treated as a thing that is unspeakable and yet . . . achieves utterance by means of a complex translation process. . . . This hieroglyphic system is what the cryptologists (Abraham and Torok) were finally able to decipher, using techniques, like those used by Champollion to decipher the Rosetta stone (their own analogy), that require translations across three languages—in this case, Russian, German, and English. . . . The cryptonomy of verbal material that the Wolf Man derived from . . . his fetish scene . . . did not operate by the usual procedures of representation—the symbolizing or hiding of one word behind another, or one thing by a word or a word by a thing. Rather, his names were generated by picking out from the extended series of 'allosemes'—the catalogue of uses available for a given word—a particular usage, which is then translated into a synonym (creating thus even greater distance from the secret name). The path from crypt to speech may follow either semantic or phonic paths, with the play between homonyms and synonyms being part of the mechanism" (*Applied Grammatology*, 62–63).

73. Elaine Pagels informs us of the details of this discovery in her scholarly feminist interpretation of the gnostic gospels. Of the Gospel of Mary, she writes: "In 1896 a German Egyptologist . . . bought in Cairo a manuscript that, to his amazement, contained the *Gospel of Mary* [Magdalene] and three other texts." "The author of the *Gospel*," she goes on to say, "interprets the resurrection appearances [of Christ] as visions received in dreams or in ecstatic trance. This gnostic gospel recalls traditions recorded in Mark and John, that Mary Magdalene was the first to see the risen Christ." See *The Gnostic Gospels* (1980; Harmondsworth, Eng., 1985), 22, 42.

74. In *Bid Me to Live*, H.D. describes translation as trade in myrrh: "If you look at a word long enough, this peculiar, its magic angle, would lead somewhere, like that Phoenician track, trod by the old traders. She was a trader in the gold, the old gold, the myrrh of the dead spirit. She was bargaining with each word" (162).

75. Freud, *Civilization and Its Discontents*, SE 21:106.

76. Sigmund Freud, "The Dynamics of Transference" (1912), SE 12:99–108.

## 2. Autobiographical Fantasy

1. "Paint It Today" (1921, unpublished), "Asphodel" (1921–22, unpublished), *HERmione* (1981 [1927]), and *Bid Me to Live* (1960 [1939, 1948–50]) mark H.D.'s first ventures into autobiographical prose. *Hedylus* (1928 [1924?]), *Palimpsest* (1926 [1924?]) and "Pilate's Wife" (1924, 1929, unpublished) are her first historical and classical adaptations of autobiography.

2. "I have tried," H.D. testifies, "to write the story or the novel of my war experience, my first, still-born child and the second, born so fortunately. . . . I have rewritten this story and others that 'ghosted' for it, as in the case of *Pilate's Wife* and *Hedylus*, both historical or classic reconstructions. . . . I have never been completely satisfied with any of my books, published or unpublished. . . . [They] are not so much still-born as born from the detached intellect. Someone spoke of *Hedylus* as being " 'hallucinated writing' " (*TF* 148–49).

3. Friedman describes H.D.'s writing of *Bid Me to Live* as a form of therapy. Freud, she claims, "seemed to have connected the repression of these memories [of 1915–19] with her loss of creative direction. His 'cure' included a therapeutic writing of events without embellishment or distancing masks." She quotes H.D. in a letter to Bryher, 15 May 1933: "Evidently I blocked the whole of the 'period' and if I can skeleton-in a vol. about it, it will break the clutch. . . . the 'cure' will be, I fear me, writing that damn vol. straight, as history, no frills as in Narthex, Palimp. [*Palimpsest*] and so on, just a straight narrative, then later, changing names and so on." See *Psyche Reborn*, 30.

4. Adalaide Morris considers the double signature of "H.D. by Delia Alton": "The title balances the names 'H.D.' and 'Delia Alton:' the first, the signature under which she gained fame as a poet; the second, the name with which she signed a cluster of late novels . . . among them *Bid Me to Live*. . . . As these notes [also catalogued under the title 'Notes on Recent Writing'] explain, 'Delia Alton' came into being through certain psychic experiences she had during World War II in London. . . . What H.D.'s title suggests and what these notes give us, then, is a shimmering and unresolved series of reflections: 'H.D.' side-by-side with the later manifestation of her writing self that she called 'Delia Alton,' 'H.D.' created through the agency or medium of 'Delia Alton,' and the meditations of a larger writing self, a self capacious enough to contain both incarnations or manifestations of her creativity but as yet without a signature." See Morris's introduction, "H.D.'s 'H.D. by Delia Alton,' " *Iowa Review* 16.3 (1986): 174, I would like to add without further speculation that "Delia Alton" reads like an anagram of "Aldington," H.D.'s married surname.

5. According to Morris, Delia Alton's notes "signal . . . H.D.'s turning back again or anew to the jumble of published and unpublished poems, short stories, novels, plays, memoirs, tributes, and translations that had accumulated across nearly forty years of creative activity." The notes themselves entail "twenty-one entries written between December 1949 and June 1950," the first step before H.D. "reassembled, reread, relived and remapped what she wryly called her 'so far uncollected Collected Works' " (ibid., 175).

6. H.D. possessed a copy of Ernest Jones, *Sigmund Freud: Life and Work*, 3 *vols*. (London, 1953, 1955, 1957), which she annotated in the margins, indi-

cating her interest in the "life" of Freud outside of her own personal acquaintance.

7. See Sigmund Freud, *The Interpretation of Dreams*, SE 4:196–97, for a self-analysis of his efficacious enactment of the Hannibal fantasy, which he had cherished since boyhood.

8. Sigmund Freud, *An Autobiographical Study* (1925 [1924]), SE 20:7.

9. See Catherine Clément, "Sorceress and Hysteric," in Hélène Cixous and Catherine Clément, *The Newly Born Woman*, trans. Betsy Wing (1975; Minneapolis, 1986), 12.

10. Michel de Certeau, *Heterologies: Discourse on the Other*, trans. Brian Massumi (Manchester, 1986), 14, hereafter cited in the text.

11. Sigmund Freud, "On the History of the Psycho-Analytic Movement" (1914), SE 14:37.

12. H.D., quoted in Guest, *Herself Defined*, 9.

13. Josef Breuer and Sigmund Freud, *Studies on Hysteria* (1893–95), SE 2:216.

14. Rachel Blau DuPlessis reads this hieroglyph as "an evocation . . . of the 'Corfu vision' of 1920. " See "Language Acquisition," 265. For a discussion of H.D.'s hieroglyph as sign of mediation between the symbolic and the semiotic, see DuPlessis, "Language Acquisition," esp. 266–68, and Lucas, "Re(reading)-Writing," esp. 53–56.

15. "It's this dreadful beauty of abstraction that's done us all in," Her exclaims later on. "What is the darn use of coping with the gracile suavity of (say) a fern, of (say) that sort of sperm-pod of moss propagating seen under the microscope." (195)

16. She would also have found reinforcement in Freud's more general evaluation of hysteria's genius: "Hysteria of the severest type can exist in conjunction with gifts of the richest and most original kind—a conclusion which is, in any case, made plain beyond a doubt in the biographies of women eminent in history and literature" (SE 2:103).

17. S. Travis derives her reading of this scene of snow writing from both Kristeva and Luce Irigaray: "The winter landscape into which Hermione emerges . . . is . . . the undifferentiated world before the separation of subject from object. Here also is the recurring image of the . . . palimpsest, written on and re-written upon. H.D.'s fascination with symbol writing, hieroglyphs, and reading bird signs appears in *HER* as Herminone's tracks in the snow signal alternative symbolic systems for woman. . . . Hermione is symbolically acting out her future as a poet, anticipating the balance she seeks in the constant confrontation between the symbolic and semiotic realms." "A Crack in the Ice: Subjectivity and the Mirror in H.D.'s *Her*," *Sagetrieb* 6.2 (1987): 135. Her's snow-writing is also discussed in Susan Stanford Friedman and Rachel Blau DuPlessis, " 'I Had Two Loves Separate': The Sexualities of H.D.'s *Her*," *Montemora* 8 (1981): 7–30; and in Susan Stanford Friedman, "Palimpsests of Origin in H.D.'s Career," *Poesis* 6.3/4 (1985): 56–73.

18. H.D., Frances Josepha Gregg, and Ezra Pound are the masked players in the lovers' triangle of *Her*; while H.D., Bryher, and Kenneth Macpherson compose the triangle of *Nights*.

19. Where off and on from 1931 to 1946 H.D. lived at Kenwin (built in 1931). Before that she lived at Riant Chateau in Territet when she was in Switzerland.

20. Part 1 was written after the 1934 analysis with Freud; part 2 was written before the 1933 analysis.

21. Quoted by Luce Irigaray, "*La Mystérique*," in *Speculum of the Other Woman*, trans. Gillian C. Gill (1974; Ithaca, N.Y., 1985), 191, hereafter cited in the text.) The translator notes that "the French title's economy and richness cannot be matched in English. Four elements are fused in Irigaray's neologism: mysticism, hysteria, mystery, and the femaleness ["*la mystérique*"] fundamental to the previous three" (191).

22. According to the card catalogue of H.D.'s books kept in the Beinecke Rare Book and Manuscript Library at Yale University, H.D. possessed a copy of Thérèse de Lisieux, *The Little Flower of Jesus: An Autobiography* (London: Burns, Oates, and Washbourne, 1927).

23. Although H.D. may have had in mind Breuer's descriptive observation that "hysterics are the flower of mankind, as sterile, no doubt, but as beautiful as double flowers" (*SE* 2:240) as well as his reference to "the patron saint of hysteria, Saint Teresa" (232).

24. Sigmund Freud, "The Economic Problem of Masochism" (1924), *SE* 19:159–60.

25. Irigaray supplies a long quotation from Saint Teresa of Avila's famous account of her ecstatic masochistic vision of the Flaming Heart (as transcribed and translated by Vita Sackville-West in *The Eagle and the Dove* ("*La Mystérique*," 201 n. 2).

26. According to Irigaray, the "crypt for the reciprocal sharing of the abyss between 'her' and God. Into which she will have to (re)descend in order to find, at last, the quietude and rest in herself-God" ("*La Mystérique*," 201).

27. Otto Rank, "The Play-Impulse and Aesthetic Pleasure," in *Art and Artist: Creative Urge and Personality Development*, trans. Charles Frances Atkinson (New York: Knopf, 1932), 91–110, 100, hereafter cited in the text.

28. Friedrich Nietzsche, "From the Souls of Artists and Writers," in *Human, All Too Human: A Book for Free Spirits*, trans. R. J. Hollingdale (1878; Cambridge, 1986), 80–81.

29. In a close analysis of *Beyond the Pleasure Principle*, Derrida deconstructs what he reads as Freud's "autobiography" into a "auto-bio-thanato-hetero-graphic scene of writing." Jacques Derrida, "Freud's Legacy," in *The Post Card: From Socrates to Freud and Beyond*, trans. Alan Bass (1980; Chicago, 1987), 336.

30. The New Directions Press edition of *The Gift* (1982), from which the Virago edition is offset, has cut out the speculative, "psychoanalytic" pas-

sages. Major cuts of this type occur in "Dark Room" and "The Dream," but the complete chapters are published elsewhere: "Dark Room," *Montemora* 8 (Aug. 1981): 57–76; "The Dream," *Contemporary Literature* 10.4 (1969): 605–26. New Directions editor Giselda Ohanessian also excised the entire second chapter: see "Fortune Teller," *Iowa Review* 16.2 (1986): 18–41. See Rachel Blau DuPlessis, " A Note on the State of H.D.'s *The Gift*," *Sulfur* 9 (1984): 178–82, for a discussion of these editorial cuts and how they substantially alter the book's "basic premises."

31. Sigmund Freud, "Childhood Memories and Screen Memories," *The Psychopathology of Everyday Life* (1901), *SE* 6:47.

32. For a discussion of H.D.'s variable use of the figure of "projection" throughout her work, see Morris, "The Concept of Projection." In addition to reading this "master-metaphor of H.D.'s" (413) as psychological "defense mechanism" (424–29), Morris reads it as "phanopoeia" (413–16), as psychic cartography (416–21), as cinematography (421–24), and as alchemical "trans-mutation" (429–36).

33. Sigmund Freud, "Instincts and Their Vicissitudes" (1915), *SE* 14:136.

34. Sigmund Freud, "Negation" (1925), *SE* 19:237.

35. Sigmund Freud, "A Metapsychological Supplement to the Theory of Dreams" (1917 [1915]), *SE* 14:223.

36. Roland Barthes, *Camera Lucida: Reflections on Photography*, trans. Richard Howard (1980; London, 1984), 106. Barthes is quoting Michel Blanchot.

37. Jacques Derrida, "Freud and the Scene of Writing," in *Writing and Difference*, trans. Alan Bass (1968; Chicago, 1978), 228. Derrida notes that in Freud's writing, "the metaphor of a photographic negative occurs frequently. Cf. 'The Dynamics of Transference' (*SE* XII). The notions of negative and copy are the principal means of the analogy. . . . In 'Notes on the Concept of the Unconscious in Psychoanalysis,' 1913 (*SE* XII, 264). Freud compares the relations between the conscious and the unconscious to a photographic process. . . . we will find [this analogy] again in the 'Note on the Mystic Writing Pad': 'Memory, compared to a camera, has the marvelous superiority of natural forces: to be able to renew by itself its means of action' " (330 n. 18).

38. H.D.'s accent on the intrapsychic emphasizes the primary technology of memory to record and recall and project, just as Freud emphasizes that "in the photographic camera [man] has created an instrument which retains the fleeting visual impressions, just as a gramophone disc retains the equally fleeting auditory ones; both are at bottom materializations of the power he possesses of recollection, his memory" (*SE* 21:91).

39. Sigmund Freud, "Dreams and Occultism," in *New Introductory Lectures* (1933 [1932]), *SE* 22:55.

40. Susan Stanford Friedman points to H.D.'s exploration of the fourth dimension in *Palimpsest*, 138, 155, 157, 162, 165. See "Exile in the American Grain: H.D.'s Diaspora," *Agenda* 25.3/4 (1987–88): 27–50. During the late twenties and early thirties, H.D. experimented with film as an expressive

medium. In addition to acting, producing, and editing she also wrote articles and reviews for the British avant-garde film journal *Close-Up*. A full bibliography of her film criticism may be found in Jackson R. Bryer and Pamela Roblyer, "H.D.: A Preliminary Checklist," *Contemporary Literature* 10.4 (1969): 632–75. For a critical history of *Close-Up*, see Anne Friedberg, *Writing about the Cinema: 'Close-Up,' 1927–1933*, Ph.D. diss., New York University, 1983 (Ann Arbor, Mich., 1986).

In his essay "The New Language of Cinematography," *Close-Up* 4.5 (1929): 10–13, Eisenstein writes that "cinematography is for the first time availing itself of the experience of literature for the purpose of working out *its own language, its own speech, its own vocabulary, its own imagery*. The period is ending when the most brilliant productions—from a dramaturgical point of view—were pronounced, from the point of view of genuine cinematography, in a childish lisp" (11).

41. Sergei Eisenstein, "The Fourth Dimension in the Kino," pt. 1, *Close-Up* 6.3 (1930): 185, hereafter cited in the text.

42. Sergei Eisenstein, *Film Form and The Film Sense*, trans. Jay Leyda (Cleveland, 1957), 29–30.

43. Pound, *Gaudier-Brzeska*, 89.

44. Freud refers to *Uncle Tom's Cabin* in his study of childhood masochism, "A Child Is Being Beaten" (1919), as a regular feature of early childhood education and an important factor in stimulating and structuring childhood fantasy (*SE* 17:180).

45. "Should we not look for the first traces of imaginative activity as early as in childhood?" Freud asks. "The child's best-loved and most intense occupation is with his play or games. Might we not say that every child at play behaves like a creative writer, in that he creates a world of his own." "Creative Writers and Day-Dreaming" (1908 [1907]), *SE* 9:143–44.

46. Sigmund Freud, "Determinism, Belief in Chance, and Superstition," in *The Psychopathology of Everyday Life* (1901), *SE* 6:258–59.

47. Morris, "Concept of Projection," 426, hereafter cited in the text.

48. Pound, "Retrospect," *Literary Essays*, 5, hereafter cited in the text.

49. Freud, *Civilization and Its Discontents*, *SE* 21:65.

50. T. S. Eliot, *The Use of Poetry and the Use of Criticism* (1933; London, 1964), 155.

51. Derrida explains that passages in these texts "do not belong to the genre of autobiography in the strict sense of the term. To be sure, it is not wrong to say that Nietzsche speaks of his 'real' (as one says) father and mother. But he speaks of them '*in Ratselform*,' symbolically, by way of a riddle; in other words, in the form of a proverbial legend, and as a story that has a lot to teach." *The Ear of the Other: Otobiography, Transference, Translation*, ed. Christie V. MacDonald, trans. Peggy Kamuf (1982; New York, 1985), 16, hereafter cited in the text. *Otobiography* is Derrida's coinage, from the Greek root *oto-*, meaning "to sound loudly."

52. "What, then, are the consequences of this double origin?" Derrida asks. "The birth of Nietzsche, in the double sense of the word 'birth' (the act of being born and family lineage), is itself double. It brings something into the world and the light of day out of a singular couple: death and life, the dead man and the living feminine, the father and the mother. The double birth explains who I am and how I determine my identity" (16).

53. Derrida does not refer to Joyce explicitly here, but Joyce is the subject of another study, "Two Words for Joyce," in *Post-structuralist Joyce: Essays from the French*, ed. Derek Attridge and Daniel Ferrer (Cambridge, 1984), 145–59.

54. James Joyce, *Ulysses* (1922, Harmondsworth, Eng.: 1975), 43, 53, 55.

55. For deconstructive readings of Freud's essay "The Uncanny" which describe the etymological and philological complexities of the work and point out Freud's possession by the uncanny themes and motifs he discloses, see Hélène Cixous, "Fiction and Its Phantoms: A Reading of Freud's *Das Unheimliche* ('The Uncanny')," trans. Robert Dennomé, *New Literary History* 7 (Spring 1976): 525–48; and Samuel Weber, "The Side Show; or, Remarks on a Canny Moment," *MLN* 88.6 (1973): 1102–33.

56. Sigmund Freud, "The Uncanny" (1919), *SE* 17:220.

57. See Sigmund Freud, "The Antithetical Meaning of Primal Words" (1910), *SE* 11:155–61. Also, see my discussion of this work in relation to *Helen in Egypt* in Chapter 4 herein.

58. Strachey adds a note to this etymological passage, saying that "according to the *Oxford English Dictionary*, a similar ambiguity attaches to the English *canny*, which may mean not only "cosy" but also "endowed with occult or magical powers."

59. Freud refers to Otto Rank's study of the double (1914), whose themes he uses, in turn, to explain the ancient Egyptians "art of making images of the dead in lasting materials" as an example of the desire to double the mortal self in immortal likenesses thereby transcending (repressing) a recognition of death" (235).

60. "Psycho-analysis has taught us," Freud writes, "that this terrifying phantasy [of being buried alive] is only a transformation of another phantasy which had originally nothing terrifying about it at all . . . the phantasy, I mean, of intra-uterine existence" (244).

61. Freud suggests that the fortune-teller in his patient's story behaves like a skilled analyst in soliciting facts from the desiring unconscious. But he cannot be sure. "How, then, did he arrive at the knowledge which enabled him to give expression to my patient's strongest and most secret wish?" he asks. "I can see only two possible explanations. Either the story as it was told me is untrue . . . or thought-transference exists as a real phenomenon" (*SE* 22:42).

62. Sigmund Freud, "A Childhood Recollection From *Dichtung und Warheit*" (1917), *SE* 17:156.

63. H.D. notes in "Advent" that, as a girl, she enjoyed playing her

mother's "Halloween games . . . such as telling the future from a small candle-end stuck in a nutshell that was set afloat on a tub of water" (*TF* 186).

64. To find out "who Christian is" without rousing Mamalie from her trance, Hilda avoids activating the dream censors by referring to him directly. Instead, when Mamalie awakens and asks, "what was I saying, Hilda?" her response is to call for a reading from Hans *Christian* Anderson, which effectively sends Mammalie back into trance. "She said, 'I thought you knew, Agnes, that I called your father Christian" (80, 82).

## 3. Mourning, Mystery, and Melancholia

1. Sigmund Freud, "Mourning and Melancholia" (1917 [1915]), *SE* 14: 245.

2. See Guest, *Herself Defined*, 6–8.

3. I borrow the term "masochistic *jouissance*" from Leo Bersani to refer to the figure of joyous self-shattering in H.D.'s text, a figure that Bersani claims to derive from Freud. See *The Freudian Body: Psychoanalysis and Art* (New York, 1986), 38–39, 41, 89, 90, 92, 98, 114.

4. Sigmund Freud, "The Dissolution of the Oedipus Complex" (1924), *SE* 19:177.

5. For other critical work concerned with the recovery of the maternal, see Deborah Kelly Kloepfer, "Flesh Made Word: Maternal Inscriptions in H.D.," *Sagetrieb* 3.1 (1983): 27–48; Kloepfer, "Mother as Muse and Desire: The Sexual Politics of H.D.'s *Trilogy*," in *H.D.*, ed. King, 191–209; Gelpi, "Remembering the Mother: A Reading of H.D.'s *Trilogy*," in *H.D.*, ed. King, 173–90; Mary K. DeShazer, " 'A Primary Intensity between Women': H.D. and the Female Muse," in *H.D.*, ed. King, 157–71; and Friedman, "Psyche Reborn."

I borrow the term "gift economy" from Adalaide Morris, "A Relay of Power and of Peace: H.D. and the Spirit of the Gift," *Contemporary Literature* 27.4 (1986): 493–524. Morris in turn refers to Lewis Hyde, *The Gift: Imagination and the Erotic Life of Property* (New York, 1983); and Marshall Sahlins, *Stone Age Economics* (Chicago, 1972). Morris observes that H.D. "seems to operate within another economy" and suggests a "rift between a market economy that works through reason and egotism and a gift economy animated by imagination and love" (499). I use the term to refer to my own understanding of H.D.'s intertextual (Freudian-Moravian) conceptualization of the gift.

6. I borrow the title of this section from Irigaray, who uses it to title one of the sections of *Speculum of the Other Woman*, 66.

7. Freud's colleague and French translator, Marie Bonaparte (Princess George of Greece), began compiling her notes for *Female Sexuality* in 1933–34, shortly after Freud had challenged analysts, particularly woman analysts, to resolve the riddle of femininity in his essay "Femininity." This was also, of course, the time of H.D.'s analysis; "femininity" was very much in the air.

Bonaparte takes a very conservative line on the subject. "The castration complex," she writes, "is mainly cultural in the boy, and arises as the representative of patriarchal morality, whereas it is mainly biological in the girl, since it represents an anatomical reality." The girl, accordingly, shows aggression to the mother, "who made her incomplete." Moreover, she harbors the "masochistic wish to be subjected to the triad castration-violation-childbirth." Conversely, she views the male "bearer of the phallus" as "self-sufficient; he has his social task which he loves and which occupies his mind and thus has more chance of satisfying and of sublimating his sexual instinct." Bonaparte, *Female Sexuality*, trans. J. Rodker 1949; (London, 1953), 29.

8. Irigaray then cross-references themes and semes from "Mourning and Melancholia" and "Femininity," deconstructing Freud's monstrous figure of "feminine melancholia," which emerges in her ironic double reading (66–67).

9. Marina Warner, *Alone of All Her Sex: The Myth and the Cult of the Virgin Mary* (1976; London, 1985), 126, hereafter cited in the text.

10. H.D.'s rhetorical "listen" is, I suggest, another telltale sign of intertextuality, and a clue to her own "subversive mimesis" or critical revision of Freud. It was Freud's later style to write as if addressing a listening audience. For instance, before venturing to illustrate his thesis on dreams and occultism, he gestures to his readers to "listen" or to "listen then" (*SE* 22:40,47). H.D.'s "listen" is the adult's cue to attend to the speculative memory of the child on the occult or uncanny nature of the dream/nightmare and to suspend belief in scientific explanation and in its rationalized oversimplifications.

11. "At first sight," Erich Neumann writes, "the character of vision and inspiration seems, because of its connection with Pythian Apollo, to stand in opposition to Dionysus. But this opposition is superficial . . . because in Apollo's Delphi the representative of manticism is Pythia, a woman. . . . Pythia originally belonged to the matriarchal province of the moon" (72n). Neumann includes the Cretan serpent goddess and the Delphic oracle (both mentioned by H.D. in her *Tribute to Freud*) among the figures of prehistoric manticism in "The Woman as Mana Figure," in *The Great Mother: An Analysis of the Archetype*, trans. Ralph Manheim (Princeton, N.J., 1963), 287–305.

12. H.D.'s nightmare pythia may derive from the totem figure of the serpent drawn by Robert Briffault in *The Mothers: The Study of the Origins of Sentiments and Institutions*, 3 vols. (London, 1927). This is one of several sensational patriarchal studies of the cult of the *magna mater* following in the wake of J. J. Bachofen's *Mother Right* (1867) and Sir James G. Frazer's *Golden Bough* (1912). The serpent, Briffault contends, was generally regarded throughout the archaic world as the guardian of the maternal waters of life. He pictures a scene of Theban women washing at sacred springs whence appear serpents that girdle round them and *lick their cheeks*, explaining that "the predilection of serpents for women was associated with the sacred

functions of women in the agricultural rites which came to be associated with Dionysus and Orpheus" (2:644). Hilda's memory of the nightmare serpent is cued by a less traumatic memory of washing clothes with Ida.

13. Sigmund Freud, "Medusa's Head" (1940 [1922]), *SE* 18:273.

14. Neumann asserts that "to this province of *inspiration mysteries*," including that of the pythia and the serpent goddesses, "belong medicine, intoxicants, and all positive stimulants." He defers his decision, however, as to whether the use of narcotics "ends in a regression of the personality and a loss of consciousness, or whether on the contrary the temporary reduction of consciousness by intoxicant or poison leads to an extension of the consciousness or personality" (*The Great Mother*, 73).

15. Sigmund Freud, "The Taboo of Virginity (Contributions to the Psychology of Love, 3)" (1918 [1917]), *SE* 11:198.

16. Sir James G. Frazer, "The Magic Art and the Evolution of Kings," in *The Golden Bough* (New York, 1917), 1.1:36, 37, quoted in M. Esther Harding, *Woman's Mysteries: Ancient and Modern* (New York 1971), 101.

17. Ernest Jones, *On the Nightmare* (London, 1931), 76, 190, 222.

18. Hoffmann's narrator leaves his readers suspended between his inconclusive observations that the hero of his story succumbs to a world haunted by demons and to the demonological delusions of obsessive theorizing. "Incensed that Clara would grant the existence of the demon only as a force within him, Nathaniel was about to launch upon an exposition of his entire mystical theory of devils and cruel powers." E. T. A. Hoffmann, "The Sandman," in *Tales of Hoffmann*, trans. R. J. Hollingdale (Harmondsworth, Eng., 1982) 104. Like "Clara," Freud attempts to clarify and demystify Nathaniel's circumstances, identifying the source of his affliction as his deluded fear of castration.

19. Through dream interpretation, Freud is able to diagnose the Wolf Man's infantile neurosis (his wolf phobia, among other things) as the "pathogenic effect of the primal scene and the alteration which its revival produced in his sexual development." "From the History of an Infantile Neurosis" (1918 [1914]), *SE* 17:43.

20. "Hoffmann is the unrivalled master of the uncanny in literature," Freud declares. "His novel, *Die Elixire des Teufels* [*The Devil's Elixir*], contains a whole mass of themes to which one is tempted to ascribe the uncanny effect of the narrative; but it is too obscure and intricate a story to venture upon a summary of it." Freud, "The Uncanny," *SE* 17:233–34.

21. This sadistic first half of the *fort:da* game might then be translated as "gone! good riddance! Only the first half really interests Freud: "the first act . . . was repeated untiringly as a game" (15).

22. Freud, "Female Sexuality" (1931), *SE* 21:239.

23. H.D.'s evocation of the three fates in this passage recalls Freud's similar evocation in his reading of the uncanny figure of femininity in classical and folk literature. This is either a double or a triple figure signifying life

or love and death: "If the third of the sisters is the Goddess of Death, the sisters are known to us. They are the Fates . . . the third of whom is called Atropos, the inexorable." He goes on: "What is represented here are the three inevitable relations that a man has with a woman—the woman who bears him, the woman who is his mate and the woman who destroys him; or . . . the three forms taken by the figure of the mother in the course of a man's life—the mother herself, the beloved one who is chosen after her pattern, and lastly the Mother Earth who receives him once more." Sigmund Freud, "The Theme of the Three Caskets" (1913), *SE* 12:296, 301.

24. This passage of H.D.'s childhood reminiscence is as scenographic as the *fort:da* passage, of which Derrida observes: "Everything is very constructed, very propped up, dominated by a system of rules and compensations. . . . The grandfather, the father of the daughter and mother, actively selects the traits of the description. I see him rushing and worried, like a dramatist or director who has a part in the play. Staging it, he has to act with *dispatch*: to control everything, have everything in order, before going off to change for his part. This is translated by a peremptory authoritarianism, unexplained decisions, interrupted speeches, unanswered questions. The elements of the *mise en scène* have been put in place. . . . [It] hastens on, the actor-dramatist-producer will have done everything himself" (308).

25. Sigmund Freud, *Jokes and Their Relation to the Unconscious* (1905), *SE* 8:128.

26. The passage of time between chapters 6 and 7 in terms of Hilda's actual age is forty-five years; I base this calculation on the narrator's statement that Hilda was ten when "the thing" happened, the double trauma in "What It Was." H.D.'s birthdate was 1886; the date of composition was 1941.

27. DuPlessis, *H.D.*, 77–78.

28. Adalaide Morris discusses the ritual exchange of women in gift economies. "It is tempting to dismiss such ceremonies as a commodification," she writes, "but we are dealing here with the gift, not with the market. The exchange H.D. describes is not social but sacred. . . . for H.D. . . . women seem to embody the spirit of the gift: its bonding into kinship, its life-sustaining mutuality, and its generative power. . . . When the Moravian Anna von Pahlen is initiated into the Indian mysteries and the Indian Morning Star is baptized Moravian, they exchange inner names and the pact between the two tribes is sealed" ("Relay of Power and Peace," 522–23).

29. Leo Bersani illustrates his notion of masochistic *jouissance* by drawing attention to Mallarmé's *Après-midi d'une faune*. It is a figure of burning, ecstatic self-immolation. "The quivering flame of the faun's lips explodes the still unity of the nymphs' bodies. But the faun himself is divided and devoured by the ironic passion of Mallarmé's poem. In his willful recreation of scenes which may never have taken place, the faun narcissistically indulges a self already burned away. Desire purifies the faun of his identity. It 'drinks' the 'secret fright' of a person, just as the poet's sublimating speech divides

the writer from himself, dissipates the oppressive themes of his being in the exuberant irony of his work" (*Freudian Body*, 50).

30. Sigmund Freud, "From the History of an Infantile Neurosis," in *The Wolf-Man by the Wolf-Man*, ed. Muriel Gardiner (New York, 1971), 153–262, 256.

31. Virginia Woolf, "Women and Fiction," in *Women and Writing: Virginia Woolf*, ed. Michèle Barrett (1979, Dunvegan, Ont., 1984), 51.

## 4. Helen's Pharmacy

1. Aeschylus, *Agamemnon*, in *Oresteia*, ed. David Grene and Richmond Lattimore, trans. Lattimore (Chicago, 1953), 82.

2. Euripides, *Orestes*, trans. William Arrowsmith, in *Eripides IV*, ed. David Grene and Richmond Lattimore (Chicago, 1958), 178, 185.

3. Euripides, *Iphigenia in Aulis*, trans. Charles R. Walker, in *Euripides IV*, 290–91.

4. Euripides, *Helen*, in *Euripides II*, ed. David Grene and Richmond Lattimore, trans. Lattimore (Chicago, 1956), 192 hereafter cited in the text.

5. Although *Helen in Egypt* is not itself historical, it may respond to historical rereadings of the Trojan War which diminish the significance of women. David Roessel suggests that H.D.'s *Helen in Egypt*, may "be read as a reaction to masculine historical thinking" (40) as represented in such contemporary works as J. B. Bury, *A History of Greece* (1913) and Walter Leaf, *A Study in Homeric Geography* (1912). These works emphasize the Trojan War as a trade war and deemphasize the role of Helen, the logic apparently being "that a real war deserves a serious cause" (38). (They follow in the wake of Herodotus, as we shall see.) The irony of this historical reevaluation is that whereas the men who fought the Trojan War become more real in the public mind, the woman who supposedly set it off "fade[s] off into the world of romance and unreality" (38). Although H.D. was "most clearly inspired by literary sources, especially Euripides," Roessel conjectures, "the trade war theory may have colored the way H.D. presented the myth, particularly the poet's depiction of Helen's loss and reclamation of identity" (40). David Roessel, "H.D.'s Troy: Some Bearings," *H.D. Newsletter* 3.2 (1990): 38–42.

6. Herodotus, *The Histories*, trans. Aubrey de Sélincourt (Harmondsworth, Eng., 1954). According to the Persian account, the conflict between Greece and Troy arose after a series of abductions of women on both sides, culminating in the rape of Helen. Herodotus, however, is not convinced that such insignificant actions could lead to war. In the spirit of disinterestedness with which he forges his new historical science, he records the Persian story before setting down his own: "*Thus far there had been nothing worse than woman-stealing on both sides*; but for what happened next the Greeks, they say, were seriously to blame; for it was the Greeks who were, in a military sense, the aggressors. Abducting young women, in their opinion, is not, indeed, a

lawful act; but it is stupid after the event to make a fuss about it. *The only sensible thing is to take no notice; for it is obvious that no young woman allows herself to be abducted if she does not wish to be*. . . . according to the Persians . . . the Greeks, *merely on account of a girl from Sparta*, raised a big army, invaded Asia and destroyed the empire of Priam. From that root sprang their belief in the perpetual enmity of the Grecian world towards them. . . . So much for what Persians . . . say. . . . I prefer to rely on my own knowledge, and to point out who it was in actual fact that first injured the Greeks" (42–43, my emphasis).

7. "If Helen is writing she is also, and emphatically, Image—the 'most beautiful woman in the world,' after all—and in the text of the poem we see her diversely reflected or projected as such in the eyes of several different men, each of whom narrates a history that constructs a tableau in which he 'sees' and 'inscribes' his very own Helen. Thus, H.D.'s Achilles, Theseus and Paris might be compared to Stesichorus, Homer, Euripides, Goethe and their anonymous precursors, each of whom narrated a tale of Helen. . . . For H.D. as for Freud, myth is the collective correlative of individual phantasy." Hirsh, "'New Eyes,'" 6.

8. For a discussion of the evolution of the Greek logos, see Julia Kristeva, "Logical Greece," in *Language, the Unknown: An Initiation into Linguistics*, trans. Anne M. Menke (Brighton, 1989), 104–16. Kristeva emphasizes Aristotle's contribution to the formation of the "discourse-logos": "The logos, for Aristotle, was an enunciation, a formula, an explanation, an explicative discourse, or a concept. *Logical* became a synonym for concept, for signification, and for the rules of truth. Any recourse to the substance of language and to the specificities of its formation was omitted" (112).

9. See *Helen in Egypt*, pt. 2 (Leuké): "I am the first in all history / to say, she died, died, died / when the Walls fell; / what mystery is more subtle than this? / what spell is more potent? (131)

10. I recall Freud: "It is fair to say that the productions of the dream-work, which, it must be remembered, *are not made with the intention of being understood*, present no greater difficulties to their translators than do the ancient hieroglyphic scripts to those who seek to read them." *Interpretation of Dreams*, SE 5:341.

11. Numerous studies of *Helen in Egypt* discuss H.D.'s feminist re-vision of classical, phallocentric literature. See in particular, L. M. Freibert, "From Semblance to Selfhood: The Evolution of Woman in H.D.'s Neo-Epic *Helen in Egypt*," *Arizona Quarterly* 36 (1979): 165–75; Susan Stanford Friedman, "Creating a Women's Mythology: H.D.'s *Helen in Egypt*," *Women's Studies* 5.2 (1977): 163–97. In "Gender and Genre Anxiety: Elizabeth Barrett Browning and H.D. as Epic Poets," *Tulsa Studies in Women's Literature* 5.2 (1986): 203–28, Friedman argues that *Helen in Egypt* "rewrites Homer's *Iliad*" partly by modeling its revisionary saga "on the interpretive patterns of psychoanalysis" (217). See also her *Psyche Reborn* for discussion of the poem's re-visionary use of mysticism as well as psychoanalysis.

12. Novelist Leslie Dick offers a writer's definition of Freud's palimpsest: "There is no time in the Unconscious. The literary strategies of superimposition and juxtaposition that we employ allow us to place disparate elements together, regardless of temporal constraint, or sequences of cause and effect. The endless analytic process of re-writing, or re-working the past is itself inscribed in the text, where the same ground is gone over and over, using repetition with slight differences to convey the layering, the complex texture of psychic reality." Leslie Dick, "Notes on Freud and Writing," *Women: A Cultural Review* 1.3 (1990): 259.

13. See Richmond Lattimore's Introduction to Euripides, *Helen*, 261.

14. Lattimore provides the story Herodotus gathered from the priests of Memphis as background to Euripides' *Helen*: "Paris did steal Helen" but rough winds forced him ashore in Egypt. The Pharaoh, Proteus, put Helen under house arrest for "safekeeping" until her husband came to retrieve her. Meanwhile, Menelaus and Agamemnon raised a "Greek Armada, sailed to Troy, and demanded Helen." When the Trojans denied that they had her, saying she was in Egypt, the Greeks besieged and destroyed the city, only to discover that Helen was indeed missing. Menelaus visited the Pharaoh, collected Helen and "(after disgracing himself and Greece by an illicit sacrifice involving two Egyptian boys) sailed home (Herodotus 2.112–20)" (261–62).

15. Euripides explains, in Helen's words, his use of Hermes Argeiphontes, as deus ex machina: "I myself was caught up by Hermes, sheathed away in films of air, for Zeus had not forgotten me, and set down by him where you see me, in the house of Proteus, chosen because, most temperate of men, he could guard my honor safe for Menelaus" (192).

16. *The Oxford Companion to Classical Literature*, ed. Paul Harvey (Oxford: Oxford University Press, 1980), 205.

17. E. A. Wallis Budge, *The Literature of the Ancient Egyptians* (London, 1914), 1–2. "Egyptian writing," Budge writes, "was believed to have been invented by the god Tehuti, or Thoth, and as this god was thought to be a form of the mind and intellect and wisdom of the God who created the heavens and the earth, the picture characters, or hieroglyphs . . . were held to be holy, or divine, or sacred" (1). Further references to this edition will appear in the text.

18. Budge, *Literature of the Ancient Egyptians*, 37. " 'Book of the Dead' is the name . . . now generally given to the large collection of 'Chapters,' or compositions, both short and long, which the ancient Egyptians cut upon the walls of the corridors and chambers in pyramids and rock-hewn tombs, and cut or painted upon the insides and outsides of coffins and sarcophagi, and wrote upon papyri, etc., which were buried with the dead in their tombs. . . . these Chapters . . . were written entirely for the dead . . . and such prayers and hymns as are incorporated with them were supposed to be said and sung by the dead for their own benefit. The author of the Chapters of the

Book of the Dead was the god Thoth. . . . The OBJECT OF THE BOOK OF THE DEAD was to provide the dead man with . . . spells, prayers, amulets . . . to enable him to . . . take his place among the subjects of Osiris in the Land of Everlasting Life (41).

19. H.D. possessed a copy of E. A. Wallis Budge, *Book of the Dead: An English Translation* (London; New York, 1938). See Smyers, "H.D.'s Books in the Bryher Library," 19. In fact, H.D. had more books by Budge than by Freud in her library. Also in her possession: *Easy Lessons in Egyptian Hieroglyphics* (1902); *The Egyptian Heaven and Hell*, 3 vols. (1905); *A Hieroglyphic Vocabulary to the Theban Recension of the Book of the Dead* (1911); *Egyptian Literature: Legends of the Gods* (1912); *Osiris and the Egyptian Resurrection*, 2 vols. (1911); *Cleopatra's Needles and Other Egyptian Obelisks* (1926). See the card catalogue to H.D.'s library collected by the Beinecke Rare Book and Manuscript Library, Yale University.

20. Freud calls attention to the marketing of a new commodity, a self-erasing writing pad, whose design and function suggest to him a dynamic figure of the memory of perception. The " 'Mystic Writing-Pad,' " he observes, is "a small contrivance that promises to perform more than the sheet of paper or the slate. It claims to be nothing more than a writing-tablet from which notes can be erased by an easy movement of the hand. But if it is examined more closely it will be found that its construction shows a remarkable agreement with my hypothetical structure of our perceptual apparatus and that it can in fact provide both an ever-ready receptive surface and permanent traces of the notes that have been made upon it." Sigmund Freud, "A Note upon the 'Mystic Writing-Pad' " (1925 [1924]), SE 19:228.

21. Jacques Derrida, "Plato's Pharmacy," in *Dissemination*, trans. Barbara Johnson (1972; Chicago, 1981), 91, hereafter cited in the text.

22. Freud does not dismiss a mystical interpretation of the psyche; in fact, he raises its viability in the same instance that he stresses the mechanical limitations of his machine metaphor: "We need not be disturbed by the fact that in the Mystic Pad no use is made of the permanent traces of the notes that have been received; it is enough that they are present. There must come a point at which the analogy between an auxiliary apparatus of this kind and the organ which is its prototype will cease to apply. It is true, too, that once the writing has been erased, the Mystic Pad cannot 'reproduce' it from within; *it would be a mystic pad indeed if, like our memory, it could accomplish that*" (SE 19:230, my emphasis).

23. Euripides offers an exemplary demonstration of the point Derrida makes while analyzing Freud's graphic metaphor of repression. "Writing is unthinkable without repression. The condition for writing is that there be neither a permanent contact nor an absolute break between strata: the vigilance and failure of censorship. It is no accident that the metaphor of censorship should come from the area of politics concerned with the deletions, blanks, and disguises of writing, even if, at the beginning of the

*Traumdeutung*, Freud seems to make only a conventional, didactic reference to it. The apparent exteriority of political censorship refers to an essential censorship which binds the writer to his own writing." Derrida, "Freud and the Scene of Writing," 226.

24. Another of H.D.'s primary sources is Denis de Rougemont, *Love in the Western World* (1940), whose book 1, "The Tristan Myth," features a section "The Love-Potion" and whose "Inconclusive and Scientifico-Polemical Post-script" features a section "Passion and Drugs." *Love in the Western World*, trans. Montgomery Belgion (Princeton, 1983).

25. "This anodyne of Egypt," the title of this section, is from H.D.'s "Secret Name: Excavator's Egypt" (*P* 176).

26. Hélène Cixous describes the oppositional logic at work in Western languages as a violence against the coupling of antithetical terms in which one of the terms, as a rule, the "feminine" one, is degraded. "Is the fact that Logocentrism subjects thought—all concepts, codes and values—to a binary system, related to "the" couple, man/woman? . . . Organization by hierarchy makes all conceptual organization subject to man. Male privilege [is] shown in the opposition between *activity* and *passivity*, which he uses to sustain himself. . . . woman is always associated with passivity in philosophy. . . . And if we consult literary history, it is the same story. . . . There is an intrinsic connection between the philosophical and the literary . . . and the phallo-centric. Philosophy is constructed on the premise of woman's abasement." Cixous and Clément, *Newly Born Woman*, 63–65, hereafter cited in the text.

27. W. S. Landor reconstructs an imaginary amorous meeting between Helen and Achilles on Mount Ida overlooking the battlefields of Troy (where the battle for Helen ensues). Landor's Achilles is not Homer's manly, man-loving warrior but an effeminate mystic, dreamer, and herbalist who woos an amazonian Helen. See his "Achilles and Helena," in *Imaginary Conversations of Greeks and Romans*, vol. 1 of *The Collected Works of Walter Savage Landor*, ed. T. Earle Welby (London, 1927), 1–5.

Consider the following passage from Goethe, *Faust, Part Two*, trans. Philip Wayne (Harmondsworth, Eng., 1959), 169–71:

Helen.
    Was all this me? Is still? And ever shall I be
    The phantom scare of them that lay proud cities waste?
Phorykas [Mephisto].
    Yet rumour has it, you assume a two-fold shape,
    Seen both in Ilium and in Egypt's lands.
Helen.
    Spare the confusion in the sad distracted mind.
    Even here, the truth of what I am, I do not know.
Phorykas.
    Again 'tis said that from the hollow realm of shades

Achilles rose in burning passion for your sake
You whom he loved of old, despite the voice of fate.
Helen.
Then was I but a wraith, and with a wraith was joined.
It was a dream, the very words declare this true.

Barbara Guest speculates that Eliza M. Butler, author of *The Fortunes of Faust* (Cambridge, 1952), referred H.D. to "Goethe's use of the legend of Helen's having fled to Egypt and her double appearing on the walls of Troy." *Herself Defined*, 291.

28. Freud, "Creative Writers and Day-Dreaming," *SE* 9:150.

29. See *The Interpretation of Dreams*, *SE* 4:323. See also "Remarks on the Theory and Practice of Dream-Interpretation" (1923), *SE* 19:120.

Jean Laplanche and J.-B. Pontalis add that "in the earliest forms of fantasy, [the subject] cannot be assigned any fixed place in it. . . . As a result, the subject, although always present in the fantasy, may be so in a *desubjectivized* form, that is to say, in the very syntax of the sequence in question." "Fantasy and the Origins of Sexuality," in *Formations of Fantasy*, ed. Victor Burgin, James Donald, and Cora Kaplan (London, 1986), 26.

30. Freud, *Beyond the Pleasure Principle*, *SE* 18:27.

31. "Achilles was one of the princely suitors for [Helen's] hand, at the court of her earthly father, Tyndareus of Sparta" (*HE* 7). According to legend, Tyndareus agreed to marry Helen to Menelaus on the condition that her many unsuccessful suitors pledge their allegiance to her husband-to-be—an agreement that mythically reflects the historical accomplishment of the patriarchal unification of Greece and the domestication of women. Moreover, it supports Freud's myth of the repressive, patriarchal foundation of civilization.

32. In his reading of "the famous legend of the death of Osiris," Derrida writes that "Isis, transformed into a vulture, lies on the corpse. . . . In that position she engenders Horus," who is, in turn, responsible for avenging his father's death and bringing him back to life and potency by collaborating with Thoth ("Plato's Pharmacy," 90).

33. "The common translation of *pharmakon* by *remedy* [remède]—a beneficent drug—is not, of course, inaccurate," Derrida observes as he traces the ambiguity of the word in the Socratic dialogues, detecting Plato's concern to expose its disturbing, double meaning. "Not only can *pharmakon* really mean *remedy*. . . . But it is . . . the stated intention of Theuth . . . that he *turns* the word on its strange and invisible pivot, presenting it from a single one, the most reassuring, of its *poles*. This medicine is beneficial; it repairs and produces, accumulates and remedies, increases knowledge and reduces forgetfulness. Its translation by "remedy" nonetheless erases, in going outside the Greek language, the other pole reserved in the word *pharmakon*. . . . when the textual center-stage of the word *pharmakon*, even while it means *remedy*, cites,

re-cites, and makes legible that which *in the same word* signifies, in another spot and on a different level of the stage, *poison* . . . the choice of only one of these renditions by the translator has as its first effect the neutralization of the citational play, of the 'anagram' " ("Plato's Pharmacy," 97–98).

34. Homer, *The Odyssey*, trans. E. V. Rieu (Harmondsworth, Eng., 1946), 70.

35. "The famous legend of the death of Osiris is well known," Derrida writes. "Tricked into being shut up in a trunk the size of his body, he is dismembered, and his fourteen parts are scattered to the winds. After many complications, he is found and reassembled by his wife Isis, all except for the phallus, which has been swallowed by an Oxyrhynchus fish" ("Plato's Pharmacy," 90).

36. Bersani elaborates Jean Laplanche's distinction between Freud's Nirvana (the pleasure of of recovering homeostasis or of returning to the quiescence of before and after life, of being inorganic, dead) and his inarticulate intuition of pleasure in excess, or *jouissance* (Jean Laplanche, *Life and Death in Psychoanalysis*, trans. Jeffrey Mehlman Baltimore, 1976), 121–24.

37. Hélène Cixous's reading of Heinrich von Kleist's *Penthesileia* celebrates a violent exchange of sexual difference that recalls H.D.'s treatment of Achilles and Helen. See "Achilles is Penthesileia is Achilles," in Cixous and Clément, *Newly Born Woman*, 112–32.

38. In his rereading of *Civilization and Its Discontents*, Bersani detects a rhetorical, if not logical, kinship between supposedly opposed terms of "Aggression" and "oceanic feeling": "Aggressiveness is now beginning to sound bizarrely like . . . the oceanic feeling, which, as we have seen, was an ecstatic sense of oneness with the universe, a breaking down of the boundaries between the ego and the world traceable to the 'limitless narcissism' of infancy. Like the oceanic feeling, aggressiveness includes an intense erotic pleasure. . . . *The oceanic feeling is a benign reformulation of 'the blind fury of destructiveness.* . . . the text obliquely yet insistently reformulates this argument [that we must sacrifice part of our sexuality and sublimate it into brotherly love] in the following way: human love is something like an oceanic aggressiveness which threatens to shatter civilization in the wake of its own shattering narcissistic pleasure" (*The Freudian Body*, 19–20, my emphasis).

39. Bersani argues that Freud's theory of sexuality obliquely points to maternal erotism as the primal source of cultural mobilization. "The maternally derived traumatic model of sexuality moves Freud toward a view of cultural symbolization as a continuation rather than a repressive substitute for sexual fantasy. Or, in other terms, it provides the genetic basis for a view of sublimation as coextensive with sexuality, as an appropriation and elaboration of sexual impulses" (45).

40. I note the implied pun, Pharos and Pharaoh's (the lighthouse of Pharos equals the Pharaoh's enlightenment), which H.D. implicitly repeats

as a way of emphasizing the resurrection of the Egyptian Mysteries. As E. M. Forster explains in the opening pages of *Pharos and Pharillon* (1930; Berkeley, 1980), "Pharos," easily confused with "Pharaoh's," is the name of the island in the canopic delta on which the lighthouse of ancient Alexandria once stood. The legend of Helen provides a dramatic context for Forster's explanation (15).

41. Bersani writes: "Freud's own text exemplifies the insistent replications of sexuality in the very process of its both constituting and evading the theory of those replications" (115).

42. I recall the role of the "secretary" In "Secret Name: Excavator's Egypt" (*Palimpsest*). On the one hand, it designates the occupation of the protagonist, Helen, a philologist of ancient languages specializing in Greek who has momentarily been employed by the famous Egyptologist Bodge-Grafton to record and research his findings on site of the Tuthankamen excavations. On the other hand, it signifes Helen's *secret* experience of the radical otherness of Egypt and of Egyptian writing as a mysterious, semiotic presence, untranslatable into Greek or any modern European language.

43. Ernest Jones reports that Freud once said: "If I had my life to live over again I should devote myself to psychical research rather than to psychoanalysis." Jones, *Sigmund Freud* 3:419.

44. Sigmund Freud, "Analysis Terminable and Interminable" (1937) "The female's wish for a penis . . . is the source of outbreaks of severe depression in her, owing to an internal conviction that the analysis will be of no use and that nothing can be done to help her. And we can only agree that she is right, when we learn that her strongest motive in coming for treatment was the hope that, after all, she might still obtain a male organ, the lack of which was so painful to her" (*SE* 23:252).

45. Luce Irigaray, *This Sex Which Is Not One*, trans. Catherine Porter with Carolyn Burke (1977; Ithaca, N.Y., 1985), 25.

46. "Heads in hieroglyphic bonnets, / Heads in turbans and black birettas, / Heads in wigs and thousand other / Wretched, sweating heads of humans (Heinrich Heine, *Nordsee*, Second Cycle, 7, "Fragen").

47. See Sarah Kofman, *The Enigma of Woman: Woman in Freud's Writings*, trans. Catherine Porter (1980; Ithaca, N.Y., 1985); Irigaray, *Speculum*; Cixous and Clément, *Newly Born Woman*; Hélène Cixous, "Castration or Decapitation," trans. Annette Kuhn, *Signs* 7.1 (1981): 41–55; Shoshana Felman, "Rereading Femininity," *Yale French Studies* 62 (1981): 19–44.

48. Freud, *The Complete Letters of Sigmund Freud to Wilhelm Fliess, 1887–1904*, ed. and trans. Jeffrey Moussaieff Masson (Cambridge, Mass., 1985), 227.

49. Freud, "Extracts from the Fliess Papers" (1950 [1892–99]), *SE* 1:242.

50. Theodor W. Adorno and Max Horkheimer, *Dialectic of Enlightenment*, trans. John Cumming (1944; London, 1979), 4, hereafter cited in the text.

51. "In the hieroglyphics of the ancient Egyptians the mother is repre-

sented by a picture of a vulture." *Leonardo DaVinci and a Memory of His Childhood* (1910), SE 11:88. Freud's reference is Horapollo, *Hieroglyphica I*.

52. Catherine Clément, *Newly Born Woman* (14–15).

53. Peggy Kamuf points out the limitations of Freud's case histories as models for women who would write themselves out of hysteria, though they may serve as a launching pad. "If . . . we are looking for . . . an inscription of the posthysterical subject in the symbolic order . . . it will have to be elsewhere. Dora, however, and the other characters in Freud's hysterical plots, will at least have given us an idea of where to look. What if one of them had left a written account of her passage out of a closed hysterical silence? As a record of this passage, the account would have to substitute for the conventions of the case history the conventions of autobiography, so that to imagine such a text is to imagine the interlocutor as the silent pole through which passes the invention of the writing subject." Peggy Kamuf, *Fictions of Feminine Desire: Disclosures of Heloise* (Lincoln, Neb., 1982), 56.

54. Barbara Guest represents H.D.'s life after World War II as lived out in the seclusion of hotels and clinics. She also suggests that throughout her entire career, H.D. was attended by analysts, including, after Freud, Walter Schmideberg (1935–38), son-in-law of Melanie Klein, and the Heideggerean analyst, Erich Heydt (1953–55). See *Herself Defined*, esp. chaps. 25 and 27.

55. Freud, "Fragment of an Analysis of a Case of Hysteria" (1905 [1901]), *SE* 7:120 n. 1.

56. For critical discussions of H.D.'s inscription of lesbianism, see Friedman and DuPlessis, " 'I Had Two Loves Separate' "; Susan Gubar, "Sapphistries," *Signs* 10.1 (1984): 43–62; and Buck, "Freud and H.D." For a less critical, more biographical discussion, see also Gillian Hanscombe and Virginia L. Smyers, "H.D.'s Triangles," in *Writing for Their Lives: The Modernist Women, 1910–1940* (London, 1987), 14–32.

57. Like H.D., Hélène Cixous recasts the hysteric as anarchic witch: "Fire! She shoots, she shoots away. Break. From their bodies where they have been buried, shut up and at the same time forbidden to take pleasure. Women have almost everything to write about femininity: about their sexuality, that is to say, about the infinite and mobile complexity of their becoming erotic, about the lightning ignitions of such a minuscule-vast region of their body, not about destiny but about the adventure of such an urge, the voyages, crossings, advances, sudden and slow awakenings, discoveries of a formerly timid region that is just now springing up. Woman's body with a thousand and one fiery hearths, when—shattering censorship and yokes—she lets it articulate the proliferation of meanings that runs through it in every direction." "Sorties," in Cixous and Clément, *Newly Born Woman*, 94.

58. Monique Wittig writes of the "psychoanalytic contract" to which homosexual patients are expected to subscribe, making treatment itself an accomplice in their oppression. "In the analytical experience there is an oppressed person, the psychoanalyzed, whose need for communication is

exploited and who (in the same way as the witches could, under torture, only repeat the language that the inquisitors wanted to hear) has no other choice, (if s/he does not want to destroy the implicit contract which allows her/him to communicate and which s/he needs), than to attempt to say what s/he is supposed to say. . . . If we believe recent testimonies by lesbians, feminists, and gay men, . . . [w]hen the general state of things is understood . . . the result is for the oppressed person to break the psychoanalytical contract." Monique Wittig, "The Straight Mind," *Feminist Issues* 1.1 (1980): 105.

59. Walter Pater, *The Renaissance: Studies in Art and Poetry*, ed. Donald L. Hill (1893; Berkeley, 1980). Although Freud refers to the first edition of this text (1873), I quote the famous *La Gioconda* passage from the 1893 edition, whose text remains the same. Pater describes the labor by which Da Vinci created his *Mona Lisa* as a dream and wonders "by [what] stroke of magic . . . the image was projected." Giving us the impression that by gazing into her painted face he can unveil her mystery, he proceeds to trace her sources in pagan prehistory: "Hers is the head upon which all 'the ends of the world are come,' and the eyelids are a little weary. It is a beauty wrought . . . of strange thoughts and fantastic reveries and exquisite passions . . . the animalism of Greece, the lust of Rome, the mysticism of the middle ages . . . the sins of the Borgias. She is older than the rocks among which she sits; like the vampire, she has been dead many times, and learned the secrets of the grave; . . . and, as Leda, was the mother of Helen of Troy, and, as Saint Anne, the mother of Mary; . . . [she] might stand as the embodiment of the old fancy, the symbol of the modern idea" (98–99).

60. For a discussion of the significance of Frazer, Briffault, and Freud in shaping the patriarchal theory of twentieth-century cultural studies and social sciences, see Rosalind Coward, *Patriarchal Precendents: Sexuality and Social Relations* (London, 1983), esp. chaps. 1, 2, and 7.

# Postscript

1. In quite a different way, Susan Stanford Friedman's *Psyche Reborn* argues the same claim that H.D.'s Freudian revisionism is both personally and culturally healing.

2. As discussed in Chapter 1, Freud distinguishes between the "symbolic" and the "decoding" methods of dream interpretation. An example of this first method is "to be seen in the explanation of Pharaoh's dream propounded by Joseph in the Bible." Since success in symbolic interpretation is a matter of "hitting on a clever idea" or "direct intuition," it was possible for it "to be exalted into an artistic activity dependent on the possession of peculiar gifts." The decoding method, however, "is far from making any such claims . . . since it treats dreams as a kind of cryptography in which each

sign can be translated into another sign having a known meaning, in accordance with a fixed key." Freud, *Interpretation of Dreams*, SE 4:97.

3. In *The Interpretation of Dreams*, Freud repeatedly paraphrases Nietzsche in referring to the "transvaluation of all psychical values" to describe the "complete reversal of all psychical values [which] takes place between the dream-thoughts and the dream" (*SE* 4:330). In one discussion of this theme, he compares the dream work to a "revolution" in which all the "noble and powerful families which had previously dominated the scene were sent into exile and all the high offices were filled by newcomers" (*SE* 5:516). H.D. adapts and develops this comparison.

4. The misprinting of hieratic as "heiratic," which is possibly H.D.'s own mistranscription, is punningly appropriate in the context of this discussion of her legacy motif (motive).

5. Jacques Derrida, "Scribble (Writing-Power)," *Yale French Studies* 58 (1979): 124.

6. Catherine Clément, *The Weary Sons of Freud*, trans. Nicole Ball (1978; London, 1987), 9–11, hereafter cited in the text.

7. Freud to Lou Andreas-Salomé, [18 May 1916]. In her letter of 11 May 1916, Lou Andreas-Salomé tells Freud that she "would like to have sent you what I produced in the years 1914/15 . . . a little book about what is most significant for me in your psycho-analysis, in which I have tried to make it palatable to wider circles." Freud and Lou Andreas-Salomé, *Letters*, ed. Ernst Pfeiffer, trans. William Scott and Elaine Robson-Scott (1966; New York, 1972), 43–44, hereafter cited in the text.

8. Lou Andreas-Salomé, "Der Mensch als Weib," *Neue Deutsche Rundschau* 10 (1899): 225–43. See Stanley A. Leavey, Translator's Introduction to Lou Andreas-Salomé, *The Freud Journal* (1964; London, 1987), 23.

9. Sigmund Freud, "Lou Andreas-Salomé" (1937), *SE* 23:297.

10. Lou Andreas-Salomé to Freud, 28 Aug. 1917, *Letters*, 62.

11. Ernst Pfeiffer, Introduction to *Letters*, 2.

12. See Lou Andreas-Salomé, *Mein Dank an Freud* (Vienna, 1931), 109.

13. H.D.'s sense of "re-value" is informed, I contend, not only by "the transvaluation of all psychical values" but also by another Nietzschean assertion of Freud's, that "in dreams 'some primaeval relic of humanity is at work which we can now scarcely reach any longer by a direct path'; and we may expect that the analysis of dreams will lead us to a knowledge of man's archaic heritage, of what is psychically innate in him." Freud, *Interpretation of Dreams*, SE 5:549.

14. Estelle Roith, *Riddle of Freud*, 174–75, hereafter cited in the text.

15. I only hint at a thematic connection between H.D. and Klein, but Elizabeth Abel outlines a similar but much clearer and more focused connection between Klein and Virginia Woolf in *Woolf and the Fictions of Psychoanalysis*, esp. 19–20.

16. "Klein," Roith continues, "not only had challenged many of Freud's

basic tenets including his theory of female sexual development but also had carried with her many of his most devoted supporters including Ernest Jones, his analysand and translator Joan Riviére, and many others. The resulting controversy with Anna Freud, whose legacy has shaped the course of the development of psychoanalysis, is a part of psychoanalytic history" (173–74).

17. See Karl Abraham, *Clinical Papers and Essays on Psycho-Analysis*, ed. H. C. Abraham, trans. H. C. Abraham and D. R. Ellison et al. (London, 1979).

18. Hirsh, " 'New Eyes,' " hereafter cited in the text.

19. Freud, "Creative Writers and Day-Dreaming," *SE* 9:150.

20. Feminist historian Joan Kelly describes the witch persecutions, which saw "the hanging or burning alive of some 100,000 or more women as witches," as the "single most horrendous expression in early modern Europe" of the cultural transformation from feudal to bourgeois society. Joan Kelly, *Women, History, and Theory* (Chicago, 1984), 93–94.

21. Adrienne Rich, "Twenty-one Love Poems [v]," in *The Dream of a Common Language: Poems, 1974–1977* (New York, 1978), 27.

# Bibliography

## Works by H.D.

H.D.'s works are listed in chronological order of the date of writing, which is provided after the title in square brackets where it differs from the date of first publication. Details of first publication are given along with those of some newer editions. Page numbers throughout the text are taken from the most recent edition listed, and the abbreviations are those used in the text.

*Collected Poems, 1912–1944*. Ed. Louis L. Martz. New York: New Directions, 1983. (Abbreviated *CP*.)

*Sea Garden*. Boston: Houghton Mifflin, 1916. Now in *CP*.

*Choruses from the Iphigenia in Aulis*. London: Egoist Press, 1916. Now in *CP*.

*Choruses from the Iphigenia in Aulis and the Hippolytus of Euripides*. Poets' Translation Series. London: Egoist Press, 1919. Now in *CP*.

*Notes on Thought and Vision*. [1919]; San Francisco: City Lights Books, 1982. (Abbreviated *NTV*.)

*Palimpsest*. [1924]; Paris: Contact Editions and Boston: Houghton Mifflin, 1926. Rev. ed. Carbondale: Southern Illinois University Press, 1968. (Abbreviated *P*).

*Hedylus*. [1924?]; Boston: Houghton Mifflin, 1928; Oxford: Basil Blackwell, 1928 and 1929. Redding Ridge, Conn.: Black Swan Books, 1980.

*HERmione*. [1926–27]; New York: New Directions, 1981. Rpt. as *Her*. London: Virago, 1984. (Abbreviated *Her*.)

*Kora and Ka*. [1930]; Dijon: Imprimerie Darantière, 1934. Berkeley: Bios, 1978.

*Nights*. [1931, 1934]; Dijon: Imprimerie Darantière, 1935 (under the pseudonym John Helforth). New York: New Directions, 1986. (Abbreviated *N*.)

*Euripides' Ion*. [1916,1919,1934,1935] Boston: Houghton Mifflin, 1937; Redding Ridge, Conn.: Black Swan Books, 1986.

"Letter to Norman Pearson, 1937 ('A Note on Poetry')." *Agenda* 25.3/4 (1987–88): 71–76.

*The Gift.* [1941–43]; Abridged by Griselda Ohanessian. New York: New Directions, 1982. Rpt. London: Virago, 1984. (Abbreviated *G*).

"Dark Room" (*The Gift*, chap. 1). *Montemora* 8 (Aug. 1981): 57–76. (Abbreviated *G1*.)

"Fortune Teller" (*The Gift*, chap. 2). *Iowa Review* 16.2 (1986): 18–41. (Abbreviated *G2*.)

"The Dream" (*The Gift*, chap. 3). *Contemporary Literature* 10.4 (1969): 605–26. (Abbreviated *G3*.)

*The Walls Do Not Fall* [pt. 1, *Trilogy*). [1942]; London: Oxford University Press, 1944; New York: New Directions, 1973. Now in *CP*. (Abbreviated *WDNF*.)

*Tribute to the Angels* (pt. 2, *Trilogy*). [1944]; London: Oxford University Press, 1945. New York: New Directions, 1973. Now in *CP*. (Abbreviated *TA*.)

"Writing on the Wall" [1944]. First published in the periodical, *Life and Letters Today*. London, 1945–46. First published in book form as *Tribute to Freud*; New York: Pantheon and Toronto: McClelland and Stewart, 1956. Now in *TF*, 1–111.

*The Flowering of the Rod* [pt. 3, *Trilogy*]. [1944]; London: Oxford University Press, 1946; New York: New Directions, 1973. Now in *CP*. (Abbreviated *FR*.)

"Advent." [1948]. In *TF*. Boston: David R. Godine and New York: New Directions, 1974, 113–87.

*Tribute to Freud.* [1944, 1948]; New York: Pantheon and Toronto: McClelland and Stewart, 1956; Boston: David R. Godine and New York: New Directions, 1974; Rpt. Manchester: Carcanet, 1985. (Abbreviated *TF*.)

"H.D. by Delia Alton" ("Notes on Recent Writing"). [1949]; *Iowa Review* 16.3 (1986): 444–74. (Abbreviated *DA*.)

*Bid Me to Live.* [1939, 1948–50]; New York: Grove Press and Toronto: McClelland and Stewart, 1960. Redding Ridge, Conn.: Black Swan Books, 1983.

*Helen in Egypt.* [1952–55]; New York: Grove Press, 1961; New York: New Directions, 1974. (Abbreviated *HE*.)

*End to Torment: A Memoir of Ezra Pound.* [1958]. Ed. Norman Holmes Pearson and Michael King. New York: New Directions, 1979; Manchester: Carcanet, 1980. (Abbreviated *ETT*).

"Hermetic Definition" [1960–61]. In *Hermetic Definition*. New York: New Directions, 1972: 1–55. (Abbreviated *HD*.)

## Works by Sigmund Freud

*The Complete Letters of Sigmund Freud to Wilhelm Fliess, 1887–1904.* Ed. and trans. Jeffrey Moussaieff Masson. Cambridge: Harvard University Press, 1985.

Freud and Lou Andreas-Salomé. *Letters*. Ed. Ernst Pfeiffer. Trans. William
  Scott and Elaine Robson Scott. New York: Norton, 1985.
*The Standard Edition of the Complete Psychological Works of Sigmund Freud*. Ed.
  and trans. James Strachey in collaboration with Anna Freud. 24 vols.
  London: Hogarth Press and Institute of Psycho-Analysis, 1953–74. (Abbre-
  viated *SE*).

References, by volume and page number, are to the *Standard Edition*. Works
in that edition are listed below in chronological order of the date of writing,
which, following Strachey's notation, is provided in square brackets after the
date of first publication in the original language where the two differ:

"Extracts from the Fliess Papers." 1950 [1892–99]. 1:177–280.
With Josef Breuer. *Studies on Hysteria*. 1893–95. 2:3–311.
*The Interpretation of Dreams*. 1900. 4:1–338, 5:339–627.
"Childhood Memories and Screen Memories." *The Psychopathology of Every-
  day Life*. 1901. 6:43–52.
"Determinism, Belief in Chance and Superstition." *The Psychopathology of
  Everyday Life*. 1901. 6:239–79.
"Fragment of an Analysis of a Case of Hysteria." 1905 [1901]. 7:7–122.
*Three Essays on the Theory of Sexuality*. 1905. 7:135–245.
*Jokes and Their Relation to the Unconscious*. 1905. 8:9–238.
"Delusions and Dreams in Jensen's *Gradiva*." 1907 [1906]. 9:7–95.
"Creative Writers and Day-Dreaming." 1908 [1907]. 9:143–53.
"Hysterical Phantasies and Their Relation to Bisexuality." 1908. 9:159–66.
" 'Civilized' Sexual Morality and Modern Nervous Illness." 1908. 9:181–204.
*Leonardo Da Vinci and a Memory of His Childhood*. 1910. 11:63–137.
"The Antithetical Meaning of Primal Words." 1910. 11:155–61.
"The Dynamics of Transference." 1912. 12:99–108.
"The Theme of the Three Caskets." 1913. 12:291–301.
*Totem and Taboo*. 1913 [1912–13]. 13:1–162.
"On the History of the Psycho-Analytic Movement." 1914. 14:7–66.
"From the History of an Infantile Neurosis." 1918 [1914]. 17:7–122.
"The Unconscious." 1915. 14:166–215.
"Instincts and Their Vicissitudes." 1915. 14:111–40.
"Mourning and Melancholia." 1917 [1915]. 14:243–58.
"A Metapsychological Supplement to the Theory of Dreams." 1917 [1915].
  14:222–35.
"The Archaic Features and Infantilism of Dreams." 1916–17 [1915–17]. 15:
  199–212.
"A Childhood Recollection from *Dichtung und Wahrheit*." 1917. 17:147–56.
"The Taboo of Virginity (Contributions to the Psychology of Love, 3)." 1918
  [1917]. 11:193–208.
"The Uncanny." 1919. 17:219–56.

"A Child Is Being Beaten: A Contribution to the Study of the Origin of Sexual Perversions." 1919, 17:179–204.
*Beyond the Pleasure Principle.* 1920. 18:7–64.
"Medusa's Head." 1940 [1922]. 18:273–74.
"Remarks on the Theory and Practice of Dream-Interpretation." 1923. 19: 109–21.
"The Economic Problem of Masochism." 1924. 19:155–70.
"The Dissolution of the Oedipus Complex." 1924. 19:173–79.
"A Note upon the 'Mystic Writing-Pad.'" 1925 [1924]. 19:227–32.
*An Autobiographical Study.* 1925 [1924]. 20:7–74.
"Negation." 1925. 19:235–39.
*Civilization and Its Discontents.* 1930 [1929]. 21:64–145.
"The Goethe Prize." 1930. 21:208–12.
"Female Sexuality." 1931. 21:225–43.
"Dreams and Occultism." *New Introductory Lectures on Psycho-Analysis.* 1933 [1932]. 22:31–56.
"Femininity." *New Introductory Lectures on Psycho-Analysis.* 1933 [1932]. 22: 112–35.
"Preface to Marie Bonaparte's *The Life and Works of Edgar Allan Poe: A Psycho-Analytic Interpretation.*" 1933. 22:254.
"Analysis Terminable and Interminable." 1937. 23:216–53.
"Lou Andreas-Salomé." 1937. 23:297–98.
"*An Outline of Psycho-Analysis.*" 1940 [1938]. 23:144–207.
"*Constructions in Analysis.*" 1940 [1938]. 23:257–69.
*Moses and Monotheism: Three Essays.* 1939 [1934–38]. 23:7–137.

## Works by Other Authors

The date provided after the title (and translator) is that of first publication in the original language.

Abel, Elizabeth. *Virginia Woolf and the Fictions of Psychoanalysis.* Chicago: University of Chicago Press, 1989.
Adorno, Theodor W., and Max Horkheimer. *Dialectic of Enlightenment.* Trans. John Cumming. 1944; London: Verso, 1979.
Aeschylus. *Agamemnon.* In *Oresteia.* Ed. David Grene and Richmond Lattimore. Trans. Richmond Lattimore. Chicago: University of Chicago Press, 1953: 35–90.
Aldington, Richard. *Death of a Hero.* 1929. London: Hogarth Press, 1984.
———, trans. *The Garland of Meleager.* London: Egoist Press, 1920.
Andreas-Salomé, Lou. *The Freud Journal.* Trans. Stanley R. Leavy. 1964; London: Quartet Encounters, 1987.
———. "Der Mensch als Weib." *Neue Deutsche Rundschau* 10 (1899): 225–43.

——. *Mein Dank an Freud*. Vienna: n.p., 1931.
Arthur, Marylin B. "Psychomythology: The Case of H.D." *Bucknell Review* 28.2 (1983): 65–79.
Bakan, David. *Sigmund Freud and the Jewish Mystical Tradition*. Princeton: Van Nostrand, 1958.
Barthes, Roland. *Camera Lucida: Reflections on Photography*. Trans. Richard Howard. 1980; London: Flamingo, 1984.
——. *The Pleasure of the Text*. Trans. Richard Miller. 1973; New York: Hill and Wang, 1975.
Baudelaire, Charles. *Les fleurs du mal*. Trans. Richard Howard. London: Picador, 1982.
Benstock, Shari. *Women of the Left Bank: Paris, 1900–1940*. London: Virago, 1987.
Bergman, David. "The Economics of Influence: Gift Giving in H.D. and Robert Duncan." *H.D. Newsletter* 2.1 (1988): 11–16.
Bernal, Martin. *Black Athena: The Afroasiatic Roots of Classical Civilization*. Vol. 1: *The Fabrication of Ancient Greece, 1785–1985*. New Brunswick: Rutgers University Press, 1987.
Bernheimer, Charles, and Claire Kahane, eds. *In Dora's Case: Freud, Hysteria, Feminism*. London: Virago, 1985.
Bersani, Leo. *The Freudian Body: Psychoanalysis and Art*. New York: Columbia University Press, 1986.
Bonaparte, Marie. *Female Sexuality*. Trans. J. Rodker. 1949; London: Imago, 1953.
——. *The Life and Works of Edgar Allan Poe: A Psycho-Analytic Interpretation*. Trans. J. Rodker. 1933; London: Imago, 1949.
Boone, Bruce. "H.D.'s Writing: Herself as Ghost." *Sagetrieb* 6.2 (1987): 17–19.
Boughn, Michael. "The Bibliographic Record of Reviews of H.D.'s Works." *H.D. Newsletter* 2.1 (1988): 27–47.
Briffault, Robert. *The Mothers: The Study of the Origins of Sentiments and Institutions*. 3 vols. London: Allen and Unwin, 1927.
Brooks, Peter. "Freud's Masterplot: Questions of Narrative." In Felman, *Literature and Psychoanalysis*, 280–300.
Brown, Chris. "A Filmography for H.D." *H.D. Newsletter* 2.1 (1988): 19–24.
Bruzzi, Zara. "'The Fiery Moment': H.D. and the Eleusinian Landscape of English Modernism." *Agenda* 25.3/4 (1987–88): 97–112.
Bryer, Jackson R. and Pamela Roblyer. "H.D.: A Preliminary Checklist." *Contemporary Literature* 10.4 (1969):632–75.
Bryher [Winnifred Ellerman]. *The Days of Mars: A Memoir, 1940–1946*. London: Marion Boyars, 1972.
——. *The Heart to Artemis*. London: Collins, 1963.
——. *Two Selves*. Paris: Contact, 1923.
Budge, E. A. Wallis. *Book of the Dead: An English Translation*. London: Keagan Paul, Trench, Trubner; New York: E. P Dutton, 1938.

———. *A Hieroglyphic Vocabulary to the Theban Recension of the Book of the Dead.* London: Kegan Paul, Trench, Trubner & Co., 1911.

———. *The Literature of the Ancient Egyptians.* London: J. M. Dent and Sons, 1914.

———. *The Rossetta Stone.* New York: Dover, 1989.

Buck, Claire. "Freud and H.D.: Bisexuality and a Feminist Discourse." *m/f* 8 (1983): 53–66.

Burgin, Victor, James Donald, and Cora Kaplan, eds. *Formations of Fantasy.* London: Methuen, 1986.

Burnett, Gary. *H.D. Between Image and Epic: The Mysteries of Her Poetics.* Ann Arbor: University of Michigan Research Press, 1990.

———. "A Poetics out of War: H.D.'s Responses to the First World War." *Agenda* 25.3/4 (1987–88): 54–63.

Butler, Eliza M. *The Fortunes of Faust.* Cambridge: Cambridge University Press, 1952.

Carroll, David. *The Subject in Question: The Languages of Theory and the Strategies of Fiction.* Chicago: University of Chicago Press, 1982.

Certeau, Michel de. *Heterologies: Discourse on the Other.* Trans. Brian Massumi. Manchester: Manchester University Press, 1986.

Chase, Cynthia. "'Transference' as Trope and Persuasion." In Rimmon-Kenan, 211–32.

Chisholm, Dianne. "H.D's Auto*hetero*graphy." *Tulsa Studies in Women's Literature* 9.1 (1990): 79–106.

Cixous, Hélène. "Castration or Decapitation." Trans. Annette Kuhn. *Signs* 7.1 (1981):41–55.

———. "Fiction and Its Phantoms: A Reading of Freud's *Das Unheimliche* ('The Uncanny')." Trans. Robert Dennomé. *New Literary History* 7 (Spring 1976): 525–48.

———. "The Laugh of the Medusa." Trans. Keith Cohen and Paula Cohen. *Signs* 1.4 (1976): 875–93.

Cixous, Hélène, and Catherine Clément. *The Newly Born Woman.* Trans. Betsy Wing. 1975; Minneapolis: University of Minnesota Press, 1986.

Clément, Catherine. *The Weary Sons of Freud.* Trans. Nicole Ball. 1978; London: Verso, 1987.

Collecott, Diana. Introduction to H.D., *The Gift.* London: Virago, 1984: vii–xix.

———. "Memory and Desire: H.D.'s 'A Note on Poetry.'" *Agenda* 25.3/4 (1987–88): 64–70.

———. "Remembering Oneself: The Reputation and Later Poetry of H.D." *Critical Quarterly* 27.1 (1985): 7–22.

Coward, Rosalind. *Patriarchal Precedents: Sexuality and Social Relations.* London: Routledge and Kegan Paul, 1983.

Culler, Jonathan. "Changes in the Study of the Lyric." *Lyric Poetry: Beyond New Criticism.* Ed. Chaviva Hosek and Patricia Parker. Ithaca: Cornell University Press, 1985: 38–54.

Dennis, Helen M. "The Eleusinian Mysteries as an Organizing Principle in the Pisan Cantos." *Paideuma* 10.2 (1981): 273–82.

Derrida, Jacques. *The Ear of the Other: Otobiography, Transference, Translation.* Ed. Christie V. MacDonald. Trans. Peggy Kamuf. 1982; New York: Schocken Books, 1985.

——. "Freud and the Scene of Writing." In *Writing and Difference.* Trans. Alan Bass. 1968; Chicago: University of Chicago Press, 1978. 196–231.

——. *Of Grammatology.* Trans. Gayatri Chakravorty Spivak. Baltimore: Johns Hopkins University Press, 1976.

——. "Plato's Pharmacy." In *Dissemination.* Trans. Barbara Johnson. 1972; Chicago: University of Chicago Press, 1981: 61–171.

——. *The Post Card: From Socrates to Freud and Beyond.* Trans. Alan Bass. 1980; Chicago: University of Chicago Press, 1987.

——. "Scribble (Writing-Power)." *Yale French Studies* 58 (1979): 117–47.

——. *Spurs: Nietzsche's Styles / Eperons: Les Styles de Nietzsche.* Trans. Barbara Harlow. 1978; Chicago: University of Chicago Press, 1979.

——. "Two Words for Joyce." In *Post-structuralist Joyce: Essays from the French.* Ed. Derek Attridge and Daniel Ferrer. Cambridge: Cambridge University Press, 1984: 145–59.

DeShazer, Mary K. "'A Primary Intensity between Women': H.D. and the Female Muse." In King, *H.D.*, 157–71.

Dick, Leslie. "Notes on Freud and Writing." *Women: A Cultural Review* 1.3 (1990): 256–60.

Doyle, Charles. "Palimpsests of the Word: The Poetry of H.D." *Queen's Quarterly* 92.1 (1985): 310–21.

Dunn, Margaret M. "Altered Patterns and New Endings: Reflections of Change in Stein's *Three Lives* and H.D.'s *Palimpsest.*" *Frontiers* 9.2 (1987): 54–59.

DuPlessis, Rachel Blau. "Family, Sexes, Psyche: An Essay on H.D. and the Muse of the Woman Writer." In King, *H.D.*, 69–90.

——. *H.D.: The Career of That Struggle.* Brighton: Harvester Press, 1986.

——. "Language Acquisition." *Iowa Review* 16.3 (1986): 252–83.

——. "A Note on the State of H.D.'s *The Gift.*" *Sulfur* 9 (1984): 178–82.

——. "Romantic Thralldom in H.D." *Contemporary Literature* 20.2 (1979): 178–203.

——. *Writing beyond the Ending: Narrative Strategies of Twentieth-Century Women Writers.* Bloomington: Indiana University Press, 1985.

DuPlessis, Rachel Blau, and Susan Stanford Friedman. "'Woman Is Perfect': H.D.'s Debate with Freud." *Feminist Studies* 7.3 (1981): 417–30.

Eder, Doris. "Freud and H.D." *Book Forum* 1 (1975): 365–69.

Eisenstein, Sergei. *Film Form and The Film Sense.* Trans. Jay Leyda. Cleveland, 1957.

——. "The Fourth Dimension in the Kino." *Close-Up* 6.3 (1930): 184–94; 6.4 (1930): 253–62.

——. "The New Language of Cinematography." *Close-Up* 4.5 (1929): 10–13.

Eliot, T. S. "Classics in English." Review of Poets' Translation Series, 1–6. *Poetry* 9 (Oct.–March 1916–17): 1–4.

——. *The Use of Poetry and the Use of Criticism*. 1933; London: Faber, 1964.

Ellmann, Maud. *The Poetics of Impersonality*. Brighton: Harvester Press, 1987.

Emerson, Ralph Waldo. *Selections from Ralph Waldo Emerson*. Ed. Stephen E. Whicher. Boston: Houghton Mifflin, 1957.

Euripides. *Helen*. Trans. Richmond Lattimore. In *Euripides II*. Ed. David Grene and Richmond Lattimore. Chicago: University of Chicago Press, 1956.

——. *Iphigenia in Aulis*. Trans. Charles R. Walker. In *Euripides IV*. Ed. David Grene and Richmond Lattimore. Chicago: University of Chicago Press, 1958.

——. *Orestes*. Trans. William Arrowsmith. In *Euripides IV*. Ed. David Grene and Richmond Lattimore. Chicago: University of Chicago Press, 1958.

Faery, Rebecca Blevins. " 'Love Is Writing': Eros in *HERmione*." *San Jose Studies* 13.3 (1987): 56–65.

Felman, Shoshana. "Rereading Femininity." *Yale French Studies* 62 (1981): 19–44.

——. "Turning the Screw of Interpretation." In Felman, *Literature and Psychoanalysis*, 94–207.

——. "Woman and Madness: The Critical Phallacy." *Diacritics* 5.4 (1975): 2–10.

——, ed. *Literature and Psychoanalysis· The Question of Reading: Otherwise*. 1977; Baltimore: Johns Hopkins University Press, 1982.

Fenollosa, Ernest. *The Chinese Written Character as a Medium for Poetry*. Ed. Ezra Pound. 1918; San Francisco: City Lights Books, 1936.

Fields, Kenneth. Introduction to H.D., *Tribute to Freud*. Boston: David R. Godine, 1974: xvii–xlv.

Fliegel, Zenia O. "Feminine Psychosexual Development in Freudian Theory: A Historical Reconstruction." *Psychoanalytic Quarterly* 42 (1973): 385–408.

Forrester, John. *Language and the Origins of Psychoanalysis*. London: MacMillan, 1980.

Forster, E.M. *Pharos and Pharillon*. 1923; Berkeley: Creative Arts, 1980.

Frappier-Mazur, Lucienne. "Desire, Writing, and Identity in the Romantic Mystical Novel: Notes for a Definition of the Feminine." *Style* 18.3 (1984): 328–54.

Freeman, Lucy, and Herbert S. Strean. "The Poet Patient." In *Freud and Women*. New York: Frederick Ungar, 1981: 117–22.

Freibert, L.M. "From Semblance to Selfhood: The Evolution of Woman in H.D.'s Neo-Epic *Helen in Egypt*." *Arizona Quarterly* 36 (1979): 165–75.

Friedberg, Anne. "Approaching *Borderline*." *Millennium Film Journal* 7.9 (1980–81): 130–39.

——. "On H.D., Woman, History, Recognition." *Wide Angle* 5.2 (1982): 26–31.

——. *Writing about the Cinema: 'Close-Up,' 1927–1933*. Ph.D. diss., New York University, 1983. Ann Arbor, Mich.: University Microfilms, 1986, 8405770.

Friedman, Susan Stanford. "Against Discipleship: Collaboration and Intimacy in the Relationship of H.D. and Freud." *Literature and Psychology* 33.3/4 (1987): 89–108.

——. "Creating a Woman's Mythology: H.D.'s *Helen in Egypt*." *Women's Studies* 5.2 (1977): 163–97.

——. Exile in the American Grain: H.D.'s Diaspora." *Agenda* 25.3/4 (1987–88): 27–50.

——. "Gender and Genre Anxiety: Elizabeth Barrett Browning and H.D. as Epic Poets." *Tulsa Studies in Women's Literature* 5.2 (1986): 203–28.

——. "H.D. Chronology: Composition and Publication of Volumes." *H.D. Newsletter* 1.1 (1987): 12–16.

——. " 'I Go Where I Love': An Intertextual Study of H.D. and Adrienne Rich." *Signs* 9 (Winter 1983): 228–45.

——. "Modernism of the 'Scattered Remnant': Race and Politics in the Development of H.D.'s Modernist Vision." In King, *H.D.*, 91–116.

——. "A Most Luscious *Vers Libre* Relationship: H.D. and Freud." *Annual of Psychoanalysis* 14 (1986): 319–41.

——. "Palimpsests of Origin in H.D.'s Career." *Poesis* 6.3/4 (1985): 56–73.

——. *Psyche Reborn: The Emergence of H.D.* Bloomington: Indiana University Press, 1981.

——. "Psyche Reborn: Tradition, Re-vision, and the Goddess as Mother-Symbol in H.D.'s Epic Poetry." *Women's Studies* 6 (1979): 147–60.

——. "The Writing Cure: Transference and Resistance in a Dialogic Analysis." *H.D. Newsletter* 2.2 (1988): 25–35.

Friedman, Susan, and Rachel Blau DuPlessis. " 'I Had Two Loves Separate': The Sexualities of H.D.'s *Her*." *Montemora* 8 (1981): 7–30.

Gardner, Frieda. "H.D.'s Palimpsests." *DAI* 44 (1983): 492A.

Garner, Shirley Nelson, Claire Kahane, and Madelon Sprengnether, eds. *The (M)other Tongue: Essays in Feminist Psychoanalytic Interpretation*. Ithaca: Cornell University Press, 1985.

Gelb, Ignace J. *A Study of Writing: The Foundations of Grammatology*. Chicago: Chicago University Press, 1952.

Gelpi, Albert. "Hilda in Egypt." *Southern Review* 18.2 (1982): 233–50.

——. "Re-membering the Mother: A Reading of H.D.'s *Trilogy*." In King, *H.D.*, 173–90.

——. "The Thistle and the Serpent." In H.D., *Notes on Thought and Vision*. San Francisco: City Lights Books, 1982: 7–14.

Goethe, Johann Wolfgang von. *Faust, Part Two*. Trans. Philip Wayne. Harmondsworth, Eng.: Penguin, 1959.

Gilbert, Sandra M. "H.D.: Who Was She?" *Contemporary Literature* 24.4 (1984): 496–511.

Gubar, Susan. "The Echoing Spell of H.D.'s *Trilogy*." In *Shakespeare's Sisters:*

*Feminist Essays on Women Poets.* Ed. Sandra M. Gilbert and Susan Gubar. Bloomington: Indiana University Press, 1979. 153–64.

——. "Sapphistries." *Signs* 10.1 (1984): 43–62.

Guest, Barbara. *Herself Defined: The Poet H.D. and Her World.* London: Collins, 1985.

Hanscombe, Gillian, and Virginia L. Smyers. *Writing for Their Lives: The Modernist Women, 1910–1940.* London: Women's Press, 1987.

Harari, Josué, ed. *Textual Strategies: Perspectives in Post-structuralist Criticism.* Ithaca: Cornell University Press, 1979.

Harding, Esther. *Woman's Mysteries: Ancient and Modern.* New York: Harper and Row, 1971.

Harrison, Jane Ellen. *Prolegomena to the Study of Greek Religion.* 1921; London: Merlin, 1962.

——. *Themis.* 1912; London: Merlin, 1977.

Herodotus. *The Histories.* Trans. Aubrey de Sélincourt. Harmondsowrth, Eng.: Penguin, 1954.

Hertz, Neil. "Freud and the Sandman." In Harari, 296–321.

Hirsh, Elizabeth A. " 'New Eyes': H.D., Modernism, and the Psychoanalysis of Seeing." *Literature and Psychology* 32.3 (1986): 1–10.

Hoffman, E. T. A. "The Sandman." In *Tales of Hoffman.* Trans. R. J. Hollingdale. 1816; Harmondsworth, Eng.: Penguin, 1982: 85–125.

Holland, Norman N. "H.D. and the 'Blameless Physician.' " *Contemporary Literature* 10.4 (1969): 474–506.

——. *Poems in Persons: An Introduction to the Psychoanalysis of Literature.* New York: Norton, 1973.

Homer. *The Odyssey.* Trans. E. V. Rieu. Harmondsworth, Eng.: Penguin, 1946.

Howdle, Andrew. "Feminine Hermeticism in H.D.'s Trilogy." *Studies in Mystical Literature* 4.1 (1984): 26–44.

Hughes, Glenn. "H.D.: The Perfect Imagist." In *Imagism and Imagists: A Study in Modern Poetry.* Stanford: Stanford University Press, 1931: 109–24.

Hunter, Dianne. "Hysteria, Psychoanalysis, and Feminism: The Case of Anna O." *Feminist Studies* 9.3 (1983): 465–88.

Hutchinson, R. W. *Prehistoric Crete.* Harmondsworth, Eng.: Penguin, 1962.

Hyde, Lewis. *The Gift: Imagination and the Erotic Life of Property.* New York: Randon House, 1983.

Irigaray, Luce. *Speculum of the Other Woman.* Trans. Gillian C. Gill. 1974; Ithaca: Cornell University Press, 1985.

——. *This Sex Which Is Not One.* Trans. Catherine Porter with Carolyn Burke. 1977; Ithaca: Cornell University Press, 1985.

Irwin, John T. *American Hieroglyphics: The Symbol of the Egyptian Hieroglyphics in the American Renaissance.* New Haven: Yale University Press, 1980.

Jackson, Rosemary. *Fantasy: The Literature of Subversion.* London: Methuen, 1981.

Jacobus, Mary. *Reading Woman: Essays in Feminist Criticism*. New York: Columbia University Press, 1986.

Jaffe, Nora Crow. " 'She Herself Is the Writing': Language and Sexual Identity in H.D." *Literature and Medicine* 4 (1985): 86–111.

Jones, Ernest. "Early Development of Female Sexuality." In *Papers in Psychoanalysis*. 5th ed. 1927; London: Ballière, Tindall, and Cox, 1950: 438–51.

——. *On the Nightmare*. The International Psychoanalytical Library 20. London: Hogarth Press and Institute of Psycho-Analysis, 1931.

——. Review of *Tribute to Freud. International Journal of Psycho-Analysis* 38 (March–April 1957): 126.

——. *Sigmund Freud: Life and Work*. 3 vols. London: Hogarth Press, 1953–57.

Jones, Peter. Introduction to H.D., *Tribute to Freud*. Manchester: Carcanet, 1985: 5–7.

Joyce, James. *Ulysses*. 1922; Hammondsworth, Eng.: Penquin Books, 1975.

Jung, C. G. *Aspects of the Feminine*. Trans. R. F. C. Hull. 1982; London: Ark, 1986.

Jung, C. G. and Carl Kerenyi. *Science of Mythology: Essays on the Myth of the Divine Child and the Mysteries of Eleusis*. 1949; Rpt. London: Ark, 1985.

Junker, Helmut. "On the Difficulties of Retranslating Freud into English." *International Review of Psycho-Analysis* 14 (July 1987): 317–20.

Kamuf, Peggy. *Fictions of Feminine Desire: Disclosures of Heloise*. Lincoln: University of Nebraska Press, 1982.

Kelly, Joan. *Women, History, and Theory*. Chicago: University of Chicago Press, 1984.

King, Michael, ed. *H.D.: Woman and Poet*. Orono: University of Maine Press, 1986.

——. Review of *HERmione. Paideuma* 11.2 (1982): 339–44.

Kloepfer, Deborah Kelly. "Flesh Made Word: Maternal Inscriptions in H.D." *Sagetrieb* 3.1 (1983): 27–48.

——. "Mother as Muse and Desire: The Sexual Politics of H.D.'s *Trilogy*." In King, *H.D.*, 191–209.

——. *The Unspeakable Mother: Forbidden Discourse in Jean Rhys and H.D.* Ithaca: Cornell University Press, 1989.

Knapp, Peggy A. "Women's Freud(e): H.D.'s *Tribute to Freud* and Gladys Schmitt's *Sonnets for an Analyst*." *Massachusetts Review* 24.2 (1983): 338–52.

Kofman, Sarah. *The Enigma of Woman: Woman in Freud's Writings*. Trans. Catherine Porter. 1980; Ithaca: Cornell University Press, 1985.

Kolokithas, Dawn. "The Pursuit of Spirituality in the Poetry of H.D." *San Jose Studies* 13.3 (1987): 66–76.

Kristeva, Julia. *Black Sun: Depression and Melancholia*. Trans. Leon S. Roudiez. 1987; New York: Columbia University Press, 1989.

——. *Desire in Language: A Semiotic Approach to Literature and Art*. Ed. Leon S. Roudiez. Trans. Thomas Gora, Alice Jardine, and Leon S. Roudiez. New York: Columbia University Press, 1980.

——. "Freud and Love: Treatment and Its Discontents." Trans. Leon S. Roudiez. In *The Kristeva Reader*. Ed. Toril Moi. Oxford: Basil Blackwell, 1986. 238–71.

——. *Language, the Unknown: An Initiation into Linguistics*. Trans. Anne M. Menke. Brighton: Harvester, 1989.

——. *Revolution in Poetic Language*. Trans. Margaret Waller. 1974; New York: Columbia University Press, 1984.

Ladimer, Bethany. "Madness and the Irrational in the Work of André Breton: A Feminist Perspective." *Feminist Studies* 6.1 (1980): 175–94.

Laity, Cassandra. "H.D.'s Romantic Landscapes: The Sexual Politics of the Garden." *Sagetrieb* 6 (Fall 1987): 57–75.

Landor, W. S. "Achilles and Helena." In *Imaginary Conversations of Greeks and Romans*. Vol. 1 of *The Collected Works of Walter Savage Landor*. Ed. T. Earle Welby. London: Chapman and Hall, 1927. 1–5.

Laplanche, Jean. *Life and Death in Psychoanalysis*. Trans. Jeffrey Mehlman. Baltimore: Johns Hopkins University Press, 1976.

Laplanche, Jean, and Jean-Bernard Pontalis. "Fantasy and the Origins of Sexuality." In Burgin, Donald, and Kaplan, 5–34.

——. *The Language of Psycho-Analysis*. Trans. Donald Nicholson-Smith. 1967; London: Hogarth Press and Institute of Psycho-Analysis, 1973.

Larsen, Jeanne. "Myth and Glyph in *Helen in Egypt*." *San Jose Studies* 13 (Fall, 1987): 88–101.

Lattimore, Richmond. "Euripides as Lyrist." Review of H.D., *Ion*. *Poetry* 51 (Dec. 1937): 160–64.

Lawrence, D.H. *Fantasia of the Unconscious / Psychoanalysis and the Unconscious, 1922/1921*. Harmondsworth, Eng.: Penguin, 1981.

——. "The Man Who Died" (originally "The Escaped Cock"). In *Love among the Haystacks*. 1930; Harmondsworth, Eng.: Penguin, 1986.

——. *The Princess*. 1925; Harmondsworth, Eng.: Penguin, 1986.

Levertov, Denise. "H.D.: An Appreciation." In *The Poet in the World*. New York: New Directions, 1973: 244–48.

Lisieux, Thérèse de. *The Little Flower of Jesus: An Autobiography*. London: Burns, Oates, and Washbourne, 1927.

Lucas, Rose. "Re(reading)-Writing the Palimpsest of Myth." *Southern Review* 21 (1988): 43–57.

Lurker, Manfred. *The Gods and Symbols of Ancient Egypt*. Trans. Barbara Cummings. 1974; London: Thames and Hudson, 1980.

Lyotard, Jean-François. "The Dream-Work Does Not Think." Trans. Mary Lydon. *Oxford Literary Review* 6.1 (1983): 3–34.

MacCannell, Juliet Flower. "Oedipus Wrecks: Lacan, Stendhal, and the Narrative Form of the Real." In *Lacan and Narration: The Psychoanalytic Difference in Narrative Theory*. Ed. Robert Con Davis. Baltimore: Johns Hopkins University Press, 1983. 910–40.

Mahoney, Patrick J. *Freud as a Writer*. Rev. ed. New Haven: Yale University Press, 1987.

Mandel, Charlotte. "Magical Lenses: Poet's Vision beyond the Naked Eye." In King, *H.D.*, 301–17.

Marcuse, Herbert. *Eros and Civilization: A Philosophical Inquiry into Freud.* 1956; London: Ark, 1987.

Mathis, Mary S., and Michael King. "An Annotated Bibliography of Works about H.D., 1969–1985." In King, *H.D.*, 393–511.

Meggison, Lauren Louise. "Keepers of the Flame: Hermeticism in Yeats, H.D., and Borges." *DAI* 48.2 (1987): 386A.

Meltzer, Françoise. "The Uncanny Rendered Canny: Freud's Blind Spot in Reading Hoffman's 'Sandman.'" In *Introducing Psychoanalytic Theory*. Ed. Sander L. Gilman. New York: Brunner/Mazel, 1982. 218–39.

Mitchell, Juliet. "Femininity, Narrative, and Psychoanalysis." In *Women: The Longest Revolution*. London: Virago, 1984. 287–94.

———. *Psychoanalysis and Feminism: Freud, Reich, Laing, and Women.* 1974; New York: Vintage, 1975.

Miyake, Akiko. "The Greek-Egyptian Mysteries in Pound's 'The Little Review Calendar' and in Cantos 1–7." *Paideuma* 7.1–2 (1978): 73–111.

Moi, Toril. *Sexual/Textual Politics: Feminist Literary Theory.* London: Methuen, 1985.

Morris, Adalaide. "Autobiography and Prophecy: H.D.'s *The Gift*." In King, *H.D.*, 227–36.

———. "The Concept of Projection: H.D.'s Visionary Powers." *Contemporary Literature* 25.4 (1984): 411–36.

———. "H.D.'s 'Fortune Teller.'" *Iowa Review* 16.2 (1986): 14–17.

———. "H.D.'s 'H.D. by Delia Alton.'" *Iowa Review* 16.3 (1986): 174–78.

———. "A Relay of Power and Peace: H.D. and the Spirit of the Gift." *Contemporary Literature* 27.4 (1986): 493–524.

Neumann, Erich. *The Great Mother: An Analysis of the Archetype.* Trans. Ralph Mannheim. 1955; Princeton: Princeton Universtiy Press, 1963.

Nietzsche, Friedrich. *Human, All Too Human: A Book for Free Spirits.* Trans. Ralph Mannheim. 1878; Cambridge: Cambridge University Press, 1986.

Ostriker, Alicia. "No Rule of Procedure: The Open Poetics of H.D." *Agenda* 25.3/4 (1987–88): 145–54.

———. "The Thieves of Language: Women Poets and Revisionist Mythmaking." *Signs* 8.1 (1982): 168–90.

———. *Writing like a Woman.* Ann Arbor: University of Michigan Press, 1983.

Pagels, Elaine. *The Gnostic Gospels.* 1980; Harmondsworth, Eng.: Penguin, 1985.

Pater, Walter. *The Renaissance: Studies in Art and Poetry.* Ed. Donald L. Hill. 1893; Berkeley: University of California Press, 1980.

Pearson, Norman Holmes. Foreword to H.D., *Hermetic Definition*. New York: New Directions, 1972.

———. Foreword to H.D., *Tribute to Freud*. New York: New Directions, 1974. x–xiv.

——. Foreword to H.D., *Trilogy*. New York: New Directions, 1973. v–xii.

Pondrom, Cyrena N. "H.D. and the Origins of Imagism." *Sagetrieb* 4.1 (1985): 73–100.

——. "*Trilogy* and *Four Quartets*: Contrapuntal Visions of Spiritual Quest." *Agenda* 25.3/4 (1987–88): 155–65.

Pound, Ezra. *The ABC of Reading*. 1934; New York: New Directions Press, 1960.

——. *Gaudier-Brzeska: A Memoir*. 1916; New York: New Directions Press, 1970.

——. "Hilda's Book." In H.D., *End to Torment*. Ed. Michael King. Manchester: Carcanet, 1980. 68–84.

——. *Literary Essays*. Ed. T. S. Eliot. 1954; London: Faber and Faber, 1985.

——. trans. (with Noël Stock). *Love Poems of Ancient Egypt*. New York: New Directions, 1962.

——. *The Spirit of Romance*. New York: New Directions Press, 1952.

——. *Selected Prose, 1909–1965*. Ed. William Cookson. 1973; London: Faber and Faber, 1973.

Rank, Otto. "The Play-Impulse and Aesthetic Pleasure." In *Art and Artist: Creative Urge and Personality Development*. Trans. Charles Frances Atkinson. New York: Knopf, 1932.

Rich, Adrienne. "When We Dead Awaken: Writing as Re-vision." In *On Lies, Secrets, and Silence: Selected Prose, 1966–1978*. London: Virago, 1984. 33–49.

——. *The Dream of a Common Language: Poems, 1974–1977*. New York: Norton, 1978.

Ricoeur, Paul. *Freud and Philosophy: An Essay on Interpretation*. Trans. Denis Savage. 1970; New Haven: Yale University Press, 1978.

Riddel, Joseph N. "Decentering the Image: The 'Project' of 'American' Poetics?" In Harari, 322–58.

——. "H.D. and the Poetics of 'Spiritual Realism.'" *Contemporary Literature* 10.4 (1969): 447–73.

——. "H.D.'s Scene of Writing: Poetry as (and) Analysis." *Studies in the Literary Imagination* 12.1 (1979): 41–59.

Rimmon-Kenan, Shlomith, ed. *Discourse in Psychoanalysis and Literature*. London: Methuen, 1987.

Riviere, Joan. "Womanliness as a Masquerade." In Burgin, Donald, and Kaplan, 35–44.

Robinson, Janice S. *H.D.: The Life and Work of an American Poet*. Boston: Houghton Mifflin, 1982.

——. "What's in a Box? Psychoanalytic Concept and Literary Technique in H.D." In King, *H.D.*, 237–57.

Roessel, David. "H.D.'s Troy: Some Bearings." *H.D. Newsletter* 3.2 (1990): 38–42.

Roith, Estelle. *The Riddle of Freud: Jewish Influences on His Theory of Female Sexuality*. London: Tavistock, 1987.

Roming, Evelyn M. "An Achievement of H.D. and Theodore Roethke: Psychoanalysis and the Poetics of Teaching." *Literature and Psychology* 28.3/4 (1978): 105–11.

Ronell, Avital. "*Goethezeit.*" In *Taking Chances: Derrida, Psychoanalysis, and Literature*. Ed. Joseph H. Smith and William Kerrigan. Baltimore: Johns Hopkins University Press, 1984. 146–83.

Rose, Jacqueline. *Sexuality in the Field of Vision*. London: Verso, 1986.

Rougemont, Denis de. *Love in the Western World*. Trans. Montgomery Belgion. 1940; Princeton: Princeton University Press, 1983.

Rousseau, Jean-Jacques. *Reveries of the Solitary Walker*. Trans. Peter France. 1782; Harmondsworth, Eng.: Penguin, 1979.

Ruddick, Lisa. "William James and the Modernism of Gertrude Stein." In *Modernism Reconsidered*. Ed. Robert Kiely. Cambridge: Harvard University Press, 1983.

Sachs, Hanns. "Film Psychology." *Close-Up* 3.5 (1928): 8–15.

Sahlins, Marshall. *Stone Age Economics*. Chicago: Aldine-Atherton, 1972.

Schafer, Roy. "The Appreciative Analytic Attitude and the Construction of Multiple Life Histories." *Psychoanalytic and Contemporary Thought* 2.1 (1979): 3–24.

——. "Narration in the Psychoanalytic Dialogue." In *On Narration*. Ed. W. J. T. Mitchell. Chicago: University of Chicago Press, 1981.

Schaum, Melita. "Lyric Resistance: Views of the Political in the Poetics of Wallace Stevens and H.D." *Wallace Stevens Journal* 13.2 (1989): 191–205.

Schoeck, R. J. "Listening to Stone: Reflections on H.D.'s *The Walls Do Not Fall.*" *H.D. Newsletter* 2.2 (1988): 15–24.

Scoggan, John William. "De(con)structive Poetics: Readings of Hilda Doolittle's *The War Trilogy.*" *DAI* 44.01 (1983): 167A.

Sievert, Heather Rosario. "H.D.: A Symbolist Perspective." *Comparative Literature Studies* 16.1 (1979): 48–57.

Smyers, Virginia. "H.D.'s Books in the Bryher Library." *H.D. Newsletter* 1.2 (1987): 18–25.

Spivak, Gayatri Chakravorty. "Displacement and the Discourse of Woman." In *Derrida: Displacement and After*. Ed. Mark Krupnick. Bloomington: Indiana University Press, 1983: 169–95.

Suleiman, Susan Rubin. "Nadja, Dora, Lol V. Stein: Women, Madness, and Narrative." In Rimmon-Kenan, 124–51.

Thoreau, Henry David. *Walden*. Ed. J. Lyndon Stanley. Princeton: Princeton University Press, 1971.

Todd, Jane Marie. "The Veiled Woman in Freud's 'Das Unheimliche.'" *Signs* 11.3 (1986): 519–28.

Travis, S. "A Crack in the Ice: Subjectivity and the Mirror in H.D.'s *Her.*" *Sagetrieb* 6.2 (1987): 123–40.

Ulmer, Gregory. *Applied Grammatology: Post(e)-Pedagogy from Jacques Derrida to Joseph Beuys*. Baltimore: Johns Hopkins University Press, 1985.

Walsh, John. "H.D., C. G. Jung, and Küsnacht: Fantasia on a Theme." In King, *H.D.*, 59–67.

Warner, Marina. *Alone of All Her Sex: The Myth and the Cult of Mary.* 1976; London: Picador, 1985.

Weber, Samuel. *The Legend of Freud.* Minneapolis: University of Minnesota Press, 1982.

——. "The Sideshow; or, Remarks on a Canny Moment." *MLN* 88.6 (1973): 1102–33.

White, Eric W. *Images of H.D.* London: Enitharmon Press, 1976.

Whitman, Walt. *Leaves of Grass.* Vol. 7 of *The Collected Writings of Walt Whitman.* Ed. Gay Wilson Allen, Scully Bradley, et al. 13 vols. New York: New York University Press, 1961–).

Wittiq, Monique. "The Straight Mind." *Feminist Issues* 1.1 (1980):103–10.

Wolf, Ernest S. "Psychoanalytic Psychology of the Self and Literature." *New Literary History* 12.1 (1980): 41–60.

Wolf-Man. *The Wolf-Man by the Wolf-Man.* Ed. Muriel Gardiner. New York: Basic Books, 1971.

Woolf, Virginia. "Women and Fiction." In *Women and Writing: Virginia Woolf.* Ed. Michèle Barrett. 1979; Dunvegan, Ont.: Quadrant Editions, 1984: 45–64.

Wright, Elizabeth. *Psychoanalytic Criticism: Theory in Practice.* London: Methuen, 1984.

Zajdel, Melody M. " 'I See Her Differently': H.D.'s *Trilogy* as Feminist Response to Masculine Modernism." *Sagetrieb* 5.1 (1986): 7–15.

Zeitlin, Froma I. "The Dynamics of Misogyny: Myth and Mythmaking in the *Oresteia*." *Arethusa* 2 (1978): 150–84.

# Index

Repression, 11, 22, 66, 70, 75, 95, 104, 106; of maternal memory and fantasy, 108–18, 122–23, 135–37, 144, 150, 175–76, 186, 230n6; of woman, 165–67, 177, 181–84, 197; of woman's language, 199
Rich, Adrienne, 226, 227n3, 261n21
Riddel, Joseph, 7–8, 29, 35, 227n1, 229nn12, 14, 233n25, 234n31
Rilke, Rainer Maria, 218
Rivière, Joan, 261n16
Robinson, Janice S., 227n1, 230n6
Roblyer, Pamela, 244n40
Roessel, David, 250n5
Roheim, Geza, 229n11
Roith, Estelle, 221–23, 234n31, 260nn14, 16
Romanticism, 43, 225; German, 200. See also Coleridge, Samuel Taylor; Laity, Cassandra; Schiller, Friedrich von; Shelley, Percy Bysshe
Roming, Evelyn M., 227n1
Ronell, Avital, 230n7
Rose, Jacqueline, 231n10
Rosetta Stone, 40, 61
Rougemont, Denis de, 234n33, 254n24
Rousseau, Jean-Jacques, 146
Ruddick, Lisa, 3, 228n5

Sachs, Hanns, 22, 33, 219
Sackville-West, Vita, 242n25
Sadism, 23, 147–49, 160–61, 185–86, 248n21. See also Death drive; Masculinity
Sahlins, Marshall, 246n5
Schiller, Friedrich von, 87
Schmideberg, Walter, 219, 258n54
Seduction, 138–40. See also Fantasy, primary
Self-analysis, 66–67, 86
Shakespeare, William, 83, 177
Shelley, Percy Bysshe, 44, 236n47
Sievert, Heather Rosario, 236n43
Smyers, Virginia, 234n35, 258n56
Socrates, 195–97
Sorceress, 7, 182–88, 200–213. See also Pharmakeus; Witch
Spivak, Gayatri Chakravorty, 229n15
Splitting of ego, 21
Stein, Gertrude, 3, 228n5
Steisichorus, 171–72
Stowe, Harriet Beecher, 98–99, 132, 244n44

Strachey, James, 245n58
Surrealism, 57, 181. See also Breton, André

Telepathy, 33, 96–98, 101–8, 113
Teresa of Avila, Saint, 83
Thetis-Isis, 186–87, 193–95
Thoreau, Henry David, 43, 48, 236n50
Thoth, 27, 36, 46, 65, 172–78, 187, 197, 252nn17–18. See also Book of the Dead; Hermes; Hermeticism; Mysteries: Egyptian; Neoplatonism
Torok, Maria, 239n72
Totemism, 145–47, 161–63. See also Animism; Demonology; Projection
Transference, 6, 10–14, 21, 65–67, 101–8, 113–14, 116–17; father, 30–32; in Helen in Egypt, 185–90; mother, 65, 101–9, 112–18; thought, 33, 108, 111–18. See also Freud, Sigmund: "Dynamics of Transference"; Memory; Mothers; Necromancy; Telepathy
Transference narrative, 69
Translation, 5–6, 10–20, 25, 33–36, 40–41, 50–51, 57–59, 81, 117, 190–92, 226; allegory of, 169–70; as analytic deconstruction, 169–70, 180–81; hermetic, 173, 188, 197. See also Dream interpretation; Hieroglyphs; Psychoanalysis: H.D.'s revision/translation of; Writing
Travis, S., 241n17

Ulmer, Gregory, 28, 51–52, 233n138, 236n54, 239n72
Uncanny, 2–3, 8, 28, 32, 70, 94, 109–18, 132, 147–59, 245nn55–56, 58–59
Uncanny ear, 104–8, 115, 126, 158–59
Uncanny feminine, 147–59, 198–213, 245n60
Unconscious, 37, 47, 55, 59, 66, 70, 72, 76–77, 83, 92, 96, 100, 104, 111, 115, 119; in melancholia, 123. See also Dream; Fantasy; Memory; Projection

Virginity, 141–47. See also Fantasy, primary; Female sexuality; Freud, Sigmund: "Taboo of Virginity"; Narcissism: feminine

Warner, Marina, 135, 247n9
Weber, Samuel, 235n39, 245n55
Whitman, Walt, 43, 48–49, 236n51

*Greatness Engendered: George Eliot and Virginia Woolf*
by Alison Booth

*Talking Back: Toward a Latin American Feminist Literary Criticism*
by Debra A. Castillo

*From Mastery to Analysis: Theories of Gender in Psychoanalytic Feminism*
by Patricia Elliot

*Feminist Theory, Women's Writing*
by Laurie A. Finke

*Colette and the Fantom Subject of Autobiography*
by Jerry Aline Flieger

*Cartesian Women: Versions and Subversions of Rational Discourse in the Old Regime*
by Erica Harth

*Narrative Transvestism: Rhetoric and Gender in the Eighteenth-Century English Novel*
by Madeleine Kahn

*The Unspeakable Mother: Forbidden Discourse in Jean Rhys and H. D.*
by Deborah Kelly Kloepfer

*Women and Romance: The Consolations of Gender in the English Novel*
by Laurie Langbauer

*Autobiographical Voices: Race, Gender, Self Portraiture*
by Françoise Lionnet

*Woman and Modernity: The (Life)Styles of Lou Andreas-Salomé*
by Biddy Martin

*In the Name of Love: Women, Masochism, and the Gothic*
by Michelle A. Masse

*Reading Gertrude Stein: Body, Text, Gnosis*
by Lisa Ruddick

**Library of Congress Cataloging-in-Publication Data**

Chisholm, Dianne, 1953–
    H. D.'s Freudian poetics : psychoanalysis in translation / Dianne Chisholm.
        p.   cm. — (Reading women writing)
    Includes bibliographical references and index.
    ISBN 0-8014-2474-7 (cloth : alk. paper). — ISBN 0-8014-8009-4 (pbk. : alk. paper)
    1. H. D. (Hilda Doolittle), 1886–1941—Knowledge—Psychology.   2. Women
poets, American—20th century—Psychology.   3. Freud, Sigmund, 1856–1939—
Influence.   4. Psychoanalysis and literature.   5. Poetics.   I. Title.   II. Series.
PS3507.O726Z6   1992
811'.52—dc20                                                                          91-55558